T0375240

When the overall economic pie is not growing, then how it is shared out becomes more important. In short, there is a demand for answers to questions such as: What is actually happening to welfare? Do the income statistics used to chart trends really give us the full picture about people's economic fortunes? Is the experience of one's own country better or worse than other countries? How does a person's well-being relate to the household in which they live; more fundamentally, how do households produce welfare? This book, a collection of new empirical and theoretical papers by a distinguished set of international authors, aims to answer these questions. Comparisons of poverty, income inequality, and income capacity across countries in Europe and North America are the basis of part I. Part II introduces subjective (non-monetary) approaches to the assessment of personal economic welfare. In part III new results about the measurement of inequality and poverty are derived. Part IV explores topics examining interactions between personal welfare and the resources derived from one's household, the labor market, and from the government through the tax and benefit system. The book reflects the interests of, and is a memorial to, the late Aldi Hagenaars, eminent analyst of the distribution of wealth and household production, who died tragically young.

The Distribution of Welfare and Household Production

International Perspectives

Aldi Hagenaars

The Distribution of Welfare and Household Production

International Perspectives

edited by
STEPHEN P. JENKINS,
ARIE KAPTEYN
and
BERNARD M.S. VAN PRAAG

CAMBRIDGE
UNIVERSITY PRESS

CAMBRIDGE
UNIVERSITY PRESS

University Printing House, Cambridge CB2 8BS, United Kingdom

Cambridge University Press is part of the University of Cambridge.

It furthers the University's mission by disseminating knowledge in the pursuit of education, learning and research at the highest international levels of excellence.

www.cambridge.org
Information on this title: www.cambridge.org/9780521623025

© Cambridge University Press 1998

First published 1998
First paperback edition 2010

A catalogue record for this publication is available from the British Library

Library of Congress Cataloguing in Publication data

The distribution of welfare and household production : international
    perspectives / edited by Stephen Jenkins, Arie Kapteyn, and Bernard
    van Praag.
        p.   cm.
    Includes index.
    ISBN 0 521 62302 2
    1. Income distribution - Cross-cultural studies.   2. Poverty - Cross-
cultural studies.   3. Welfare economics - Cross-cultural studies.
    I. Jenkins, Stephen P.   II. Kapteyn, Arie.   III. Praag, Bernard M. S. van.
HC79.15D5319   1998
339.2-dc21   97-25538   CIP

ISBN 978-0-521-62302-5 Hardback

Contents

Figures

Tables

Acknowledgments

This book could not have been produced without the help and support of many persons and organizations. The papers in this volume are a selection of the papers presented at a memorial conference held at Leiden University in the autumn of 1994. We thank Joke van Oost, Hedy Braun, and Josette van Muijden for their logistic support for the meeting and Hedy Braun for the smooth local organization. The organizers of the meeting gratefully acknowledge financial and logistic support from: the Foundation for Household Economics, Rotterdam; the Tinbergen Institute; the Department of Economics of Leiden University; and the Center for Economic Research of Tilburg University. Final production of the manuscript was undertaken at CentER, Tilburg University, by Josette van Muijden with notable efficiency and tolerance. The editors are most grateful to her (and hope that she never has such a task again). The editors also thank the external referees who assisted with the anonymous reviewing of the chapters.

Notes on the contributors

Yoram Amiel is Head of the Department of Economics and Management, and former Academic Director, of the Ruppin Institute, Israel. He is author of numerous articles on theoretical and experimental approaches to the analysis of income distribution.

Anthony Atkinson is Warden of Nuffield College, Oxford. He has written on poverty, income distribution, and public economics.

Richard Blundell is Professor of Economics at University College London and Director of Research at the Institute for Fiscal Studies. He is a co-editor of *Econometrica* and his current research interests include micro-econometrics, household labor supply, semiparametric analysis of consumer behavior and the analysis of tax reform.

Richard V. Burkhauser is a Professor of Economics and Associate Director of the Center for Policy Research at Syracuse University. He has published widely on US and European social welfare policy, and has particular interests in the economics of disability, aging, the labor market, and the distribution of economic well-being.

Frank A. Cowell is Professor of Economics at the London School of Economics, where he directs the Distributional Analysis Research Programme and is a Research Associate of the Centre for the Analysis of Social Exclusion. He is editor of *Economica* and author of numerous books and articles about income distribution measurement.

Sadettin Erksoy is an Assistant Professor of Economics at Brock University. His current research interests include income distribution, social security programs, and microsimulation.

Gary Fields is Professor of Labor Economics and Economics at Cornell University. He specializes in labor markets and income distribution in developing countries. His current research is on the distributional consequences of economic growth.

James E. Foster is Professor of Economics at Vanderbilt University. His research interests include the measurement of poverty, inequality, well-being, literacy, and freedom.

Karen Gardiner is Senior Research Officer at the Centre for the Analysis of Social Exclusion at the London School of Economics, with research interests in the areas of income distribution, social exclusion, and social policy, including welfare-to-work schemes.

Thesia I. Garner is a Senior Research Economist in the Division of Price and Index Number Research, at the US Bureau of Labor Statistics. Her current research interests span the distribution of expenditures and income and poverty (including subjective approaches), household-specific price indices, and the impact of economic transition.

Joop Hartog is Professor of Economics at the University of Amsterdam, and editor of *Labour Economics*. His research focuses on topics in labor economics, such as wage structure, allocation, and education, and training. Recently, he has investigated the effects of labor market institutions on labor market performance using international comparisons.

Robert Haveman is John Bascom Professor of Economics and Public Affairs at the University of Wisconsin–Madison. His current research focuses on the determinants of the schooling and fertility choices of young adults and the concept of poverty viewed as the "inability to be self-reliant."

Douglas Holtz-Eakin is Professor and Chairman of the Department of Economics, and Associate Director, Center for Policy Research, at Syracuse University. He has interests in the economics of public policy, with recent research centering on the productivity effects of public infrastructure, income mobility, and entrepreneurial ventures.

Stephen P. Jenkins is a Professor at the ESRC Research Centre on Micro-Social Change at the University of Essex. His current research interests include the distribution of income, social security, and the labor market, especially their longitudinal dimensions.

Jim Yong Jin is a Research Fellow at the Science Centre Berlin (WZB), in the department of Market Processes and Corporate Development. His main interest is in theoretical industrial organization, concentrating on topics related to imperfect information and uncertainty, such as information sharing.

David S. Johnson is a Research Economist in the Division of Price and Index Number Research at the US Bureau of Labor Statistics His research interests include the allocation of resources within the family, the estimation of equivalence scales, and the measurement of inequality and poverty.

Arie Kapteyn is Director of the CentER for Economic Research and of the Economics Institute Tilburg, both associated with Tilburg University. His current research interests include savings and consumption of households, labor markets, social security, subjective measures of well-being, and psychological extensions of neoclassical models of behavior.

Peter Kooreman is a Professor of economics at the University of Groningen. He has written extensively on the economics of the household and the use of subjective information in explaining choices.

Valerie Lechêne is Research Fellow at the Insitut National de la Recherche Agronomique (INRA) in Paris. Her research interests include economics of the family, labor supply, income distributions, poverty, and youth unemployment.

Inge O'Connor is a part-time Assistant Professor at Syracuse University. Her research interests focus on cross-national comparisons of education and earnings.

Nigel O'Leary is a Research Fellow in the Economics Department at the University of Wales, Swansea. His current research interests are in the field of labor economics and include the economics of discrimination, the economics of trade unions and public sector wage determination.

Lars Osberg is McCulloch Professor of Economics at Dalhousie University. He has a long-time interest in income distribution, poverty, and social policy. In recent years his research has emphasized structural change in labor markets, the determinants of economic insecurity, and social cohesion.

Shelley Phipps is Professor of Economics at Dalhousie University. Her current research focuses on the well-being of children and behavior within families. She is particularly interested in cross-national comparisons of social policy.

Bernard M. S. van Praag is a Professor and Managing Director of the Foundation of Economic Research at the University of Amsterdam. His research interests span labor economics, marketing research, and poverty and welfare measurement, with a focus on approaches utilizing subjective information.

Stephen Rhody, formerly at Syracuse University, is currently an economic consultant in Evanston, Illinois. He has published in the area of cross-national comparisons of income mobility. His current research interests include the determinants of self-employment, econometric estimation of duration models, and public policy issues.

Peter Saunders is Professor and Director of the Social Policy Research Centre at the University of New South Wales in Sydney. His main research interests are poverty and income distribution, with special emphasis on cross-national comparisons.

Anthony F. Shorrocks is a Research Professor at the University of Essex. His current research interests include living standards, inequality, poverty, taxation, unemployment, asset holdings, and inter-generational transfers.

Timothy M. Smeeding is Professor of Economics and Public Administration, and Director of the Center for Policy Research, at Syracuse University. He is the Director of the Luxembourg Income Study project, which he founded in 1983. His research focuses on poverty, inequality and public policy for vulnerable groups such as children, the aged, and the disabled.

Holly Sutherland is Director of the Microsimulation Unit in the Department of Applied Economics at the University of Cambridge. She is interested in the effect of social and fiscal policy on the income distribution, and currently coordinates a project to compare the impact of such policy across the countries of the European Union.

Jules J. M. Theeuwes is Professor of Applied Economics and Co-Director of the Foundation for Economic Research at the University of Amsterdam, and was formerly at the University of Leiden. His publications are in labor economics, with special interests in human capital, unemployment, labor market instruments, and the economics of aging and retirement.

Klass de Vos is a researcher at the econometrics section of the Economics Institute, Tilburg. His current research interests include the international comparison of poverty, social security, and pension arrangements.

Kathryn S. Wilson is Assistant Professor of Economics at Kent State University. Her research interests include education, disability, and teen pregnancy, with an emphasis on public policy effectiveness.

Isolde Woittiez is Assistant Professor at the Economics Department of Leiden University. Her current research interests include retirement issues, the influence of firm behaviour on labor supply and microeconometric analysis on well-being.

Barbara Wolfe is a Professor in the Departments of Economics and Preventive Medicine at the University of Wisconsin–Madison, and is currently Director of the Institute for Research on Poverty. Her research interests are in health economics, economics of poverty and income distribution, human capital, and public economics more generally.

M. Asghar Zaidi, formerly a researcher at Erasmus and Tilburg Universities, is now a PhD student at the University of Oxford. His current research interests include the measurement of poverty and inequality, especially among the elderly population of European countries.

1 Introduction

**Stephen P. Jenkins, Arie Kapteyn and
Bernard M.S. van Praag**

The measurement and explanation of household welfare is a multi-faceted undertaking. If one wants to study the well-being of households, one needs to understand household behavior and one needs to devise measures of well-being. The distribution of welfare across households is dispersed in any society, and the additional question arises how to characterize and evaluate this dispersion. Moreover, there are various ways in which one can learn more about the behavior and well-being of households: from pure reflection to broad-based empirical international comparisons; from looking at behavior only to the additional use of an array of subjective indicators of well-being. The chapters in this volume reflect many of, but certainly not all, the facets of household well-being and behavior, and the various approaches one can take to learn more about them.

The choice of approaches and facets is largely inspired by the scientific program adopted by Aldi Hagenaars in her all-too-brief career. This book reflects her interests and her methodological stance. A beautifully written and balanced review of Aldi Hagenaars' scientific program is given by Joop Hartog in chapter 2. It is at the same time an apt summary of the plan and the philosophy of this book. Aldi Hagenaars' work dealt with just about every conceivable economic aspect of household behavior. The starting point may have been a neoclassical one, but it was only a starting point and not a straitjacket. Hartog describes Aldi's work as an attempt to leave the neoclassical citadel in many directions simultaneously. The "citadel" metaphor can be fruitfully developed further: the neoclassical economics citadel is too small to hold all the insights to be acquired about household behavior, and so the fort needs to expand. If we are to make real progress in understanding household behavior and welfare, the city has to grow and gradually the old town walls will become obsolete: interesting relics for tourists or the archae-ologist rather than offering true protection against the outside world.

1

So what are the directions in which the neoclassical paradigm has to be extended? Some of them are non-controversial and have been dealt with by various authors: dynamics, more than one decision maker in the household, non-linear wage schedules, incomplete information, constraints on working hours, joint production. Others such as preference interdependence across households, or deviations from rationality generate more discussion. Even more controversial than some of the elements of theory that have to be amended are the tools that are used to do it.

Aldi Hagenaars was one of the members of what is sometimes referred to as the "Leiden School" (economists associated with Bernard van Praag), a group well known for recommending that welfare (or utility, if you prefer) be measured by means of direct questions. By its very nature, this "subjective" approach relates to central questions of social policy such as poverty, income inequality, and welfare, and it generates an interest in the use of household surveys to learn more about personal behavior and welfare. These elements not only characterize Aldi Hagenaars' work, they also sum up the approach of the chapters in this book.

Cross-national comparisons of the distribution of welfare

The approach of wanting to learn about the real world not hindered by preconceptions (or at least as few as possible), leaves plenty of room for the exploitation of diverse and rich data sources. Chapter 3, by Aldi herself and two co-authors, Klaas de Vos and Asghar Zaidi, is a prime example. It constitutes a report on a pioneering effort to construct poverty statistics for the European Community (EC). The sheer work of getting together microdata from twelve countries, processing them and solving the numerous inconsistencies that exist between them is mind-boggling. Just for a start, it turned out that data on household incomes in various countries were of too poor quality to be used in the analysis. Hence the authors were forced to use expenditure data instead. This may well prove to have been a blessing in disguise, for if one assumes that households are lifetime consumption smoothers, consumption may be a better reflection of life cycle resources than current income. Not surprisingly, this chapter pays considerable attention to issues of data quality, different definitions of poverty, different equivalence scales to compare the level of resources of different households, etc. The conclusions that one draws about the incidence of poverty in the EC are quite sensitive to the various choices that can be made, and policy makers should be aware of this.

The same point is made by the authors of chapter 4, Tony Atkinson, Karin Gardiner, Valerie Lechêne, and Holly Sutherland. They compare poverty rates between France and the United Kingdom and investigate the implications of a number of measurement choices. These include the use of expenditure versus income, defining the poverty line as a percentage of the median versus mean income, using persons versus households as the income-receiving unit, measuring income prior to or net of housing costs, using a variety of equivalence scales, and several fractions of median or mean income (40 percent, 50 percent, or 60 percent) to define the poverty line. They show that, for some choices, poverty rates in France and the United Kingdom are virtually identical, and in other cases poverty in France appears to be at least twice as high as in the United Kingdom. The upshot of their analysis is that politicians asking statisticians to calculate poverty rates on the basis of a rather loose definition may get very different answers, depending on how the statisticians fill in the details. This conclusion is strengthened further if one considers alternative poverty measures such as the poverty gap. It is then not difficult to "prove" that either France or the United Kingdom has the "most poverty," just by choosing the "right" measure and the "right" operationalization of it.

Neither income nor consumption expenditure are ideal statistical measures of material well-being for poverty measurement because both ignore variations across households in preferences for leisure or differences in the level of household production. Assuming that the ultimate concern with poverty derives from concerns about the welfare of households and their members, such neglect may be serious. Chapter 5, by Peter Saunders, Inge O'Connor, and Tim Smeeding, tries to correct for this omission by employing the concept of earnings capacity, originally introduced by Garfinkel and Haveman (1977). The basic idea is to look at the income people would have were everyone to spend the same amount of time in market work, in particular if each person were in full-time employment during the full year (so-called FYFT employment). This is earnings capacity. In order to operationalize such a concept, one has to impute the FYFT earnings for everyone who does not already work full time for the full year. This can be done by regressing log annual earnings on a set of explanatory variables using data for the people observed with FYFT employment. Next the estimated regression coefficients and error variance can be used to predict, and therefore impute, the earnings of everyone else not in FYFT employment.

The method is applied using data for the mid-1980s for five countries: Australia, Canada, West Germany, the Netherlands, and the United States. (The data derive from the Luxembourg Income Study (LIS) and only married couples are considered.) These countries vary quite substantially in terms of unemployment and participation rates, so it comes as no surprise that moving from actual earnings to earnings capacity has different effects in different countries. For instance, mean earnings go up by 28 percent in the United States if we move from actual earnings to earnings capacity. In the Netherlands the corresponding amount is 53 percent. The adjustments reduce inequality in all countries concerned, but again the change is much larger in the Netherlands than in the United States or Canada.

Besides the issues concerning analysis of income and earnings distributions across and within countries cited so far, there is one dimension – income mobility – which has not been mentioned at all. In addition to cross-section shapshots on income, one also needs longitudinal movies. In chapter 6, Richard Burkhauser, Douglas Holtz-Eakin, and Stephen Rhody add this additional twist to the study of income distributions, and compare the perspectives derived.

The relevance of mobility for distributional assessments can be brought home by considering a very simple example. Imagine a society consisting of 100 individuals, with an income distribution which is completely fixed over time. Assume furthermore that individuals live for 100 periods, and that incomes are permuted systematically over time in such a way that in each period individuals have a different income. Thus after 100 periods, the income history of every individual differs only in the order in which incomes were received. If, furthermore, the interest rate is zero and capital markets are perfect, everyone has the same lifetime income equal to the mean income in the society. This would be an example of a society with constant cross-sectional income inequality, substantial mobility, and complete lifetime equality of resources. In a somewhat less stylized world one could at least imagine that a society with a high income inequality at any given point in time and high mobility could actually exhibit a distribution of lifetime resources as equal as that of another society with lower cross-sectional income inequality and lower mobility.

Burkhauser, Holtz-Eakin, and Rhody compare income inequality and mobility in Germany and the United States in the second half of the 1980s. They find higher income inequality in the United States than in Germany (which is not unexpected), but surprisingly they do not find very large differences in mobility across the two countries. (The conclusions vary somewhat, depending on the exact definition of "mobility" and the income measure considered.) Why the greater competitiveness of the US labor market did not lead to higher mobility as well as higher inequality is an intriguing finding, deserving of further investigation. Whatever the case, the authors' results underscore the importance and relevance of analyzing mobility as well as inequality when contemplating social policy.

Subjective approaches

A crucial issue for virtually any anti-poverty policy is how to define "poverty" in the first place. This issue has several aspects, including the choice of a poverty line (identification) and the summarizing of the information about individual material deprivation (aggregation). Rather than telling us what in their opinion the correct, or at least a reasonable, approach should be, Yoram Amiel and Frank Cowell in chapter 7 asked a group of 340 students in six countries about their perceptions of poverty. They showed the respondents various hypothetical income distributions and poverty lines, and then asked them to compare these situations in terms of the severity of poverty associated with these hypothetical situations. In this way, they were able to uncover different dimensions in the perception of poverty – for instance, whether "poverty" is perceived mainly to be a relative or an absolute concept, the difference between a change in poverty implied when all incomes change proportionally or by the same amount, etc. The empirical results are not clear cut, but they are intriguing. It appears, for instance, that slight manipulation of the hypothetical situations offered to the respondents may have quite an effect on judgments about poverty. These subtleties justify extensive further research into what shapes our perception of "poverty."

Peter Kooreman investigates the explanatory power of subjective information in the modeling of consumer choices in chapter 8. This is another example of the many ways in which one may cross the boundaries of traditional neoclassical revealed preference territory and learn something on the way. Kooreman starts out by building a neoclassical model of consumer choice, in this case relating to the choice of a country in which to spend a vacation. Since different countries provide different characteristics, a utility function defined in terms of vacation characteristics (and other consumption) can be employed to model the choice of destination country as a constrained utility maximization problem. The availability of a data set with respondents' subjective statements about the importance of various vacation characteristics (e.g. whether there are many possibilities for sightseeing, the quality of food and drink) permits empirical modeling. Although some methodological caveats have to be kept in mind, the overall impression is that the subjective data contribute significantly to an explanation of destination country choices.

Whereas Kooreman uses subjective measures as explanatory variables, Isolde Woittiez and Jules Theeuwes (chapter 9) use a subjective measure of well-being (a score on the Cantril scale) as a dependent variable. They try to explain variations in self-reported well-being by a host of variables: labor market status, income, education, age, sex, housing variables, variables referring to the respondent's partner, labor market history, and various proxies for preferences for work. There are many reasons why such analyses are of interest. For instance, one may want to look at income maintenance policies, family policies, and the like. The authors concentrate on the effects of labor market status, using the other variables as controls. Generally non-workers (unemployed, disabled, pensioners, non-participants) are less happy than workers, with the exception of the early retired. A closer analysis, using further subjective information, suggests that the main reason for this is the involuntary nature of these non-working states. This also explains why the early retired are about as happy as the working population: freedom to choose breeds happiness.

Summarizing welfare

What is "inequality?" Or, to put it in Gary Fields' terms, "Do inequality measures measure inequality?" Most of the economic literature on inequality looks at income distributions (or distributions of anything else) from a social welfare viewpoint. Famous examples are the inequality measures developed by Atkinson (1970) and Dalton (1920). In chapter 10 Fields abstracts from this, and tries to arrive at reasonable criteria by which one distribution can be judged more equal than another. Alongside the generally accepted Lorenz criteria, Fields develops criteria based on the concepts of "elitism of the rich" and "isolation of the poor." This leads to a class of inequality measures which may be narrowed or broadened depending on which further specific criteria one may find reasonable to impose when considering inequality. The chapter nicely traces out where consensus among observers may be likely and where different people will hold different opinions on what "inequality" really means.

A different approach is taken by Tony Shorrocks in chapter 11. He considers the distribution of "bads" (as opposed to "goods") and introduces what he labels "deprivation profiles." The deprivation profile is related to the distribution function of bads (and therefore also to a transformation of the generalized Lorenz curve). Examples of bads include personal material deprivation, earnings discrimination, and horizontal inequity. Shorrocks' chapter usefully draws attention to common elements in measurement methods used in a variety of contexts, and shows how different distributions of bads may be ranked in terms of the amount of deprivation they entail. He considers a number of basic desirable properties which any aggregate summary measure should possess and thence defines a class of aggregate deprivation indices (which encompasses the Hagenaars–Dalton family). Shorrocks shows how unanimous deprivation index orderings are equivalent to orderings by deprivation curves, and illustrates his arguments with a specific application to poverty measurement. Shorrocks then applies this apparatus to the study of poverty and the properties of classes of poverty indices. The deprivation profiles are very helpful in investigating circumstances in which different poverty indices will yield similar rankings of poverty across countries or over time.

The robustness of poverty rankings to the choice of summary measure is also James Foster's and Yong Jin's starting point in chapter 12. They consider the influence on measured poverty of both the choice of poverty line and the sensitivity of the poverty index to differences in the distribution of resources below it. The authors concentrate on so-called Dalton utility-gap indices, i.e. indices that are additive functions of the shortfalls between each individual's utility of poverty line income and the utility of actual income. They show that poverty comparisons can be undertaken by considering the associated utility of income distributions and invoking well known theorems on stochastic dominance. One particularly nice example of robustness of the Dalton utility-gap measures is provided by their theorem 2, which says that if we use two different utility functions to operationalize the index and we find for one utility function that a given income distribution exhibits less poverty than another, then this conclusion will remain unchanged if we replace the utility function by one which is more risk averse.

The economies in transition in Eastern Europe are a fascinating laboratory to study how changes in economic structure and social policy affect the distribution of well-being. In her chapter on the changes that took place in the Czech and Slovak republics between 1989 and 1992, Thesia Garner (chapter 13) explores the evolution of income and expenditure inequality during this period. Most western observers would probably guess that inequality would increase substantially when capitalism was introduced. Surprisingly, this does not seem to have happened; certainly not in the Czech republic, and only a little in the Slovak republic. Garner ascribes the slower than expected movement in inequality to a conscious policy, especially in the Czech republic, which reputedly has a strong preference for equality. Combined with the relative prosperity of the Czech republic compared to other economies in transition, the results suggest that economic transition in the Czech republic may be one of the smoothest in existence.

The household, income, and welfare

Describing or characterizing income inequality or the incidence of poverty is one thing; influencing it is another. A prominent policy instrument for influencing the distribution of personal economic well-being is unemployment insurance (UI). In chapter 14, Lars Osberg, Sadettin Erksoy, and Shelley Phipps consider the change in the distribution of well-being associated with UI reforms in Canada. In particular, they compare the 1971 UI regime with the 1994 UI reforms. The 1994 reform substantially reduced the role of the welfare state in income maintenance policies. Such changes not only have incentive effects, e.g. on labor supply, and redistributive effects (the usual focus), but they also affect the income uncertainty people face. The incidence of uncertainty, and hence the impact of the reform, will be different for different groups of people. To evaluate the impact of reforms on economic well-being, one has to simulate behavior under both the old and the new regime, and to evaluate the welfare cost of increased uncertainty. This is exactly what the authors do, using an elaborate micro-simulation model with a database of some 20,000 Canadians (respondents to Statistics Canada's 1984 Survey of Assets and Debts). The labor supply part of the simulation model is based on a Stone–Geary specification for the utility function of individuals, and the same Stone–Geary specification is used to evaluate the welfare loss due to increased uncertainty. The chapter's findings indicate that the UI cutbacks increased inequality and may have decreased average economic well-being.

Although the parameters of the Stone–Geary utility function have been estimated from the behavorial model underlying the simulations, there is one piece of information missing. The labor supply model is static, and hence any monotonic transformation of the utility function will yield identical labor supply, but not identical risk premia. The authors compare the risk aversion implied by their utility specification with estimates from other sources (e.g. the financial literature) and conclude that the Stone–Geary specification employed probably entails too little risk aversion. This implies that their estimate of the welfare loss due to increased uncertainty is a conservative one.

Educational attainment is a primary determinant of the income an individual may expect to enjoy during his or her life. Conversely, decisions to invest in schooling may be expected to be influenced by the extra expected income it generates. In chapter 15, Robert Haveman, Kathryn Wilson, and Barbara Wolfe build a structural model in which an individual's decision to invest in schooling is a function of individual characteristics, family characteristics, neighborhood characteristics, and the expected income stream associated with the schooling choice made. To properly operationalize such a model requires an extremely rich data set. Haveman, Wilson, and Wolfe use the US Panel Study of Income Dynamics (PSID) and add neighborhood information by matching small area data from the 1970 and 1980 Censuses to the location of the children in the sample. The panel nature of the data set makes it possible, amongst other things, to construct expected income streams conditional on decisions to graduate or not for young people with varying characteristics. These expected income streams feed into a structural model of schooling choice. In terms of significance of estimates and plausibility of results the model appears to work extremely well. Expected income has a significant effect on schooling choice. For instance, the authors estimate that if one were able to increase the future expected income of high school graduates by 10 percent, this would reduce drop out rates by somewhere between 6 and 18 percent. Conversely, income maintenance schemes that gave more support to high school drop outs (either by design, or inadvertently), would increase drop out rates.

One problem intrinsic to any empirical study of welfare across households is the choice and construction of equivalence scales to account for differences in household size and composition (or more generally, "needs"). Chapters 3 and 4, by Aldi Hagenaars, Klaas de Vos, and Asghar Zaidi, and by Tony Atkinson, Karen Gardiner, Valerie Lechêne, and Holly Sutherland, draw attention to the sensitivity of empirical conclusions to the choice of equivalence scale. However, rather than having to choose an equivalence scale, one would prefer to let the data, in combination with some well established theory, tell us what equivalence scale to choose. Unfortunately, as the chapter by Richard Blundell (chapter 16) bears out, the story told by theory is largely a negative one: finding unique equivalence scales is impossible, at least on the basis of the data usually available. In essence, the problem is that information on expenditures of households can tell us a fair amount about the costs of children, but not a lot about their benefits. This fundamental identification problem has been known for some time, at least since Pollak's and Wales' (1979) paper. Blundell characterizes this identification problem borrowing from his important work with Arthur Lewbel (Blundell and Lewbel, 1991), and reminds us that the identification problem can be solved only by invoking extra information. This information may refer to preferences for different family compositions, subjective information, or it may come from "reasonable" restrictions imposed on preferences by the investigator.

To these possibilities Blundell adds exploitation of information about intertemporal choices. It is well known that, intra-temporally, a utility function can be identified only up to a monotonic transformation, and since the transformation may depend on family composition, this is the root of the identification problem. However, it is also well known that intertemporal choice restricts the number of transformations of a utility function consistent with observed behavior to a much smaller class. Hence, if one has intertemporal data on consumption and demographics, further headway may be made. This is a neat idea worth pursuing.

The chapter by Blundell is theoretical. By contrast David Johnson's chapter (chapter 17) is empirical, looking at inequality across households and persons. In doing so, Johnson has to address at least two significant issues, namely the choice of equivalence scales to deflate income (or consumption) of different households, and how to account for income inequality within each household. Both issues are practical and fundamental. The fundamental part has to do with an observational problem: generally we do not observe intra-household allocation, nor do we know, as Blundell's chapter shows, how family composition itself influences welfare. One way of handling these problems is to make a range of different assumptions and to explore the extent to which these affect the conclusions of one's analysis, and Johnson does precisely this. He estimates eight different equivalence scales (using the US Consumer Expenditure Survey) and assumes four different sharing rules for consumption within the household. For these various possibilities he then considers four different inequality measures. Not perhaps surprisingly, the estimates of the inequality measures vary considerably across scales and sharing rules. This forcefully drives home the point that we need to know much more about what is going on within the household if we want to have a really reliable basis for social policy.

A similar issue is taken up by Stephen Jenkins and Nigel O'Leary in chapter 18 when studying trends in the income differences between men and women in the United Kingdom between 1971 and 1991. Jenkins and O'Leary consider only two polar sharing rules: the first (equal sharing) assumes that within a family all incomes are shared equally, whereas the second (minimal sharing) assumes that no sharing takes place at all. It seems safe to assume that the truth is somewhere in between these extremes. Observe nonetheless that virtually all income distribution analyses, including official ones, use the equal sharing rule. It is interesting to note that the evidence for a closing of the gender gap is much more clear cut under the minimal sharing than under the equal sharing rule. Since the number of women earning an income in the labor market increased over these two decades, and since women tend to earn more than before on average, their income distribution became more similar to the income distribution for men. The situation under an equal sharing assumption is more complex, because the outcomes are now directly affected by changes in the male distribution. For instance, if higher incomes of wives coincide with lower incomes of husbands, then under equal sharing the income distribution of females may not change, even if females have more own income than before. The change in female income distribution will then be dependent on a number of inter-related factors, including the number of couples, the number of single females, trends in male and female earnings, etc. To avoid these complexities, one may be tempted to assume only minimal sharing. However, where some sharing does occur, this would not be an accurate picture and hence one must accept the somewhat blurred picture that equal sharing causes. Under equal sharing, the share of females among the very poor appears to be clearly falling. For the rest, the evidence is mixed. Combining the evidence under the two assumptions, the gender gap does appear to be closing, but at an irritatingly slow rate.

The reader should have no problem in discerning the common thread in the multitude of topics and approaches offered in this volume. In the end, it is all about how to better understand individual behavior and individual and social welfare, and how these interact. By improving our understanding we may ultimately be able to improve the human lot. In the Netherlands, this ideal has become firmly entrenched through Tinbergen's shining example (see Jolink, Kapteyn and Keuzenkamp, forthcoming), and has motivated many young economists in the Netherlands for decades. In her short academic career, Aldi Hagenaars accepted Tinbergen's academic mission and undertook it with engaging enthusiasm and notable success, nationally and internationally. Sadly she did not have the opportunity to carry out the mission to the fullest of her capacities. This volume is not only a tribute to her and her work, but also an attempt to keep the flame she lit burning.

References

Atkinson, A.B., 1970. "On the measurement of inequality," *Journal of Economic Theory*, 2, 244–63

Blundell, R. and A. Lewbel, 1991. "The information content of equivalence scales," *Journal of Econometrics*, 150, 49–68

Dalton, H., 1920. "The measurement of the inequality of incomes," *Economic Journal*, 30, 348–61

Garfinkel, I. and R. Haveman, 1977. "Earnings capacity, economic status, and poverty," *Journal of Human Resources*, 12, 49–70

Jolink, A., A. Kapteyn and H. Keuzenkamp, forthcoming. "Jan Tinbergen (1903–1994), a pragmatic utopian," *Economic Journal*

Pollak, R.A. and T.J. Wales, 1979. "Welfare comparisons and equivalence scales," *American Economic Review*, 69, 216–21

Van Dalen, H. and A. Klamer, 1996. *Telgen van Tinbergen – Het verhaal van de Nederlandse Economen* (Tinbergen offspring – a story of Dutch economists), Uitgeverij Balans

2 Escape from *cittadella neoclassica*: reflections on the work of Aldi Hagenaars

Joop Hartog

Further research should certainly be carried out in the area of female labor supply, but it is to be recommended not to narrow the area of research to economic models and economic variables only. A thoughtful combination of economic, psychological and sociological variables, obtained from survey questions, is a fruitful research strategy. It may be time, after the economic revolution, for a behavioral revolution in economics. I would recommend the two types of revolutionaries to join forces and thus to understand better one of the most challenging developments of this century. (Hagenaars, 1988c)

This is an edited extract from a paper on female labor supply that Aldi Hagenaars wrote in 1988, but it contains references to all the features that characterized her work. A focus on female labor supply, showing one of the most challenging developments in this century in terms of the nature of work and the diversion between home and market time. A strong emphasis on the use of up-to-date econometrics, applied to large data sets. Surveys specifically designed for the research issue, instead of using second-hand data. And always trying to break away from the narrow confines of highly stylized neoclassical models.

On September 8, 1988, Aldi accepted the Chair of Professor of the Economics of the Household Sector with an inaugural lecture in the Auditorium of the Erasmus University in Rotterdam. Such an inaugural address serves to take a stand, to assess the quality of the conquered plot in the academic field. It is an opportunity to explain to the audience where the weeds grow and where the crop flourishes, and to unfold plans for further cultivation. In this memorial reflection, I will look over Aldi's shoulder from the perspective of that day, see where she came from, and see where she planned to go. I found it not difficult to discover a unity in her work, to observe how separate threads were spun into a single garment. But of course, as in all the everyday papers we write, it may be just a fantasy.

Her inaugural address, a companion research paper and a related textbook all express the same views. The textbook she wrote (in Dutch) with Sophia Wunderink-van Veen (1990) presents lectures on production and consumption in households under the title "Easy Won, Easy Gone." The book starts out from the neoclassical theory on the allocation of time and from there moves on to consider the weaknesses of that model and the possibilities for improvement. The narrative easily shows how Aldi's own work fits in and how she tried to contribute to better models.

Aldi accepts Becker's theory on household consumption and production, and states that the objections that one may have can be overcome, but at a high cost in terms of model complexity and data requirements. Eight objections are listed. The model is about a single person rather than a household, it is static, assumes full information on income and prices, neglects constraints on working hours, assumes rational choice, neglects preference dependences, neglects variations in the hourly wage rate, and ignores the reality that in the household joint production is a fact of life. As far as I can judge, Aldi attempted explicitly to deal with all of these eight objections. In hindsight, we can say that she had been seeking the gates of the *cittadella neoclassica* for a long time. Perhaps she was now planning to leave the city through all the gates simultaneously?

Aldi's experiences had certainly prepared her for a major attempt to break out. After her graduation in Rotterdam, she started her academic career in Leiden. And her magistrate at that time, Bernard van Praag, can hardly be said to have imposed a neoclassical reign. She got infected with the individual Welfare Function of Income (WFI) virus, an infection that is known to be permanent. She wrote her thesis, *The Perception of Poverty* (1986a), with a concept of poverty based on the WFI; it would prepare her for her later attempts to break out.

The WFI was introduced by Bernard van Praag, in his own thesis (1968). The theoretical foundation has become buried these days under a mountain of empirical work, but it is interesting to note that a basic presumption is the consumer's limited capacity to solve optimization problems. Van Praag follows Lancaster's (1966) approach of decomposing consumption services of goods as services derived from the characteristics of those goods, an approach that Aldi clearly sympathizes with when she outlines her encompassing structural model of the household.

In her (1986) book, Aldi defines the poverty line as that income which just yields a specified utility level. For utility, she uses the WFI, with a poverty threshold at 0.5, halfway along the utility scale. The welfare evaluation of income depends on actual income ("preference drift"), but this is solved out. Of course the other parameters remain: the poverty level depends on family size and reference group. Aldi applies and estimates these concepts for eight countries of the EC, using a survey she helped design that generated some 24,000 observations. The result is a wealth of empirical information on poverty in Europe. Aldi calculates the elasticity of the poverty line across the European countries to national median income at about 0.5. That puts the poverty line halfway between perfectly absolute and perfectly relative (with elasticities of 0 and 1). The elasticity to the log standard deviation falls between 0.3 and 0.6: welfare evaluations are clearly sensitive to national environments.

With the use of a cardinal measure of welfare Aldi has left the *cittadella neoclassica* through the *porta gustatus*, the Gate of Taste, and we see later that she is willing to travel quite far along that road, all the way to "Happiness." In the book she edited with Ruut Veenhoven (1989d), on the scars left by the 1980–82 recession, she wants to know whether people remain equally happy throughout a recession. And in that book she states that we do not have one measure of "welfare or happiness" that is sufficiently accepted to be used as a single measure. Hence, we should collect as much information as possible, from as many sources as we can get.

Aldi also explored the countryside through the *porta familiaris*, the Gate of the Household. In a number of studies she estimated labor supply and allocation of time behavior for partners in a household. In joint work with Homan and van Praag (1983c) she used the WFI to derive the shadow price of household production as the marginal rate of substitution between consumption and time devoted to household production. This uses the rate of substitution to estimate the value of household production.

With the same authors (1984a) Aldi estimated a consumption-cum-time allocation model with a dominant distinction between short-run and long-run choices. Time spent in a labor market and expenditures on housing are assumed to be fixed in the short run, while time spent on home production and expenditures on food and clothing are assumed to be variable. This was another experience that would later return in the master plan.

Aldi dealt with issues on imperfect information by considering the prospects of obtaining a job. Jointly with Gusta Renes (1989a), she tried to discover through what sort of a lens the unemployed perceive their job offers. The authors use the observations from a questionnaire published in a newspaper read by 700,000 people, and returned by 23,000 (clearly, Aldi was not too fond of small samples). They set up an econometric model to analyze expectations of finding a job, desired working hours and reservation wages. They concluded that there were marked differences between married men and women. Men based their perception of the probability of obtaining a job on a comparison between reservation wage and the perceived distribution of offered wages. Women, however, looked at the distribution of offered hours and the relative position of the hours they would prefer to offer.

With van Praag and van Eck (1983a), Aldi explored the rugged terrain of errors in measuring income inequality. The authors use two observations on an individual's income, one from an oral interview measured in intervals, and one from a mail-back questionnaire left after the interview. Inequality measures can be seriously biased, with measurement error inflating measured inequality and classification error deflating it. This was perhaps the only piece of research that did not fit a training plan for a revolutionary who planned to break away from a city she was suffocating in.

In 1988 Aldi was ready to take the Chair of the Economics of the Household Sector. She climbed on the walls and pointed to the beautiful fields that surround the city, and to other cities on the horizon. She explained how she wanted to move forward. Her plan is laid out in the paper she wrote on "The economics of household activities" (1988c), the paper from which she derived her inaugural lecture. Yes, the neoclassical model of consumer behavior has mathematical elegance, but it is a poor description of human behavior. The assumptions have been criticized by economists and by other social scientists, in marketing research the model is almost completely rejected, the new discipline of economic psychology has contributed substantially to better understanding. Many extensions have been made, but we lack an integrated framework. And that is precisely what Aldi set out to present in her paper, a synthesis of theories of human behavior and a research plan deriving from it. From the simplest model of spending a given income on given commodities, she moves to Becker's New Home Economics, because time is the essential constraint. She embraces Lancaster's characteristics model, because it can deal with new products, as new bundles of the old characteristics which *a priori* can be recognized as substitutes. Here, she also perceives an opening towards market research for consumer goods, by dwelling on a well known model in psychology and marketing, the Fishbein model (Fishbein and Aizen, 1975). In Fishbein's model, a consumer chooses a specific brand to maximize the attribute score, weighted by perceptions and relative importance. Aldi subscribes to the need to model the influence of different members of a household explicitly, e.g. by game theory, although she does not yet include that in the formalized model she presents. She appreciates an extension of Becker's model to make prices, wages, and utility dependent on the time of day, to explain the activity patterns across the day (most people sleep during night hours), but she is unhappy with a model that assumes unconstrained optimization across all available hours. Instead, she borrows activity analysis from transport studies. Combining it with the concept of social settings and allowing for life cycle variation, she makes it to the core of the new model she wants to develop.

Activities, like shopping, taking care of children, enjoying leisure activities like listening to music or reading a novel, are of course subject to the common constraints of time and income. But there are also many restrictions deriving from biological, institutional, and social settings of time and place. Shops are open only during particular hours (at least in the Netherlands), children should be taken to school at the pre-set time on pre-set days, cooking has to be done before dinner. In a household, the results of the activities can be shared, giving them the character of public goods, and members can be substituted in the production, or the time pattern of each member's production can be varied.

Aldi wanted to build her model on the basis of detailed description of these activities. Salient features are the assignment to specific time slots and the distinction between obligatory and optional activities. It is here that the constraints manifest themselves – biological, institutional, and social. In the obligatory activities, there is only a choice of technology: cooking at home or going out for dinner, father or mother taking the child to school. The specific time slots for activities add constraints to the choice problem. Teaching an evening class and going to the theatre are not feasible on the same evening. To make any progress with this model we need large-scale panel observations on time use: what are the activities that households and household members engage in, how are they spaced in time, how are they influenced by the stages of the life-cycle, by the social environment of the household? For each household type, an inventory should be made of obligatory activities and of available technologies. Obligatory activities are only subject to technological choice, free activities can be chosen to maximize utility, given the time and money left over after the obligatory activities have been performed, and subject to the constraints of time slots.

The (1986c) paper indicated how Aldi perceived her journey outside the *cittadella neoclassica*, and it stipulates her hopes. She expected the model to provide openings towards work done in consumer marketing research, as her observations on activities would lay out life styles, and show the effects of life cycle stages. For analyzing aggregate effects of changes in household formation, labor market participation and consumer behavior, she proposed to build a micro-simulation model of households and their activity patterns. And she outlined how all the issues that occupied her might find a place in the framework of the activity model: labor supply behavior, preferences subject to social norms, choice patterns within the household from the interaction of the partners, analysis of poverty related to earnings capacity left over after obligatory activities have taken their share.

In the end, of course, it is not a magic plan to leave the *cittadella neoclassica* through eight gates simultaneously. Neither should that be a surprise: we do not work by magic. Even revolutionaries have to implement their great designs by solid work. And rather than pipe dreams of fancy magic, Aldi had a smart strategy. With the periscope of the questionnaire, she recommended spying on the grandest scale possible. Watching carefully what the enemy is doing, taking good notes, drawing inferences and, finally, coming out when victory is unavoidable.

It would have been so good to watch her battle, to see where she would lose and retreat, and where she could fiercely plant her banner, proud and smiling. To see how far she would have extended her periscope and what areas she would have abandoned, adjusting her plans along the way. Re-reading her papers and writing this little essay, inevitably many images of her came back. There is a memory from many years ago, when we both had left a conference dinner, at some Econometric Society meeting. We walked down the stairs of a century-old *pallazzo*. At my feet, on one of the steps, a rose was lying. It was still fresh, so I picked it up and gave it to Aldi: gallantry, you know, comes easy after a convivial meal. "Ah", she said with a smile, "finally."

I dedicate this little essay as my final rose to her.

References

Fishbein, M. and I. Aizen, 1975. *Belief, Attitude and Behavior: An Introduction to Theory and Research*, Amsterdam: Addison-Wesley

Hagenaars, A., 1978. "Missing data: a multivariate approach," report 78.09, Center for Research in Economics of the Public Sector (with B.M.S. van Praag)

1979. "Income inequality: measurement and reality," report 79.09, Center for Research in Economics of the Public Sector (with B.M.S. van Praag and N. Bouma)

1980. "Poverty in Europe," *Economisch Statistische Berichten*, 65, 1236–9 (with B.M.S. van Praag and J. van Weeren)

1982. "Poverty in Europe," *Review of Income and Wealth*, 28, 345–59 (with B.M.S. van Praag and J. van Weeren)

1983a. "The influence of classification and observation errors on the measurement of income inequality," *Econometrica*, 5, 1093–1108 (with B.M.S. van Praag and W. van Eck)

1983b. "Meetfout gemeten" (Measuring measurement errors), *Kwantitatieve Methoden*, 12, 20–31 (with B.M.S. van Praag)

1983c. "Monetaire waardering van huishoudelijke produktie met behulp van subjectieve substitutievoeten" (Monetary valuation of household production by means of subjective marginal rates of substitution), report 83.27, Center for Research in Economics of the Public Sector (with M.E. Homan and B.M.S. van Praag)

1984a. "The female participation decision, household cost functions and the shadow price of household production," report 84.08, Center for Research in Economics of the Public Sector (with M.E. Homan and B.M.S. van Praag)

1984b. "De monetaire waardering van huishoudelijke produktie" (The monetary valuation of household production), report 84.10, Center for Research in Economics of the Public Sector (with M.E. Homan and B.M.S. van Praag)

1984c. "Draagkrachtverschillen tussen huishoudens met één, resp. twee kostwinners" (Differences in ability to pay between one- and two-earner households), *Economisch Statistische Berichten*, 69, 552–9 (with M.E. Homan and B.M.S. van Praag)

1985a. "Household cost functions and the value of home production in one- and two-earner families," report 85.10, Center for Research in Economics of the Public Sector (with M.E. Homan and B.M.S. van Praag)

1985b. "The perception of poverty," PhD thesis, Leiden University

1985c. "A synthesis of poverty line definitions," *Review of Income and Wealth*, 31, 139–53 (with B.M.S. van Praag)

1986a. *The Perception of Poverty*, Amsterdam: North-Holland

1986b. "Inkomens bestedingen en schulden in Nederland" (Incomes, expenditures, and debts in the Netherlands), Ministry of Social Affairs and Employment (with K. de Vos)

1986c. "Perceptie en realiteit op de arbeidsmarkt" (Perception and reality in the labour market), *Economisch Statistische Berichten*, 71, 520–6 (with G. Renes and B.M.S. van Praag)

1986d. "Interhuishoudelijke vergelijkinen van consumptie, welvaart en tijdsallocatie" (Inter-household comparisons of consumption, welfare and the allocation of time), Ministry of Economic Affairs (with M.E. Homan and B.M.S. van Praag)

1986e. "Am en arm is twee – een empirische vergelijking van armoededefinities" (An empirical comparison of poverty definitions), Ministry of Social Affairs and Employment (with K. de Vos and B.M.S. van Praag)

1986f. "Non cash income in the Netherlands," report for the Luxembourg Income Study Noncash Project

1986g. "Poverty and relative deprivation: note on a class of decomposable poverty indices," report no. 86.16, Center for Research in Economics of the Public Sector

1986h. "Classificatie van armoede" (Classification of poverty), in J.W. de Beus and J.A.A. van Doorn (eds.), *De Geconstrueerde Samenleving*, Meppel: Boom

1987a. "A class of poverty indices," *International Economic Review*, 28, 583–607

1987b. "Armoede, arbeid en sociale zekerheid" (Poverty, labour, and social insurance), Ministry of Social Affairs and Employment (with K. de Vos and B.M.S. van Praag)

1987c. "Report on changes in the population of poor, the Netherlands, 1977–1985," report for the European Program to Combat Poverty

1987d. "Betaalde an onbetaalde arbeid van de vijftienjarigen van nu" (Paid and unpaid work of fifteen year olds), *Sociaal Maandblad Arbeid* (with R. de Zwart)

1987e. "Draagkracht en vrijetijdsbesteding" (Ability to pay and the allocation of leisure), *Economisch Statistische Berichten*, 72, 562–3 (with M.E. Homan, P.S.A. Renaud, and J.J. Siegers)

1987f. "The distribution of cash and noncash income in the Netherlands," report for the Luxembourg Income Study (with C.A. de Kam, F. van Herwaarden, and L. Ruitenberg)

1987g. "Poverty and welfare in eight European countries," paper presented at the Atlantic Economic Society meeting, Munich

1987h. "Improving the Luxembourg Income Study (LIS) income measure: microdata estimates of the size distribution of cash and noncash income in eight countries," Luxembourg Income Study Noncash Project (with B. Buhmann, R. Hauser, P. Hedstrom, C.A. de Kam, M. O'Higgins, P. Saunders, G. Schmaus, T. Smeeding, and M. Wolfson)

1988a. "Representativteit van een dagbladenquête" (Representativeness of a newspaper survey), *Kwantitatieve Methoden*, 29, 13–47 (with E.P. van Duin)

1988b. "The definition and measurement of poverty," *Journal of Human Resources*, 23, 211–22 (with K. de Vos)

1988c. "The economics of household activities," report of the Department of Household Economics, Erasmus University, Rotterdam

1988d. *Huishoudens in de Economie* (Households in the economy), inaugural lecture, Leiden: Stenfert Kroese Vitgevers

1989a. "The perceived distribution of job characteristics," *European Economic Review*, 33, 845–62 (with G. Renes)

1989b. "Arbeidsmarktparticipatie en leeftijd van de vrouq bij geboorte van het eerste kind" (Labour force participation and age at birth of the first child), Central Bureau of Statistics, The Hague (with L. Rombouts)

1989c. "Poverty research using LIS datasets," Eurostat, Poverty Working Group, Indicators of Poverty, Direction of Social and Regional Statistics

1989d. "Did the crisis really hurt? Introduction to the problem" in R. Veenhoven (ed.), *Did the Crisis Really Hurt?*, Rotterdam: Rotterdam University Press, 1–23 (with R. Veenhoven)

1990. *Soo Gewonne, soo Verteert. Economie van de Huishoudelijke Sector* (Easy Won, Easy Gone. Economics of the Household Sector), Leiden and Antwerp: Stenfert Kroese, Vitgevers (with S.W. Wunderink-van Veen)

1991. "Family equivalence scales," *Discussion Paper*, EURDP 91–06, Department of Economic Sociology and Psychology, Erasmus University, Rotterdam

1992a. "Family equivalence scales," *Discussion Paper*, Department of Economic Sociology and Psychology, Erasmus University, Rotterdam (with K. de Vos and S.W. Wunderink-van Veen)

1992b. "Labour supply in micro-simulation models," in Y.K. Brunner and H.-G. Petersen (eds.), *Simulation Models in Tax and Transfer Policy*, Frankfurt and New York: Campus Verlag, 479–507

1994. "Poverty statistics in the late 1980s: research based on microdata," Eurostat publication, Theme 3, Series D, Office for Official Publications of the European Commuinities, Luxembourg (with K. de Vos and M.A. Zaidi)

Lancaster, K.J. 1966. "A new approach to consumer theory," *Journal of Political Economy*, 74, 132–7.

Van Praag, B.M.S. 1968, *Individual Walfare Functions and Consumer Behavior*, Amsterdam: North Holland

Part I
Cross-national comparisons of the distribution of welfare

3   Patterns of poverty in Europe

Aldi Hagenaars, Klaas de Vos and Asghar Zaidi

Introduction

This chapter presents the main results of a research project that aims to provide statistical information on poverty in countries of the European Community (EC). The research has been carried out by the Department of Economic Sociology and Psychology of Erasmus University, Rotterdam, the Netherlands, under the umbrella of the so-called Poverty-3 programme of the European Community and under the auspices of Eurostat, the Statistical Office of the European Community.[1]

In providing information on poverty in the European Community countries, two rather contradictory objectives are pursued. The first is to provide statistics. Researchers should not restrict themselves to one limited definition of poverty, but should present a range of statistical information, associated with a number of different concepts of poverty. The second objective is to provide information that helps to monitor the living conditions of the least privileged. For this second purpose the researchers are usually asked to present a clear cut choice, one specific poverty definition and one poverty rate, that can be followed in time to trace changes in patterns of poverty across Europe.

The final report "Poverty statistics in the late 1980s: research based on microdata" (Hagenaars, de Vos and Zaidi, 1994) may be said to meet the first objective. This chapter seeks to present the results of our research in a more compact (and thus more limited) way, by choosing one particular concept of poverty out of the range presented in the full report.

The results of the research may be characterized by the great care that has been taken in harmonizing the concepts and definitions used across countries. For the first time in the history of European research on poverty, micro-databases on all European Community countries have been accessible to researchers. This allows us to define "total expenditures" and "total income" in a consistent and comparable way in all

European Community countries. It also allows us to analyze what the effect is on the population of poor of particular ways to compensate for the cost of additional household members. Moreover, it allows us to look at the effect of a number of characteristics on the odds of being poor, rather than having to rely on one- or two-dimensional tables.

Although we present patterns of poverty for a particular choice of the poverty definition, it will be shown that some elements of this choice are essentially arbitrary, and cannot therefore be justified by scientific arguments: the choice is made in order not to overburden the reader with information. Moreover, even the greatest care in harmonizing the concepts used cannot always overcome differences in the methodologies of the data sources. An accessible micro-database on household resources in European Community countries, based on a common methodology, should in future be made available to provide information on living conditions and poverty. We hope that this report is a step in that direction.

What is "poverty"?

Numerous books and articles have been written on the definition and measurement of poverty. We have chosen not to enter that debate in the context of the present project, although the authors have contributed to the discussion elsewhere.[2] We will, however, briefly sketch the position of the definition of poverty used in this research in relation to other definitions. In this section we will also describe the way this definition has been put into practice, and we will give some examples of the sensitivity of the results for the choices made in this journey from theory to practice.

An "economic" or "social" definition of poverty?

In "economic" definitions of poverty,[3] poverty is defined as lack of (household) resources, for instance measured by total household income. In "social" definitions, reflected in the term "social exclusion" often used in the poverty programs of the EC, the emphasis is put on the lack of participation in society. Indicators of social exclusion may be bad housing, bad health, inadequate education, lack of participation, etc. The two different approaches may both be said to be included in the definition of the Council Decision of December 19, 1984:

The poor shall be taken to mean persons, families and groups of persons whose resources (material, cultural and social) are so limited as to exclude them from the minimum acceptable way of life in the Member States in which they live.

There is a definite link to resources in this definition, but these resources are more widely defined than the material resources which are the basis of economic definitions. In this study, we nevertheless restrict ourselves to material resources; not by choice, but because no data on social and cultural resources of household members are available in our data sets. This does not mean that by using an "economic" definition we deny the existence of cultural and social aspects of poverty: we hope that future data collection will extend beyond measuring monetary resources into the above-mentioned indicators of health, housing, education, etc. However, we do believe that these other dimensions of poverty ought to be studied in combination with the material resources: if a household was found to be living in inadequate housing, but with sufficient material resources to be able to afford adequate accommodation, we do not consider this household "poor." In this respect, we maintain an economist's value judgment (Watts, 1968, p. 322) in respecting diversity of tastes and values.

An "absolute" or "relative" definition of poverty?

"Absolute" definitions of poverty start from the notion that poverty is a situation in which people are below a certain threshold, usually based on a "basket" of basic necessities, which is the same in different times and places, while according to relative definitions the borderline between poor and non-poor depends on the society and the time period to which it pertains. In practice, a totally absolute poverty cut-off point cannot usually withstand the pressures of changing circumstances. In this chapter, we will use a relative definition of poverty, with the cut-off point fixed at a certain percentage of average expenditures (per adult equivalent). However, the percentage at which this threshold is fixed is essentially arbitrary; in our main report we have therefore presented poverty statistics using three different threshold levels, based on 40 percent, 50 percent and 60 percent of average expenditures. It is important to realize the effect of this choice; the population of poor in Europe according to the 40 percent cut-off point would be about half as large as the population of poor according to the 50 percent cut-off point. Increasing the cut-off point to 60 percent would imply an increase in the population of poor of more than 30 million poor persons. In this summary, we will restrict ourselves largely to the presentation of statistics associated with 50 percent of average expenditures.

The choice of this particular relative poverty definition implies that countries with a large inequality in the distribution of resources within the country itself will be found to have high poverty rates, whereas countries with little inequality will have low poverty rates. This particular way of defining poverty does not take account of differences in the average living standard across countries: a country with a low income *per capita*, that has distributed national income fairly evenly, will therefore be found, according to this definition, to be less poor than a country with a high income *per capita* that has a large inequality of incomes. We therefore supplement these "inequality-based" poverty rates with additional information on the average resources in the various countries in terms of a single *numéraire*, and poverty statistics based on a single poverty line for all countries.

An "objective" or "subjective" definition of poverty?

"Objective" poverty definitions use objective information about the population for the assessment of poverty, whereas subjective poverty definitions make use of "subjective" opinions expressed by the target population. The latter approach has been the basis of another research project initiated by Eurostat (van Praag and Flik, 1992). The present research project uses information on expenditures and income to identify people as poor, rather than opinions of these people on the adequacy of their income, and therefore falls under the heading "objective."

A "country-specific" or "community-specific" definition of poverty?

The choice of a relative, rather than an absolute, poverty definition almost automatically implies that for each EC Member State a country-specific poverty cut-off point is defined, as relative poverty definitions specifically refer to the living conditions in the society concerned. The choice for a country-specific line is also explicitly made in the Council decision on the definition of poverty, quoted on p. 26 above. Determining relative poverty lines solely on the basis of national average expenditures (or income) results in large differences across countries: the purchasing power of the poverty line in Luxembourg (the richest of the Member States of the EC) is more than twice the purchasing power in Portugal (the poorest), as may be seen in table 3.1 (p. 33). Although we consider the notion of relative poverty to be the relevant concept for national social policy within EC countries, we think that distributional issues at the EC level cannot be solved without keeping these international differences in mind. For this reason, we have chosen to present poverty statistics based on three Community poverty lines (fixed at 50 percent of average adult equivalent expenditures in Portugal, the EC as a whole, and Luxembourg, respectively) in addition to the country-specific poverty lines. Although these European poverty lines lack the connotation of the cost of a "basket" of basic necessities valid for all times and places, they give an indication of poverty across Europe in a more absolute sense.

Income or expenditures?

The choice of resources as the basis for the poverty line needs to be further operationalized. Given the data sets that we can use, we have to choose either expenditures or income as the basis for our statistics. Theoretically, a compelling argument to prefer income is that it actually measures resources, whereas expenditures can be said to measure the actual level of living, which implies that households who voluntarily spend only a small part of their income can be counted as poor. However, in the Household Budget Surveys (HBSs) in use, targeted toward measuring expenditures in particular, income is highly under-reported in a number of Member States. This is shown, for instance, by the fact that in five out of twelve Member States the average level of expenditures in the sample is higher than the average income level. Moreover, more detailed analysis shows that in most of the surveys households headed by self-employed and non-manual workers in particular under-report their income.[4] In addition, in some countries, there is a high and selective partial non-response with respect to income data.

In the main report, total expenditures are therefore used as the most reliable measure of resources. In line with the Eurostat definition of total expenditures, imputed rent is added instead of mortgage payments. Whenever possible, income in kind and consumption of goods from own firm or farm are included as well. For most Member States we also present poverty statistics using income instead of expenditures as the indicator of resources. As definition of income we have used the total after-tax income,[5] including estimated imputed rent of owner-occupied houses.

In our empirical work, it appeared that the harmonization of income and expenditure definitions was extremely important in obtaining truly comparable results across Europe. Whether mortgage payments are included in expenditures, or an estimate of imputed rent, makes a notable difference for the poverty percentage, as well as for the composition of the poor population.[6] The information available in the data sets at this moment does not always allow for accurate measurement of the housing conditions that influence imputed rent.

We realize that our measures of resources by no means give a complete picture of the circumstances of the households. Household wealth is lacking, as well as home production.[7] Information on access to education and health is not available. In future research, one should, in our opinion, try to extend this measure of resources to include wealth and a monetary evaluation of provisions in kind, such as health services, education, etc.[8]

Households or persons?

In this section we will discuss the choice of the measurement unit which is the basis of the poverty statistics presented in this chapter. Theoretically, several choices are possible.[9] One may be interested in poverty in terms of individual *persons*. The average number of persons will vary across other measurement units (e.g. households) and therefore equal poverty rates in terms of other measurement units may imply different poverty rates in terms of persons. Moreover, theoretically, one might take into account that the poverty status of individuals within other measurement units might not be equal.

However, since most expenditure data from the HBSs are available for households only, and we lack information about the exact distribution of resources within households, it is not possible to differentiate the poverty status of individuals within households. Therefore, the poverty statistics in this chapter will primarily be presented in terms of *households*. Poverty statistics in terms of persons will also be given, but they are based on the assessment of the poverty status of the households to which the persons belong.

How to compare households of different size?

Irrespective of the choice of persons or households as the appropriate measurement unit, the comparison of household resources between households of different size and composition always requires some correction procedure, to make these different entities more "equivalent." The use of family equivalence scales for this purpose has become a standard practice for statisticians and social scientists. Sharply contrasted to the "*communis opinio*" that such a correction procedure is necessary is the large difference in opinion with regard to the choice of the particular equivalence scale to be used. Several researchers have recently pointed out the vast difference the choice and definition of a particular equiva-

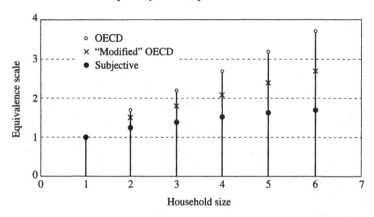

Figure 3.1 OECD, "modified" OECD, and subjective equivalence scales

lence scale may make in the study of the least privileged in a community.[10] In this study, we have followed their example by taking a variety of equivalence scales, and by analyzing the sensitivity of the poverty percentage and the composition of the population of poor for the scale chosen. In our main report we have tried the use of a single equivalence scale (the OECD scale and "modified" OECD scale), as well as different equivalence scales, although based on the same methodology, for different countries. For the latter objective we used the subjective methodology and methodologies based on cost functions, derived from microeconomic theory. Figure 3.1 illustrates this point by showing the difference between the two extreme equivalence scales in our range, the OECD scale (series 1) and the subjective scale (series 3). We have added a "modified" OECD scale that is somewhere in the middle of these two extremes.[11]

Another way of looking at the difference between the three scales is to calculate the *equivalence elasticity* (Buhmann *et al.*, 1988; Johnson, 1995), that is, the relative increase in the scale divided by the relative increase in household size. The equivalence elasticity equals 0.73 for the OECD scale, 0.55 for the "modified" OECD scale, and 0.30 for the subjective scale (for France). It appears, therefore, that the elasticity of the "modified" OECD scale is a little over the middle of the two extremes of the range.

In this chapter, we mainly present statistics based on the "modified" OECD scale. In order to show the changes in the composition of the population of poor as a result of the choice of another equivalence scale, we have added poverty rates for selected household types according to all three equivalence scales.

Data sets used

The data sets used in our calculations are the HBSs carried out in the Member States around 1988. These data sets are at present the only source of information on household resources available in all EC countries. The definitions of variables and methods of data collection differ over the Member States, although a process of harmonization of variables, initiated by Eurostat, is underway. We have tried to make the definitions of the relevant variables as comparable as possible, given the differences in the extent to which detailed information was available in the data sets provided.[12]

The representativeness of the HBSs for the whole population, and therewith its usefulness for a study like ours, has sometimes been questioned. We have therefore spent extra care on the analysis of the distribution of the survey over the population. This is mainly done by comparing the survey population with the characteristics of another survey, the Labour Force Survey (LFS). In some countries, the National Statistical Institutes (NSIs) have already provided weights to adjust the HBS to certain characteristics of the population. In other countries, we have calculated these weights on the basis of the distributions of households according to household type and region from the LFS of the same year. In spite of these attempts to make the data representative for the population, the reader should be aware of the fact that certain parts of the population, such as the homeless and the institutionalized, have not been included in the sample design, and therefore are not represented in the results.

One additional drawback of the HBSs is that expenditures are usually recorded during a short reference period. Although this can be assumed not to bias the estimate of average expenditures, it unavoidably leads to inaccuracies in the assessment of the poverty status of individual households.

It should also be mentioned that, despite the efforts to harmonize definitions of total expenditures and total income, comparison with National Accounts figures casts some doubt with respect to the reliability and comparability of the data sets used (de Vos and Zaidi, 1994a). In particular, this affects the results using income as the measure of resources and the results using a common poverty line for all Member States.

Results

After this description of concepts and data used, we can now turn to a presentation of our main results.

Table 3.1 *Overall results for all EC Member States, based on average equivalent expenditures, using the "modified" OECD equivalence scale (households), 1987–9*

Country	Av. equiv. exp. (per eq. adult)		Poor households (40% cut-off)		Poor households (50% cut-off)		Poor households (60% cut-off)	
	Nat. curr.	1988 PPS	%	abs. no. (000)	%	abs. no. (000)	%	abs. no. (000)
	(1)	(2)	(3)	(4)	(5)	(6)	(7)	(8)
1 France (1989)	86,726	13,966	7.5	1,630	14.9	3,238	24.5	5,324
2 Spain (1988)	834,764	10,341	9.3	1,021	17.5	1,920	27.1	2,974
3 Portugal (1989)	677,652	8,546	17.3	547	26.5	836	35.2	1,112
4 Italy (1988)	13,848,505	12,210	12.5	2,553	22.0	4,494	32.2	6,577
5 Greece (1988)	1,004,841	10,593	13.0	444	20.8	711	29.8	1,019
6 Ireland (1987)	6,092	10,202	7.9	80	16.4	166	26.9	272
7 Belgium (1987–8)	432,858	12,007	1.7	67	6.6	261	14.1	557
8 Luxembourg (1987)	617,205	18,920	3.7	5	9.2	12	17.2	22
9 Denmark (1987)	93,262	11,324	1.4	33	4.2	98	13.3	310
10 Netherlands (1988)	24,540	12,984	1.9	108	6.2	366	13.9	817
11 United Kingdom (1988)	6,729	14,018	7.4	1,658	17.0	3,819	28.0	6,310
12 Germany (1988)	26,441	13,771	5.3	1,442	12.0	3,250	21.2	5,766
EUR-12			*7.8*	*9,587*	*15.6*	*19,170*	*25.3*	*31,060*

Overall results

Columns (1) and (2) of table 3.1 give the average equivalent expenditures, expressed in national currency and in 1988 purchasing power standards (PPS). Columns (3)–(8) give the percentages and absolute numbers of poor households, for the poverty lines drawn at 40, 50, and 60 percent of national average equivalent expenditures.

As is to be expected, it makes a lot of difference where the cut-off percentage to define the poverty line is chosen. On the other hand, the ranking of the different Member States is hardly affected. Portugal has the highest poverty rates, followed by Greece and Italy. Four countries have poverty rates close to the overall average: the United Kingdom, Ireland, Spain, and France. Germany has a poverty percentage below the average, and in Belgium, Denmark, the Netherlands, and Luxembourg we find rather low poverty percentages.

Table 3.2 gives the percentages of poor persons. These percentages are almost all below the poverty rates in terms of households. Obviously, this implies that poverty is relatively concentrated in small households. The

Table 3.2   *Overall results for all EC Member States, based on average equivalent expenditures using the "modified" OECD equivalence scale (persons), 1987–9*

Country	Av.equiv.exp. (per eq. adult)		Poor households (40% cut-off)		Poor households (50% cut-off)		Poor households (60% cut-off)	
	Nat. curr.	1988 PPS	%	abs. no. (000)	%	abs. no. (000)	%	abs. no. (000)
	(1)	(2)	(3)	(4)	(5)	(6)	(7)	(8)
1 France (1989)	85,685	13,798	6.9	3,865	14.7	8,234	25.0	14,004
2 Spain (1988)	830,586	10,290	8.7	3,370	16.9	6,546	26.6	10,304
3 Portugal (1989)	679,442	8,568	15.5	1,597	24.5	2,525	33.3	3,431
4 Italy (1988)	13,798,358	12,166	11.6	6,658	21.1	12,111	31.4	18,023
5 Greece (1988)	1,004,168	10,586	11.4	1,139	18.7	1,868	27.6	2,757
6 Ireland (1987)	5,938	9,944	7.5	266	15.7	556	26.3	932
7 Belgium (1987–88)	426,043	11,818	2.2	217	7.4	729	15.5	1,528
8 Luxembourg (1987)	603,523	18,500	4.8	18	11.1	41	20.0	74
9 Denmark (1987)	93,499	11,353	1.1	56	3.9	200	11.5	589
10 Netherlands (1988)	24,327	12,871	1.5	221	4.8	706	11.4	1,677
11 United Kingdom (1988)	6,694	13,946	6.4	3,648	14.8	8,436	25.3	14,420
12 Germany (1988)	26,291	13,693	4.5	2,756	10.9	6,675	19.9	12,186
EUR-12			7.3	23,810	15.0	48,628	24.6	79,926

exceptions are Belgium and Luxembourg. In absolute numbers, the 50 percent cut-off defines over 19 million households as poor, containing almost 49 million poor persons. Some 85 percent of the poor live in the five large countries: Italy, the United Kingdom, France, Germany, and Spain.

Who are at risk of being poor?

Table 3.3 gives a beginning of an answer to the question: who are the poor? It presents the poverty percentages in a number of subgroups of households. In these subgroups the poverty percentages are above the average in most of the Member States, or in other words, these subgroups are what is usually referred to as "risk groups."

Before discussing table 3.3 some important limitations of its figures need to be mentioned. First, the table does not contain information on the relative sizes of the different groups. In other words, one can conclude that many single elderly are poor, but one cannot infer how many of the poor are single elderly. For that information, we refer to the full report.

Table 3.3 Poverty percentages in risk groups[a]

	Fra	Spa	Por	Ita	Gre	Ire	Bel	Lux	Den	Net	UK	Ger
Total population (households)	*14.9*	*17.5*	*26.5*	*22.0*	*20.8*	*16.4*	*6.6*	*9.2*	*4.2*	*6.2*	*17.0*	*12.0*
Socio-economic category head:												
Farmer/agricultural worker	25.0	27.4	39.8	31.2	28.8	9.8	15.6	24.4	17.9	1.4	16.5	6.7
Unemployed	34.8	29.3	47.5	35.7	24.5	43.6	28.9	44.1	2.7	22.8	47.9	13.9
Retired	21.9	27.3	48.5	35.7	33.4	19.2	7.6	11.3	6.4	12.6	30.1	(24.2)
Home maker/unoccupied	31.0	23.8	34.5	36.6	30.5	30.9	(19.6)	14.0	0.0	(10.9)	37.2	24.0
Household type:												
One person, 65 and older	33.8	37.9	59.9	40.3	44.5	35.7	7.9	11.2	5.8	20.6	40.2	21.7
Couple with 4 or more child.	36.9	22.7	37.6	42.9	27.6	22.3	21.3	25.0	25.6	8.0	28.9	24.4
Single-parental household	18.3	22.8	27.8	22.9	17.5	23.8	14.9	17.5	2.7	14.0	25.3	24.0
Economic situation:												
Nobody working	26.0	32.0	47.5	35.0	35.1	37.1	6.4	10.6	7.4	11.8	37.7	21.4
Age of head:												
Below 25	11.3	19.9	33.8	19.8	7.8	17.3	14.4	10.6	11.1	17.9	19.8	18.5
65 and older	26.1	29.1	49.5	37.1	38.9	23.3	7.3	10.5	7.1	13.8	31.5	17.8
Sex of head:												
Female	22.6	25.2	33.9	28.8	29.3	24.2	6.7	9.9	5.4	13.5	30.2	16.5
Size of community:												
Small/rural	20.1	30.6	32.3	–	36.1	–	6.2	–	4.7	–	18.0	12.8
Type of tenure:												
Main tenant	18.7	24.2	26.8	24.0	13.2	26.8–46.9	12.3	16.1	3.8	10.1	28.8–39.5	16.8

Table 3.3 (*cont.*)

	Fra	Spa	Por	Ita	Gre	Ire	Bel	Lux	Den	Net	UK	Ger
Subtenant/rented furnished	31.6	–	18.7	–	–	9.2	–	–	28.3	20.2	14.7	18.3
Rent free/reduced rent	23.7	9.4–24.8–		–	–	28.6	5.0	–	0.0	–	17.2	–
Region:												
Poorest	19.5	–	70.3	39.0	25.8	25.4	7.8	–	–	–	26.6	–
2nd poorest	19.0	–	56.3	37.4	25.5	20.2	7.7	–	–	–	25.3	–
3rd poorest	18.1	–	31.4	32.3	25.0	18.4	–	–	–	–	22.5	–
Education:												
Lowest	30.1	47.7	61.9	–	44.1	31.0	12.2	–	5.5	19.5	45.1	–
1 but lowest	17.1	31.1	46.1	–	23.8	17.7	6.0	–	5.4	5.3	29.1	–
Persons: total	*14.7*	*16.9*	*24.5*	*21.1*	*18.7*	*15.7*	*7.4*	*11.1*	*3.9*	*4.8*	*14.8*	*10.9*
Persons below 14	16.0	16.8	22.3	19.5	15.0	21.0	6.2	11.4	3.3	4.3	18.5	14.4
Persons between 14 and 16	19.4	21.1	25.0	22.7	19.8	–	12.8	18.0	4.2	3.9	14.5	(10.8)
Persons between 65 and 74	17.2	21.4	39.1	29.8	37.8	20.0	4.4	11.9	5.5	11.0	23.8	14.7
Persons of 75 and older	31.0	34.1	49.3	41.4	–	–	13.1	11.1	12.0	16.6	37.3	22.0
Non-working persons	18.8	19.3	28.9	24.6	–	20.1	8.9	11.9	5.1	6.1	23.2	14.8

Note:
[a] Poverty line defined as 50 percent of average equivalent expenditures ("modified" OECD scale).

Second, the table only gives poverty percentages according to the 50 percent cut-off. Conclusions might be different when another cut-off percentage was chosen. Therefore, we have also included poverty rates according to the 40 percent and 60 percent cut-offs in the full report. However, it appears that most of the groups with high poverty rates remain the same.

A third important limitation is that the table does not contain any error margins for the figures. It is clear that the figures are subject to errors. First, especially in small groups a sample may easily produce results which differ from the actual population. Second, the way expenditures are recorded may imply that we make measurement errors, for instance when we simply multiply a weekly amount by 52 to obtain a yearly amount. We have put some effort into looking for a reliable way to correct for this kind of error. However, so far, we have not found a methodology to obtain statistics which we are certain are better. Therefore, we tend to conclude that, given the available data, these are the most acceptable poverty figures.

If we now turn to the actual figures, we see that despite the different survey methodologies we find the same risk groups in almost all Member States, namely, households headed by unemployed persons, retired persons and home makers, single elderly and large households, households in which nobody is working, female-headed households, households headed by an elderly person, households with heads with low levels of education, and households living in certain regions. In a number of countries, farmers and agricultural workers also have a high poverty percentage, and the same holds for households living in rural areas and for single-parent households.

All in all, we see that the poverty percentages differ considerably between countries, but that there is a fairly high degree of similarity with respect to the risk groups. However, we can also note a number of differences. The most remarkable is the fact that in Belgium, and also in Luxembourg, the households with a retired head are less of a risk group than in all other countries.[13] Another source of differences is the type of tenure classification. Here, the way in which imputed rent is computed may affect the results.

In terms of persons, in almost all countries we find the highest poverty rates for elderly persons. In particular, the poverty rates for the very old are very high. Child poverty seems to be less widespread; children younger than 14 have poverty rates above the average in five countries, and persons between 14 and 16 in eight. This result will be related to the choice of the equivalence scale, and we will come back to equivalence scales later in this section.

Table 3.4   *Poverty and employment status, 1987–9*

	$(1)^a$	$(2)^b$	$(3)^c$	$(4)^d$	$(5)^e$
France (1989)	33.6	14.9	9.1	26.4	59.4
Spain (1988)	25.7	17.5	12.5	32.0	47.0
Portugal (1989)	27.0	26.5	18.7	47.5	48.5
Italy (1988)	30.4	22.0	16.3	35.0	48.5
Greece (1988)	31.0	20.8	14.3	35.1	52.4
Ireland (1987)	33.1	16.4	6.1	37.1	74.9
Belgium (1987–8)	35.4	6.6	6.7	6.4	34.6
Luxembourg (1987)	30.0	9.2	8.6	10.6	34.5
Denmark (1987)	33.6	4.2	2.6	7.4	58.9
Netherlands (1988)	31.2	6.2	3.7	11.8	58.7
United Kingdom (1988)	32.7	17.0	6.9	37.7	72.7
Germany (1988)	39.7	12.0	5.8	21.4	70.6
EUR-12	*33.2*	*15.6*	*9.6*	*27.9*	*59.2*

Notes:
[a] Percentages of households without members in paid employment.
[b] Overall poverty percentages (poverty line: 50 percent of average equivalent expenditures).
[c] Poverty percentages in households with members in paid employment.
[d] Poverty percentages in households without members in paid employment.
[e] Poor households without members in paid employment as a percentage of total population of poor.

Table 3.4 highlights one important characteristic of the poor in most Member States, namely that they are often households in which nobody is doing paid work. Of course that is no real surprise, but it is interesting to see the size of the differences. In almost all countries there is a clear gap between the poverty rates of columns (3) and (4), that is households with and without members in paid employment. Again the exceptions are Belgium and Luxembourg. In the main report we also present the differences between these groups with and without working members within different subgroups. In most cases we find that the difference remains, independent of the other characteristics.

Column (5) of table 3.4 shows how many of the poor do not have a member in paid employment. It is clear that there are substantial differences in the composition of the poor population: the share of households with nobody working in the total number of poor varies from about 35 percent in Belgium and Luxembourg to more than 70 percent in Ireland, the United Kingdom, and Germany.

Implications of the choice of equivalence scale

An important point, mentioned on p. 30, is the choice of equivalence scales. So far, the statistics have been based on what we have called the "modified" OECD scale. It assumes that for every additional adult a household needs 0.5 of the resources for the first adult, and 0.3 for every child younger than 14, to be on the same welfare level. The choice of this scale was mainly made for pragmatic reasons: it is about halfway along the original OECD scale and subjective scales, and in a pilot study for the United Kingdom (Hagenaars, 1991) it came quite close to equivalence scales computed by other methods, based on consumer demand models. We have also tried to repeat this pilot study for other Member States, but the results have not been very promising. This is probably due to the problems with the income data for many of the surveys.

In table 3.5 we present the most striking results of the sensitivity analysis with respect to the equivalence scales. The table compares the poverty percentages of the 50 percent cut-off using the original OECD scale, the "modified" OECD scale, and a subjective equivalence scale. The subjective scales are based on the computations from the research project on subjective poverty of van Praag and his colleagues (van Praag and Flik, 1992), but for some countries which were not included in that project we have used scales based on an earlier study (van Praag, Hagenaars and van Weeren, 1981). Table 3.5 gives the poverty percentages for the total population and the percentages for the groups who are likely to be the most affected by the choice of the equivalence scale, namely single-person households and large families.

Column (1) makes it clear that for the total poverty percentage the differences between the OECD scale and the modified OECD scale are not very large. The poverty rates for the subjective equivalence scales are usually somewhat higher than those for the other two scales. Columns (2)–(4) show that for the composition of the poverty population the choice of equivalence scale is crucial. The OECD scale results in very high poverty figures for large families and relatively low poverty rates for small households. The subjective scales produce the opposite picture. The "modified" OECD scale picks up both single elderly persons and large families as groups with poverty percentages above the average in almost all Member States. The results of this table show that such a sensitivity analysis is very useful, particularly since the actual choice of the equivalence scale is likely to remain a subject of debate.

Table 3.5   *Poverty percentages, 1987–9[a]*

		Total average (1)	Single pers. below 65 (2)	Single pers. 65 and older (3)	Couples with 4 or more child. (4)
France (1989)	OECD	14.0	8.7	22.6	49.6
	Mod. OECD	14.9	13.6	33.8	36.9
	Subj.	17.8	25.7	53.1	9.5
Spain (1988)	OECD	16.7	13.2	25.8	27.9
	Mod. OECD	17.5	20.4	37.9	22.7
	Subj.	21.2	43.3	70.8	11.0
Portugal (1989)	OECD	25.2	23.4	47.2	44.2
	Mod. OECD	26.5	30.5	59.9	37.6
	Subj.	29.2	50.7	81.4	19.7
Italy (1988)	OECD	20.6	10.7	28.7	51.5
	Mod. OECD	22.0	16.9	40.3	42.9
	Subj.	24.8	28.4	59.2	24.1
Greece (1988)	OECD	20.6	11.1	33.1	35.0
	Mod. OECD	20.8	16.4	44.5	27.6
	Subj.	21.6	23.9	57.7	16.0
Ireland (1987)	OECD	16.9	13.7	23.2	29.9
	Mod. OECD	16.4	20.7	35.7	22.3
	Subj.	20.0	40.1	64.3	8.8
Belgium (1987–8)	OECD	6.1	3.4	2.7	29.8
	Mod. OECD	6.6	8.0	7.9	21.3
	Subj.	8.3	18.2	18.0	2.4
Luxembourg (1987)	OECD	8.8	1.4	6.1	25.0
	Mod. OECD	9.2	4.9	11.2	25.0
	Subj.	11.2	13.5	36.6	0.0
Denmark (1987)	OECD	3.6	2.9	2.4	25.6
	Mod. OECD	4.2	5.6	5.8	25.6
	Subj.	5.5	9.2	11.8	6.3
Netherlands (1988)	OECD	4.3	2.4	7.4	19.1
	Mod. OECD	6.2	8.5	20.6	8.0
	Subj.	12.7	30.6	46.6	0.0
United Kingdom (1988)	OECD	14.6	9.1	23.7	39.5
	Mod. OECD	17.0	16.3	40.2	28.9
	Subj.	23.3	36.2	73.3	8.1
Germany (1988)	OECD	10.8	7.2	14.6	30.1
	Mod. OECD	12.0	13.0	21.7	24.4
	Subj.	17.3	30.2	40.7	5.1

Note:
[a] Poverty line is defined as 50 percent of average equivalent expenditures, for three household types, using three different equivalence scales.

Table 3.6   *Comparison of overall poverty statistics, based on total expenditures and total income as measure of resources, 1987–9[a]*

	Average equiv. expenditure (nat.curr.) (1)	Average equiv. income (nat.curr.) (2)	Poverty rate (exp.) (3)	Poverty rate (inc.) (4)	Poverty rate (both) (5)
France (1989)	86,726	79,817	14.9	14.0	6.2
Spain (1988)	834,764	766,834	17.5	12.9	6.8
Portugal (1989)	677,652	658,107	26.5	20.2	14.5
Italy (1988)	13,848,505	15,085,142	22.0	12.8	10.7
Greece (1988)	1,004,841	873,911	20.8	18.6	–
Ireland (1987)	6,092	5,544	16.4	14.9	8.0
Belgium (1987–8)	432,858	452,960	6.6	6.0	3.6
Luxembourg (1987)	617,205	626,447	9.2	5.1	2.3
Denmark (1987)	93,262	119,807	4.2	11.9	2.4
Netherlands (1988)	24,539	28,359	6.2	7.4	1.7
United Kingdom (1988)	6,729	7,486	17.0	22.4	12.4
Germany (1988)	26,441	29,703	12.0	13.6	8.5

Note:
[a] Poverty line is 50 percent of average equivalent income/expenditures.

Implications of the choice of resources

Apart from this choice of the equivalence scale, we also had to make a choice between income and expenditures as a measure of resources. As mentioned in the Introduction, we have chosen expenditures, mainly because income appears to be under-reported in a number of Member States. We have, however, also computed poverty statistics based on the income data, and the results are summarized in table 3.6. Columns (1) and (2) compare average equivalent income and average equivalent expenditures. In five of the countries average income ends up lower than average expenditures. In general, except for a few Member States, we do not have much faith in the income figures.

Columns (3) and (4) compare the overall poverty rates using expenditures and income. In France, Greece, Ireland, Belgium, the Netherlands, and Germany the difference is not very large, but in all other countries the poverty rates differ more than 4 percent. The extremes are Italy, where the poverty rate drops more than 9 percent when we take income instead of expenditures, and Denmark, where the poverty rate more than doubles. As a consequence, the ranking of the Member States also changes quite dramatically. The most remarkable result is that the

United Kingdom obtains the highest poverty rate when income is taken as the measure of resources. In view of the low quality of the income information, it is questionable whether this result should be taken seriously.[14]

Column (5) of table 3.6 gives the percentages of households who are poor according to both the income- and the expenditure-based poverty lines. The figures imply that in most Member States there are more households who are poor according to only one of the two poverty lines than households who are poor according to both poverty lines. Further research, differentiating according to subgroups, shows that in some countries this can partly be attributed to low consumption of certain subgroups, especially elderly, on the one hand, and under-reporting of income by other groups, such as the self-employed, on the other.

In the full report we have included still more types of sensitivity analysis. We have used different indices of poverty instead of the poverty percentage or headcount measure, and in some Member States we have used different measures of total expenditures and different weights. For a discussion of those results, we refer to the report.

Overall results using Community-specific poverty lines

In contrast to the main report, we also include a brief discussion of results using Community-specific poverty lines. The relevance of these poverty lines has already been explained on p. 28. Given the remaining problems with respect to the reliability and comparability of the data (see p. 32), the exercise in this section should be viewed as merely illustrative, and should not be considered as a basis for drawing solid policy conclusions.

We present poverty rates using three different Community-specific poverty lines. The first is 50 percent of the national average of Portugal, the lowest among the twelve country-specific poverty lines. The usage of this poverty line shows the relative positions of the Member States when Portuguese standards of living are taken as the reference point. The second poverty line is defined as 50 percent of the Community average, calculated as the weighted average of the national averages of the twelve Member States. Using this poverty line, more interesting comparisons can be made with the results of the country-specific poverty lines. The third Community-specific poverty line is the 50 percent poverty line of Luxembourg, which is the highest of all poverty lines. The usefulness of applying the lowest and the highest of all poverty lines is obvious: this gives a good indication of the range of poverty rates that Community-specific poverty lines could produce.

Table 3.7 *Overall results for the twelve EC Member States, using Community-specific poverty lines (households), 1987–9*

Country	% of nat. % avg. (1)	Poverty % (2)	abs. no. (000) (3)	% of nat. % avg. (4)	Poverty % (5)	abs. no. (000) (6)	% of nat. % avg. (7)	Poverty % (8)	abs. no. (000) (9)
1 France (1989)	39	2.9	628	46	11.9	2,586	68	32.4	7,040
2 Spain (1988)	41	10.3	1,127	62	29.5	3,237	92	55.8	6,123
3 Portugal (1989)	50	26.5	839	75	49.3	1,563	111	70.4	2,231
4 Italy (1988)	35	8.2	1,671	53	24.8	5,065	78	48.5	9,912
5 Greece (1988)	40	12.9	442	61	30.0	1,028	89	54.9	1,880
6 Ireland (1987)	42	9.5	97	63	29.8	302	93	56.2	569
7 Belgium (1987–8)	36	1.0	40	54	9.0	356	71	34.6	1,368
8 Luxembourg (1987)	23	0.2	0	34	1.4	2	50	9.2	12
9 Denmark (1987)	38	1.0	23	57	10.3	240	84	41.4	965
10 Netherlands (1988)	33	0.4	21	50	6.0	352	73	27.9	1,636
11 United Kingdom (1988)	30	1.7	383	46	12.9	2,906	68	35.6	8,022
12 Germany (1988)	31	1.5	413	47	9.3	2,530	69	30.6	8,293
EUR-12		*4.6*	*5,683*		*16.4*	*20,166*		*39.2*	*48,051*

Table 3.7 shows that for the first poverty line both the overall extent of poverty and the ranking of the Member States are affected. Most important are the differences in the poverty rates. The poverty rate for Portugal stays 26.5 percent, simply because the poverty line remains the same, but the poverty rates for all other countries are less than half of this percentage, with Spain, Italy Greece, and Ireland having poverty rates between 8 and 13 percent and the remaining Member States having poverty rates of less than 3 percent. In other words, only Portugal has high poverty. This seriously undermines the plausibility of this Community-specific poverty line. It also implies, however, that Portugal does not rank first only in terms of relative poverty, but also in terms of absolute poverty.

The basis of the second Community-specific poverty line is the average expenditures per equivalent adult of the twelve Member States, calculated as about 12,896 PPS in 1988 prices. The results show that the ranking of the countries is roughly the same as the one given by the first Community-specific poverty line. According to this poverty line, almost half of the total population in Portugal is poor. In Spain, Greece, and Ireland the poverty rate is around 30 percent, which is clearly higher than the poverty rates based on the country-specific poverty lines. This can be expected since these three countries, as well as Portugal, have national averages which are clearly lower than the Community average. Italy, Belgium, and Denmark have slightly higher poverty rates compared to the results of the national poverty lines. On the other hand, the countries with average equivalent expenditure higher than the "Community average" (France, Luxembourg, the United Kingdom, and Germany) have a lower poverty rate for this poverty line compared to the country-specific poverty lines.

The third Community-specific poverty line is the 50 percent poverty line of Luxembourg. Again, the relative positions of the countries as obtained for the second Community-specific poverty line remain largely unaffected. However, the absolute differences in the poverty rates should also be noted. Luxembourg remains the country with the lowest poverty rate, but all other countries have a poverty rate of above 27 percent. These poverty rates are even higher than those based on the country-specific 60 percent poverty lines.

In conclusion, we see that the application of the Community-specific poverty lines does not only alter the incidence of poverty but also affects the relative positions of the Member States as obtained from the country-specific poverty lines, in particular where the latter ranking does not follow the ranking according to average equivalent expenditures.

Table 3.8 presents the results in terms of persons. The conclusions with respect to the relative positions of the countries remain the same. On the whole, about 20 million households are counted as poor when the poverty line is set at 50 percent of the Community average (see table 3.7). This figure is about a million higher than that of the national poverty lines. According to the same Community-specific poverty line, over 53 million persons are poor: a figure which is about 5 million higher than according to the corresponding country-specific poverty lines. More interesting is to see how the shares of the countries in the total poor population in the EC change. For the country-specific poverty lines, Spain, Portugal, Greece, and Ireland contain about 24 percent of all poor persons in the twelve Member States, whereas for the Community-specific poverty lines this share increases to almost 37 percent.

Finally, a few words about the group-specific poverty. We have analyzed whether shifting from country-specific to Community-specific poverty lines changes the relative positions of the different socio-economic groups. If we restrict ourselves to the 50 percent poverty lines, we find that on the whole the composition of the poor population is only marginally affected. In most of the Member States, the groups identified as the "risk groups" according to the Community-specific poverty lines are the same as for the country-specific poverty lines.

Table 3.8   *Percentages and absolute numbers of poor persons in the twelve EC Member States, using Community-specific poverty lines, 1987–9*

Country	Poverty line of Portugal		Weighted average		Poverty line of Luxembourg	
	%	abs. no. (000)	%	abs. no. (000)	%	abs. no. (000)
	(1)	(2)	(3)	(4)	(5)	(6)
1 France (1989)	2.5	1,400	11.2	6,274	33.2	18,598
2 Spain (1988)	9.7	3,757	29.2	11,311	56.8	22,002
3 Portugal (1989)	24.5	2,532	47.7	4,930	69.6	7,193
4 Italy (1988)	7.5	4,305	24.0	13,776	48.4	27,781
5 Greece (1988)	11.0	1,099	27.9	2,787	54.0	5,394
6 Ireland (1987)	9.0	319	29.4	1,041	57.0	2,019
7 Belgium (1987–8)	1.3	128	10.1	997	37.3	3,684
8 Luxembourg (1987)	0.2	1	1.9	7	11.1	41
9 Denmark (1987)	0.8	41	9.0	461	38.8	1,988
10 Netherlands (1988)	0.4	59	4.6	677	27.5	4,047
11 United Kingdom (1988)	1.4	798	11.2	6,384	33.1	18,866
12 Germany (1988)	1.2	735	8.5	5,205	29.0	17,820
EUR-12	*4.7*	*15,174*	*16.6*	*53,850*	*39.9*	*129,433*

Evaluation and recommendations

In the previous section we saw that there were substantial differences between the overall poverty rates in the Member States of the EC and, on the other hand, considerable similarities with respect to the characteristics of the poor population. In this section we will tentatively evaluate these results, and present some recommendations for further research.

In our view, the poverty statistics in this chapter present a quite reliable picture of the incidence of poverty across the Member States of the EC. In fact, for the first time, poverty statistics have been derived for almost all Member States using comparable definitions and data sets. Nevertheless, given the unavoidable limitations in the quality and the comparability of the data, and the arbitrariness of a number of choices with respect to the definition of poverty, the poverty statistics should not be taken as exact measures of the incidence of poverty. For example, the result that we have four Member States with low poverty (Denmark, the Netherlands, Belgium, and Luxembourg), four Member States with average poverty (France, Ireland, the United Kingdom, and Spain), with Germany in between these two groups, two Member States with high poverty (Greece, Italy), and one Member State with very high poverty

(Portugal), can be viewed as quite robust. However, not too much value should be attached to the ranking of the individual Member States within these groups with low, average, and high poverty. Similarly, the identification of "risk groups" can be seen as an important result, whereas the differences in the poverty rates between certain risk groups in a country should be taken seriously only if they are fairly large, since these figures have substantial error margins.

The main outcome of the study summarized in this chapter is a detailed set of comparable poverty statistics based on one common poverty concept, and the elaborate sensitivity analysis of these statistics for several, partly arbitrary, choices with respect to the operationalization of these choices. Nevertheless, as mentioned several times, the study suffers from a number of serious limitations, on which further research would be desirable.

The quality of the poverty statistics depends crucially on the data from which they are to be derived. At this moment, the HBSs are the only source of more or less comparable statistics on poverty in all Member States of the EC. However, with respect to the extent, the quality, and the comparability of the information, the HBSs have considerable shortcomings. For one thing, institutionalized and homeless people are not represented in the HBSs. The latter group in particular, which appears to be growing in most of the EC Member States, would seem to be a relevant part of the target group of the least privileged. A special effort to quantify the extent of this phenomenon would be worthwhile.

A second shortcoming, determining our choice for expenditures as a measure of resources, concerns the quality of the income data in many of the HBSs. In our view, the initiative of Eurostat to set up an independent community-wide panel survey on income data should be supported. Moreover, the absence of information on social and cultural resources in the HBSs, forcing us to limit ourselves to material resources, also justifies efforts to come up with independent information on non-material resources, particularly, if the Council decision to view poverty as a lack of sufficient material, social, and cultural resources remains the relevant starting point for the definition of poverty.

With respect to the expenditure data obtained from the HBSs, the efforts to harmonize the methodology should also be supported unconditionally. This should also include a harmonized procedure for computing imputed rent and taking account of rent subsidies. Moreover, more research is needed into the possibility of correcting for unavoidable measurement errors as a result of the limited reference period.

The value of the poverty statistics would increase if they were calculated on the most recent available data. Therefore, it is recommended that NSIs give Eurostat access to the latest HBS data as soon as possible. This would serve the purpose both of getting a more complete picture from an intertemporal comparison, and of producing poverty statistics more relevant for the European Commission.

Finally, most HBSs lack information on wealth and also on a number of non-cash additions to household resources, such as provision of education and health facilities, and subsidies on housing and public transport by the government. Since the level of these benefits can be expected to be quite different in different countries, a Community-wide study on the extent of these benefits, and the consequences of taking them into account in the poverty statistics, should be regarded as highly necessary.

Notes

This chapter is a summary of the report "Poverty statistics in the late 1980s: research based on microdata" by the same authors. This report was written for the project "Living conditions of the Least Privileged in the EC," carried out at the Department of Economic Sociology and Psychology, Erasmus University, Rotterdam, under the auspices of Eurostat within the Poverty-3 program of DG-V (contract number PCR3/63). We thank Eurostat and the National Statistical Institutes for their efforts to make this research project possible. Final revisions to the chapter were made at the Economics Institute, Tilburg. We gratefully acknowledge comments made by Tony Atkinson and by an anonymous referee.

The statistics presented in this chapter are the results of research, for which the sole responsibility rests with the authors. The results do not necessarily reflect the views of national governments or the European Commission.

1   The full results of the research are presented in the report "Poverty statistics in the late 1980s: research based on micro data" (Hagenaars, de Vos and Zaidi, 1994). The present chapter merely presents a summary of the main results and an indication of the considerations that have guided us in making the numerous choices that needed to be made. For a more detailed description of both we refer to the aforementioned final report.
2   See Hagenaars (1986), Hagenaars and de Vos (1988), de Vos (1991), Zaidi and de Vos (1993).
3   Watts (1968, p. 321) emphasized the importance of "command over resources" as the basis for a poverty definition, rather than the actual consumption of goods and services deemed minimally necessary.
4   See the synthesis report on trend analysis of poverty statistics based on HBS data (de Vos and Zaidi, 1994a) and the country reports summarized there.
5   As constructed in Ménard, Pearce and Verma (1991).
6   See pp. 139–40 of the final report (Hagenaars, de Vos and Zaidi, 1994).
7   The consequences of taking home production into account in a cross-

country comparison of household resources are discussed in chapter 5 in this volume (Saunders, O'Connor and Smeeding, 1995).

8   See, for example, Smeeding *et al.* (1993) for an international comparison of living standards including non-cash income.

9   See, for example, Atkinson (1991).

10 See especially Buhmann *et al.* (1988).

11 The OECD scale (OECD, 1982) equals 1 for the first person, adds 0.7 for each additional adult, and 0.5 for each child (defined as persons younger than 14). The "modified" OECD scale equals 1 for the first person, 0.5 for each additional adult, and 0.3 for each child (defined as a person younger than 14). The subjective scale varies per country; for France, for instance, it equals 1, 1.232, 1.391, 1.517, 1.622, 1.713 for households of size 1,. .,6. (Refer to pp. 15–27 of the final report for further details on these scales.) See also Hagenaars, de Vos and Wunderink-van Veen (1992) for a detailed description of procedures and results.

12 For an illustration of some of the issues in obtaining comparable variables, see also chapter 4 in this volume (Atkinson *et al.* 1995).

13 Further research (de Vos and Zaidi, 1994b) suggests that, at least in Belgium, this outlying result is caused by selectivity of the sample of elderly.

14 Research by the Department of Social Security (DSS) suggests that the income information from the 1988 HBS is out of line with that of other years. To reduce the effects of random fluctuations on the statistics of households below average income, the DSS itself combines information from 1988 and 1989 (DSS, 1992).

References

Atkinson, A.B., 1991. "Comparing poverty rates internationally: lessons from recent studies in developed countries," *World Bank Economic Review*, 5, 3–21

Atkinson, A.B, K. Gardiner, V. Lechêne and H. Sutherland, 1995. "Comparing poverty rates across countries: a case study of France and the United Kingdom," chapter 4 in this volume

Buhmann, B., L. Rainwater, G. Schmaus and T.M. Smeeding, 1988. "Equivalence scales, well-being, inequality, and poverty: sensitivity estimates across ten countries using the Luxembourg Income Study (LIS) database," *Review of Income and Wealth*, 34, 115–42

Department of Social Security (DSS), 1992. *Households below Average Income. A Statistical Analysis 1979–1988/89*, London: HMSO

De Vos, K., 1991. "Micro-economic definitions of poverty," dissertation, Rotterdam: Erasmus University

De Vos, K. and M.A. Zaidi, 1994a. "Trend analysis of poverty in the European Community – synthesis of country reports for the United Kingdom, Spain, France, Portugal, Belgium and Greece," report submitted to Eurostat, Department of Economic Sociology and Psychology, Erasmus University, Rotterdam, and the Economics Institute, Tilburg

1994b. "Trend analysis of poverty in Belgium (1978/79–1987/88)," report submitted to Eurostat, Department of Economic Sociology and Psychology, Erasmus University, Rotterdam, and the Economics Institute, Tilburg

Eurostat, 1990. *Poverty in Figures: Europe in the early 1980s*, Theme 3, Series C, Luxembourg: Office for Official Publications of the European Communities

Hagenaars, A.J.M., 1986. *The Perception of Poverty*, Amsterdam: North-Holland

1991. "Family equivalence scales," *Discussion Paper*, EURDP91.06, Department of Economic Sociology and Psychology, Erasmus University, Rotterdam

Hagenaars, A.J.M. and K. de Vos, 1988. "The definition and measurement of poverty," *Journal of Human Resources*, 23, 211–22

Hagenaars, A.J.M., K. de Vos and S.R. Wunderink-van Veen, 1992. "Family equivalence scales," *Discussion Paper*, Department of Economic Sociology and Psychology, Erasmus University

Hagenaars, A.J.M., K. de Vos and M.A. Zaidi, 1994, *Poverty Statistics in the Late 1980s: Research Based on Microdata*, Eurostat publication, Theme 3, Series D, Luxembourg: Office for Official Publications of the European Community

Johnson, D. 1995. "Equivalence scales and the distribution of well-being across and within households," chapter 17 in this volume

Ménard, B., M. Pearce and V. Verma, 1991. "Construction of standardised variables: illustrations," Harmonisation of Family Budget Surveys, Doc BF 52/91, report to the Statistical Office of the European Community

OECD, 1982. *The OECD List of Social Indicators*, Paris: OECD

Saunders, P., I. O'Connor and T. Smeeding, 1995. "The distribution of welfare: inequality, earnings capacity, and household production in a comparative perspective," chapter 5 in this volume

Smeeding, T.M., P. Saunders, J. Coder, S. Jenkins, J. Fritzell, A.J.M. Hagenaars, R. Hauser, and M. Wolfson 1993. "Poverty, inequality and family living standards impacts across seven nations: the effects of non-cash subsidies for health, education and housing," *Review of Income and Wealth*, 39, 229–56

Van Praag, B.M.S. and R.J. Flik, 1992. "Subjective poverty," report to the Statistical Office of the European Community

Van Praag, B.M.S., A.J.M. Hagenaars and J. van Weeren, 1981. "Poverty in Europe," *Review of Income and Wealth*, 28, 345–59

Watts, H. 1968. "An economic definition of poverty," in D.P. Moynihan (ed.), *On Understanding Poverty*, New York: Basic Books, 316–29

Zaidi, M.A. and K. de Vos, 1993. "Research on poverty statistics in Pakistan: some sensitivity analyses," *Pakistan Development Review*, 2, 1171–86

4 Comparing poverty rates across countries: a case study of France and the United Kingdom

Anthony B. Atkinson, Karen Gardiner,
Valerie Lechêne and Holly Sutherland

Introduction: poverty in the European Union

Concern about poverty in the European Union (EU) means that it is important that we are able to monitor its development over time and across countries. The estimates made by the European Commission of the number of people living in poverty in Europe have already played a powerful role in promoting public and political support for the extension of the social responsibilities of the Community. The function of the statistics was in this case to *mobilize* policy, but poverty statistics are also used in its *execution*. The incidence of low incomes may be used to identify subgroups of the population, such as the elderly or lone parents, where policy initiatives are required. Just as unemployment rates are used in determining the need for labor market intervention, so too poverty rates by region may be used in the allocation of the Social Fund or other programs. With such uses in policy execution, issues of comparability across Member States become particularly important. The use of such an indicator to allocate European funds may provide national or local governments with an incentive to over-state the degree of poverty, counter-balancing their natural political desire to minimize the extent of the problem.

The European Commission has taken an active role in the development of measures of poverty in Europe. In the evaluation report of December 1981 on the first European Action Programme to combat poverty, the Commission made an estimate of the number of poor people in the Community in 1975, an estimate based on the definition of "poverty" as having less than 50 percent of the average disposable (after-tax) income per equivalent adult in the country in question. This relative poverty criterion was the concrete implementation of the definition adopted by the Council of Ministers as those persons whose resources (material, cultural and social) are so limited as to exclude them from the minimum acceptable way of life in the Member States in which they live. (Council Decision, December 19 1984)

Subsequently, the interim report on the Second European Poverty Programme (European Commission, 1989), based on the work of O'Higgins and Jenkins (1989), estimated that the number of poor had increased from 38 million in 1975 to 44 million in 1985.

The Report on the Second Programme, taking expenditure rather than disposable income as the indicator of resources, reached the alternative estimate for 1985 of 50 million people, or 15.4 percent of the total Community population. This figure was virtually unchanged compared with 1980, but the Commission noted that this stability in the number at the Community level was the net result of different developments at the national level. More recently, the report on the Poverty-3 programme (European Commission, 1993) included the provisional results of research carried out by Aldi Hagenaars and her colleagues at Erasmus University, Rotterdam (see chapter 3 in this volume), giving estimates of poverty (again based on expenditure) in Member States around the year 1988. The total is again broadly the same, with 53 million people estimated to be living at below 50 percent of the average expenditure per equivalent adult, but the findings for individual countries are rather different.

These statistics have served to heighten public and governmental awareness of the problem of poverty. The statistics do, however, raise a number of questions and the answers are important in assessing how far the statistics are sufficiently firmly based to provide an accurate instrument for monitoring the evolution of poverty in Europe and for policy decisions.

First, in order to obtain Union-wide figures, and to make comparisons between Member States, it is necessary to have *sources and methods that are comparable*. The more recent Commission estimates are based on the same kind of source – Household Budget Surveys (HBSs) – but these surveys themselves vary across countries. The way in which questions are posed may differ across countries and the same questions may have different connotations in different social and economic contexts. The methods of analysis may differ: for example, the procedures for grossing-up for differential non-response, or for the omission of atypical households, or for the treatment of durable expenditure.

Secondly, the *implementation of the poverty measure* itself raises a number of important issues. A criterion of 50 percent of average income, or expenditure, may appear at first sight unambiguous, but it leaves a number of matters to be decided. These include the definition of "average," the choice of equivalence scale, and the weighting of households according to their size. Such matters may seem ones that can be relegated to footnotes, but in fact they can have an appreciable effect on the relative poverty measures in different countries. Examination of the sensitivity of the estimates is a major contribution of the work of Hagenaars, de Vos and Zaidi (1994).

Thirdly, we have to consider the relation between Europe-wide estimates and *national studies* of poverty, that is studies from individual Member States. In a number of European countries there have been studies carried out by government statisticians, independent research institutions, or by academics. It is natural to ask how the numbers presented by the European Commission correspond to the findings of these national studies. To the extent that they are different, how can the differences be explained? Such an investigation is necessary, among other reasons, to ensure confidence in European level statistics.

The aim of this section is to contribute to the investigation of these questions by making a case study of France and the United Kingdom. This case study approach is based on the belief that further progress requires examination in depth of the situation in individual countries, particularly when it comes to the relationship with national studies. In this respect, our approach may be seen as complementary to that examining all (or most) Member States.

The chapter first examines in more detail the basis for the Commission's estimates with particular reference to France and the United Kingdom, and to the relation with French and British official studies of low incomes. It then takes up the question of the comparability of sources, and focuses on the issues of definition, demonstrating that different choices can change the conclusions drawn as to the relative extent of poverty in the two countries. This in turn brings out the role of differences in social policy in France and the United Kingdom in affecting the measurement of poverty, and these are the subject of the final section.

Relation between the Commission's estimates and national studies

The main features of the European Commission's poverty estimates for 1980, 1985, and 1988 are shown in table 4.1, where the Member States have been ranked in order of their poverty rate in 1988. In considering these estimates, it should be noted that the estimates relate to the *household* population and thus exclude those living in institutions and the homeless. Some of the most deprived members of the Community are

Table 4.1 *European Commission estimates of poverty rates, 1980, 1985 and 1988 (percent)*

	Percentage of persons below 50% of the "national mean"		
	1980	1985	1988[a]
Portugal	32.4	32.7	25.1
Italy	14.1	15.5	22.0
Greece	21.5	18.4	20.5
Ireland	18.4	19.5	19.4
Spain	20.9	18.9	17.7
France	19.1	15.7	16.5
United Kingdom	14.6	18.2	15.3
Germany[b]	10.5	9.9	11.9
Luxembourg	n/a	n/a	11.5
Belgium	7.1	5.9	9.4
Netherlands	9.6	11.4	4.8
Denmark[c]	7.9	8.0	4.3
Total	*15.5*	*15.4*	*16.0*

Notes:
[a] The estimates for 1988 are not comparable with those for 1980 and 1985.
[b] The estimates for Germany relate to West Germany before unification.
[c] The Danish national statistical institute has expressed reservations about the quality of its national HBS for the year in question.
Sources: 1980 and 1985 from Eurostat (1990, table 1); 1988 from European Commission (1993, p. 100). In some cases the year covered for a particular country differs from that shown.

therefore missing from the statistics. Similarly, it should be noted that the estimates treat the household as a single, unified entity. A person is not "poor" unless the total expenditure of the household falls below the appropriate figure. This takes no account of the *distribution of expenditure within the household.* There may be inequality within the household which means that the husband, say, enjoys a standard of living above the poverty line, while his wife and children fall below.

The European Commission (1993) emphasizes that the estimates for 1988 are not comparable with those for the earlier years, and for this reason a vertical line is drawn in the table. For certain countries, notably Portugal, Italy, Belgium, the Netherlands, and Denmark, there are large differences between the estimates for 1985 and 1988. The difference for Denmark may be due to shortcomings in the data, but a number of the figures seem to merit closer examination. In such an examination one useful benchmark is provided by the national studies of poverty to which reference was made earlier.

The present case study of two countries – France and the United Kingdom[1] – was motivated by the existence of such national studies undertaken by official statisticians. With one important exception, these studies follow the same broad approach as the European Commission. In the United Kingdom, the Department of Social Security (DSS) has for several years carried out a study of "Households Below Average Income" (HBAI), which gives estimates of the percentage of households below different percentages of average disposable income. This is the source of the figures shown in table 4.2. They are based on the same data set – the Family Expenditure Survey (FES) – as the Commission's estimates. In France, the study by Assémat and Glaude (1989) makes use of data from two sources: the income tax declarations, and the HBS. It is the latter – the Enquête sur les Budgets Familiaux or EBF – which is used by the Commission, and it is on this that we focus here. (The relation of the results from the two sources is examined in Atkinson *et al.*, 1993.) The results for France in 1985 and 1988 are shown in table 4.2.

The national studies do, however, differ in that they take *disposable income* as the indicator of resources. In making the choice there are issues of principle and issues of practice. The issues of principle are important ones (see Atkinson, 1989). There are different conceptions of poverty. If one views poverty in terms of the right to a minimum level of resources, then disposable income appears the appropriate choice; if one views poverty in terms of a minimum standard of living, then consumption appears appropriate. The Commission in its statement regarded income as the right choice *in principle*, but adopted expenditure on practical grounds. Expenditure is seen as a more reliable indicator than income, although it can be debated how far this is true of countries such as Great Britain and France. There is undoubtedly under-reporting of income, particularly of certain types, but expenditure, too, poses problems of under-reporting.[2]

The difference between disposable income and expenditure is one reason for the divergence between the national and Commission estimates shown in table 4.2. In particular, the choice of indicator is a major reason for the difference between the Commission's estimates and those in the DSS study in Great Britain shown in table 4.2. (A further reason for the difference between the Commission's estimates and those in the DSS study is that the latter related to Great Britain, which excludes Northern Ireland. The DSS estimates now cover the whole of the United Kingdom, but did not at this time.) Johnson and Webb (1991) find that

Table 4.2 *National and European Commission estimates: United Kingdom, 1985 and 1988, France, 1985 and 1988 and Great Britain, 1987 and 1988/89*

	United Kingdom, % population below 50% of average	France, % population below 50% of average
European Commission		
1985	18.2	15.7
1988	15.3	16.5
National studies		
1985	9.2	10.1
	(Great Britain)	
1987	15.7	–
1988/89	18.6	–

Sources: European Commission estimates from Eurostat (1990, table 1) and European Commission (1993, p. 100); United Kingdom and Great Britain estimates from DSS (1990, p. 21) (before housing costs), and DSS (1992, table F1(BHC)); France national estimates from Assémat and Glaude (1989, p. 5).

in 1985 the distributions of income and expenditure look quite different: the estimated proportion below 50 percent on an income basis is about 0.6 of the figure obtained on an expenditure basis. But the relationship varies from year to year, and for 1988 Hagenaars, de Vos and Zaidi (1994) find the reverse. In the appendix (p. 72), we show their expenditure-based and income-based estimates. In the case of France and the United Kingdom, we have the percentages below 50 percent of the national mean shown in table 4.3.

The difference between expenditure and income is, however, only part of the story, as is shown below, where we concentrate solely on the income-based estimates.

What can we conclude from these different estimates about the relative extent of low incomes in the two countries? Is poverty lower in France, as indicated by the EC (1985) estimates (expenditure-based) and by the income-based estimates for 1988–9 of Hagenaars, de Vos and Zaidi? Or are poverty rates similar in the two countries, as indicated by the EC (1988) estimates (expenditure-based) and by the national studies? Account has to be taken of the sampling errors which surround these estimates. According to the Department of Social Security (DSS, 1992, p. 141), the 95 percent confidence interval for the proportion of the population below 50 percent of average income in 1988/89 (with a sample

Table 4.3   *Percentages "below 50 per cent of the national mean": France, 1989 and United Kingdom, 1988*

	Expenditure-based	Disposable income-based
France (1989)	14.7	14.4
United Kingdom (1988)	14.8	19.0

about twice the size of that in 1985) was about ± 1 percentage points. Our own approximate calculations (Atkinson *et al.*, 1993) suggest that we are looking for differences of $1\frac{1}{2}$ percentage points for significance at the 5 percent level.

Before we can reach any definite conclusion, we have to investigate the issues set out in the Introduction.

Comparability of data sources in France and the United Kingdom

The fact that the surveys for the two countries used by the Commission, and used here, are both HBSs does not mean that we can assume that they are identical. There may be differences in sample coverage and design; there may be variation in response rates, item non-response, and in methods of imputation; the surveys may differ in the accuracy of recording and in the extent of re-coding.

In the United Kingdom, the Family Expenditure Survey (FES) is a continuous household budget survey, the primary purpose of which is to collect expenditure information necessary to construct the weights for the Retail Prices Index (RPI), but which also collects a substantial quantity of income data, together with other information on household composition, housing costs, etc. There are extensive questions covering the income of each household member from a wide range of sources and taxes paid. In 1985 the Income Schedule for each person has 81 questions specifically about income; there are $3\frac{1}{2}$ pages for the self-employed; there are detailed questions on individual state benefits. The whole schedule covers 39 pages. The FES is a representative sample of United Kingdom private households. The sample size is about 11,000, equivalent to around a 1 in 2,000 sample of all private households. The response rate in 1985 was 67 percent, giving a total of 7,012 households.

In France, the Enquête sur les Budgets Familiaux (EBF), is conducted periodically and here we refer to the 1984–5 survey carried out between mid-1984 and mid-1985. Information is obtained by interview on expenditure, income, and other variables. The income section contains 10 questions and is less detailed than the United Kingdom survey, although there is scope for adding supplementary information (for example, describing sources of income). The French sample of 20,000 households is about twice the size of that in the United Kingdom FES, representing approximately 1 in 1,000 households. About a third of the sample could not be contacted, refused to participate, or failed to complete the survey (Assémat and Glaude, 1989). This led to 11,977 cases being included in the INSEE database from which we started. In our analysis below, we use only those returns where the income questions were answered, and discarded those for which simply a range of income was given. The size of the effective sample is further reduced by the fact that there are households which answered the income questions but for which there are missing values for certain items of income. We use only those returns where there was a full answer to the income questions, leading to a final sample of 9,837. It should be noted that the United Kingdom FES uses imputation procedures in the case of item non-response, and it is possible that the exclusion from the FES of households where there had been imputation would affect the conclusions drawn in our comparison.

In the United Kingdom, there is evidence that the characteristics of non-respondents differ from those of respondents. A special study in 1981 (Redpath, 1986) found a lower response among households without children and where the head was self-employed; there was a fall in response with the age of the head of household. In order to adjust for differential non-response, differential grossing-up weights are applied which vary with family composition and age of the head. In France, to adjust for differential non-response between different types of household in the EBF, a grossing-up procedure is applied to yield results representative of the population. The weights are calculated for households grouped into 115 categories based on the type of commune (local authority district), socio-economic category of the household head, and number of persons in the household (Moutardier, 1988, p. 12). In our analysis, we have applied these weights, but it is not clear that they apply to the particular sample that we are using. The exclusion of households with item non-response for income may not be adequately allowed for.

In the sample studied here for the United Kingdom, all households interviewed are included. Unlike the official analysis by the Department of Social Security (DSS, 1992, p. 122), we have not, for example, excluded families where an absent spouse is recorded. We have however re-coded a number of cases where a detailed examination shows there to be inconsistencies (e.g. where the woman is coded as married with spouse absent and the man is coded as married with spouse present). We have re-coded foster children to show them as dependents, rather than as separate family units; and we have re-coded certain students living at home as separate units. Similarly in France we have made various re-codings. The need may be illustrated by the case of family benefits paid as part of the wage. Respondents were first asked (Question 26) about their wage, and then about family benefits, including whether (Question 29) these are included in the wage reported in response to the earlier question. Where the benefit was reported as included, it is then subtracted from the wage, the benefit appearing as a separate item. In certain cases, this procedure generates a negative net income, and we have assumed that the second question was not answered correctly. This example is mentioned, not because it is quantitatively important, but because it illustrates the difficulty in replicating the calculations of others; quite a lot has to be done to the data tape before it can be used to prepare tabulations. The issues of replication have been discussed in the economics profession, but arise particularly severely with microdata. It is virtually impossible to document these adjustments, short of supplying the full computer program.

In studying disposable income, our aim is to measure the total net flow of resources accruing to the household in a specified period, but inevitably we fall short of this ideal and the degree of shortfall may differ in the two countries. While in both France and the United Kingdom there is evidence that certain forms of income tend to be under-stated in the budget surveys (interest and dividend income, and the income of the self-employed), the relative importance of these differs across the two countries. This applies in particular to the income of farmers in France, reckoned to be under-reported by about 50 percent in the EBF (Assémat and Glaude, 1989, p. 12), where home production may also be more important. One tends to think that such under-statement of income will lead to poverty being *over-stated*. However, it has to be remembered that the measure is one of *relative* poverty. Adjustments for missing income affect both those at the bottom *and* the mean income. Increasing recorded investment income, for example, may increase the mean more than it shifts the bottom part of the distribution, thus increasing rather than reducing recorded poverty.

The time period over which income is measured differs both by type of income and across the two countries. In France, where earnings are not regular, the question asks for a monthly average; in the United Kingdom, the calculations are based on "normal" earnings. In the case of non-earned income, more categories are collected on an annual basis in France than in the United Kingdom, and altogether the French definition is closer to an annual than to a current basis.

To sum up, the fact that both the EBF and FES are HBSs should not be allowed to obscure the fact that there may be significant respects in which they are not comparable. Access to microdata allows researchers to go a considerable way towards harmonizing cross-country studies, but there remain differences between the sources which have to be borne in mind when considering the results. In some cases these differences could be eliminated by changes in the surveys in the two countries, but in other cases they reflect differences in structure between the countries, such as the relative importance of farm income.

Agreeing on definitions

In this section, we accept that poverty is to be measured in terms of household disposable income relative to the average, with particular reference to those below 50 percent of the average. While one may quite reasonably challenge this choice of definition, it is taken here simply to be politically given. The main point of this section is to show how, if one takes this particular definition as given, there is still considerable room for disagreement.

We do this by starting from the approach adopted in the study by Assémat and Glaude, which is shown in line A of table 4.4. If you look first at the 9.6 percent figure, this corresponds to the 10.1 percent figure cited from their study. The difference shows that we have not succeeded fully in reproducing their calculations; nonetheless it is close. There are on this basis about 10 percent of the French population in poverty, a figure which may be contrasted with the much smaller proportion – around 4 percent – in the United Kingdom when measured in this way. This difference is certainly larger than the $1\frac{1}{2}$ percentage points we identified as necessary for significance at the 5 percent level. The Assémat and Glaude definition is, however, a different interpretation of "50 percent of the average" from that adopted in the British study by the Department of Social Security (DSS). We now examine the effect of moving step by step towards the British definition. There are four main ingredients:

Choice of mean or median

The simplest difference is that the French take the median as the measure of the average, whereas the DSS study in the United Kingdom, and the Commission in their estimates, take the mean. The choice between these is in part a matter of their relative statistical properties, and it may be argued that the median is less subject to sampling fluctuations (this of

Table 4.4 *Estimated size of low income population on different defini-tions: France, 1984–5 and United Kingdom, 1985*

		France: proportion less than			United Kingdom: proportion less than		
Definition		40%	50%	60%	40%	50%	60%
A:	median households OECD scale before housing	5.3	9.6	16.8	1.7	4.1	9.9
	Median	48,937 FF per year			£70.44 a week		
B:	*mean* households OECD scale before housing	7.0	13.5	22.5	3.1	9.2	20.9
	Mean	54,604 FF per year			£83.09 a week		
C:	mean *individuals* OECD scale before housing	6.4	12.5	22.0	3.8	10.3	21.0
	Mean	51,356 FF per year			£80.01 a week		
D:	mean individuals *DSS scale* before housing	6.5	11.9	20.1	2.6	8.6	19.9
	Mean	57,188 FF per year			£86.58 a week		
E:	mean individuals DSS scale *after housing*	7.4	13.0	21.2	5.3	13.6	25.0
	Mean	44,739 FF per year			£67.13 a week		

course makes certain assumptions about the form of the income distribution). We should also note that, while the median is unaffected by the top or bottom coding of observations, it is affected by the deletion of observations, such as those with zero incomes.

The choice is however also a question of the *level* of the poverty line. As may be seen from table 4.4, the median is 85 percent of the mean in the United Kingdom and 90 percent in France. Taking 50 percent of the median is like taking a cut-off of 42.5 percent or 45 percent of the mean. The figures are therefore higher with 50 percent of the mean, and they are higher to a different extent in the two countries. Poverty is now – with definition *B* in table 4.4 – around half as much again in France, rather than twice as much, although it is still clearly significantly different.

Weighting of different units

The second difference concerns the weights to be applied to each individual household. As has been highlighted by O'Higgins and Jenkins (1989), the mean or median can be calculated in different ways depending on how the units are weighted, and the same applies to the calculation of the proportion with low incomes. For each household we calculate the disposable income per equivalent adult. (We discuss the equivalence scales below.) If the total disposable income of household h is y_h, and the number of equivalent adults e_h, then the equivalent income is y_h/e_h, and it is according to this that the households are ranked. The question is now: how do we weight these households when adding them up? There are at least three possibilities: a weight of unity to each household, a weight of e_h to household h, and a weight equal to the number of individuals in household h. As is pointed out in Atkinson and Cazes (1990), the first of these methods has been applied in French studies; the second in estimates for Germany; the third is that applied in the DSS study in the United Kingdom.

This might not appear to be a question of much importance. However, it may be seen from a comparison of lines *B* and *C* in Table 4.4 that while the difference between the estimates for each country individually is fairly small – of the order of 1 percentage point – they move the two countries in opposite directions. The poverty count is reduced in France and increased in the United Kingdom, so that it is now only around a quarter higher in France. The difference falls to 2.2 percentage points, or only slightly above the amount for which we are looking for significance at the 95 percent level.

Choice of equivalence scale

Thirdly there is the choice of equivalence scale. The equivalence scale applied in the analysis of the French EBF by Assémat and Glaude (1989) is very simple: 1 for the first adult, adds 0.7 for each additional adult, and 0.5 for each child (defined as persons younger than 14). This scale is that recommended by the OECD (1982), and for shorthand we refer to it as the OECD scale (although the OECD has used other scales; see also chapter 3 in this volume).

The OECD scale tends to be relatively generous to large families; it can also be criticized for not being sufficiently finely graduated. The scale applied in the DSS study in the United Kingdom varies the amount per additional adult according to the number in the household (and is less for the spouse of the household head), and the amount per child is graded with age, with a child aged under 2 receiving only a third of the amount allowed for a child aged 13–15.[3] The effect of adopting this scale in both countries is shown in line *D* of table 4.4. This goes in the opposite direction to the previous change, reducing both poverty counts and widening the interval again, so that poverty in France is now 40 percent higher than in the United Kingdom. The difference is more than twice the $1\frac{1}{2}$ percentage points that we are treating as significant at the 95 percent level.[4]

Before or after housing costs

The calculations carried out by the Department of Social Security in Britain are made on two bases: before and after housing costs. In the former case, the figures relate to the distribution of equivalent disposable income, which includes housing benefit but makes no deduction for housing costs. In the latter case, what is measured is net resources, defined as disposable income *minus* housing expenditure, again expressed per equivalent adult. For owner-occupiers, housing costs include the interest paid on loans for house purchase (net of income tax relief); no account is taken of imputed rent in either income or housing costs.

The second of these calculations – that of net resources after housing costs – may appear rather strange to observers from outside the United Kingdom. It can, however, be justified on the grounds that housing expenditure is a relatively exogenous element of a household's outgoings and one which varies across households in a way which reflects accidents of geographical location and tenure rather than the quality of the accommodation occupied. Moreover, changes in housing policy over time mean that the after-housing costs' estimates may provide a more consistent picture.

Viewed in terms of comparisons across countries, the case for considering net resources is that differences in disposable incomes could represent differences between the countries in their housing policies. One country may pursue a policy of low rents (either via low rents in the public sector or via rent control legislation in the private sector); the other may provide increased income transfers. The proportion in poverty may be lower in the latter country when measured in terms of disposable income, even though the situation after housing cost is identical in the two countries. This does not mean that we should concentrate *solely* on net resources, but a case can be made for considering its implications. These are shown in line E of table 4.4. In France the impact of the change in definition is small, but in the United Kingdom it is large, and the poverty percentage is now not significantly different from that in France. In both countries, the proportion below 50 percent of the average is around 13 percent.

Conclusion

The different findings with regard to the proportion of the population below 50 percent of average disposable income are summarized in figure 4.1, which demonstrates that the choice of definition can make a noticeable difference to the results. If we imagine the politicians as having agreed on a "50 percent of average" target, and then left the details to their statisticians, then the latter could come up with very different pictures depending how they interpreted the brief. Adopting a definition like that in the Assémat and Glaude study – with 50 percent of the median, weighting households as 1, applying the OECD equivalence scale, and taking disposable income before housing costs – we find poverty to be more than twice as high in France as in the United Kingdom. Adopting the definition used in the official British study, with 50 percent of the mean, counting people not households, with the DSS equivalence scale, and taking income after housing costs, there seems to be little difference in the extent of poverty. In the text we have concentrated on the 50 percent cut-off. It may be seen from table 4.4 that a higher (60 percent) or lower (40 percent) cut-off leads to different quantitative results but to the same broad conclusion regarding their sensitivity to the choice of definition.

Differences in social policy in France and the United Kingdom

It is a feature of figures such as these that they raise more questions than they answer. This section comments on some of the issues of interpret-

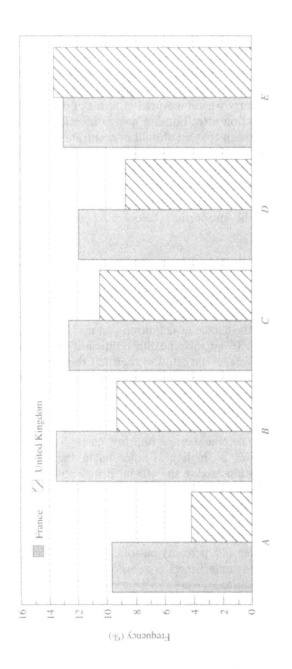

Figure 4.1 Five interpretations of "below 50 percent of the average"

Notes:

A French definition, median/households/OECD scale/before housing costs

B Mean for median

C Individuals for households

D DSS equivalence scale for OECD scale

E After rather than before housing costs

ation which arise from differences in social policy between the two countries. There are of course many other problems of interpretation, such as the whole role of public provision of health care or education. And there are interesting questions with regard to the *composition* of the low income population, where we discuss only the role of household size.

We comment on three aspects:
• Extent of safety net provision
• Family policy and equivalence scales
• Role of housing benefit.

Extent of safety net provision

One important difference between the two countries, at least in 1985, was that the United Kingdom had a general income safety net, then known as Supplementary Benefit. This did not cover those in full-time work, but otherwise provided a guaranteed minimum income to those out of the labor force or who were unemployed or sick. The level of the guarantee was then between 40 and 50 percent of average disposable income. It cannot be described as fully effective, in part because it was conditional (for example on not refusing appropriate job offers) and was in part because there is a problem of incomplete take-up. Nonetheless, the United Kingdom social security system, while less generous than France in terms of social insurance, can be seen as having a relatively more effective safety net. Since 1985 the French have introduced the *Revenu Minimum d'Insertion* (RMI), but this did not apply at the time studied.

This difference in the degree of social protection is probably one for the explanations of the difference between the distributions of income at the bottom end in the two countries. Figure 4.2 shows the cumulative distribution, in relation to mean disposable income, for equivalent income, using the DSS scale, before housing costs. (These figures correspond to line *D* in table 4.4.) The solid line relates to France. It may be seen from the axis that the frequencies are in general higher until we reach 45 percent of mean income, there appear to be more really low incomes in France. In contrast, in the United Kingdom (dashed line) frequencies are more concentrated in the range 45–70 percent of the mean, it being in this range that the two curves approach one another and intersect at around 65 percent of the mean. This highlights the impact of the safety net. About 1 in 8 of the population were living in families in receipt of Supplementary Benefit at this time.

The difference in the shape of the cumulative distributions for France

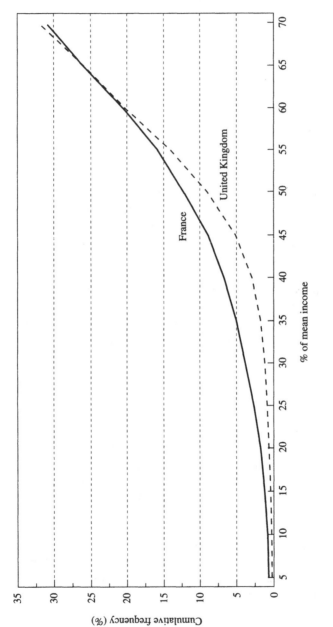

Figure 4.2 Cumulative income frequency distribution, France and the United Kingdom (definition *D*)

and the United Kingdom means that the results depend not only on the selection of the cut-off (and the choice between mean and median), but also on the choice of poverty *measure*. So far, we have used the head-count: the percentage below the poverty line. An alternative is the poverty gap: the amount of the income shortfall. The implications of adopting the poverty gap may be seen from figure 4.2, since the difference in the poverty gap is the integral of the difference in the cumulative distribution (Atkinson, 1987), so we can immediately deduce that the poverty gap is larger in France for all poverty lines up to 65 percent of the mean, and for some range above. Calculations (based on the same definitions as line *D* in table 4.4) show that the poverty gap is indeed higher for all poverty cut-offs up to the mean disposable income. The poverty gap gives more weight to those at some distance below the poverty line, and this is taken further by more elaborate measures such as those proposed by Sen (1976) and Foster, Greer and Thorbecke (1984). We can thus add the choice of poverty measure to the list of sources of differences in the estimates. If one wants to show more poverty in France, one chooses a measure that gives a greater weight to the largest poverty gaps.

Family policy and equivalence scales

We have seen that the change in equivalence scales from the OECD to the DSS scale affected not just the level of poverty but also the relative poverty rates in the two countries. This is not perhaps surprising in view of what we know about the differences in policy towards families of different sizes in the two countries. People tend to think in terms of French policy being more generous to larger families, whether in the form of income tax allowances (the *quotient familial*) or child benefits.

Although household size is not the same as family size, it may be useful to examine the treatment of household size in the low income calculations. In order to look at this in more detail, we have followed the approach suggested by Buhmann *et al.* (1988), who parameterized the equivalence scales as n^s, where n is the number of household members. So a value of 0 for s means that no adjustment is being made for household size and a value of 1 for s gives a *per capita* scale.

The exponent s is a valuable method of summarizing differences in scales. Buhmann *et al.*, show, for example, that scales based on benefit parameters tend to have values of s around 0.55; estimates based on observed consumption patterns and identifying restrictions tend to be lower (Buhmann *et al.*, take a value of 0.36 as representative); scales based on subjective evaluations (of what is needed "to get along") tend to be lower still (around 0.25). At the same time, the parameterization is only very approximate and does not capture the variation by age or other characteristics that one finds within a household of a specified size. Even the simple OECD scale, for example, for a household of 5 people ranges from 3.0 to 3.8, which would mean s varying from 0.68 to 0.83. The DSS scale could in principle range from 1.89 (assuming a single parent with children aged 0, 1, 2, and 3) to 3.62, which would mean s varying from 0.4 to 0.8.

Figure 4.3 illustrates how the poverty measures vary with s, taking the equivalence scale as given by n^s. These estimates are otherwise the same as in lines C and D in table 4.4. If we take the 50 percent lines, which are both dashed, then we can see that they have a U-shape, as has been examined in depth in work by Coulter, Cowell and Jenkins (1992). The trough in France appears to be around 0.55, that in the United Kingdom rather higher, around 0.65. It is the difference between the countries which is of particular interest here. The two curves intersect at a value of s around 0.6, with poverty higher in the United Kingdom if we take values below this. If one were to take a value of 0.25, as with the scales based on subjective evaluation, then the United Kingdom would have a poverty rate of 15.4 percent compared with 13.0 percent in France. On a *per capita* basis, the poverty rate in France is 16.5 percent compared with 14.3 percent in the United Kingdom.

Why do we get this intersection? There are two effects as s changes which have to be taken into account when considering the position of an individual household. The first is that, for all households except those consisting of just a single person, there is a change in their calculated equivalent income. Suppose that one considers the extreme cases of $s = 0$ (no adjustment for household size) and $s = 1$ (a *per capita* calculation). Then, if the household total income is Y, its equivalent income is Y on the former basis and Y/n on the latter basis, where n is the number of household members. The second effect is that the poverty line changes, since average equivalent income changes. In both countries the average equivalent income is reduced by broadly a factor of 3 in moving from $s = 0$ to $s = 1$.

We can therefore deduce how households of different sizes are affected. For single-person households, only the second effect operates. The rise by a factor of 3 in average equivalent income in moving from $s = 0$ to $s = 1$ means that for a single-person household the poverty line is reduced to a third relative to their incomes. This reduces measured poverty in both countries, but the effect is larger in the United Kingdom, since the United Kingdom distribution is steeper – as we have seen in aggregate. In the case of two-person households, both effects operate,

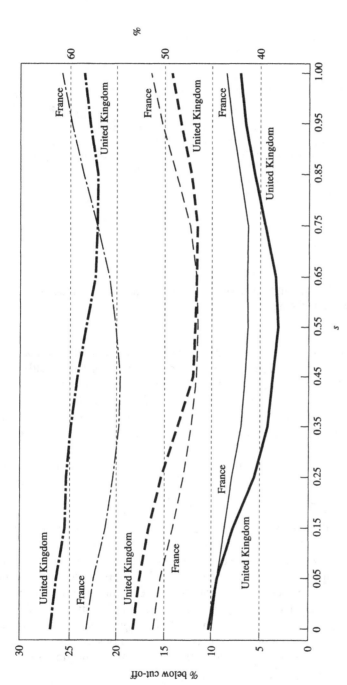

Figure 4.3 Sensitivity of headcounts to equivalence scales, France and the United Kingdom (definition *C* and *D*)

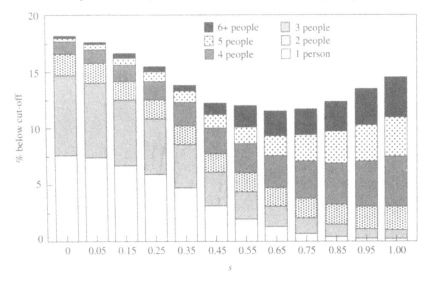

Figure 4.4 Sensitivity of 50 percent headcount to equivalence scales, household composition, United Kingdom

but the second is larger. In moving from $s = 0$ to $s = 1$, their income is halved but the poverty line falls to a third. It is only for households of 4 persons or larger that the first effect is larger. The reason why the curves intersect for the two countries appears therefore to be that the United Kingdom estimates are more sensitive to variations in the poverty line, and that the effects for small households outweigh those for larger households.

It is not just the total in poverty which is affected but also the *composition*. Figure 4.4 shows the breakdown by size of household for the United Kingdom. With $s = 0$, single-person households account for 42 percent of the total, whereas with $s = 1$, they are only some 1 percent, and those with 5 or more people account for a half. One gets a quite different picture of the problem, depending on the value of s selected.

The comparisons made above assume that the same equivalence scale should be applied in both countries, but the appropriate equivalence scale may vary from country to country. Where, for instance, the fixed costs of a household are relatively low, then standard of living considerations may point to a scale which is close to *per capita*. In another country, where fixed costs, such as those for housing, heating, and property taxes, are relatively larger, then the costs of additional household members may be less.

Role of housing benefit

The treatment of housing is particularly important, in view of differences across countries in relative prices and in the arrangements for finance. We have already seen the effect of subtracting housing costs, but we now consider the treatment of income-related subsidies to housing, known in the United Kingdom as housing benefit. These are related to housing costs, and indeed may be paid direct to the landlord where the accommodation is rented.

This raises the question of the appropriate treatment of housing benefit. Is it an income supplement, or is it a subsidy to spending? The latter would be parallel, for example, to transport subsidies, which simply show up in lower prices. In our estimates, housing benefit has been treated as income, but this can affect the comparison. The exclusion of housing benefit from income makes little difference to the French estimates (calculated on the same basis as line *D* in table 4.4), but increases those for the United Kingdom very significantly. The proportion below 50 percent of the mean rises from 8.6 percent to 16.0 percent. The cumulative distribution now intersects between 40 and 45 percent of the mean, although the poverty gap remains smaller in the United Kingdom until about 65 percent of the mean. This is a further illustration of the potential sensitivity of the conclusions.

Conclusions

In this section we have not attempted to discuss in any fundamental way what we mean by "poverty". Nor have we explored in depth the substantive findings, which lead to further questions, such as how our results are affected by the year chosen for the comparison (1985) and whether absolute poverty measures, as discussed on p. 27, may be less sensitive than relative poverty measures. Instead, our aim has been to emphasize the importance of what may seem to be relatively technical aspects of measuring poverty. These technical matters are not minor questions to be left to the footnotes. As we have tried to show, apparently innocuous differences in definitions can make a major difference to the conclusions. The degree of poverty in two countries such as France and the United Kingdom can be made to appear quite different depending on the choice of central tendency, on whether we count in terms of households or individuals, on the equivalence scale, and on the treatment of housing costs and housing benefit. Nor is it easy to ensure comparability of the data sources, even when they are both apparently of the same type. These reasons for lack of comparability may in turn have major implications for the identification of policy priorities and for the allocation of social or structural adjustment funds. Millions of ECU may depend on the choice of definition, and the way in which the data are analyzed.

Appendix: European poverty rates

Table 4A.1 *Comparisons of expenditure-based and income-based estimates, 1987–9*

Country		% of persons below 50% of the national mean	
		Expenditure-based[c]	Income-based
3 Portugal	(1989)	24.5	17.2
4 Italy	(1988)	21.1	13.0
5 Greece	(1988)	18.7	17.3
6 Ireland	(1987)	15.7	16.9
2 Spain	(1988)	16.9	13.7
1 France	(1989)	14.7	14.4
11 United Kingdom	(1988)	14.8	19.0
12 Germany[a]	(1988)	10.9	10.6
8 Luxembourg	(1987)	11.1	5.7
7 Belgium[b]	(1987–8)	7.4	n/a
10 Netherlands	(1988)	4.8	7.1
9 Denmark	(1987)	3.9	8.8

Notes:
[a] The estimates for Germany relate to West Germany before unification.
[b] Income data not available for Belgium.
[c] Expenditure-based results differ from those in table 4.1 on account of difference in equivalence scale.
Sources: Hagenaars, de Vos and Zaidi (1994), expenditure-based estimates from table 3.2 and income-based estimates from appendix tables A4.4.

Notes

The research reported in this chapter has been supported by the Nuffield Foundation, STICERD, the ESRC (Programme Grant X206 32 2001), the Institut National de Recherche Agronomique, and the European Community Human Capital and Mobility Programme (Network on Comparative Social Policy and Taxation Modelling). We are grateful to the CSO and the ESRC Data Archive for permission to use the FES data for the United Kingdom. Neither the CSO nor the ESRC Data Archive bear any responsibility for the analysis or interpretation of the data reported here. Earlier versions of the chapter have been presented by Gardiner to the Cross-National Research Seminar at LSE, by

Sutherland to the Institute for Fiscal Studies Seminar, the Social Policy Research Unit at York, and at a conference of the Social Policy Research Centre at the University of New South Wales; by Gardiner and Sutherland to the Welfare State Seminar at the LSE, and by Atkinson as an invited lecture at the Gmunden meeting of the European Society for Population Economics (June 1992). We are most grateful to all those who have made helpful comments, and particularly to John Hills for his careful reading and to the editors and referees for their suggestions which have improved the chapter.

1 Comparison with a third country – Spain – is made by Mercader (1994).

2 McGregor and Borooah (1992) have analyzed the income and expenditure data from the 1985 FES in the United Kingdom, combined with the information on durable ownership. They argue that more confidence can be placed in the expenditure measure, although this refers to a standard of living approach to measuring poverty.

3 The scale used by the DSS is that known as the "McClements" scale. It allows 0.64 for the spouse and an amount ranging from 0.15 to 0.59 for children (DSS, 1992, p. 125, the scale quoted there in terms of a couple = 1.00).

4 It is the 8.6% figure for the United Kingdom in line *D* of table 4.4 which should be compared with the 9.2 percent estimate by the DSS quoted in table 4.2 There are, however, several reasons why the figure may differ, apart from our failure to reproduce exactly their calculations. Among these are the fact that we include Northern Ireland, and that we have tried to align the definition of income with that in the French data, including certain lump-sum payments such as that for redundancy.

References

Assémat, J. and M. Glaude, 1989. "Source fiscale et/ou enquête par interview: l'experience française en matière de mesure des bas revenus," Paper presented at Eurostat Conference, Noordwijk

Atkinson, A.B., 1987. "On the measurement of poverty," *Econometrica*, 55, 749–64

1989. *Poverty and Social Security*, Hemel Hempstead: Harvester Wheatsheaf

Atkinson, A.B. and S. Cazes, 1990. "Mesures de la pauvreté et politiques sociales," *Observations et Diagnostics Economiques*, Revue de l'OFCE, 33, 105–30

Atkinson, A.B., K. Gardiner, V. Lechêne and H. Sutherland, 1993. "Comparing low incomes in France and the United Kingdom: evidence from Household Expenditure Surveys," Micro-simulation Unit, *Discussion Paper* MU9301, Cambridge: Department of Applied Economics

Buhmann, B., L. Rainwater, G. Schmaus and T. Smeeding, 1988. "Equivalence scales, well-being, inequality, and poverty: Sensitivity estimates across the countries using the Luxembourg Income Study (LIS) database," *Review of Income and Wealth*, 34, 115–42

Coulter, F., F.A. Cowell and S.P. Jenkins 1992. "Equivalence scale relativities and the extent of inequality and poverty," *Economic Journal*, 102, 1067–82

Department of Health and Social Security (DHSS) 1988. *Low Income Statistics: Report of a Technical Review*, London: Government Statistical Service

Department of Social Security (DSS) 1988. *Social Security Statistics 1988*, London: HMSO

1990. *Households below Average Income 1981–87*, London: Government Statistical Service

1992. *Households below Average Income: A Statistical Analysis 1979–1988/89*, London: HMSO

European Commission, 1989. Interim Report on the Second European Poverty Programme, *Social Europe*, Supplement 2, Brussels

1991. Final Report on the Second European Poverty Programme 1985–1989, Brussels

1993. Report of the Implementation of the Community Program for the Social and Economic Integration of the Least Privileged Groups (1989–1994), Brussels

Eurostat, 1990. "Inequality and poverty in Europe (1980–1985)," *Rapid Reports, Population and Social Conditions*, 7

Foster, J.E., J. Greer and E. Thorbecke, 1984. "A class of decomposable poverty indices," *Econometrica*, 52, 761–76

Hagenaars, A.J.M., K. de Vos and M.A. Zaidi, 1994. "Poverty statistics in the late 1980s: research based on microdata," Luxembourg: Eurostat

Johnson, P. and S. Webb, 1990. "Poverty in official statistics: two reports," *IFS Commentary*, 24, London

1991. "United Kingdom poverty statistics: a comparative study," *IFS Commentary*, 27, London

McGregor, P.P.L. and V.K. Borooah, 1992. "Is low spending or low income a better indicator of whether or not a household is poor?: some results from the 1985 Family Expenditure Survey," *Journal of Social Policy*, 21, 53–69

Mercader, M., 1994. "The low income population in Spain and a comparison with France and the United Kingdom," Welfare State Programme, *Discussion Paper*, 95, London: LSE

Moutardier, M., 1988. "Les budgets des ménages en 1984–1985," Paris: INSEE

OECD, 1982. *Social Indicators*, Paris: OECD

O'Higgins, M. and S. Jenkins, 1989. "Poverty in Europe: estimates for 1975, 1980 and 1985," paper presented at Eurostat Conference, Noordwijk

Redpath, R.U., 1986. "A second study of differential response comparing Census characteristics of FES respondents and non-respondents," *Statistical News*, 72

Sen, A.K., 1976. "Poverty: an ordinal approach to measurement," *Econometrica*, 44, 219–31

Townsend, P., 1990. "The poor are poorer: a statistical report on changes in the living standards of rich and poor in the United Kingdom 1979–1989," University of Bristol: Statistical Monitoring Unit

5   The distribution of welfare: inequality, earnings capacity and household production in a comparative perspective

Peter Saunders, Inge O'Connor and Timothy Smeeding

Introduction

One area of income distribution analysis of increasing research interest and policy relevance concerns the contribution that the earnings of a second earner in families (normally the wife) make to the level and distribution of family earnings and income. Recent studies for a range of countries suggest that the earnings of wives have had, and continue to have, an equalizing effect on the distribution of family income, including in Australia (Saunders, 1993), the Netherlands (Nelissen, 1990), Sweden (Bjorklund, 1992) the United Kingdom (Machin and Waldfogel, 1994) and the United States (Danziger, 1980; Cancian, Danziger and Gottschalk, 1993). Several of these studies also reveal that the distributional impact of wives' earnings is not stable over time, while the Luxembourg Income Study (LIS)-based work by Cancian and Schoeni (1992) reveals that it is also not stable across countries.

This evidence raises questions about the extent to which the observed cross-country differences in the distribution of income among households reflect differences in married women's labor force participation and earnings in each country. The counterpart to the increased market earnings of married women is a decline in either the number of hours worked in the home or in leisure. The resulting changes in the value of home production and leisure act to offset the increase in money income, so that the change in the economic welfare of the family is over-stated by money income alone. Furthermore, the degree of such over-statement is likely to vary across families within and between countries, thus affecting the interpretation of national and cross-national differences in the distribution of (money) income. Such considerations in turn raise issues about the extent to which public policies (e.g. tax and transfer systems and child care provisions and costs) influence the labor force decisions of second earners (whether by intent or not) and about the

75

implications of the rise of the two-earner couple for the design of such policies.

In addition to married women's labor force behavior, observed differences in household earnings may also be due to the influence of the macroeconomy on patterns of married men's employment status. Hence, differences in part- and full-time work and unemployment may also have a large effect on measured earnings differences across countries.

The empirical results we present below are intended to indicate the contribution that LIS data can make to understanding this aspect of cross-country differences in the distribution of income. Although several aspects of our methodology remain open to debate, our results are primarily intended to illustrate one particular approach and its empirical consequences. Central to the topic we address is the question of how best to estimate the impact of the value of household production on the distribution of welfare among families. This question has received considerable attention in many countries, and at many different levels. Some have seen it as important in providing alternative aggregate measures of economic product to those derived from the National Accounts. In contrast, we focus attention at a more microeconomic level on the consequences of the value of household production for the level of economic well-being within the household, and for its distribution among households and across nations.

The chapter is organized as follows: we first briefly review some of the relevant literature and canvas the conceptual and practical issues involved in estimating earnings capacity. The range of potential distributional consequences of substituting actual earnings by earnings capacity is also discussed. We then explain how and why our sample (of countries and, within countries, of families) was selected and outline our methodology in a little more detail, focusing on aspects where conceptual elegance had to be sacrificed on the altars of comparative research – practicality and data availability. Our main results are then presented, analyzed and discussed before some main conclusions are drawn.[1]

Earnings capacity and the distribution of welfare

The earnings function

The limitations of using market income (even when adjusted for need using an equivalence scale) to measure economic welfare are well known. These include the fact that market income reflects tastes and preferences for leisure as compared with work, and macroeconomic influences on employment, and that survey-based measures of market income contain transitory elements which cannot be separated from permanent income. In addition, money income reflects only the financial return to labor supplied to the market economy and thus takes no account of the value of work undertaken in the domestic economy – the value of household production. For these reasons, comparisons of the monetary incomes of different families at a point in time, or of the income of a given family at different points in time, are likely to provide misleading indications of the relative level (and hence the distribution) of economic welfare, and how this is changing over time. Gottschalk and Mayer (1994) have noted, for example, that the increased incomes of many families in the United States reflect the increased labor force participation of married women, yet associated with this rise in money income is a fall in the value of household production (and/or leisure). An implication is that the change in money income over-states the gain in economic welfare.

Taking account of changes in the value of home production thus has the potential to cause prevailing views on the size and trend in inequality to be re-considered. The two approaches to estimating the value of home production are the service price (or replacement cost) method, in which domestic work is valued at the market price of the equivalent services performed in the domestic economy, and the opportunity cost method, in which the potential market wage is used to value hours worked in the domestic economy.[2]

Our preferred approach, the earnings capacity method, involves identifying the factors which determine the wages of those who are in paid employment and using the resulting model to predict the forgone wages of those who are not in paid employment. These earnings capacity estimates can then be used to replace the actual earnings of those actually in employment (who may not be working to their full capacity) and to impute earnings for those not actually receiving market earnings. Ideally, the method is used to estimate the hourly wage, from which the value of home production can be calculated given information on the time spent performing household tasks. Where such information is not available (as is the case with the LIS database), weekly or annual earnings capacity can be calculated from data on the earnings of full-year, full-time (FYFT) workers. An estimate of the value of home production can then be calculated as being equal to the earnings capacity of those who are not participating in the labor market. This is the income that these people could earn if they were participating in the labor market, but it must be recognized as an imprecise estimate of the value of home production because it takes no account of how much time is *actually* spent on household work while they are not participating in the labor market. The limitations of the earnings capacity approach are acknowledged and should be kept in mind when reviewing our results.[3]

Methodology and sample selection

Methodology

Having provided a justification for our use of the earnings capacity approach, we now describe in a little more detail how we have applied the method. Here, we have been guided by the methodology developed by Garfinkel and Haveman (1977) and its more recent application by Haveman and Buron (1993). Central to the method is the application of the human capital model to estimate an earnings function in which earnings (e) is a function of a vector of human capital variables ($h_1 \cdots h_m$), a vector of personal characteristics variables ($p_1 \cdots p_n$), and a vector of job characteristics ($c_1 \cdots c_k$. Thus:

$$\log(e) = f(h_1 \cdots h_m; p_1 \cdots p_n; c_1 \cdots c_k) \qquad (5.1)$$

where $\log(e)$ is the logarithm of annual gross wage and salary income.

In estimating the earnings function (5.1) we included all FYFT workers, single people as well as those in couple families. As noted earlier, the LIS database does not make it generally possible to derive estimates of the hourly wage rate, so we were forced to use total (annual) wage and salary income. However, we decided to focus on FYFT workers only so as to minimize the effect of variations in hours worked. We included in the sample single people (aged 25 to 55) as well as couples in this age range, in order to obtain better point estimates of the parameters of the earnings function. We excluded the self-employed and earnings from self-employment because of the conceptual problems of separating this into a return to labor and a return to capital, as well as the practical limitations on the accuracy of household income survey data on self-employment incomes (Atkinson and Micklewright, 1983; Atkinson, Rainwater and Smeeding, 1995).[4]

Once estimated, the parameters of (5.1) were used to predict the earnings capacity ($e*$) of each individual in our sample of couple families (described below), given data on their human capital, personal and other relevant characteristics. These estimates of earnings capacity then replaced the actual earnings (whether positive or zero) of *all* partners in our sample of couples and the resulting distribution was compared with that of actual earnings.

This latter step in the exercise was undertaken in a series of separate stages. First, we replaced the earnings of FYFT workers with earnings capacity, then we extended the exercise in several sequenced steps to include part-time (PT) workers (defined as part-time in terms of either hours worked per week or weeks worked per year), then to those people who were unemployed (UN) and, finally, to those who were not in the labor force (NILF).[5] At each stage in this sequence, the actual earnings of each individual in each group was replaced by the estimate of earnings capacity, the implied distribution of earnings capacity was derived and the degree of inequality calculated.[6] At the stage of estimating these various distributions, the unit of analysis switches from the individual to the family (in our case couple families only; see below). This is partly because the family is a more appropriate unit of analysis for distributional purposes, and partly because we wish to investigate the impact of differences in individual earnings (and earnings capacity) on inequality among families.

To summarize, we thus have the following five distributions to estimate and compare:

$D1$ = the distribution of actual gross annual wage and salary income (hereafter earnings) among prime-aged (25 to 55) couples

$D2$ = the distribution of earnings among couples where the actual earnings of all FYFT workers are replaced by their estimated earnings capacity

$D3$ = as for $D2$, with the actual earnings of all PT workers also replaced by their estimated FYFT earnings capacity

$D4$ = as for $D3$, with the estimated FYFT earnings capacity included as earnings for the unemployed

$D5$ = as for $D4$, with the estimated FYFT earnings capacity included as earnings for those not in the labor force.

This structure allows us to estimate the overall distributional impact of replacing actual earnings by earnings capacity as we move sequentially from those with strongest attachment to the labor force to those with weaker or no such attachment.

One of the problems with comparing the distributions of observed earnings and earnings capacity is that the latter is derived from an estimated model which leaves a good deal of the actual variation in earnings unexplained. Unless some account is taken of this, it will be virtually impossible to ascribe the differences which emerge in the two distributions to differences in labor force participation behavior (which cause actual earnings to be below earnings capacity) as compared with differences which are a consequence of the weak predictive performance of the model used to derive earnings capacity. This explains why, in the first step described above, we replace actual earnings by earnings capacity for our sample of FYFT workers. This gives an indication of the extent to which poor model prediction alone accounts for differences between the levels and distributions of actual earnings and earnings capacity. By then using the latter distribution (D2) as a benchmark against which to compare our subsequent distributions, the impact of the accuracy of the regression predictions on the distributional differences is minimized (though admittedly not avoided altogether).

One final adjustment to the method draws on the analysis of earnings capacity and poverty undertaken by Garfinkel and Haveman (1977), and more recently by Haveman and Buron (1993). The latter authors observe that use of the human capital earnings predictions to replace actual earnings omits several important factors known to influence earnings, and note that the procedure assigns an identical earnings capacity to each. In order to overcome these problems, we followed the procedure applied by Haveman and Buron and varied each individual earnings prediction within a cell by a randomized component drawn from a normal distribution with zero mean and standard deviation based on the standard error of the regression equation estimated for all FYFT workers.[7] The results described on p. 87 have thus all been derived after this randomization procedure was applied to the actual earnings regression predictions of earnings capacity.

Once the five alternative distributions (D1–D5) had been derived, the differences between them were compared, both within and across countries. For this part of the analysis, we relied on comparisons of decile mean incomes (more accurately, mean earnings) to get an assessment of the absolute levels of the earnings capacity adjustments at each stage, and on the decile shares, Gini coefficient and percentile ratios in our distributional analysis. It is also worth emphasizing that our earnings capacity estimates enter cumulatively as we move from distribution D1 to distribution D5.

One of the issues which motivated this chapter was to try and assess, in a comparative cross-country context, the distributional consequences of including an estimate of the value of home production into conventional earnings distribution comparisons. Our results allow us to approach this through a comparison of distributions D4 and D5, where the latter imputes earnings capacity to those not in the labor force, while the former assumes FYFT earnings capacity earnings for all members of the labor force. The great majority (though not all) of those entered at this last stage of the analysis will be married women currently engaged in domestic (or voluntary) work. However, some domestic work will also have been performed by women (and men) who enter the comparisons at an earlier stage in the chain of comparisons, while some of those who enter at the final stage may not necessarily have been engaged in home production. However, without time use data at our disposal, assumptions concerning use of time for home production versus leisure must be made as we move through the analysis.[8]

Sample selection

The broad structure and features of the LIS database have been described elsewhere (e.g. Smeeding, O'Higgins and Rainwater, 1990) and will not be repeated here. In choosing our sample of countries from the LIS database, we were guided by the objectives of our analysis and restricted by what could be achieved in practice. Because one of our main interests was in investigating the different contributions of the earnings of wives to earnings inequality among families, we restricted ourselves to couple families where earnings were most likely to be the primary source of family income. Thus we included only those couples where both partners were aged between 25 and 55 years (inclusive) and who were not identified as containing at least one partner with a disability which prevented participation in the labor market.[9]

We included couples both with and without children, but did not use an equivalence scale to adjust for differences in need. Although the use of an equivalence scale can be justified in providing better estimates of economic welfare, our emphasis is on comparing alternative distributions of earnings rather than investigating how earnings and other sources of income influence living standards.[10] In our framework, the presence or absence of children is likely to influence labor force behavior and hence earnings, and we attempt to capture such an effect in our earnings model. However, we do not go beyond this to investigate the demands placed on those earnings by the needs arising from the existence of the children themselves.[11]

Finally, we restricted ourselves to countries with data available in the 'second wave' (c. 1985) of the LIS database and to those countries for whom it was possible to derive comparable estimates of the earnings function. This left us with the following five countries (years in brackets): Australia (1986); Canada (1987); (West) Germany (1984); the Netherlands (1987); and the United States (1986).[12]

Table 5.1 presents a breakdown of the *unweighted* samples in each country, by family type and labor force status. Our sample size ranged from around 1,300 couples in Germany to over 3,500 in Canada. Comparison of the different national sample structures reveals some substantial differences in the pattern of labor force attachment in each

Table 5.1 *Married couples, both partners aged 25 to 55, in five nations: unweighted sample size, by gender and labor force status*[a]

	United States (1986)		Canada (1987)		Australia (1985)		Netherlands (1987)		Germany (1984)	
	Number	%	Number	%	Number	%	Number	%	Number	%
Couples: both with and without children										
Husbands	3,284	100.0	3,587	100.0	2,351	100.0	1,705	100.0	1,345	100.0
Employed FYFT[b]	2,402	73.1	2,617	73.0	2,111	89.8	1,491	87.4	1,078	80.1
Employed < FYFT	543	16.5	418	11.7	68	2.9	106	6.2	169	12.6
Unemployed	243	7.4	255	7.1	95	4.0	76	4.9	66	4.9
Not in labor force	96	2.9	297	8.2	77	3.3	32	1.9	32	2.4
Wives	3,284	100.0	3,587	100.0	2,351	100.0	1,705	100.0	1,345	100.0
Employed FYFT[b]	1,052	32.0	1,129	31.5	654	27.8	187	11.0	267	19.9
Employed < FYFT	982	29.9	1,094	30.5	687	29.2	392	23.0	408	30.3
Unemployed	210	6.4	263	7.3	103	4.4	216	12.7	84	6.2
Not in labor force	1,040	31.7	1,101	30.7	907	38.6	910	53.4	586	43.6
Couples with children										
Husbands	2,324	100.0	2,616	100.0	1,781	100.0	1,231	100.0	920	100.0
Employed FYFT[b]	1,717	73.9	1,915	73.2	1,609	90.3	1,079	87.7	753	81.8
Employed < FYFT	378	16.3	300	11.5	38	2.1	74	6.0	109	11.8
Unemployed	169	7.3	183	7.0	81	4.5	58	4.7	43	4.7
Not in labor force	60	2.6	218	8.3	53	3.0	20	1.6	15	1.6

	N	%	N	%	N	%	N	%	N	%
Wives	2,324	100.0	2,616	100.0	1,781	100.0	1,231	100.0	920	100.0
Employed FYFT[b]	601	25.9	689	26.3	351	19.7	39	3.2	111	12.1
Employed < FYFT	738	31.8	847	32.4	576	32.3	267	21.7	273	29.7
Unemployed	150	6.5	203	7.8	94	5.3	163	13.2	60	6.5
Not in labor force	835	35.9	877	33.5	760	42.7	762	61.9	476	51.7
Couples without children										
Husbands	960	100.0	971	100.0	570	100.0	474	100.0	425	100.0
Employed FYFT[b]	685	71.4	702	72.3	502	88.1	412	86.9	325	76.5
Employed < FYFT	165	17.2	118	12.2	30	5.3	32	6.8	60	14.1
Unemployed	74	7.7	72	7.4	14	2.5	18	3.8	23	5.4
Not in labor force	36	3.8	79	8.1	24	4.2	12	2.5	17	4.0
Wives	960	100.0	971	100.0	570	100.0	474	100.0	425	100.0
Employed FYFT[b]	451	47.0	440	45.3	303	53.2	148	31.2	156	36.7
Employed < FYFT	244	25.4	247	25.4	111	19.5	125	26.4	135	31.8
Unemployed	60	6.3	60	6.2	9	1.6	53	11.2	24	5.6
Not in labor force	205	21.4	224	23.1	147	25.8	148	31.2	110	25.9

Notes:

a The sample includes individuals aged 25 to 55 (inclusive).

b FYFT = full-year, full-time.

Source: LIS database; see table 5A.1 (p. 100) for definition of labor force status.

country. In total, between 73 percent (Canada) and 90 percent (Australia and Germany) of husbands were in employment, although the prevalence of part-time male employment was more variable, being highest (16.5 percent) in the United States, but very much lower in Australia (2.9 percent) and the Netherlands (6.2 percent), with Canada and Germany in between with a figure of around 12 percent. Not surprisingly, cross-country variations in employment rates are much greater for wives than for husbands. In the three non-European countries, the total employment rate of wives was between 57 percent and 62 percent: in Germany, it was around 50 percent and in the Netherlands less than 34 percent. Much of this difference is explained by differences in the full-time employment rate of wives, with the rate of part-time employment varying in a relatively small range, from 23 percent (in the Netherlands) to 32 percent (in Canada and the United States). An illustration of the size of these differences among wives' employment can be gained by noting that if the Netherlands were to conform to the same patterns as those in the United States, an additional 359 married women (out of a total of 1,705 – equivalent to over 21 percent) would have been in FYFT employment and a further 118 wives (7 percent) would be employed part-time. Clearly, these differences have the potential to have a considerable impact on the distribution of family earnings in the Netherlands, and how it compares with that in the United States.

Further comparison of the employment ratios of wives according to whether or not there are children in the family provides additional insight into the differences shown in table 5.1. In all five countries, full-time work is greater for wives without children than for those with children. However, the differential percentage of full-time workers among each group varies considerably across countries, from a factor of almost 10:1 in the Netherlands, to around 3:1 in Germany, about 2.7:1 in Australia, to around 1.7:1 in North America. Generally, the rate of part-time work among wives shows much less variation with the presence or absence of children, although the rate is generally higher for those with children (except in the Netherlands and Germany). These patterns suggest that part-time work is the preferred option for most married women in all five countries and that this option (unlike full-time work) is not greatly constrained by the presence of children.

In summary, table 5.1 reveals that the biggest cross-country differences in employment rates occur among wives and in relation to the prevalence of full-time work for those with children. These differences are likely to reflect prevailing social values and attitudes to the role of women as mothers or workers, combined with factors such as the availability, quality and cost of child care and the nature of the incentives built into the tax and transfer systems. These and other facilitative mechanisms shape and reinforce prevailing social attitudes by constraining the nature of labor market choices and influencing the terms on which those choices can be exercised.

Results

Earnings regressions

As explained previously, the first step in our analysis involves estimating the human capital earnings function shown in general terms in (5.1). In undertaking this, we decided for reasons of cross-national comparability to include only those variables which could be specified in a broadly comparable way for each country. In some instances, this required us to aggregate variables into a smaller (but common) list of classifications than we would have chosen if we had been studying only one country. In others, we were forced to omit variables entirely in order to maintain the comparability of our estimates. The full list of explanatory variables used is specified and defined in table 5A.1 in the appendix (p. 100), while the resulting earnings function regression estimates are provided in tables 5A.2 and 5A.3 (pp. 101–3) for wives and husbands, respectively.[13]

The two key human capital variables used in the earnings model are years of experience and level of education. The former variable was constructed by assuming that schooling began at age 6 and that there had been continual labor force attachment for all individuals since leaving the education system.[14] This is known to be an invalid approximation, particularly for women, though increasingly for men, but it was the best that could be done with the available data.[15] The education, occupation and industry variables were also fairly rudimentary, but were specified with a view to maximizing the degree of cross-country comparability. We experimented with a number of other personal characteristics variables (see below) but those shown in table 5A.1 – place of birth, marital status, and the presence and age of children – performed consistently best overall (though not necessarily always in each individual country).

Turning briefly to the results themselves, it is important to recall that we estimated the earnings functions on *all* individuals aged 25 to 55 years who were FYFT workers in each country. This explains why the sample sizes shown in tables 5A.2 and 5A.3 differ from those which define our samples of couples shown in table 5.1.[16]

Our preferred results for women indicate that the human capital variables (experience and education) are generally significant, except in Australia where only the college education variable was statistically significant (table 5A.2). For the remaining four countries, the earnings–experience profile follows an inverted U-shape which reaches its maximum value after 22 years (in the United States), 24 years (in Canada), 31 years (in the Netherlands), and 26 years (in Germany). The education variables generally conform to the anticipated pattern, with higher financial returns associated with higher levels of formal education. Our estimates indicate that the return to college education is a good deal higher in North America than in Europe. Those with no or very low education in the Netherlands appear to face a particular disadvantage in terms of earnings. Native-born women have slightly lower earnings than overseas-born women in three out of four countries, but the differences are not significant. Women who are married tended to have significantly lower earnings than single women, but the presence of children has an even larger (negative) impact on female earnings than marriage itself.[17]

Turning to the results for men in table 5A.3, we again found the human capital variables performed well, even in Australia. The earnings-experience profile reaches its peak after 33 years (in the United States and Canada), 27 years (in Australia, and Germany), and 36 years (in the Netherlands). In all cases these peaks occur some years later than the earnings peak for women.[18] Again, the estimated returns to education are highest for males in the United States, while males with no or very low education in the United States and in the Netherlands have very low earnings relative to those with more education. There is a pronounced earnings differential in favor of native-born (or majority) as compared to overseas-born (or minority) men. This differential is particularly large in the United States where it refers to white versus non-white men, regardless of place of birth.

Our estimates indicate that married men have higher earnings than single men with the same characteristics in all five countries, significantly so in three of them. This contrasts with the negative effects of marriage on female earnings in three countries shown in table 5A.2. Only in the United States was the marital status significant for both men and women, indicating a positive effect on male earnings which, in absolute terms, is considerably larger than the negative effect on female earnings. Finally, nowhere did either of the two child variables have a significant effect on male earnings. In combination with the estimated negative impact of children on female earnings, it is clear that, in terms of earnings at least, women bear most of the financial burden associated both with getting married and with child rearing. Neither event has a negative effect on male earnings; in fact, there is a clear "marriage premium" in the male earnings structures in all five countries.[19]

Distributional analysis

Having presented and discussed our estimated earnings regressions, we now use these to estimate the distributional impact of earnings capacity in the series of stages described earlier. The focus of our analysis is now narrowed to the samples of prime-aged couple families summarized in table 5.1. We discuss our results in two stages, focusing first on the level of mean earnings, followed by a more explicit assessment of their distributional implications.

Mean earnings

We first show (see column (1) in table 5.2) how the level of mean earnings varies in each country as we move from the distribution of actual family earnings to the progressive replacement of actual earnings by earnings capacity in the series of stages described earlier.[20] As previously noted, the first stage in this process involves the replacement of actual earnings by earnings capacity for FYFT workers only (column (2)), and provides evidence on the predictive accuracy of the estimated earnings functions. This step causes mean earnings to rise overall in all five countries, though to varying degrees.[21] The change in mean earnings within each decile is, however, not always positive (e.g. in Canada) and the effect tends generally to be smaller in the middle of the distribution than at either extreme. The largest proportionate increase in decile mean earnings occurs in the lowest decile in all five countries.

Columns (3)–(5) in table 5.2 allow an estimate to be made of the impact of replacing actual earnings by estimated (FYFT) earnings capacity for part-time workers, the unemployed and those not in the labor force, respectively. In general, the smallest effects are associated with including earnings capacity for the unemployed, while the largest effects occur when estimated earnings capacity is incorporated for those who are not in the labor force.[22] Since the great majority of those not in the labor force are women working in the domestic economy, these aspects of the results illustrate the overall magnitude of the value of home production relative to market earnings. The overall cumulative effect of the four sequenced earnings adjustments causes mean earnings to rise by 28 percent from their observed value in the United States, 28 percent in Canada, 38 percent in Australia, 53 percent in the Netherlands and 44 percent in Germany.

Table 5.2 *Decile mean earnings for actual earnings and alternative earnings capacity populations[a] (national currencies)*

Country/decile	Actual family earnings (1)	FYFT (2)	<FYFT (3)	UN (4)	NILF (5)	NILF/ Actual (6)	NILF/ FYFT (7)
			Earnings capacity				
United States (1986)							
First	7,836	7,607	10,896	12,533	20,618	2.63	2.71
Second	17,829	16,794	20,577	21,929	27,960	1.57	1.66
Third	23,548	22,095	26,255	27,318	32,933	1.40	1.49
Fourth	27,940	26,837	30,885	31,937	37,809	1.35	1.41
Fifth	32,228	31,440	35,886	37,200	42,428	1.32	1.35
Sixth	37,111	36,773	41,370	42,624	47,446	1.28	1.29
Seventh	42,210	42,780	47,082	48,669	53,816	1.27	1.26
Eighth	48,513	50,630	55,311	56,659	61,071	1.26	1.21
Ninth	58,221	62,076	66,539	68,372	72,577	1.25	1.17
Tenth	85,726	94,064	98,616	99,981	103,760	1.21	1.10
Total	*38,116*	*39,110*	*43,342*	*44,722*	*50,042*	*1.31*	*1.28*
Canada (1987)							
First	7,959	8,896	13,004	15,821	26,001	3.27	2.92
Second	21,517	20,423	24,812	26,849	34,054	1.58	1.67
Third	27,870	26,480	30,696	32,282	39,199	1.41	1.48
Fourth	33,301	31,338	36,214	37,655	43,931	1.32	1.40
Fifth	38,363	36,307	41,906	43,494	48,454	1.26	1.33
Sixth	43,294	42,036	47,495	49,049	53,384	1.23	1.27
Seventh	48,947	48,254	53,735	54,910	58,993	1.21	1.22
Eighth	55,399	56,131	61,340	62,239	66,182	1.19	1.18
Ninth	64,448	66,948	72,291	73,040	76,568	1.19	1.14
Tenth	90,565	95,942	101,895	103,175	106,343	1.17	1.11
Total	*43,166*	*43,276*	*48,339*	*49,851*	*55,311*	*1.28*	*1.28*
Australia (1985)							
First	3,630	6,304	7,223	10,520	19,010	5.24	3.02
Second	16,800	15,601	17,014	18,775	25,450	1.51	1.63
Third	21,379	20,003	22,153	23,580	29,323	1.37	1.47
Fourth	25,147	24,062	26,506	27,481	33,452	1.33	1.39
Fifth	28,377	27,989	30,503	31,407	37,688	1.33	1.35
Sixth	31,608	32,512	35,445	36,302	41,893	1.33	1.29
Seventh	34,891	37,539	40,975	41,557	45,958	1.32	1.22
Eighth	39,109	42,987	46,418	46,896	51,284	1.31	1.19

Country/decile	Earnings capacity						
	Actual family earnings (1)	FYFT (2)	<FYFT (3)	UN (4)	NILF (5)	NILF/ Actual (6)	NILF/ FYFT (7)
Ninth	45,197	51,539	54,420	55,005	59,733	1.32	1.16
Tenth	63,139	74,541	78,037	79,708	84,255	1.33	1.13
Total	*30,928*	*33,308*	*35,869*	*37,123*	*42,805*	*1.38*	*1.29*
Netherlands (1987)							
First	17,972	17,185	18,513	27,996	56,440	3.14	3.28
Second	34,932	34,188	34,856	38,034	65,587	1.88	1.92
Third	39,921	40,308	41,242	45,416	72,046	1.80	1.79
Fourth	44,501	45,652	47,858	53,815	77,982	1.75	1.71
Fifth	49,735	51,490	55,254	62,283	82,903	1.67	1.61
Sixth	55,537	57,534	63,812	70,930	87,768	1.58	1.53
Seventh	63,522	64,704	73,533	79,680	93,749	1.48	1.45
Eighth	72,609	73,488	83,118	88,045	102,102	1.41	1.39
Ninth	84,420	86,160	96,275	100,483	112,942	1.34	1.31
Tenth	119,701	116,716	126,264	129,257	140,412	1.17	1.20
Total	*58,285*	*58,743*	*64,073*	*69,594*	*89,193*	*1.53*	*1.52*
Germany (1984)							
First	20,390	19,361	22,948	27,001	46,490	2.28	2.40
Second	32,833	32,219	34,793	38,188	55,205	1.68	1.71
Third	37,887	38,295	42,514	45,579	61,780	1.63	1.61
Fourth	42,492	43,564	49,203	51,862	67,532	1.59	1.55
Fifth	47,780	48,576	55,625	58,300	72,468	1.52	1.49
Sixth	53,537	54,523	62,033	64,566	77,859	1.45	1.43
Seventh	60,443	60,847	68,594	71,399	84,144	1.39	1.38
Eighth	68,417	67,859	76,882	79,506	92,259	1.35	1.36
Ninth	79,315	79,567	89,520	91,716	104,006	1.31	1.31
Tenth	106,800	110,887	120,477	121,825	130,326	1.22	1.18
Total	*54,989*	*55,570*	*62,259*	*64,994*	*79,207*	*1.44*	*1.43*

Note:
[a] The structure of this table is explained in the main text. All figures have been rounded to the nearest 10 currency units.

Earnings shares and inequality

We next show (in table 5.3) the effects of including earnings capacity on the distribution of earnings at each stage, while the final distributional results (table 5.4) show the percentile ratios which summarize the degree of inequality in each of the distributions. In terms of the overall distributional impact of including earnings capacity, a similar pattern emerges within each country. The replacement of actual earnings by earnings capacity for FYFT workers has an ambiguous effect on inequality, the Lorenz curves of the two distributions intersecting in the middle ranges in all five countries. Each of the next three steps causes a decline in inequality in the United States and Canada, while this is not always true for each pairwise comparison in the other three countries. In Australia, the final distribution of earnings capacity always Lorenz dominates the actual distribution of earnings among FYFT workers, while in the Netherlands and Germany this is not true for less than FYFT workers.

Some interesting and informative patterns emerge from the Gini coefficients shown in table 5.3. In all countries except the Netherlands, the replacement of earnings by earnings capacity for FYFT workers causes the Gini coefficient to increase. This occurs despite the higher earnings capacity estimates in the lower deciles, these being more than offset by the changes at the upper end of the distribution. Imputing earnings capacity for part-time workers causes the Gini coefficient to decline except in Germany. Imputing earnings capacity to the unemployed and to those not in the labor force causes the Gini coefficient to decline further in all countries, with the largest effects arising from non-participation. The results thus indicate that the existence of *both* unemployment *and* non-participation cause actual earnings inequality to be greater than it would be if all labor was fully utilized at market earnings capacity.

The effect on inequality of non-participation alone can be estimated from the Gini coefficients in columns (4) and (5) in table 5.3. These show that this adjustment causes a decline in the Gini coefficient of around 15 percent in the United States, 18 percent in Canada and Australia, 39 percent in the Netherlands, and 27 percent in Germany. These reductions explain much of the overall decline in the Gini coefficients between the first and last stages shown in column (7) of table 5.3 and point to the quantitative significance for inequality of our estimates of the value of home production. Perhaps of greater significance than the overall size of these effects, however, is its variation across countries, specifically the very large effects estimated for the Netherlands.

Overall, these results thus indicate that both non-employment (due to either unemployment or the absence of labor force participation) and under-employment (due to part-time work) cause the distribution of earnings to be more unequal than would be the case if everyone worked FTFY and earned to the limits of their capacity. The summary statistics in table 5.4 reinforce those in table 5.3, and also serve to highlight the fact that the biggest distributional effects occur at the bottom of the distribution and that those associated with part-time work and non-participation in the labor force dominate those associated with unemployment.[23]

The earnings capacity estimates included in the final stage of the analysis refer to those who are not in the labor force, the great majority of whom are women. Comparison of the estimates in the columns of tables 5.2, 5.3, and 5.4 (see below) is thus relevant to assessing the effects on the distribution of earnings of including a value for home production when it is estimated using the earnings capacity approach.

Inequality comparisons: a summary

Our first interest lies in assessing the distributional impact of the value of household production (and the other adjustments), in particular in seeing how this value varies across countries and thus affects cross-country comparisons of inequality. To do this, we compared the observed distributions shown in column (1) of tables 5.3 and 5.4 with the full earnings capacity distributional estimates shown in the last column of each table. On the basis of the actual distributions of earnings, table 5.3 shows Germany to have the most equal distribution of earnings, followed by the Netherlands and Australia. The United States and Canada have the most earnings inequality, with the distribution in the United States less equal than that in Canada, and with the Australian distribution less equal than that in the Netherlands.

Thus, even given the lower participation rates of married women in Germany and the Netherlands, in combination with the fact that wives' earnings tend to have an equalizing effect on family earnings, the distributions of family earnings in Germany and the Netherlands are still relatively equal compared with those in Australia, Canada and the United States. This observation suggests that a clearer earnings inequality ranking should emerge when cross-country variations in under-employment and non-employment are eliminated by replacing actual earnings by earnings capacity.

Table 5.3 *Decile earnings for actual earnings and alternative earnings capacity populations (%)*

	Earnings capacity						
Country/decile	Actual family earnings (1)	FYFT (2)	<FYFT (3)	UN (4)	NILF (5)	NILF/ Actual (6)	NILF/ FYFT (7)
United States (1986)							
First	2.1	1.9	2.5	2.8	4.1	2.0	2.2
Second	4.7	4.3	4.7	4.9	5.6	0.9	1.3
Third	6.2	5.6	6.1	6.1	6.6	0.4	1.0
Fourth	7.3	6.9	7.1	7.1	7.6	0.3	0.7
Fifth	8.5	8.0	8.3	8.3	8.5	0.0	0.5
Sixth	9.7	9.4	9.5	9.5	9.5	−0.2	0.1
Seventh	11.1	10.9	10.9	10.9	10.8	−0.3	−0.1
Eighth	12.7	12.9	12.8	12.7	12.2	−0.5	−0.7
Ninth	15.3	15.9	15.4	15.3	14.5	−0.8	−1.4
Tenth	22.5	24.1	22.8	22.4	20.7	−1.8	−3.4
Gini coefficient	*0.310*	*0.337*	*0.308*	*0.300*	*0.256*	*−17.4*	*−24.0*
Canada (1987)							
First	1.8	2.1	2.7	3.2	4.7	2.9	2.6
Second	5.0	4.7	5.1	5.4	6.2	1.2	1.5
Third	6.5	6.1	6.4	6.5	7.1	0.6	1.0
Fourth	7.7	7.2	7.5	7.6	7.9	0.2	0.7
Fifth	8.9	8.4	8.7	8.7	8.8	−0.1	0.4
Sixth	10.0	9.7	9.8	9.8	9.7	−0.3	0.0
Seventh	11.3	11.2	11.1	11.0	10.7	−0.6	−0.5
Eighth	12.8	13.0	12.7	12.5	12.0	−0.8	−1.0
Ninth	14.9	15.5	15.0	14.7	13.8	−1.1	−1.7
Tenth	20.9	22.2	21.1	20.7	19.2	−1.7	−3.0
Gini coefficient	*0.291*	*0.309*	*0.283*	*0.269*	*0.222*	*−23.7*	*−28.2*
Australia (1985)							
First	1.2	1.9	2.0	2.8	4.4	3.2	2.5
Second	5.4	4.7	4.7	5.1	5.9	0.5	1.2
Third	6.9	6.0	6.2	6.4	6.9	0.0	0.9
Fourth	8.1	7.2	7.4	7.4	7.8	−0.3	0.6
Fifth	9.2	8.4	8.5	8.5	8.8	−0.4	0.4
Sixth	10.2	9.8	9.9	9.8	9.8	−0.4	0.0
Seventh	11.3	11.3	11.4	11.2	10.7	−0.6	−0.6
Eighth	12.6	12.9	12.9	12.6	12.0	−0.6	−0.9

Country/decile	Earnings capacity					NILF/ Actual (6)	NILF/ FYFT (7)
	Actual family earnings (1)	FYFT (2)	<FYFT (3)	UN (4)	NILF (5)		
Ninth	14.6	15.5	15.2	14.8	14.0	−0.6	−1.5
Tenth	20.4	22.4	21.8	21.5	19.7	−0.7	−2.7
Gini coefficient	*0.282*	*0.313*	*0.303*	*0.285*	*0.233*	*−17.4*	*−25.6*
Netherlands (1987)							
First	3.1	2.9	2.9	4.0	6.3	3.2	3.4
Second	6.0	5.8	5.4	5.5	7.4	1.4	1.6
Third	6.8	6.9	6.4	6.5	8.1	1.3	1.2
Fourth	7.6	7.8	7.5	7.7	8.7	1.1	0.9
Fifth	8.5	8.8	8.5	8.9	9.3	0.8	0.5
Sixth	9.5	9.8	10.0	10.2	9.8	0.3	0.0
Seventh	10.9	11.0	11.5	11.4	10.5	−0.4	−0.5
Eighth	12.5	12.5	13.0	12.7	11.4	−1.1	−1.1
Ninth	14.5	14.7	15.0	14.4	12.7	−1.8	−2.0
Tenth	20.5	19.9	19.7	18.6	15.7	−4.8	−4.2
Gini coefficient	*0.261*	*0.258*	*0.269*	*0.240*	*0.147*	*−43.7*	*−43.0*
Germany (1984)							
First	3.7	3.5	3.7	4.2	5.9	2.2	2.4
Second	6.0	5.8	5.6	5.9	7.0	1.0	1.2
Third	6.9	6.9	6.8	7.0	7.8	0.9	0.9
Fourth	7.7	7.8	7.9	8.0	8.5	0.8	0.7
Fifth	8.7	8.7	8.9	9.0	9.1	0.4	0.4
Sixth	9.7	9.8	10.0	9.9	9.8	0.1	0.0
Seventh	11.0	10.9	11.0	11.0	10.6	−0.4	−0.3
Eighth	12.4	12.2	12.3	12.2	11.6	−0.8	−0.6
Ninth	14.4	14.3	14.4	14.1	13.1	−1.3	−1.2
Tenth	19.4	20.0	19.4	18.7	16.5	−2.9	−3.5
Gini coefficient	*0.244*	*0.251*	*0.246*	*0.230*	*0.169*	*−30.7*	*−32.7*

Table 5.4 *Indicators of inequality in five distributions in five countries[a]* *(percentile ratios)*

Country/decile	Actual family earnings (1)	FYFT (2)	<FYFT (3)	UN (4)	NILF (5)
		Earnings capacity			
United States (1986)					
P_{90}/P_{50}	1.87	2.07	1.94	1.91	1.79
P_{50}/P_{10}	2.38	2.54	2.25	2.17	1.77
P_{90}/P_{10}	4.45	5.28	4.37	4.14	3.17
P_{80}/P_{50}	1.49	1.64	1.55	1.53	1.48
P_{50}/P_{20}	1.68	1.72	1.63	1.61	1.47
P_{80}/P_{20}	2.50	2.83	2.52	2.46	2.17
Canada (1987)					
P_{90}/P_{50}	1.75	1.92	1.77	1.73	1.66
P_{50}/P_{10}	2.36	2.38	2.14	1.98	1.63
P_{90}/P_{10}	4.11	4.58	3.78	3.43	2.72
P_{80}/P_{50}	1.46	1.57	1.48	1.46	1.92
P_{50}/P_{20}	1.63	1.65	1.60	1.56	1.38
P_{80}/P_{20}	2.38	2.58	2.36	2.28	1.92
Australia (1985)					
P_{90}/P_{50}	1.64	1.91	1.82	1.80	1.67
P_{50}/P_{10}	2.32	2.41	2.43	2.11	1.73
P_{90}/P_{10}	3.81	4.61	4.42	3.79	2.89
P_{80}/P_{50}	1.39	1.54	1.50	1.48	1.38
P_{50}/P_{20}	1.54	1.67	1.67	1.58	1.44
P_{80}/P_{20}	2.15	2.58	2.52	2.34	1.99
Netherlands (1987)					
P_{90}/P_{50}	1.77	1.74	1.77	1.64	1.42
P_{50}/P_{10}	1.62	1.78	1.92	1.96	1.38
P_{90}/P_{10}	2.87	3.09	3.41	3.22	1.96
P_{80}/P_{50}	1.49	1.45	1.50	1.39	1.26
P_{50}/P_{20}	1.40	1.46	1.55	1.60	1.24
P_{80}/P_{20}	2.08	2.12	2.32	2.23	1.56
Germany (1984)					
P_{90}/P_{50}	1.74	1.75	1.68	1.63	1.51
P_{50}/P_{10}	1.69	1.79	1.89	1.83	1.46
P_{90}/P_{10}	2.95	3.12	3.17	2.99	2.20
P_{80}/P_{50}	1.44	1.40	1.41	1.38	1.29
P_{50}/P_{20}	1.42	1.46	1.51	1.44	1.29
P_{80}/P_{20}	2.05	2.04	2.12	1.99	1.66

Note: [a] The distributions are described in the main text.
Source: LIS database.

The inequality measures in tables 5.2, 5.3 and 5.4 bear out this expectation. When the full earnings capacity distributions are compared across countries, an unambiguous inequality ranking emerges, with Netherlands now exhibiting the least inequality of earnings capacity, followed by Germany, Canada, Australia and the United States (in that order). These results thus confirm that the earnings inequality ranking of countries produced in other studies using the LIS database are not purely a result of country differences in the degree of labor market attachment among members of the workforce-aged population. Indeed, the methods we have used to standardize these differences provide not only a clearer cross-country ranking of family earnings inequality, but one which reinforces the picture which others (e.g. Gottschalk, 1993) have already documented.

Value of home production

The second major objective of this chapter is to ascertain the gross value of home production using the earnings capacity approach to measure the opportunity cost of home production. We have not tried to estimate a net value of added market work, e.g. taking gross earning capacity and netting out the additional costs of working (e.g. transportation, work clothing), the costs of replacement services (e.g. child care, home services, etc.), or the taxes on additional earnings, to arrive at a true net added value of out-of-home work. Our objective is much simpler at this stage, i.e. just to get an idea of the gross value of home production relative to actual earnings by determining its opportunity costs. Our home production values come from time under-employed (part-time), time unemployed, and time not in the labor force. Moreover, the aggregate values include home production by both men and women. We then disaggregate the contribution of each sex to this aggregate value.

Aggregate values

We begin (table 5.5) by taking actual overall average earnings and overall average earnings capacity from table 5.2 and placing each in a ratio format. Thus, we estimate home production relative to prime-age men and women working FYFT (panel *A*) and relative to our estimate of earnings capacity for these same FYFT men and women (panel *B*).[24]

As might be expected, the overall value of estimated home production (as a percentage of earnings or earnings capacity) varies inversely with unemployment, part-time work, and non-labor force participation (the latter of particular importance for married women). Based on actual earnings, the Netherlands and Germany tend to have the highest overall value added for home production, with Canada having the least. Here, the total value added (column (4)) varies from 28 to 53 percent of earnings. If the basis on which home production is calculated is earnings capacity (and not actual earnings), total value added runs from 28 to 52 percent of the base, with the Netherlands and Germany still highest, but with the other three nations more closely bunched just below 30 percent value added. The contribution of various types of workers to home production is also quite varied. In Australia, home production for part-time workers is 16 percent of total earnings all by itself (panel *A*, column (2)). Unemployment adds 3–9 percent as a separate factor, while the largest adjustment is for those not in the labor force where 13–34 percent of the total value of home production is added to the other components.

Table 5.5   *Gross values of home production*

Country	Actual family earnings (1)	Earnings capacity		
		<FYFT (2)	UN (3)	NILF (4)
Panel A: Home production relative to actual earnings				
United States (1986)	100	114	117	131
Canada (1987)	100	112	115	128
Australia (1985)	100	116	120	138
Netherlands (1987)	100	110	119	153
Germany (1984)	100	113	118	144

	Earnings capacity			
	FYFT	<FYFT	UN	NILF
Panel B: Home production relative to earnings capacity				
United States (1986)	100	111	114	128
Canada (1987)	100	112	115	128
Australia (1985)	100	108	111	129
Netherlands (1987	100	109	118	152
Germany (1984)	100	112	117	143

Production by men and women

The total value of home production can be separated for men and women as shown in table 5.6. Here, the estimates of home production relative to either FYFT earnings or estimated earnings capacity from table 5.5 are broken down by gender. To obtain the percentage of value added attributed to men and to women at each stage, an additional step was added to the calculations in table 5.5. When moving from actual earnings to the value added of part-time workers and in sequence to those not in the labor force, the value added was first calculated for men and then for both men and women, with the difference being attributed to women.

The percentage of the total value of home production attributable to women (based on actual earnings) ranged from around 70 percent in the United States and Canada to around 87–88 percent in the Netherlands. If the basis on which home production is calculated is earnings capacity, the general trend remains the same, though the actual percentage of the value added attributable to women is slightly higher in most countries. Whichever base is used, countries with the highest total value added (Germany and the Netherlands) are also the countries with the largest percentage of the value attributable to women.

The contribution of various types of workers to the components of home production varies substantially by gender. A larger percentage of the value of household production comes from men when looking at time not worked due to part-time working and unemployment than when looking at those not in the labor force. For all countries, most of the value of home production of those not in the labor force is by women. This ranges from 96 percent to 77 percent depending on country and base used (column (6), NILF), i.e. 1–0.04 for Germany and 1–0.23 for Canada. The value of home production for part-time workers and the unemployed is less easily generalized to men or women. The value added of part-time workers (using the earnings capacity base) generally shows a majority due to female part-time workers. The value added to household production from unemployed workers shows little gender pattern.

Summary and conclusion

This chapter has produced the first comparable estimates of earnings capacity across five nations using the LIS database. While our methods and results should be taken as a first attempt, several interesting findings

Table 5.6 *Gross values of home production: percentage change attributable to men and women*

				Earnings capacity				% total change	
Country	Actual family earnings (1)	<FYFT (2)	% male (3)	UN (4)	% male (5)	NILF (6)	% male (7)	Male (8)	Female (9)
Panel A: Home production relative to actual earnings									
United States	100	114	50	117	67	131	14	32	68
Canada	100	112	33	115	33	128	23	29	71
Australia	100	116	50	120	50	138	11	19	81
Netherlands	100	110	20	119	22	15	39	13	87
Germany	100	113	23	118	60	144	4	16	84

				Earnings capacity				% total change	
	FYFT (1)	<FYFT (2)	% male (3)	UN (4)	% male (5)	NILF (6)	% male (7)	Male (8)	Female (9)
Panel B: Home production relative to earnings capacity									
United States	100	111	36	114	66	128	14	29	71
Canada	100	112	33	115	66	128	15	29	71
Australia	100	108	9	111	66	129	11	16	84
Netherlands	100	109	11	118	22	15	29	12	88
Germany	100	112	17	117	40	14	34	12	88

Source: LIS database.

emerge with respect to the overall gross value of home production and its effect on cross-national comparisons of inequality among married couple households.

Measures of inequality in market earnings and household production (earnings capacity) reinforce patterns found in market earnings alone when large differences in unemployment, part-time work and non-labor force participation in each nation have been leavened by the earnings capacity methodology. Moreover, the gross value of home production (including both men and women with no adjustments for costs of working, child care, or household work forgone) is both large and varies substantially across nations. The earnings capacity measure of the gross value of time not spent in work is equal to 53 percent of total actual earnings in the Netherlands in 1987, and was at a minimum 28 percent of total earnings in Canada in the same year (table 5.2).

The source of the majority of the value added by home production depends on the country studied and the source of the value added, be it part-time work, unemployment, or non-labor force participation. In the United States and Canada, women appear to contribute about 70 percent of the total value of home production; with more than 80 percent of the total value coming from women in the other nations studied (table 5.6). Men's contributions are larger only when considering home production of those who are unemployed. In all nations, married women make by far the largest contribution to home production based on non-labor force participation.

Additional research will be aimed at refining these estimates, netting out various work-related costs, and considering more carefully the net value added from home production. We might also attempt to adjust for time paid for but not worked (vacations and holidays). Germany and the Netherlands which have the highest overall value of home production (relative to earnings), also have the highest total number of vacation days and holidays.

Appendix: the earnings modes

Table 5A.1   *Explanatory variables included in the estimated earnings functions[a,b]*

Variable name	Definition
EXPER	Age in years *minus* years of education *minus* six
EXPSQD	*EXPER* squared
EDUC1	No or very low education
EDUC2	Low education
EDUC3[*]	Education to high school level or equivalent
EDUC4	Education beyond high school but below college level
EDUC5	College level education or higher
OCC1	Professional or administrative occupation
OCC2	Sales, service or clerical occupation
OCC3[*]	Blue collar occupation
IND1	Primary industry
IND2[*]	Manufacturing industry
IND3	Commerce industry
IND4	Other service industry
IND6	Utilities industry
IND7	Construction industry
NATIVE	Equals 1 if native born; 0 otherwise (i.e. overseas born)[c]
MARRIED	Equals 1 if married; 0 otherwise
YNGCHILD	Equals 1 if youngest child aged under 6; 0 otherwise
OLDCHLD	Equals 1 if youngest child aged 6 or over; 0 otherwise

Notes:
[a] Variables indicated with an asterisk (*) were used as the reference categories in the estimated regression equations.
[b] Labor force variables are given in table 5A.1.
[c] In the United States this variable separates non-white minorities from the white majority.

Table 5A.2 *Regression estimates for women aged 25 to 55 who worked FYFT[a]*

	United States (1986)	Canada (1987)	Australia (1985)	Netherlands (1987)	Germany (1984)
Sample size	1,811	1,747	951	267	405
Constant	9.398* (0.070)	9.581* (0.096)	9.42* (0.134)	10.003* (0.081)	10.060* (0.116)
Experience	0.034* (0.006)	0.029* (0.007)	0.009* (0.011)	0.052* (0.007)	0.019* (0.010)
Experience squared ($\times$ 10,000)	−7.912* (1.341)	−5.132* (1.615)	−1.251 (2.718)	−8.322* (1.660)	−2.826 (2.459)
Low/No education[b]	−0.254* (0.096)	−0.307* (0.071)	na	−0.371* (0.041)	na
Low education	−0.135* (0.049)	−0.186* (0.043)	−0.019 (0.065)	−0.135* (0.036)	−0.222* (0.051)
Other education	−0.138* (0.031)	0.108* (0.034)	0.095 (0.065)	na	−0.010 (0.061)
College education	0.366* (0.034)	0.330* (0.043)	0.321* (0.082)	0.299* (0.053)	0.268* (0.072)
Professional[b]	0.254* (0.049)	0.375* (0.065)	0.405* (0.072)	na	0.309* (0.078)
Sales, service, clerical	0.034 (0.056)	0.094 (0.062)	0.155* (0.058)	na	0.119* (0.058)
Primary[b]	−0.194* (0.106)	−0.045 (0.097)	0.222 (0.151)	0.211 (0.220)	0.430 (0.347)
Commerce	−0.308* (0.045)	−0.218* (0.060)	−0.193* (0.072)	−0.079 (0.054)	−0.109 (0.072)
Other service	−0.172* (0.038)	−0.148* (0.053)	−0.100 (0.062)	0.099* (0.044)	−0.053 (0.054)
Financial service	−0.074 (0.048)	−0.142* (0.064)	0.093 (0.080)	na	0.070 (0.074)
Utilities	0.122* (0.057)	0.014 (0.071)	−0.034 (0.099)	0.113 (0.074)	0.092 (0.132)
Construction	0.106 (0.115)	−0.016 (0.126)	0.126 (0.209)	0.065 (0.105)	0.234 (0.162)

Table 5A.2 (*cont.*)

	United States (1986)	Canada (1987)	Australia (1985)	Netherlands (1987)	Germany (1984)
Native born	0.019 (0.027)	−0.009 (0.037)	0.006 (0.042)	na	0.001 (0.050)
Married	−0.037 (0.027)	−0.085* (0.029)	0.022 (0.042)	0.039 (0.028)	0.005 (0.040)
Child < age 6	−0.104* (0.036)	0.000 (0.042)	−0.338* (0.065)	0.007 (0.084)	−0.138* (0.066)
Child age ⩾ 6	−0.126* (0.027)	−0.156* (0.032)	−0.150* (0.048)	−0.155* (0.052)	−0.128* (0.043)

Notes: na = not available.
a Dependent variable = log wage; standard errors in parentheses.
b The missing education category is high school, occupation is blue collar, and industry is manufacturing.
* Statistically significant at the 10 percent level.

Table 5.A.3 *Regression estimates for men aged 25 to 55 who worked FYFT* *a*

	United States (1986)	Canada (1987)	Australia (1985)	Netherlands (1987)	Germany (1984)
Sample size	3,352	3,460	2,709	1,776	1,603
Constant	9.483* (0.055)	9.835* (0.051)	9.572* (0.067)	10.203* (0.051)	10.005* (0.151)
Experience	0.029* (0.005)	0.033* (0.004)	0.026* (0.006)	0.051* (0.004)	0.043* (0.004)
Experience squared (× 10,000)	−4.287* (1.063)	−5.135* (0.842)	−4.851* (1.370)	−6.984* (0.819)	−8.010* (0.098)
Low/No education*b*	−0.492* (0.079)	−0.221* (0.034)	na	−0.479* (0.025)	na
Low education	−0.252* (0.034)	−0.090* (0.024)	−0.059* (0.035)	−0.173* (0.025)	−0.119* (0.025)
Other education	0.168* (0.027)	0.087* (0.022)	0.025 (0.033)	na	0.090* (0.023)

	United States (1986)	Canada (1987)	Australia (1985)	Netherlands (1987)	Germany (1984)
College education	0.411* (0.028)	0.286* (0.028)	0.220* (0.042)	0.271* (0.031)	0.290* (0.028)
Professional[b]	0.147* (0.027)	0.107* (0.023)	0.236* (0.026)	na	0.276* (0.026)
Sales, service, clerical	−0.035 (0.029)	−0.058* (0.024)	0.78* (0.031)	na	0.102* (0.020)
Primary[b]	−0.224* (0.061)	0.069* (0.032)	−0.209* (0.045)	−0.085 (0.062)	−0.013 (0.050)
Commerce	−0.165* (0.031)	−0.170* (0.027)	−0.113* (0.034)	0.001 (0.024)	−0.062* (0.026)
Other service	−0.228* (0.027)	−0.156* (0.025)	−0.070* (0.031)	−0.002 (0.020)	−0.096* (0.021)
Financial services	0.019 (0.051)	−0.101* (0.045)	0.012 (0.041)	na	0.140* (0.038)
Utilities	0.083* (0.034)	−0.003 (0.027)	0.095* (0.033)	−0.014 (0.030)	0.061* (0.028)
Construction	−0.043 (0.039)	−0.154* (0.036)	−0.015 (0.043)	−0.032 (0.028)	−0.096* (0.029)
Native born	0.178* (0.025)	0.062* (0.024)	0.018 (0.023)	na	0.060* (0.024)
Married	0.112* (0.025)	0.054* (0.023)	0.090* (0.029)	0.057* (0.022)	0.018 (0.022)
Child < age 6	0.014 (0.027)	0.002 (0.023)	0.002 (0.028)	0.022 (0.021)	0.025 (0.022)
Child ≥ age 6	0.029 (0.022)	0.005 (0.020)	−0.004 (0.027)	0.021 (0.020)	0.005 (0.017)

Notes: na = not available.
[a] Dependent variable = log wage; standard errors in parentheses.
[b] The missing education category is high school, occupation is blue collar, and industry is manufacturing.
* Statistically significant at the 10 percent level.

Table 5A.4 *Derivation of labor force status*

	Australia (1985)	Canada (1987)	Germany (1984)	Netherlands (1987)	United States (1986)
HRSHD/HRSSP	0 Non-worker 1 < 10 hours 2 3 4 5 6 7 8 9	Number of hours 10–19 hours 20–24 hours 25–29 hours 30–34 hours 35–39 hours 40–44 hours 45–49 hours 50+ hours	Number of hours	Number of hours	Number of hours
WEEKHDFT/ WEEKSPFT	Number of weeks	Number of weeks	Number of weeks	Number of weeks	Number of weeks
Head/Spouse 1. *FYFT* 2. *<FYFT* 3. No Work	*HRSHD(SP)* ge 35 and *WEEKSHD(SP)FT* ge 48 *HRSHD(SP)* 1–34 and *WEEKHD(SP)FT* ge 48 or *HRSHD(SP)FT* ge 48 and *HRSHD(SP)* gt 0 and *WEEKHD(SP)FT* lt 48 *HRSHD(SP)* = 0				
LFSHD/LFSSP	−1 No spouse 3 NILF school 4 Unpd. volunteer 5 Employed FT 6 Employed PT	−1 No spouse 1 Employed 2 Unemployed 3 NILF	−1 No spouse 0 Missing/na 1 NILF 2 Looking or layoff 3 Employed civilian	−1 No spouse 0 Not labeled 1 NILF 2 Looking for work 3 In labor force	−1 No spouse 1 Employed + working 2 Employed, not at work 3 Unemployed 4 NILF keeping house

	Australia (1985)	Canada (1987)	Germany (1984)	Netherlands (1987)	United States (1986)
	7 Unemployed 8 NILF		4 School 5 Mandatory military 6 Professional soldier	4 School	5 NILF school 6 NILF disabled/ill 7 NILF other
Labor force status					
1. *FYFT*	*LFSHD* = 5	*LFSHD* = 1 and *HEAD* = 1	*LFSHD* = 3 and *HEAD* = 1	*LFSHD* = 3 and *HEAD* = 1	*HEAD* = 1
2. < *FYFT*	*LFSHD* = 6	*LFSHD* = 1 and *HEAD* = 2	*LFSHD* = 3 and *HEAD* = 2	*LFSHD* = 3 and *HEAD* = 2	*HEAD* = 2
3. *Unemployed*	*LFSHD* = 7	*LFSHD* = 2	*LFSHD* = 2 or *LFSHD* = 3 and *HEAD* = 3	*LFSHD* = 2 or *LFSHD* = 3 and *HEAD* = 3	*LFSHD* = 2 or *LFSHD* = 3
4. *NILF*	*LFSHD* = 3 or *LFSHD* = 4 or *LFSHD* = 8	*LFSHD* = 3	*LFSHD* = 0 or *LFSHD* = 1 or *LFSHD* = 4	*LFSHD* = 0 or *LFSHD* = 1 or *LFSHD* = 4	*LFSHD GT* = 3

Notes

Support for this chapter was provided to the Luxembourg Income Study under US National Science Foundation Grant no. SES91–23675, and to the Center for Advanced Study in the Behavioral Sciences under US National Science Foundation Grant no. SBR-9022192. An earlier version of this chapter appeared in *LIS Working Paper* 122 (December 1994). The authors are grateful to two anonymous referees and to Stephen Jenkins for helpful comments, but retain responsibility for all errors of omission and commission.

1 Readers who wish to obtain more information about the larger study of which this chapter forms part should consult Saunders, O'Connor and Smeeding (1994).
2 The two methods are discussed by Chadeau (1992) and Goldschmidt-Clermont (1993). They have been evaluated and compared by the Australian Bureau of Statistics (ABS, 1990). The ABS estimated the value of household work in Australia (in 1986–7) using each method. The estimates derived using the opportunity cost method exceed those derived using the replacement cost method by an amount equivalent to around 5 percent of GDP (out of a total estimated value of household work of around 60 percent of GDP).
3 Most of these limitations are discussed in the original study undertaken by Garfinkel and Haveman (1977) and in Haveman and Buron (1993).
4 The self-employed were excluded from our sample by excluding all families which earned any self-employment income. Data limitations prevented us from attributing the self-employment earnings to an individual within the family.
5 It was possible to identify fairly precisely FYFT workers on the LIS data tapes. Part-time (PT) workers were defined to include all other individuals with positive wage and salary income over the year. The unemployed (UN) and those not in the labor force (NILF) were identified as those individuals with zero *annual* wage and salary income whose *current* status (i.e. at the time of the survey) was unemployed or not in the labor force, respectively. Table 5A.1 (p. 100) presents the derivation of the labor force variables for each nation studied.
6 This sequenced analysis of inequality is similar to that recently undertaken by Gottschalk (1993).
7 Haveman and Buron note (1993, n. 7, p. 145) that there are in fact two components of the earnings residual, one related to unmeasured individual-specific human capital variables and the other related to random fluctuations in earnings. Following them, we assumed that each component is normally distributed with a zero mean and constant (and independent) variance. The authors would like to thank Larry Buron for his advice and assistance on this aspect of the chapter.
8 In order to separate out the differences in value due to household production by spouses, we estimated the sum of earnings capacity for the male *plus*

actual wife's earnings as a substage between $D4$ and $D5$. The results are available from the authors. They show that at least 80 percent (Canada) and up to 95 percent (Germany) of the difference between $D4$ and $D5$ is due to married women with no earnings who are not in the labor force.

9 This focus on those in prime workforce-age range accords with studies of earnings distribution undertaken by Green, Coder and Ryscavage (1992), Bradbury (1993), and Saunders and Fritzell (1993).

10 Gottschalk and Mayer (1994) show that the use of an equivalence scale correction does not affect their earnings capacity estimates to any substantial degree.

11 Here we depart from Garfinkel and Haveman (1977) and Haveman and Buron (1993), both of whom deduct an estimate of child care costs in deriving net (as opposed to gross) earnings capacity. While netting out the additional costs of working, including not only child care costs but also other costs, is theoretically appropriate, we have not carried out such an imputation at this time. To do so would require information on the net costs of child care which will vary widely across countries due to differences in subsidy rates by age of children, tax treatment and non-profit provisions (e.g. German and Dutch kindergartens) and additional information on the cost of work-related clothing, transportation, and other goods and services.

12 The Australian data refer to the financial year (beginning July 1) 1985/86, but the survey was actually conducted in the latter months of 1986. It is worth noting that our sample is a subset of the sample of countries included in the recent LIS-based study by Cancian and Schoeni (1992).

13 While it would be theoretically preferred to correct the female regressions for the probability of being in the labor force, data constraints limited our ability to do this. Standard practice (e.g. the Heckman procedure) would take account of whether or not women were in the labor force. However, since we run our regressions only on those working FYFT, it is more appropriate to correct for whether or not women work FYFT as opposed to whether or not they work. This is possible for four of the five countries studied, but for the Netherlands, where so few women work FYFT, the maximum likelihood functions do not converge. For consistency's sake, then, we did not correct any of the equations for the probability of working FYFT.

14 While they do not consider women in their analyses, Lorenz and Wagner (1990) include a similar experience variable in their earnings functions using the LIS database, as do many others who have examined both men and women (e.g. Phipps, 1993; Knudsen and Peters, 1994).

15 This is particularly the case for those who have remained out of the labor force for long periods.

16 This also explains the inclusion of the marital status variable in the estimated earnings models. In addition, to be included in the regression sample only the individual needed to be age 25 to 55 while to be included in the sample of couples, both partners had to meet the age restriction.

17 Saunders, O'Connor and Smeeding (1994) describe some of the specifications of the model which were explored but rejected in favor of those shown. Our preferred specifications and the general features of our results contain a number of similarities with the earnings functions estimated for married women from the LIS data by Phipps (1993) and Knudsen and Peters (1994).
    This last finding is consistent with that derived from the LIS data by McLanahan, Casper and Sorensen (1992) who conclude that a woman's risk of poverty is increased by motherhood or child-bearing, rather than by marriage or paid employment.

18 This finding is likely to be influenced by the limitations of our experience variable specifications for women, particularly for married women.

19 This is consistent with the LIS work by Schoeni (1990), who found that married men earn more than single men, all else being equal.

20 When earnings capacity was predicted from the estimates in tables 5A.2 and 5A.3 (pp. 101–3) for the unemployed and those not in the labor force, the omitted category was assigned for the occupation and industry variables (i.e. blue collar occupation and manufacturing industry).

21 Part of the reason for this is that the self-employed now have an earnings capacity attributed to them, whilst previously (as explained earlier) their self-employment income was excluded.

22 Earnings capacity can be less than actual earnings for several reasons, including because of good fortune, or the possibility that earnings capacity is over-utilized. We made no attempt to adjust hours of work for those who were working beyond the full-time limit in each country.

23 This may be due to the fact that the unit of analysis being used is the couple rather than the individual, combined with the relatively low incidence of unemployment compared with part-time work and non-participation (see table 5.1).

24 Recall that our estimates of FYFT earnings capacity (D2) differed from actual earnings for various reasons, e.g. more than FYFT earnings for some men, estimation error, treatment of the self-employed, etc.

References

Atkinson, A.B. and J. Micklewright, 1983. "On the reliability of income data in the Family Expenditure Survey 1970–77," *Journal of the Royal Statistical Society*, Series A, 146, 33–61

Atkinson, A.B., L. Rainwater and T.M. Smeeding, 1995. *Income Distribution in OECD Countries: The Evidence from the Luxembourg Income Study*, Paris: OECD

Australian Bureau of Statistics (ABS), 1990. *Measuring Unpaid Housework: Issues and Experimental Estimates*, catalogue no. 5236.0, Canberra: ABS

Björklund, A., 1992. "Rising female labor force participation and the distribution of family income – the Swedish experience," *Acta Sociologica*, 35, 299–309

Bradbury, B., 1993. "Male wage inequality before and after tax: a six country comparison," *Discussion Paper*, 42, Social Policy Research Centre, University of New South Wales

Cancian, M. and R.F. Schoeni, 1992. "Female earnings and the level and distribution of household income in developed countries," *LIS–CEPS Working Paper*, 84, The Luxembourg Income Study

Cancian, M., S. Danziger and P. Gottschalk, 1993. "Working wives and family income inequality among married couples," in S. Danziger and P. Gottschalk (eds.), *Uneven Tides: Rising Inequality in America*, New York: Russell Sage Foundation, 195–221

Chadeau, A., 1992. "What is households' non-market production worth?," *OECD Economic Studies*, 18, 85–103

Danziger, S., 1980. "Do working wives increase family income inequality?," *Journal of Human Resources*, 15, 444–51

Garfinkel, I. and R. Haveman, 1977. *Earnings Capacity, Poverty and Inequality*, New York: Academic Press

Goldschmidt-Clermont, L., 1993. "Monetary valuation of non-market productive time: methodological considerations," *Review of Income and Wealth*, 39, 419–33

Gottschalk, P., 1993. "Changes in inequality of family income in seven industrialized countries," *American Economic Review, Papers and Proceedings*, 83, 136–42

Gottschalk, P. and S. Mayer, 1994. "Changes in home production and trends in economic inequality," paper presented to the RAND Conference on "Reshaping the Family: Social and Economic Changes and Public Policy" (January)

Green, G., J. Coder and P. Ryscavage, 1992. "International comparisons of earnings inequality for men in the 1980s," *Review of Income and Wealth*, 38, 1–15

Haveman, R. and L.F. Buron, 1993. "Escaping poverty through work – the problem of low earnings capacity in the United States, 1973–88," *Review of Income and Wealth*, 39, 141–58

Knudsen, C. and E. Peters, 1994. "An international comparison of married women's labor supply," *LIS–CEPS Working Paper* 106, The Luxembourg Income Study

Lorenz, W. and J. Wagner, 1990. "A note on returns to human capital in the eighties: evidence from twelve countries," *LIS–CEPS Working Paper*, 54, The Luxembourg Income Study

Machin, S. and J. Waldfogel, 1994. "The decline of the male breadwinner: evidence on the changing shares of the earnings of husbands and wives in family income in the UK," University College, London, mimeo

McLanahan, S.S., L.M. Casper and A. Sorensen, 1992. "Women's roles and women's poverty in eight industrial countries," *LIS–CEPS Working Paper*, 77, The Luxembourg Income Study

Nelissen, J.H.M., 1990. "The effect of increased labor force participation of married women on the distribution of family income in the Netherlands," *De Economist*, 38, 47–62

Phipps, S., 1993. "Determinants of women's labor force participation: an econometric analysis for five countries," *LIS–CEPS Working Paper*, 99, The Luxembourg Income Study

Saunders, P., 1993. "Married women's earnings and family income inequality in the eighties," *Australian Bulletin of Labour*, 19, 199–217

Saunders, P. and J. Fritzell, 1993. "Wage and income inequality in two welfare states: Australia and Sweden," paper presented to the Conference on "Comparative Research on Welfare States in Transition," Oxford (September)

Saunders, P., I. O'Connor and T. Smeeding (1994). "The distribution of welfare: inequality, earnings capacity and household production in a comparative perspective," *Discussion Paper*, 51, Social Policy Research Centre, University of New South Wales, Sydney

Schoeni, R., 1990. "The earnings effect of marital status: an international comparison," *LIS–CEPS Working Paper*, 43, The Luxembourg Income Study

Smeeding, T.M., M.O'Higgins and L. Rainwater (eds.), 1990. *Poverty, Inequality and Income Distribution in Comparative Perspective: The Luxembourg Income Study*, Hemel Hempstead: Harvester Wheatsheaf

6 Mobility and inequality in the 1980s: a cross-national comparison of the United States and Germany

Richard Burkhauser, Douglas Holtz-Eakin and Stephen Rhody

Introduction

Both the popular press and professional journals have devoted enormous attention to changes in the distribution of labor earnings and income in the United States during the 1980s. There has been much less attention devoted to issues of *mobility*, yet mobility may importantly temper attitudes about inequality *per se*. For example, while persistent low earnings of workers or the poverty of their families is undesirable, short spells of either, followed by rapid upward mobility, may be less alarming. Moreover, a direct study of mobility is essential because a particular pattern of cross-sectional inequality may be consistent with a wide variety of mobility patterns. This chapter begins to link inequality and mobility patterns by looking at overall changes in labor earnings and income distributions over the 1980s and then following the outcomes of individuals over this period.

In doing so, we employ cross-national comparisons between the United States and Germany. This cross-national perspective allows us to move beyond characterizing mobility as "large" or "small" to whether the earnings mobility of workers, and more generally the household-based income mobility of working-age persons in the United States, is "relatively large" or "relatively small" compared to that of workers in another western industrialized country.

Mobility and inequality

Most studies of inequality in the United States are based on repeated cross-sectional observations of labor earnings or income distributions. (For excellent reviews of these studies, see Levy and Murnane, 1992, or

111

Karoly, 1993.) While cross-sectional data are useful in measuring inequality at a moment in time, they are unsuitable for analyzing movements in individual earnings or incomes over time.[1] Such movements are of interest because a given pattern of cross-sectional inequality may be consistent with a wide variety of mobility patterns. For instance, greater cross-sectional inequality may be caused by an increase in the "spread" of a static distribution, or by an increase in the variability of income received by individuals who are perfectly mobile within the distribution.[2] Thus, observed changes in the cross-sectional distribution may be the consequence of changes in the relative income of individuals, or the result of changes in the pattern of income mobility for individuals, or some combination of both. Of course, the lifetime welfare of each individual is determined both by his or her mobility among income levels and by the income levels themselves. Hence, in the same way that inequality alone cannot serve as a sufficient basis for welfare judgments, neither can a study of mobility alone settle issues of well-being.

A second difficulty in evaluating the dynamics of inequality is the absence of a standard for comparison. An appealing, if not definitive, approach is to compare the experiences of individuals in one country with those in another comparable country. Several cross-national studies have used cross-sectional data to compare relative inequality and movements in inequality over time. (For examples, see Atkinson, Rainwater and Smeeding, 1994; Gottschalk, 1993.)

A final issue is choosing the appropriate measure of income. Many studies, including some of those cited above, use labor earnings or household income unadjusted for taxes as the basis of their inequality measure. Yet some government budgetary and tax policies are designed to mitigate labor earnings inequality and, hence, to reduce inequality in the overall income distribution. These same policies may affect mobility as well. Even a large degree of instability – and hence mobility – in labor earnings or other private sources of income might be buffered by the design of transfer programs, resulting in a relatively static distribution of after-government (post-transfer and post-tax) income. And income sharing is hardly restricted to government programs. In examining the income prospects of individuals it is important to allow for private transfers among individuals, particularly those in the same household. The growth of multiple labor earners in a single household makes the labor earnings distribution a relatively inaccurate measure of either the before-government (pre-transfer and pre-tax) or after-government household size-adjusted income distribution.

Objectives

This chapter provides a cross-national comparison of income dynamics in the United States and Germany during the 1980s, with particular focus on alternative measures of income. We build upon earlier work (Burkhauser, Holtz-Eakin and Rhody, 1995) that focused on labor earnings alone by extending the analysis to more comprehensive measures of economic resources.

We lay the foundation for our dynamic analysis in the larger cross-sectional literature on inequality in labor earnings and household income. We look at working-age men and women (aged 25 to 55) in the United States and Germany and compare changes in the distribution of labor earnings in the two countries over the 1980s. We then compare changes in the labor earnings distribution with those of the before- and after-government household income distributions for the same age group in the two countries. In this way, we are able to characterize the net impact of government tax and transfer policy on inequality in each country.

Germany provides an ideal point of comparison for our analysis of the United States. Germany is also a large, advanced western economy, and we focus our analysis on the period of business cycle expansion in both countries. However, labor market policies (indeed, social policies more generally) differ greatly between the two countries. (See Abraham and Hauseman, 1993, 1995 for a discussion of the German labor market.) Our comparisons provide a useful perspective on the effect of these differences in policies and programs on the relative mobility of working-age individuals in the United States.

Our analysis employs longitudinal data drawn from the Panel Study of Income Dynamics (PSID) for the United States and the German Socio-Economic Panel (GSOEP) for Germany. Hence, we are able to go beyond our cross-sectional look at inequality by following the relative fortunes of individuals of working age over time. We show the movement across the labor earnings, and the before- and after-government income distributions of individuals of working age over the six-year period 1983 through 1988.

Organization of the chapter

The next section describes the longitudinal data sets we employ in our analysis. We then present our cross-sectional analysis of the United States and Germany, while the following section contains our analysis of mobility rates. In particular, we focus on contrasting the mobility patterns generated using alternative measures of income. The final section is a summary of our findings.

To anticipate the results, our data support the conventional view that cross-sectional inequality was substantially greater in the United States than in Germany in the 1980s regardless of whether the unit measured was labor earnings, before-government income, or after-government income. We find that inequality in labor earnings grew modestly in both countries over the period, with a slightly greater increase in Germany. Despite this, inequality in both before- and after-government income grew faster in the United States than in Germany.

When we take full advantage of our longitudinal data, however, we find remarkable similarities in mobility patterns for the two countries. To the extent that they differ, we find suggestive evidence that the probability of changing quintiles in the labor earnings distribution is slightly greater in Germany than in the United States, but the probability of changing before- or after-government income quintiles is slightly larger in the United States than in Germany. Interestingly, the differences derive largely from differences between American and German women; American and German men have virtually the same mobility patterns over the period. This suggests that it is a spread in the relative economic well-being of the quintiles in the United States, rather than differences in the individual dynamics of their members, that is responsible for the relative increases in inequality between the United States and Germany over the latter years of the 1980s.

Data

Our empirical results are based on two longitudinal data sets. For the United States we use the Cross-Year 1989 Response–Nonresponse File of the PSID. For Germany we use the 1993 Syracuse University English Language Public Use File of the GSOEP. Since 1968, the PSID has interviewed annually a representative sample of some 5,000 families. At least one member of each family was either part of the original families interviewed in 1968 or born to a member of one of these families. Partial information on individuals who ceased to be respondents prior to 1989 is included in our analysis whenever possible. (For a more complete discussion of these data, see Hill, 1992.) We look at economic information for the calendar years 1983–8.

The GSOEP is a more recent longitudinal data set developed at the Universities of Frankfurt and Mannheim in cooperation with the Deutsches Institut für Wirtschaftsforschung, Berlin (DIW), and initially financed by the German National Science Foundation. In 1990 the DIW assumed control of the panel with funding from the Bund-Länder-Kommission für Forschungförderung. The National Institute on Aging has provided funding to Syracuse University to translate the documentation and make a public use file of the data available to English-speaking researchers. The panel started in the spring of 1984. It comprises about 6,000 families, for which 11 yearly waves have been conducted (1984–94). Six waves (1984–89) are used here, providing information on calendar years 1983–8. The data are representative of the German population, including "guest workers." (For a more complete discussion of the public use version of these data, see Wagner, Burkhauser and Behringer, 1993.)

As noted above, we look at three types of distributions. The first is individual pre-tax yearly labor earnings. Data on yearly pre-tax labor earnings are directly available in the PSID. There is no such direct measure in the GSOEP. We use a constructed measure of annual labor earnings from all employment. This construct is the product of the number of months in the income year that a respondent received payments from a given source multiplied by the average monthly amount they estimate receiving from that source in the income year. The sum of these products forms the base of an estimate of yearly gross labor earnings. To the degree that fluctuations in workers' monthly earnings are not fully captured by their reported average, this raises the possibility that our measure of earnings could smooth differences in actual yearly variations in labor earnings.

The yearly labor earnings measure also includes overtime and bonus pay. These irregular payments include 13th and 14th month pay, holiday pay, Christmas pay, and profit sharing. In addition, we include any other earnings that the respondent classifies as job-related – amounts reported as "other bonus income" in the survey questionnaire.

Ideally, other types of compensation such as health insurance, pension accrual and other fringe benefits should be included in labor earnings, but such information is not available in either data set. A more detailed discussion of the constructed GSOEP yearly labor earnings variable and other constructed variables which are used for cross-national comparisons using PSID and GSOEP data can be found in Burkhauser, Butrica and Daly (1995).

Our next two distributions also use the individual as the unit of analysis, but do so in a household context. In constructing these, we depart somewhat from conventional procedures. Pre-tax, post-transfer household income, including cash government transfers, is the most common yardstick of economic status in the United States. We are interested, however, in measuring the net impact of government in this study, and this measure includes elements of both household and government resources. We use as our second measure of income household income in the absence of government taxes and transfers ("before-government" income). It is obtained by summing all sources of income for all family members during a calendar year and adding the imputed rental value of owner-occupied housing.[3] To gauge the impact of government, we use as our final measure household income *plus* government transfers and net of personal taxes and social security contributions ("after-government income").[4] For the United States, this measure includes the in-cash value of food stamps received.[5]

Household income measures of the type suggested above are less than ideal measures of economic status (Moon and Smolensky, 1977). For one thing, there is no universally accepted household size-adjusted equivalence scale (see Buhman *et al.*, 1988 for a discussion of the sensitivity of cross-national comparisons to different equivalence scales). We adopt the scale used in the United States for the computation of poverty thresholds.[6] We then assume that all household members share household income equally during the period when they are together.[7] Our unit of analysis, however, is the individual, since we are interested in tracing outcomes over several years. While household composition may change, the individual can be followed consistently over time.

We assume those who report no labor earnings during our sample period (1983–8) are not actively participating in the labor market, and we exclude them from our analysis of labor earnings mobility. Some individuals, however, report both zero and non-zero labor earnings during the time period under examination. It can be argued that movements from non-zero to zero earnings (and vice versa) are an important type of dynamics, and these individuals are included in our basic results. However, to ensure that such transitions are not the sole source of earnings dynamics, we conducted a sensitivity analysis that excluded these transitions in our samples. Our substantive conclusions are essentially unaffected by this decision.[8]

By definition, anyone in our labor earnings distribution will be in our income distributions, but not vice-versa. We include anyone in our income distribution with positive household size-adjusted income over the period.[9] The differences between wage mobility and income mobility in our analysis are in part related to changes in the type of income measured and in part to changes in the sample size. In appendix B (p. 154) we show how our result differs when we include in the income distributions only those in our wage distributions.[10]

Each of our longitudinal data sets contains weights permitting one to replicate the population in each year, and cross-sectional computations may straightforwardly use these weights. Mobility analyses, however, require comparisons across sample years and raise the issue of which weight (or weights) to use. We follow the recommendations of the PSID staff and weight each dynamic measure using the sample weights in the terminal year of the comparison. For example, comparisons using data for 1985 and 1986 employ the weights for the 1986 sample year. By weighting in this manner, we retain a focus on the outcomes of dynamic processes. For consistency, we follow the same practice in our analysis of the GSOEP data.

Many aspects of the German work experience vary from that in the United States. The school-to-work transition, the transition into retirement, and the labor force participation of women are all likely to be different. To separate these effects from those of other forces and to make our analysis more comparable with previous studies of mobility in the United States, we look only at working-age individuals who can be expected to have already entered into full-time permanent employment and to have not yet retired (aged 25 to 55), and we segment our sample by gender.[11] In this way, our analysis attempts to abstract from differences in job market entry and exit as determinants of "mobility" and to isolate gender differences. In the PSID we include individuals who were either heads of households or their partners; for Germany, we include both Germans and guest workers.[12]

Changes in cross-sectional inequality, 1983–8

Unemployment rates reached decade highs of 9.5 percent in the United States and 8.0 percent in Germany in 1983 (OECD, 1990). But that year also marked the beginning of a recovery that lasted for the rest of the decade in both countries. Table 6.1 provides a cross-sectional look at changes in the distribution of labor earnings and household income for working-age men and women in the two countries over the recovery period (columns (1) and (2)).[13]

In the United States in 1983, workers (men and women aged 25 to 55 in that year who earned at least $1 over the year) in the lowest 20 percent of the labor earnings distribution received only 0.9 percent of all labor earnings. In contrast, the highest 20 percent earned 48.0 percent of all labor earnings. Five years later both ends of the distribution increased their share of labor earnings at the expense of the middle two groups; the lowest quintile received 1.5 percent of labor earnings in 1988, the next lowest increased from 8.6 percent to 9.1 percent, and the top 20 percent accounted for 48.8 percent. This "shrinking" of the labor earnings of

Table 6.1 Distribution of labor earnings, before- and after-government income: US and German individuals aged 25 to 55, 1983 and 1988 (%)

	United States						Germany					
	Labor earnings[a]		Before-government income[b]		After-government income[c]		Labor earnings[a]		Before-government income[b]		After-government income[c]	
Quintile	1983 (1)	1988 (2)	1983 (3)	1988 (4)	1983 (5)	1988 (6)	1983 (7)	1988 (8)	1983 (9)	1988 (10)	1983 (11)	1988 (12)
Lowest	0.9	1.5	3.2	3.1	4.4	4.1	1.7	1.0	6.7	6.3	9.3	8.2
Next lowest	8.6	9.1	8.4	7.8	9.1	8.3	11.6	10.8	13.4	13.4	14.3	14.2
Middle	16.7	16.1	13.3	12.4	13.7	12.8	18.9	19.3	17.6	17.8	17.9	18.2
Next highest	25.8	24.5	22.8	22.2	23.2	22.5	24.6	25.1	22.8	23.5	22.4	23.2
Highest	48.0	48.8	52.3	54.5	49.6	52.3	43.3	43.8	39.5	39.0	36.0	36.2
Gini	0.47	0.47	0.48	0.50	0.45	0.48	0.41	0.43	0.32	0.33	0.27	0.28

Notes:
[a] Includes all persons who received positive labor earnings during the year.
[b] Includes all persons with positive household size-adjusted, non-government income during the year.
[c] Includes all persons with positive household size-adjusted income, including net government transfers during the year.
Source: the 1989 Cross-Year Response–Nonresponse File of the PSID and the 1993 Syracuse University English Language Public Use File of the GSOEP.

middle class workers is a much discussed concern in the United States (see Duncan, Smeeding and Rogers, 1993). However, summarizing the change in inequality using an index such as the Gini coefficient indicates the shift was quite modest over the period. Indeed, the Gini was unchanged at 0.47.

As noted above, one would anticipate that government programs would tend to offset pre-existing inequality and in doing so would focus on income (not just labor earnings). Columns (3)–(6) in table 6.1 address these issues. Turning to the columns labeled "Before-government income," one can see that in 1983 the share of income accruing to the lowest income quintile is higher (3.2 percent) than the share of labor earnings.[14] The Gini coefficient for before-government income inequality in 1983 is comparable to that for labor earnings inequality. However, unlike labor earnings, the before-government Gini showed a perceptible increase over the five-year period.[15] In both 1983 and 1988, after-government income inequality is lower than before-government inequality, showing that government tax and transfer policy is pro-equality. But after-government inequality also rose over the period, with those in the top quintile increasing their share at the expense of all of the other quintiles.

The cross-sectional picture of Germany has both similarities and differences when compared to that of the United States. Confirming other studies, cross-sectional inequality in Germany is uniformly smaller than in the United States in 1983 and 1988 across all three income measures. The growth in cross-sectional inequality over this period is more surprising. Despite the major concern about growing labor earnings inequality in the United States, the very modest increase we find in the United States over this period is less than that experienced in Germany.[16] The major difference in inequality growth between the two countries is the rise in the middle quintiles shares of before- and after-government income in Germany. As noted above, the highest quintile's share rose substantially in the United States.

In short, the data reveal a modest increase in labor earnings inequality in both countries. For broader measures of income, however, the United States and Germany moved even further apart during our sample period.

Mobility analysis

Conceptual framework

In this section we look at the individual level underpinnings of the changes in the labor earnings and income distributions reported above by examining quintile-to-quintile transition rates for each country. We compute these mobility rates as follows. For each year we rank individuals according to their labor earnings or household size-adjusted incomes and assign each to a quintile of the distribution. Such rankings are at the heart of cross-sectional measures of inequality. However, we use our panel data to measure movements by individuals within the distribution by defining an indicator variable t^i_{qr}, which is equal to 1 if individual i made a transition from quintile q to quintile r and is equal to zero otherwise. For the sample as a whole, our estimate of the probability of moving between quintiles q and r is given by

$$p_{qr} = \frac{\sum_{i=1}^{i=N} w^i t^i_{qr}}{\sum_{i=1}^{i=N} w^i} \tag{6.1}$$

where w^i is the sample weight for individual i.

Transition probabilities provide insights into the nature of the dynamics that underlie inequality observed in cross-sections. One possibility is that the distribution of individuals is quite static, and changes in inequality stem from changes in earnings or incomes *per se*. In such a distribution one would anticipate large probabilities of remaining in the same quintile ($p_{qr} \approx 1$ for $q = r$) and low probabilities of mobility ($p_{qr} \approx 0$ for $q \neq r$). Alternatively, changes in inequality may be driven by changes in the individuals in each quintile of the distribution. In a dynamic, flexible society one would expect a greater probability of changing quintiles, and a correspondingly lower probability of remaining in the same location in the distribution.

Variation in earnings or income that move individuals across the distribution may be permanent or transitory phenomena. Our data permit us to compute the transition probabilities for time periods of one–five years and to shed light on the relative permanence of shocks for individuals.[17] Consider a simple example in which income for each individual consists of two components: a fixed, permanent component and yearly, transitory fluctuations. That is, $y_{it} = \mu_i + \varepsilon_{it}$. In these circumstances, the probability of making a transition from one quintile to another depends only upon the relative sizes of the yearly shocks (the εs) for the two years under consideration. Suppose that an individual receives a positive fluctuation in income in year t ($\varepsilon_{it} > 0$) and a negative shock in year $t + k$ ($\varepsilon_{it+k} < 0$). The change in income is given by $y_{it+k} - y_{it} = \varepsilon_{it+k} - \varepsilon_{it} < 0$. Thus, the probability of making a downward transition among the quintiles of the income distribution depends upon the sizes of the transitory disturbances.

The logic of this example applies not just to adjacent years ($k = 1$), but to comparisons across all time periods, i.e. for any k. Only the relative size of the transitory shocks in the comparison years affects the probability of making a transition across quintiles. Given a probability distribution for the transitory disturbances, the corresponding probabilities of changing quintiles will be fixed, not dependent upon the length of the time period under consideration. The probability of moving, say, from the middle to the highest quintile is the same over a three-year as over a one-year period. All that matters is the shocks to income in each of the comparison years.

In contrast, to the extent that fluctuations in income are driven by persistent, or even permanent, changes for each individual, the probability of making a transition rises with the length of time considered. Longer time periods permit a greater number of shocks to move the individual across the income distribution.[18]

Mobility patterns across the entire population

Table 6.2 summarizes labor earnings mobility in the United States and Germany. In this table we focus on the direction and magnitude of mobility by consolidating quintile-by-quintile transition rates. For example, we compute for the United States the fraction of the individuals in all quintiles, and for all years, who remain in the same quintile one year later. We repeat the analysis, allowing longer time periods to make the transition, and report these as our global measures of immobility for the United States (see the row labelled "No mobility"). We then repeat this procedure for Germany.

We next extend our summary measures to incorporate mobility using the "off-diagonal" transitions. In both countries, we compute the fraction of the sample in all quintiles, and for all years, that had moved up one quintile by the next year. Notice that individuals in the highest quintile are not eligible for this transition and must be excluded from the computation. As a result, our sample sizes will differ; we report the number of observations used to compute each transition rate in square brackets in the table. At the same time, however, we effectively normalize our measure so that it reflects the propensity to move up one quintile among those who have the possibility of doing so.

We repeat this analysis to yield an analogous measure of the fraction that moved up two quintiles, that moved up three quintiles, and so forth. We also compute the transition rates for downward movements of one or

Table 6.2 *Labor earnings mobility, United States and Germany, individuals aged 25 to 55[a] (%)*

		Transition period				
Change in quintile		$t+1$	$t+2$	$t+3$	$t+4$	$t+5$
Down 4	United States	1.0 [38]	1.4 [51]	2.1[***] [59]	2.7[***] [56]	2.8 [37]
	Germany	0.7 [27]	1.0 [34]	0.9 [24]	1.2 [16]	1.5 [8]
Down 3	United States	1.5 [146]	2.2 [180]	2.6 [163]	3.1 [133]	3.3 [88]
	Germany	1.3 [117]	1.9 [144]	2.4 [130]	2.8 [92]	3.4 [56]
Down 2	United States	3.0 [494]	4.3 [576]	5.1 [520]	5.7 [420]	6.2 [296]
	Germany	2.9 [420]	4.5 [472]	5.2 [372]	6.2 [272]	6.9 [134]
Down 1	United States	14.3[**] [3,423]	16.2[***] [3,076]	17.4[***] [2,532]	17.4[***] [1,824]	18.0[***] [1,171]
	Germany	12.9 [2,663]	13.3 [2,075]	14.2 [1,509]	14.2 [909]	13.3 [421]
No mobility	United States	69.3[***] [19,369]	62.9[***] [13,909]	58.3[***] [9,796]	55.8 [6,654]	52.6 [3,953]
	Germany	71.2 [16,483]	65.5 [11,247]	60.4 [7,383]	57.1 [4,364]	53.8 [1,907]
Up 1	United States	17.7[**] [4,038]	20.5 [3,640]	22.9 [3,030]	24.1 [2,241]	25.7 [1,511]
	Germany	16.5 [3,338]	19.6 [2,992]	22.7 [2,367]	24.4 [1,594]	27.4 [835]
Up 2	United States	3.1 [521]	4.8 [629]	5.9 [590]	7.0 [490]	8.0 [350]
	Germany	3.5 [487]	5.2 [554]	6.7 [480]	7.3 [319]	7.8 [169]

	United States	1.3	2.3*	2.8	3.4***	4.1
		[127]	[178]	[169]	[151]	[114]
Up 3						
	Germany	1.6	2.8	3.3	5.2	5.4
		[127]	[169]	[153]	[141]	[80]
	United States	0.4**	1.0	1.2**	1.4**	1.6***
		[18]	[35]	[36]	[29]	[19]
Up 4						
	Germany	0.8	1.5	2.4	2.9	4.8
		[29]	[40]	[39]	[36]	[28]

Notes:
a   Each entry shows the number of individuals making the transition as a
     fraction of those eligible to make the transition (see text, p. 121). Column
     totals will *not* sum to 1 as a result.
*** Indicates that the US and German rates are significantly different at the
     1 percent level.
**   Indicates that the US and German rates are significantly different at the
     5 percent level.
*   Indicates that the US and German rates are significantly different at the
     10 percent level.
Source: The 1989 Response–Nonresponse File of the PSID and the 1993 Syracuse
University English Language Public Use File of the GSOEP.

more quintiles across the labor earnings distribution. The end result of
these efforts is a set of probabilities for immobility, upward mobility, and
downward mobility for each of the five transition periods in both
countries.

What do these probabilities reveal? As can be seen from table 6.2,
global immobility rates for the two countries are surprisingly similar
across all transition periods. For example, the immobility rate over a one-
year horizon is 69.3 percent in the United States versus 71.2 in Germany.
While the difference is significant at the 1 percent level, the magnitude of
the difference is quite small. Moreover, both the magnitude and statistical
significance of the differences decline as one looks over longer horizons.
In both countries the vast majority of workers do not experience a shift in
quintile after one period, and a majority remain in the same quintile over
all five periods. In the United States the immobility rate over five years is
52.6 percent compared with 53.8 percent in Germany.

Of course, any differences in immobility imply corresponding differences in transitions among the quintiles. As shown in the remaining rows
of table 6.2, the major difference is a greater propensity for small

downward moves in the US earnings distribution. In every period, workers in the United States are more likely than their German counterparts to make a one-quintile decline in the earnings distribution.

Any set of mobility findings is to some extent an artifact of definitions, as there is an element of arbitrariness in any attempt to "draw the lines" for a mobility analysis. To check the importance of quintiles to the substantive conclusion we conducted a sensitivity analysis employing an alternative scheme. We divide the labor earners into three groups. "Low earners" consists of all those with labor earnings below 50 percent of median earnings, "Middle earners" consists of those with earnings between 50 percent of median earnings and 150 percent of median earnings and "High earners" consists of the remainder with earnings above 150 percent of median earnings.[19] Given this alternative definition of "groups," we define transitions among the groups in a fashion analogous to that for quintiles and, correspondingly, derive a set of mobility and immobility rates. These transition rates are presented in table 6.3.[20]

Because the distribution of labor earnings is much tighter in Germany than in the United States, an absolute change in earnings will propel a German worker much further up or down the distribution than in the United States. The quintile scale is much more sensitive to this type of concern since its boundaries are purely relative. The advantage of segmenting the sample based on borders around the median is that the borders have an absolute component to them.

Not surprisingly, the alternative definition directly affects the absolute level of measured immobility. Using this approach, 81.9 percent of individuals are immobile over a one-year horizon in the United States; the corresponding rate in Germany is 84.8 percent. On the whole, however, the pattern is quite similar, especially over horizons of three years or more. Our measures of immobility tend to be higher in Germany, with the mobility differences showing up as slightly greater probabilities in the United States of making a one-group downward move in the earnings distribution.

As noted at the outset, changes in labor earnings represent only a portion of the shifts in resources that individuals face and may, as a result, give an incomplete or misleading picture of income mobility. To gauge the magnitude of this possibility, we use the same methods as discussed in table 6.2 to summarize before- and after-government household size-adjusted income mobility in the United States and Germany. These results are presented in tables 6.4 and 6.5 respectively. In these instances, measured immobility in before-government and after-government income is greater in the United States than in Germany. However,

Table 6.3 *Labor earnings mobility, United States and Germany, individuals aged 25 to 55[a], median-based groupings (%)*

		Transition period				
Change in quintile		$t+1$	$t+2$	$t+3$	$t+4$	$t+5$
Down 2	United States	1.3 [97]	2.0 [137]	2.7[*] [137]	3.3 [112]	3.4 [73]
	Germany	1.2 [46]	1.7 [59]	1.9 [44]	2.4 [32]	2.1 [14]
Down 1	United States	11.0[***] [2,316]	13.9[***] [2,254]	15.8[***] [1,939]	16.8[***] [1,475]	17.6[**] [949]
	Germany	9.3 [1,624]	11.4 [1,485]	12.6 [1,159]	14.4 [804]	15.1 [403]
No mobility	United States	81.9[***] [23,032]	77.4[***] [17,237]	74.1[***] [12,531]	72.2[***] [8,632]	69.7[*] [5,284]
	Germany	84.8 [20,129]	80.8 [14,369]	77.7 [9,718]	74.4 [5,833]	71.8 [2,641]
Up 1	United States	9.4[***] [2,650]	11.3[***] [2,511]	12.9 [2,160]	13.9 [1,676]	15.8 [1,163]
	Germany	7.9 [1,838]	10.1 [1,741]	12.1 [1,469]	13.8 [1,020]	15.7 [544]
Up 2	United States	0.3 [79]	0.6 [135]	0.7 [128]	0.9 [103]	1.0 [70]
	Germany	0.3 [54]	0.5 [73]	0.8 [67]	0.9 [54]	1.3 [36]

Notes:
[a] Each entry shows the number of individuals making the transition as a fraction of those eligible to make the transition (see text, p. 121). Column totals will *not* sum to 1 as a result.
[***] Indicates that the US and German rates are significantly different at the 1 percent level.
[**] Indicates that the US and German rates are significantly different at the 5 percent level.
[*] Indicates that the US and German rates are significantly different at the 10 percent level.
Source: The 1989 Response–Nonresponse File of the PSID and the 1993 Syracuse University English Language Public Use File of the GSOEP.

Table 6.4 *Before-government income mobility, United States and Germany, individuals aged 25 to 55[a] (%)*

Change in quintile		Transition period				
		$t+1$	$t+2$	$t+3$	$t+4$	$t+5$
Down 4	United States	0.7 [36]	1.1 [47]	1.5[*] [48]	2.0[***] [42]	1.6[***] [23]
	Germany	1.1 [47]	1.6 [58]	2.3 [53]	3.8 [45]	4.7 [27]
Down 3	United States	1.9 [275]	3.5 [352]	4.6 [333]	5.7 [283]	6.5[**] [195]
	Germany	1.7 [160]	3.4 [253]	4.6 [248]	5.1 [181]	4.7 [82]
Down 2	United States	4.2[***] [830]	6.0[***] [882]	7.6 [835]	8.6 [654]	9.3[*] [428]
	Germany	5.3 [836]	7.1 [867]	8.4 [723]	9.4 [515]	11.1 [276]
Down 1	United States	14.0[***] [3,486]	15.6[***] [3,093]	16.5[***] [2,462]	16.7[***] [1,747]	16.9[***] [1,104]
	Germany	17.5 [3,911]	19.0 [3,221]	19.7 [2,278]	19.6 [1,376]	20.0 [623]
No mobility	United States	67.9[***] [21,581]	60.0[***] [15,162]	53.6[***] [10,392]	48.9[***] [6,823]	45.0[***] [3,988]
	Germany	62.5 [16,864]	54.7 [10,953]	49.5 [7,033]	45.7 [4,070]	41.8 [1,803]
Up 1	United States	17.3[***] [4,251]	20.3[***] [3,928]	23.1[**] [3,338]	24.9 [2,541]	26.2[**] [1,703]
	Germany	19.6 [4,335]	22.6 [3,767]	24.6 [2,852]	26.1 [1,850]	28.8 [924]
Up 2	United States	4.4 [883]	7.3 [1,114]	9.5 [1,095]	11.6 [958]	14.0[**] [740]
	Germany	4.8 [729]	7.5 [855]	9.5 [759]	11.6 [592]	11.5 [295]

Up 3	United States	2.1** [288]	3.2 [345]	4.2 [351]	5.3 [310]	5.8 [203]
	Germany	1.6 [173]	2.7 [208]	3.7 [188]	4.4 [142]	5.0 [87]
Up 4	United States	0.4*** [27]	0.9*** [47]	1.2* [53]	1.5* [42]	1.7* [30]
	Germany	1.1 [43]	1.8 [66]	2.1 [63]	2.7 [43]	3.9 [23]

Notes:
a   Each entry shows the number of individuals making the transition as a fraction of those eligible to make the transition (see text, p. 121). Column totals will *not* sum to 1 as a result.
*** Indicates that the US and German rates are significantly different at the 1 percent level.
** Indicates that the US and German rates are significantly different at the 5 percent level.
* Indicates that the US and German rates are significantly different at the 10 percent level.
Source: The 1989 Response–Nonresponse File of the PSID and the 1993 Syracuse University English Language Public Use File of the GSOEP.

the overall pattern is quite similar, with measured differences in immobility becoming smaller as the length of the time horizon is extended.

Mobility across before- and after-government income is greater than mobility across labor earnings. While roughly 60 percent or more of both German and US individuals remain in the same before- (after-) government income quintile after one period, by the fifth year a majority have shifted to another quintile.

The basic patterns in tables 6.4 and 6.5 are quite similar. In both tables, mobility takes the form of a greater probability in Germany of a one-quintile movement up or down in the distribution than in the United States. And glancing at movements of three quintiles (for which the sample sizes remain at least modest) the propensity for "big" moves appears greater in the United States. Perhaps more interesting than the patterns themselves is the fact that they are comparable for before-government and after-government income in both countries. Despite the large apparent differences in the magnitude and structure of government

Table 6.5 *After-government income mobility, United States and Germany, individuals aged 25 to 55[a] (%)*

		Transition period				
Change in quintile		$t+1$	$t+2$	$t+3$	$t+4$	$t+5$
Down 4	United States	0.8***	1.2***	1.4***	1.8***	1.4***
		[44]	[49]	[47]	[42]	[21]
	Germany	1.7	3.0	3.5	5.1	7.1
		[74]	[82]	[72]	[63]	[38]
Down 3	United States	2.1	3.9*	5.1	6.6**	7.0*
		[316]	[394]	[370]	[319]	[210]
	Germany	2.5	3.2	4.7	5.3	5.4
		[205]	[229]	[211]	[145]	[72]
Down 2	United States	4.2*	5.8**	7.3*	8.2	9.6*
		[840]	[892]	[823]	[632]	[439]
	Germany	4.7	7.4	8.1	8.8	8.0
		[742]	[832]	[667]	[465]	[215]
Down 1	United States	13.6***	15.0***	15.9***	15.7***	15.5***
		[3,453]	[3,033]	[2,412]	[1,683]	[1,029]
	Germany	18.7	19.3	19.7	19.5	21.4
		[4,031]	[3,124]	[2,238]	[1,333]	[657]
No mobility	United States	68.1***	60.0***	53.7***	49.0***	44.7***
		[21,529]	[15,073]	[10,363]	[6,806]	[3,963]
	Germany	59.8	52.9	48.3	45.3	41.4
		[16,474]	[10,889]	[6,981]	[4,072]	[1,749]
Up 1	United States	17.3***	20.8***	23.2***	25.1	26.5**
		[4,315]	[4,039]	[3,383]	[2,569]	[1,734]
	Germany	21.3	23.2	25.3	25.6	29.0
		[4,610]	[3,876]	[2,913]	[1,861]	[974]
Up 2	United States	4.3**	7.2***	9.5*	11.9**	14.5
		[895]	[1,138]	[1,105]	[992]	[772]
	Germany	5.0	8.7	10.4	13.5	13.1
		[801]	[984]	[891]	[707]	[347]

	United States	2.3	3.4*	4.7*	5.9***	6.7**
		[334]	[374]	[404]	[350]	[242]
Up 3						
	Germany	2.0	2.8	3.9	4.2	4.5
		[182]	[218]	[207]	[146]	[77]
	United States	0.5***	1.0**	1.3	1.4	1.5
		[32]	[54]	[54]	[45]	[29]
Up 4						
	Germany	1.1	1.8	1.6	2.1	2.7
		[42]	[57]	[45]	[37]	[18]

Notes:
a   Each entry shows the number of individuals making the transition as a
    fraction of those eligible to make the transition (see text, p. 121). Column
    totals will *not* sum to 1 as a result.
*** Indicates that the US and German rates are significantly different at the
    1 percent level.
**   Indicates that the US and German rates are significantly different at the
    5 percent level.
*   Indicates that the US and German rates are significantly different at the
    10 percent level.
Source: The 1989 Response–Nonresponse File of the PSID and the 1993 Syracuse
University English Language Public Use File of the GSOEP.

programs in these two countries, they have similar (non-)effects on
mobility.[21]

When making comparisons across tables 6.2, 6.4, and 6.5 one must be
aware that the underlying samples differ. That is, individuals who have
no labor income were excluded from table 6.2 but lived in households
with incomes and were included in table 6.4 and table 6.5. Since table 6.4
excludes persons who live in households with only non-government
income, the population in this sample is slightly different from that in
table 6.5 At this point two objectives of this chapter conflict somewhat.
On the one hand, we wish to be comprehensive in our analysis, suggesting
the broadest possible sample for each income measure. At the same time,
we wish to understand how measured mobility changes as the focus shifts
from labor income to before-government income, and finally to post-
government income. Unfortunately, as the income measure changes, the
sample does as well. Are our substantive results driven by the former, not
the latter?

To address this issue, we replicated the analysis in tables 6.2, 6.4 and
6.5 using a common sample. Since those who have labor earnings will

always have before- or after-government income, but the reverse is not true, this sample consists of all individuals who qualify for our labor earnings analysis (i.e. had labor earnings in at least one year). The results indicate that in practice the choice of sample is not the dominant influence in our results. Eliminating men and women of working age who do not work from our income distribution tends to raise our measures of mobility in both countries, but slightly more so in Germany.[22]

What picture emerges from tables 6.2, 6.4 and 6.5? First, patterns of mobility within each country accord with intuition. Both upward and downward mobility across a fixed number of quintiles rise essentially monotonically as the time period lengthens, emphasizing the persistence of shocks. Similarly, for any given time period the probability of making a transition across two quintiles is smaller than the probability of moving across one quintile, the probability of moving three quintiles is smaller still, and so forth. That is, large movements are less common than small movements. Finally, immobility is smaller for after-government than for before-government income, which in turn is less than that for labor income.

Comparing rates between the two countries, one finds that the United States displays about the same mobility in labor earnings, but slightly less mobility in before- and after-government income than does Germany. The difference in mobility manifests itself mostly as "small" (one-quintile) moves in Germany. The probability of moving three quintiles is somewhat greater in the United States. Finally, this characterization of mobility differs in magnitude but not character as one examines longer time periods. Hence, our results provide no evidence that the relative growth in income inequality found in our cross-sectional data in table 6.1 is being caused by differences in mobility across quintiles rather than by a relative pulling apart of quintiles in the United States.[23]

Mobility patterns and gender

The similarity in overall mobility patterns across labor earnings quintiles in the United States and Germany is surprising, given the much less regulated US labor markets, as is the greater immobility in pre- and post-government income found for the United States, given the larger tax and transfer systems in place in Germany. One possibility is that our broad level of aggregation, while providing an accurate summary, conceals the sources of these patterns. To investigate these comparisons further, we repeat our analysis but disaggregate our sample along gender lines.

In doing the mobility analysis for a subset of workers there are two ways to define the cut-off points for quintiles of the distribution. Either one could retain the same quintiles as the entire sample and examine mobility of men and women across these income levels, or compute separate quintiles in a fashion analogous to those for the sample as a whole, and examine the distribution of men and women separately. We adopted the latter approach, thus avoiding the possibility (especially among women) of small sample sizes in some of the quintiles. However, we emphasize that these analyses represent only the mobility of men (women) among the distribution of men (women).

Tables 6.6, 6.7 and 6.8 report labor earnings, before-government, and after-government income mobility for working-age men in the United States and Germany. For tables 6.6 and 6.7, a single best descriptor of the tables is similarity. With few exceptions, the differences in the labor earnings or before-government income mobility of men in the two countries is neither large nor significant. In table 6.8, the differences in mobility measured by after-government income reflect the pattern in table 6.5 and are more frequently significant. As in our analysis of the entire populations, mobility is somewhat higher in Germany; the immobility rates are uniformly higher for men in the United States. Moreover, the difference in mobility appears to take the form of a larger probability of a small movement in Germany.

Tables 6.9, 6.10 and 6.11 report labor earnings, before-government, and after-government income mobility for working-age women in the United States and Germany. Once again, the overall mobility patterns for working-age women in the two countries are similar. US women are about as mobile as German women with respect to labor earnings, with the differences concentrated in downward movements of roughly one quintile. Again, however, moving to before-government income shows greater immobility in the United States, with the larger mobility in Germany taking the form of one-quintile moves up or down. Once more, using after-government income in table 6.11, German women are significantly more mobile than US women, despite a much more extensive tax and transfer system. While German women are more likely to experience upward mobility than US women, they are significantly more likely to experience very large downward mobility, especially over long transition periods, although the sample sizes are quite small.

Summary

In this chapter we contribute several new dimensions to the discussion of inequality in the United States in the 1980s. First, unlike most of the

Table 6.6 *Labor earnings mobility, United States and Germany, men aged 25 to 55[a] (%)*

		Transition period				
Change in quintile		$t+1$	$t+2$	$t+3$	$t+4$	$t+5$
Down 4	United States	1.4 [29]	2.4 [41]	3.1 [39]	3.2 [32]	4.3 [24]
	Germany	1.4 [33]	2.4 [43]	3.1 [33]	3.1 [19]	4.0 [10]
Down 3	United States	2.0 [86]	2.7 [96]	3.1[***] [83]	4.0 [74]	4.0 [55]
	Germany	2.0 [98]	2.3 [96]	1.7 [65]	3.0 [60]	4.5 [34]
Down 2	United States	3.8 [274]	4.8 [276]	5.7 [253]	6.0 [188]	6.4[*] [128]
	Germany	3.8 [339]	4.2 [289]	5.3 [250]	4.9 [159]	4.5 [90]
Down 1	United States	15.0 [1,545]	15.4 [1,288]	15.9 [1,018]	15.3 [708]	14.9 [431]
	Germany	14.2 [1,747]	15.6 [1,431]	16.0 [1,017]	16.4 [637]	15.6 [270]
No mobility	United States	65.0 [8,457]	59.2 [6,083]	54.9 [4,267]	52.3 [2,868]	49.2 [1,704]
	Germany	66.2 [8,497]	59.9 [5,702]	55.3 [3,729]	51.1 [2,156]	47.8 [952]
Up 1	United States	20.0[**] [2,002]	23.5[***] [1,834]	25.4[**] [1,504]	27.7 [1,154]	29.1 [761]
	Germany	18.4 [2,142]	21.0 [1,799]	23.4 [1,380]	26.0 [940]	28.4 [474]
Up 2	United States	4.5 [330]	6.4[**] [370]	8.0[*] [353]	9.0 [283]	11.0 [215]
	Germany	5.2 [431]	7.7 [483]	9.5 [393]	9.9 [259]	11.3 [143]

	United States	1.8*	2.4***	3.1***	3.7***	4.6**
		[75]	[88]	[94]	[83]	[58]
Up 3						
	Germany	2.5	4.4	5.8	7.7	8.5
		[116]	[140]	[129]	[100]	[55]
	United States	1.0	2.1	3.1	3.0*	3.3**
		[27]	[39]	[42]	[29]	[23]
Up 4						
	Germany	1.5	2.4	3.2	5.6	7.7
		[32]	[40]	[40]	[41]	[27]

Notes:

a   Each entry shows the number of individuals making the transition as a fraction of those eligible to make the transition (see text, p. 121). Column totals will *not* sum to 1 as a result.

***   Indicates that the US and German rates are significantly different at the 1 percent level.

**   Indicates that the US and German rates are significantly different at the 5 percent level.

*   Indicates that the US and German rates are significantly different at the 10 percent level.

Source: The 1989 Response–Nonresponse File of the PSID and the 1993 Syracuse University English Language Public Use File of the GSOEP.

Table 6.7 *Before-government income mobility, United States and Germany, men aged 25 to 55[a] (%)*

Change in quintile		Transition period				
		$t+1$	$t+2$	$t+3$	$t+4$	$t+5$
Down 4	United States	1.1 [27]	1.7 [31]	1.9 [28]	2.3 [24]	2.5 [15]
	Germany	0.7 [19]	1.3 [27]	1.8 [27]	2.2 [20]	3.4 [14]
Down 3	United States	2.8*** [179]	4.6*** [212]	6.7*** [207]	8.3*** [171]	9.2*** [116]
	Germany	1.9 [84]	3.1 [126]	4.7 [123]	4.5 [84]	4.8 [38]
Down 2	United States	4.6 [426]	7.0 [478]	8.8 [452]	10.0 [363]	10.5 [240]
	Germany	5.1 [410]	7.6 [453]	8.8 [379]	9.9 [274]	12.2 [146]
Down 1	United States	14.9** [1,711]	15.5*** [1,432]	16.4*** [1,121]	16.1*** [762]	16.6* [487]
	Germany	18.2 [2,040]	19.2 [1,671]	19.8 [1,194]	20.3 [737]	19.2 [335]
No mobility	United States	65.8*** [9,136]	58.4*** [6,407]	51.3** [4,314]	47.0 [2,832]	43.3 [1,648]
	Germany	61.7 [8,405]	54.4 [5,432]	49.2 [3,480]	45.3 [1,991]	42.1 [879]
Up 1	United States	17.4*** [1,995]	20.2** [1,790]	23.1 [1,531]	24.6 [1,113]	25.8 [754]
	Germany	19.7 [2,173]	22.0 [1,856]	24.1 [1,390]	25.9 [915]	28.1 [456]
Up 2	United States	4.8 [444]	7.4 [535]	9.9 [507]	12.1 [446]	13.9 [325]
	Germany	5.1 [392]	8.1 [444]	10.4 [399]	11.7 [288]	12.7 [146]

Up 3	United States	2.9*** [187]	4.4*** [208]	5.5*** [211]	6.7** [174]	7.1* [114]
	Germany	1.7 [87]	2.8 [104]	3.4 [80]	4.6 [72]	4.7 [44]
Up 4	United States	0.7 [20]	1.1* [28]	1.4 [25]	1.2** [18]	1.5* [13]
	Germany	1.0 [19]	2.1 [36]	2.3 [36]	3.2 [25]	4.3 [12]

Notes:
a Each entry shows the number of individuals making the transition as a fraction of those eligible to make the transition (see text, p. 121). Column totals will *not* sum to 1 as a result.
*** Indicates that the US and German rates are significantly different at the 1 percent level.
** Indicates that the US and German rates are significantly different at the 5 percent level.
* Indicates that the US and German rates are significantly different at the 10 percent level.
Source: The 1989 Response–Nonresponse File of the PSID and the 1993 Syracuse University English Language Public Use File of the GSOEP.

Table 6.8 *After-government income mobility, United States and Germany, men aged 25 to 55[a] (%)*

		Transition period				
Change in quintile		$t+1$	$t+2$	$t+3$	$t+4$	$t+5$
Down 4	United States	1.2 [28]	1.7[*] [32]	1.8[**] [26]	2.8 [29]	2.6[**] [17]
	Germany	1.4 [34]	2.8 [40]	3.5 [37]	4.7 [32]	6.2 [19]
Down 3	United States	3.1 [199]	5.4[***] [243]	7.4[***] [233]	8.9[***] [184]	9.8[***] [122]
	Germany	2.8 [111]	3.5 [116]	4.7 [108]	4.8 [73]	5.4 [36]
Down 2	United States	4.5 [426]	6.3 [456]	8.6 [450]	9.4 [346]	11.0 [246]
	Germany	4.8 [373]	7.2 [424]	8.7 [366]	9.7 [250]	9.6 [121]
Down 1	United States	14.2[***] [1,657]	15.1[***] [1,418]	15.9[***] [1,081]	15.9[***] [761]	15.8[***] [475]
	Germany	18.9 [2,063]	19.9 [1,616]	19.8 [1,136]	19.2 [691]	20.5 [333]
No mobility	United States	66.6[***] [9,224]	59.0[***] [6,421]	51.8[***] [4,357]	47.2[*] [2,825]	43.2 [1,637]
	Germany	59.7 [8,266]	52.7 [5,428]	48.2 [3,495]	45.1 [2,011]	41.5 [879]
Up 1	United States	17.2[***] [1,947]	20.0[***] [1,781]	22.6[**] [1,494]	24.2 [1,143]	25.1 [747]
	Germany	20.9 [2,270]	22.7 [1,903]	24.9 [1,409]	25.7 [915]	27.4 [459]
Up 2	United States	4.4[**] [447]	7.2[**] [537]	9.8 [517]	11.6 [429]	14.1 [328]
	Germany	5.3 [423]	8.7 [498]	10.5 [442]	13.2 [348]	13.9 [175]

Up 3	United States	3.1***	4.5***	6.1***	8.0***	8.6***
		[198]	[218]	[221]	[195]	[134]
	Germany	1.9	2.9	3.8	4.2	4.9
		[90]	[106]	[101]	[72]	[41]
Up 4	United States	0.9	1.4	1.7	1.4	1.5
		[22]	[31]	[29]	[21]	[13]
	Germany	1.3	2.3	1.9	2.6	3.2
		[23]	[34]	[25]	[20]	[10]

Notes:
a   Each entry shows the number of individuals making the transition as a fraction of those eligible to make the transition (see text, p. 121). Column totals will *not* sum to 1 as a result.
***   Indicates that the US and German rates are significantly different at the 1 percent level.
**   Indicates that the US and German rates are significantly different at the 5 percent level.
*   Indicates that the US and German rates are significantly different at the 10 percent level.
Source: The 1989 Response–Nonresponse File of the PSID and the 1993 Syracuse University English Language Public Use File of the GSOEP.

Table 6.9 *Labor earnings mobility, United States and Germany, women aged 25 to 55[a] (%)*

Change in quintile		Transition period				
		$t+1$	$t+2$	$t+3$	$t+4$	$t+5$
Down 4	United States	1.1 [24]	2.5 [45]	3.8 [54]	4.1[*] [43]	3.8[**] [22]
	Germany	1.7 [26]	3.7 [49]	5.3 [51]	6.8 [40]	8.8 [23]
Down 3	United States	1.9 [101]	2.9[***] [134]	4.1[***] [133]	5.6[*] [129]	7.6 [111]
	Germany	2.5 [102]	5.1 [162]	6.7 [149]	7.7 [108]	9.0 [56]
Down 2	United States	4.1[**] [381]	6.5 [468]	7.6 [432]	8.2[*] [342]	8.5 [229]
	Germany	5.2 [321]	6.7 [317]	8.2 [251]	10.0 [171]	8.8 [91]
Down 1	United States	16.0[***] [2,094]	18.4[***] [1,937]	19.5[***] [1,564]	21.0[***] [1,211]	20.8[***] [762]
	Germany	13.9 [1,169]	14.7 [911]	15.1 [661]	14.1 [394]	15.7 [189]
No mobility	United States	66.3 [10,080]	57.9[*] [6,968]	52.9 [4,864]	48.4 [3,163]	45.8 [1,898]
	Germany	66.9 [6,789]	59.5 [4,472]	52.8 [2,812]	49.8 [1,622]	44.6 [661]
Up 1	United States	18.2 [2,220]	20.6 [2,002]	22.5 [1,623]	23.5 [1,190]	24.1 [765]
	Germany	17.2 [1,465]	19.8 [1,298]	23.0 [1,028]	24.2 [693]	26.8 [375]
Up 2	United States	3.9[*] [349]	6.2[**] [426]	7.3[***] [393]	9.0[*] [343]	10.5[*] [237]
	Germany	4.7 [283]	7.2 [345]	9.7 [331]	11.1 [242]	13.7 [130]

	United States	1.3**	3.3	4.7	5.2	6.1
		[80]	[145]	[143]	[117]	[90]
Up 3						
	Germany	2.0	4.1	4.5	5.0	5.9
		[86]	[122]	[109]	[78]	[45]
	United States	0.7	1.5	2.0	3.2	3.7
		[20]	[34]	[36]	[41]	[26]
Up 4						
	Germany	1.1	1.6	2.6	3.4	2.2
		[15]	[28]	[29]	[24]	[13]

Notes:

[a] Each entry shows the number of individuals making the transition as a fraction of those eligible to make the transition (see text, p. 121). Column totals will *not* sum to 1 as a result.

*** Indicates that the US and German rates are significantly different at the 1 percent level.

** Indicates that the US and German rates are significantly different at the 5 percent level.

* Indicates that the US and German rates are significantly different at the 10 percent level.

Source: The 1989 Response–Nonresponse File of the PSID and the 1993 Syracuse University English Language Public Use File of the GSOEP.

Table 6.10 *Before-government income mobility, United States and Germany, women aged 25 to 55[a] (%)*

		Transition period				
Change in quintile		$t+1$	$t+2$	$t+3$	$t+4$	$t+5$
Down 4	United States	0.4***	0.8**	1.2***	1.6***	1.1***
		[11]	[19]	[22]	[16]	[8]
	Germany	1.6	1.8	3.1	5.4	5.4
		[26]	[27]	[30]	[26]	[13]
Down 3	United States	1.5	2.6**	2.8**	3.9	4.2
		[121]	[140]	[123]	[117]	[76]
	Germany	1.6	3.8	4.2	5.0	5.3
		[79]	[132]	[115]	[88]	[44]
Down 2	United States	3.5***	5.2***	6.7***	6.7**	7.7
		[367]	[437]	[400]	[284]	[195]
	Germany	5.1	6.6	8.6	8.9	9.8
		[391]	[410]	[354]	[242]	[127]
Down 1	United States	13.5***	15.5***	16.7**	17.4	17.3
		[1,845]	[1,665]	[1,338]	[986]	[616]
	Germany	16.9	18.5	18.5	19.2	19.0
		[1,907]	[1,525]	[1,057]	[654]	[288]
No mobility	United States	69.5***	61.1***	55.0***	50.5***	46.7**
		[12,301]	[8,614]	[6,006]	[3,965]	[2,329]
	Germany	63.7	55.4	50.5	46.1	42.9
		[8,475]	[5,551]	[3,559]	[2,036]	[912]
Up 1	United States	17.1***	20.6***	23.3	25.0*	25.9**
		[2,307]	[2,213]	[1,856]	[1,426]	[936]
	Germany	19.0	22.8	24.5	27.1	29.9
		[2,148]	[1,910]	[1,464]	[979]	[481]
Up 2	United States	4.2	7.1	9.1	11.2	13.7**
		[463]	[592]	[572]	[501]	[403]
	Germany	4.5	6.8	9.3	10.4	10.3
		[348]	[405]	[386]	[297]	[145]

Up 3	United States	1.4	2.7	3.7	4.7	6.0
		[107]	[154]	[172]	[162]	[122]
	Germany	1.4	2.8	3.7	4.1	5.2
		[73]	[110]	[99]	[68]	[50]
Up 4	United States	0.3***	0.5***	0.9*	1.3	2.1
		[10]	[15]	[22]	[20]	[17]
	Germany	1.1	1.7	1.9	2.6	3.3
		[22]	[29]	[25]	[18]	[10]

Notes:

[a] Each entry shows the number of individuals making the transition as a fraction of those eligible to make the transition (see text, p. 121). Column totals will *not* sum to 1 as a result.

*** Indicates that the US and German rates are significantly different at the 1 percent level.

** Indicates that the US and German rates are significantly different at the 5 percent level.

* Indicates that the US and German rates are significantly different at the 10 percent level.

Source: The 1989 Response–Nonresponse File of the PSID and the 1993 Syracuse University English Language Public Use File of the GSOEP.

Table 6.11 *After-government income mobility, United States and Germany, women aged 25 to 55[a] (%)*

Change in quintile		Transition period				
		$t+1$	$t+2$	$t+3$	$t+4$	$t+5$
Down 4	United States	0.5*** [17]	0.8*** [20]	1.0*** [20]	1.2*** [15]	1.2*** [9]
	Germany	2.0 [39]	2.9 [40]	3.3 [33]	4.9 [29]	7.4 [18]
Down 3	United States	1.5*** [120]	2.7 [150]	3.3** [135]	4.7 [133]	4.4 [81]
	Germany	2.5 [107]	3.2 [117]	4.7 [101]	5.6 [68]	5.7 [36]
Down 2	United States	3.5*** [374]	5.2*** [439]	6.3* [397]	6.2*** [273]	7.5 [190]
	Germany	4.5 [351]	7.3 [399]	7.5 [306]	8.5 [223]	6.8 [94]
Down 1	United States	13.0*** [1,851]	14.5*** [1,603]	15.4*** [1,283]	16.0*** [933]	16.1*** [578]
	Germany	18.5 [1,979]	18.9 [1,526]	19.8 [1,108]	19.4 [641]	20.7 [320]
No mobility	United States	69.9*** [12,294]	61.6*** [8,680]	56.0*** [6,036]	51.1*** [3,982]	46.1** [2,314]
	Germany	60.0 [8,203]	52.9 [5,437]	48.4 [3,474]	45.4 [2,054]	41.9 [878]
Up 1	United States	16.9*** [2,358]	20.9*** [2,234]	23.2** [1,881]	25.2 [1,449]	27.2 [978]
	Germany	21.3 [2,330]	23.6 [1,981]	25.6 [1,508]	25.9 [963]	29.4 [506]
Up 2	United States	4.2 [458]	7.0*** [597]	9.2 [588]	11.5* [520]	14.2 [424]
	Germany	4.8 [386]	8.7 [488]	10.3 [449]	13.2 [350]	13.8 [183]

	United States	1.6	2.8	4.0	5.2	6.3[***]
Up 3		[127]	[166]	[190]	[177]	[128]
	Germany	2.1	2.9	4.3	4.5	3.5
		[93]	[113]	[108]	[74]	[32]
	United States	0.3[**]	0.6[*]	0.9	1.2	1.8
Up 4		[11]	[20]	[23]	[23]	[18]
	Germany	1.0	1.4	1.4	1.5	2.0
		[20]	[25]	[19]	[15]	[7]

Notes:
[a]   Each entry shows the number of individuals making the transition as a fraction of those eligible to make the transition (see text, p. 121). Column totals will *not* sum to 1 as a result.
[***] Indicates that the US and German rates are significantly different at the 1 percent level.
[**] Indicates that the US and German rates are significantly different at the 5 percent level.
[*]   Indicates that the US and German rates are significantly different at the 10 percent level.
Source: The 1989 Response–Nonresponse File of the PSID and the 1993 Syracuse University English Language Public Use File of the GSOEP.

literature, we look at changes in both the distribution of labor earnings and in the distribution of pre- and post-government income. Second, we do so from a cross-national perspective by comparing distributions of earnings and income in the United States, with those in another highly industrialized western economy – Germany. Third, and most important, we use the panel nature of our data to follow the labor earnings and household income patterns of working-age people in both countries to measure mobility differences across the two countries.

Our cross-sectional results confirm what others have found. Inequality was greater in the United States than in Germany during the 1980s, whether measured across the distribution of labor earnings, the distribution of before-government, or the distribution of after-government income. We also found that labor earnings inequality rose slightly in both countries, but slightly more so in Germany than in the United States. However, inequality in before- and after-government household size-adjusted income in the United States rose both absolutely and relative to Germany over the period.

Individual mobility patterns in the two countries are surprisingly similar, with the United States displaying slightly greater mobility in labor earnings but less mobility in pre- and post-government income. Labor earnings mobility is less than before- or after-government income in both countries. Mobility increases over time for all three measures, but the patterns are remarkably similar. The mobility patterns of US and German men are virtually the same. Despite very different labor market institutions, and very different tax and transfer systems, the dynamic outcomes of working-age men and women are remarkably similar. While overall patterns of income mobility for US and German women are similar, there are more significant differences between them than between men.

We believe the introduction of mobility into the public policy debate over inequality is important. But we find little evidence that differences in mobility patterns can explain the differences in cross-sectional inequality that occurred over the 1980s.

Appendix A: Mobility rates, median-based groupings

As noted in the text, we also compute mobility rates using an alternative to our quintile groupings. In this analysis, we divide individuals in each country into three groups: those below 50 percent of median income; those with income between 50 percent of median income and 150 percent of median income; and those with income above 150 percent of median income. This appendix contains tables analogous to tables 6.2 and 6.4–6.11 in the text (and numbered so as to facilitate direct comparison) containing estimated mobility rates using these groupings.

Table 6A.2 *Labor earnings mobility, United States and Germany, individuals aged 25 to 55[a], median-based groupings (%)*

		Transition period				
Change in group		$t+1$	$t+2$	$t+3$	$t+4$	$t+5$
Down 2	United States	1.3 [97]	2.0 [137]	2.7[*] [137]	3.3 [112]	3.4 [73]
	Germany	1.2 [46]	1.7 [59]	1.9 [44]	2.4 [32]	2.1 [14]
Down 1	United States	11.0[***] [2,316]	13.9[***] [2,254]	15.8[***] [1,939]	16.8[***] [1,475]	17.6[**] [949]
	Germany	9.3 [1,624]	11.4 [1,485]	12.6 [1,159]	14.4 [804]	15.1 [403]
No mobility	United States	81.9[***] [23,032]	77.4[***] [17,237]	74.1[***] [12,531]	72.2[***] [8,632]	69.7[*] [5,284]
	Germany	84.8 [20,129]	80.8 [14,369]	77.7 [9,718]	74.4 [5,833]	71.8 [2,641]
Up 1	United States	9.4[***] [2,650]	11.3[***] [2,511]	12.9 [2,160]	13.9 [1,676]	15.8 [1,163]
	Germany	7.9 [1,838]	10.1 [1,741]	12.1 [1.469]	13.8 [1,020]	15.7 [544]
Up 2	United States	0.3 [79]	0.6 [135]	0.7 [128]	0.9 [103]	1.0 [70]
	Germany	0.3 [54]	0.5 [73]	0.8 [67]	0.9 [54]	1.3 [36]

Notes:
[a] Each entry shows the number of individuals making the transition as a fraction of those eligible to make the transition (see text, p. 121). Column totals will *not* sum to 1 as a result.
[***] Indicates that the US and German rates are significantly different at the 1 percent level.
[**] Indicates that the US and German rates are significantly different at the 5 percent level.
[*] Indicates that the US and German rates are significantly different at the 10 percent level.
Source: The 1989 Response–Nonresponse File of the PSID and the 1993 Syracuse University English Language Public Use File of the GSOEP.

Table 6A.4 *Before-government income mobility, United States and Germany, individuals aged 25 to 55[a], median-based groupings (%)*

		Transition period				
Change in group		$t+1$	$t+2$	$t+3$	$t+4$	$t+5$
Down 2	United States	1.6*** [187]	2.6*** [224]	3.3*** [219]	4.3*** [187]	4.5 [120]
	Germany	0.7 [33]	1.1 [43]	1.6 [35]	2.4 [28]	3.5 [17]
Down 1	United States	11.0*** [2,854]	13.9*** [2,849]	15.8*** [2,434]	16.6*** [1,797]	17.6*** [1,170]
	Germany	9.1 [2,237]	11.0 [1,983]	12.3 [1,545]	13.2 [1,012]	13.9 [505]
No mobility	United States	80.5*** [25,188]	74.2*** [18,304]	69.4*** [13,013]	66.1*** [8,804]	62.4*** [5,272]
	Germany	83.3 [22,411]	78.7 [15,872]	75.7 [10,698]	72.8 [6,429]	70.8 [2,947]
Up 1	United States	9.9*** [3,253]	13.3*** [3,357]	16.2*** [3,015]	18.6*** [2,429]	21.3*** [1,732]
	Germany	8.4 [2,385]	11.1 [2,305]	12.9 [1,881]	14.7 [1,315]	15.7 [657]
Up 2	United States	0.5*** [175]	0.8*** [236]	1.0*** [226]	1.1*** [183]	1.3*** [120]
	Germany	0.2 [32]	0.3 [45]	0.3 [38]	0.4 [30]	0.4 [14]

Notes:
[a] Each entry shows the number of individuals making the transition as a fraction of those eligible to make the transition (see text, p. 121). Column totals will *not* sum to 1 as a result.
*** Indicates that the US and German rates are significantly different at the 1 percent level.
Source: The 1989 Response–Nonresponse File of the PSID and the 1993 Syracuse University English Language Public Use File of the GSOEP.

Table 6A.5 *After-government income mobility, United States and Germany, individuals aged 25 to 55[a], median-based groupings (%)*

Change in group		Transition period				
		$t+1$	$t+2$	$t+3$	$t+4$	$t+5$
Down 2	United States	1.3**	2.0*	2.7	3.7	3.9
		[163]	[179]	[181]	[164]	[104]
	Germany	0.8	1.5	2.4	3.1	3.1
		[36]	[44]	[40]	[30]	[14]
Down 1	United States	10.5***	13.6***	15.3***	15.8***	16.8***
		[2,921]	[2,973]	[2,509]	[1,805]	[1,201]
	Germany	8.1	9.4	10.2	10.9	12.3
		[1,993]	[1,689]	[1,260]	[815]	[431]
No mobility	United States	80.9***	74.3***	69.8***	66.7***	62.7***
		[25,234]	[18,280]	[13,036]	[8,881]	[5,280]
	Germany	84.5	81.1	78.9	77.5	75.0
		[22,996]	[16,537]	[11,345]	[6,911]	[3,170]
Up 1	United States	9.8***	13.4***	16.2***	18.6**	21.7***
		[3,285]	[3,416]	[3,042]	[2,446]	[1,761]
	Germany	7.8	9.8	11.0	11.6	12.5
		[2,117]	[1,999]	[1,563]	[1,063]	[524]
Up 2	United States	0.4***	0.7***	0.8***	0.9**	1.0***
		[155]	[198]	[193]	[142]	[93]
	Germany	0.1	0.1	0.1	0.2	0.3
		[19]	[22]	[17]	[10]	[8]

Notes:
[a] Each entry shows the number of individuals making the transition as a fraction of those eligible to make the transition (see text, p. 121). Column totals will *not* sum to 1 as a result.
*** Indicates that the US and German rates are significantly different at the 1 percent level.
** Indicates that the US and German rates are significantly different at the 5 percent level.
* Indicates that the US and German rates are significantly different at the 10 percent level.
Source: The 1989 Response–Nonresponse File of the PSID and the 1993 Syracuse University English Language Public Use File of the GSOEP.

Table 6A.6 *Labor earnings mobility, United States and Germany, men aged 25 to 55[a], median-based groupings (%)*

		Transition period				
Change in group		$t+1$	$t+2$	$t+3$	$t+4$	$t+5$
Down 2	United States	1.5**	2.3**	2.9**	3.1*	4.1*
		[33]	[41]	[41]	[32]	[23]
	Germany	0.6	1.0	1.3	1.7	1.6
		[11]	[19]	[15]	[10]	[5]
Down 1	United States	9.8***	10.5***	11.5***	11.6***	11.3*
		[1,047]	[887]	[728]	[530]	[335]
	Germany	6.3	7.1	8.0	9.2	9.3
		[697]	[591]	[477]	[332]	[159]
No mobility	United States	80.6***	77.0***	73.5***	71.3***	68.6***
		[10,326]	[7,794]	[5,649]	[3,873]	[2,340]
	Germany	87.0	84.0	81.3	77.5	74.8
		[11,851]	[8,564]	[5,834]	[3,500]	[1,610]
Up 1	United States	10.9***	13.6***	15.9***	17.9***	20.5***
		[1,389]	[1,351]	[1,192]	[948]	[670]
	Germany	7.2	9.2	11.1	13.6	15.9
		[858]	[824]	[691]	[510]	[269
Up 2	United States	0.2	0.4	0.6**	0.7	0.9
		[30]	[42]	[43]	[36]	[31]
	Germany	0.2	0.3	0.3	0.4	0.7
		[18]	[25]	[19]	[19]	[12]

Notes:
[a] Each entry shows the number of individuals making the transition as a fraction of those eligible to make the transition (see text, p. 121). Column totals will *not* sum to 1 as a result.
*** Indicates that the US and German rates are significantly different at the 1 percent level.
** Indicates that the US and German rates are significantly different at the 5 percent level.
* Indicates that the US and German rates are significantly different at the 10 percent level.
Source: The 1989 Response–Nonresponse File of the PSID and the 1993 Syracuse University English Language Public Use File of the GSOEP.

Table 6A.7 *Before-government income mobility, United States and Germany, men aged 25 to 55[a], median-based groupings (%)*

Change in group		Transition period				
		$t+1$	$t+2$	$t+3$	$t+4$	$t+5$
Down 2	United States	2.0***	2.8***	3.8***	5.0***	5.3**
		[111]	[118]	[111]	[99]	[63]
	Germany	0.4	0.8	1.2	1.5	2.5
		[13]	[19]	[14]	[11]	[9]
Down 1	United States	11.5***	14.5***	16.8***	17.7***	18.8***
		[1,426]	[1,417]	[1,200]	[869]	[573]
	Germany	8.8	10.5	11.6	12.5	14.4
		[1,106]	[993]	[755]	[503]	[260]
No mobility	United States	78.9***	72.6***	67.3***	63.6***	60.1***
		[10,869]	[7,860]	[5,562]	[3,734]	[2,233]
	Germany	83.9	79.3	76.6	74.0	70.8
		[11,331]	[7,988]	[5,404]	[3,244]	[1,480]
Up 1	United States	10.7***	13.9***	16.9***	19.5***	21.8***
		[1,620]	[1,612]	[1,419]	[1,147]	[794]
	Germany	8.1	10.9	12.6	14.2	15.3
		[1,164]	[1,126]	[911]	[630]	[314]
Up 2	United States	0.6***	0.9***	1.0***	1.1***	1.3***
		[89]	[114]	[104]	[74]	[49]
	Germany	0.2	0.3	0.4	0.4	0.5
		[15]	[23]	[24]	[18]	[7]

Notes:
[a]   Each entry shows the number of individuals making the transition as a fraction of those eligible to make the transition (see text, p. 121). Column totals will *not* sum to 1 as a result.
***   Indicates that the US and German rates are significantly different at the 1 percent level.
**   Indicates that the US and German rates are significantly different at the 5 percent level.
Source: The 1989 Response–Nonresponse File of the PSID and the 1993 Syracuse University English Language Public Use File of the GSOEP.

Table 6A.8 *After-government income mobility, United States and Germany, men aged 25 to 55[a], median-based groupings (%)*

Change in group		Transition period				
		$t+1$	$t+2$	$t+3$	$t+4$	$t+5$
Down 2	United States	1.8***	2.4	3.4	4.9	5.0
		[101]	[98]	[100]	[89]	[56]
	Germany	0.7	1.8	2.8	3.2	3.2
		[17]	[26]	[24]	[16]	[7]
Down 1	United States	10.7***	13.8***	15.8***	16.6***	17.8***
		[1,402]	[1,422]	[1,194]	[877]	[574]
	Germany	7.9	8.8	9.7	10.3	12.1
		[984]	[829]	[616]	[399]	[217]
No mobility	United States	79.7***	73.3***	68.4***	64.6***	61.0***
		[10,951]	[7,914]	[5,616]	[3,765]	[2,249]
	Germany	84.8	81.5	79.3	77.9	75.1
		[11,611]	[8,310]	[5,711]	[3,463]	[1,590]
Up 1	United States	10.3***	13.7***	16.5***	19.2***	21.6***
		[1,602]	[1,603]	[1,406]	[1,136]	[797]
	Germany	7.7	9.9	11.0	11.6	12.5
		[1,029]	[987]	[756]	[526]	[254]
Up 2	United States	0.6***	0.8***	0.9***	0.9***	1.1**
		[92]	[100]	[92]	[66]	[43]
	Germany	0.1	0.1	0.2	0.3	0.4
		[12]	[13]	[12]	[8]	[5]

Notes:
[a] Each entry shows the number of individuals making the transition as a fraction of those eligible to make the transition (see text, p. 121). Column totals will *not* sum to 1 as a result.
*** Indicates that the US and German rates are significantly different at the 1 percent level.
** Indicates that the US and German rates are significantly different at the 5 percent level.
Source: The 1989 Response–Nonresponse File of the PSID and the 1993 Syracuse University English Language Public Use File of the GSOEP.

Table 6A.9   *Labor earnings mobility, United States and Germany, women aged 25 to 55[a], median-based groupings (%)*

Change in group		Transition period				
		$t+1$	$t+2$	$t+3$	$t+4$	$t+5$
Down 2	United States	2.9[*]	4.7[***]	7.1[***]	7.9[***]	9.4[**]
		[127]	[163]	[192]	[157]	[117]
	Germany	3.8	7.6	10.4	12.8	15.2
		[135]	[212]	[185]	[133]	[67]
Down 1	United States	13.9	18.0[***]	19.6[***]	21.5[**]	22.0[*]
		[1,459]	[1,477]	[1,237]	[943]	[620]
	Germany	14.2	15.2	16.9	18.2	18.4
		[980]	[780]	[595]	[383]	[202]
No mobility	United States	79.1	72.6	68.8	66.1	63.7
		[12,128]	[8,855]	[6,407]	[4,422]	[2,673]
	Germany	79.0	73.7	68.5	65.2	63.3
		[8,015]	[5,566]	[3,673]	[2,188]	[975]
Up 1	United States	10.0	12.5	13.9	14.8[*]	15.6[*]
		[1,533]	[1,506]	[1,247]	[921]	[621]
	Germany	9.4	12.2	15.2	16.6	18.2
		[1,020]	[1,006]	[844]	[583]	[295]
Up 2	United States	0.7[**]	1.4	1.9	2.3	3.2[*]
		[102]	[158]	[159]	[136]	[109]
	Germany	1.1	1.8	2.2	2.6	2.2
		[106]	[140]	[124]	[85]	[44]

Notes:
[a]   Each entry shows the number of individuals making the transition as a fraction of those eligible to make the transition (see text, p. 121). Column totals will *not* sum to 1 as a result.
[***]   Indicates that the US and German rates are significantly different at the 1 percent level.
[**]   Indicates that the US and German rates are significantly different at the 5 percent level.
[*]   Indicates that the US and German rates are significantly different at the 10 percent level.
Source: The 1989 Response–Nonresponse File of the PSID and the 1993 Syracuse University English Language Public Use File of the GSOEP.

Table 6A.10 *Before-government income mobility, United States and Germany, women aged 25 to 55[a], median-based groupings (%)*

Change in group		Transition period				
		$t+1$	$t+2$	$t+3$	$t+4$	$t+5$
Down 2	United States	1.2 [79]	2.1 [96]	2.5 [91]	3.1 [80]	3.9 [57]
	Germany	0.9 [18]	1.4 [23]	1.8 [19]	3.2 [17]	4.9 [10]
Down 1	United States	10.6** [1,439]	13.7*** [1,465]	15.6*** [1,255]	16.3** [927]	16.2* [584]
	Germany	9.4 [1,121]	11.7 [1,013]	12.9 [778]	14.1 [518]	13.9 [251
No mobility	United States	81.6** [14,295]	75.1*** [10,408]	70.8*** [7,455]	67.5*** [5,071]	64.3*** [3,052]
	Germany	82.8 [11,120]	78.1 [7,879]	75.5 [5,345]	72.4 [3,210]	70.9 [1,469]
Up 1	United States	9.5** [1,646]	13.1*** [1,768]	15.6*** [1,587]	18.1*** [1,299]	21.0*** [941]
	Germany	8.6 [1,195]	11.2 [1,161]	12.6 [933]	14.3 [650]	15.4 [332]
Up 2	United States	0.4*** [73]	0.7*** [112]	1.0*** [123]	1.1*** [100]	1.3*** [68]
	Germany	0.2 [15]	0.3 [23]	0.2 [14]	0.3 [13]	0.4 [8]

Notes:
[a] Each entry shows the number of individuals making the transition as a fraction of those eligible to make the transition (see text, p. 121). Column totals will *not* sum to 1 as a result.
*** Indicates that the US and German rates are significantly different at the 1 percent level.
** Indicates that the US and German rates are significantly different at the 5 percent level.
* Indicates that the US and German rates are significantly different at the 10 percent level.
Source: The 1989 Response–Nonresponse File of the PSID and the 1993 Syracuse University English Language Public Use File of the GSOEP.

Table 6A.11 *After-government income mobility, United States and Germany, women aged 25 to 55[a], median-based groupings (%)*

Change in group		Transition period				
		$t+1$	$t+2$	$t+3$	$t+4$	$t+5$
Down 2	United States	1.0	1.8**	2.1	2.6	3.3
		[68]	[83]	[80]	[74]	[50]
	Germany	0.8	1.0	1.9	2.7	2.7
		[16]	[17]	[15]	[12]	[6]
Down 1	United States	9.9***	12.4***	14.4***	15.0***	14.8
		[1,475]	[1,465]	[1,267]	[915]	[589]
	Germany	8.3	9.8	10.7	11.5	13.1
		[1,010]	[860]	[648]	[421]	[221]
No mobility	United States	82.1***	76.3***	71.6***	68.3***	65.0***
		[14,284]	[10,482]	[7,484]	[5,107]	[3,048]
	Germany	84.3	81.0	79.0	77.2	74.7
		[11,401]	[8,236]	[5,648]	[3,446]	[1,575]
Up 1	United States	9.5***	12.7***	15.7***	18.3***	21.6***
		[1,724]	[1,786]	[1,622]	[1,329]	[980]
	Germany	7.8	9.6	10.7	11.5	12.4
		[1,075]	[1,004]	[790]	[536]	[269]
Up 2	United States	0.3***	0.6***	0.7***	0.8***	0.9***
		[59]	[93]	[100]	[80]	[53]
	Germany	0.0	0.1	0.1	0.1	0.2
		[6]	[9]	[5]	[2]	[3]

Notes:
[a] Each entry shows the number of individuals making the transition as a fraction of those eligible to make the transition (see text, p. 121). Column totals will *not* sum to 1 as a result.
*** Indicates that the US and German rates are significantly different at the 1 percent level.
** Indicates that the US and German rates are significantly different at the 5 percent level.
Source: The 1989 Response–Nonresponse File of the PSID and the 1993 Syracuse University English Language Public Use File of the GSOEP.

Appendix B: Sensitivity analysis: calculations for individuals with labor earnings for at least one year

As noted in the text, we also compute mobility rates using a sample restricted to those individuals with labor earnings for at least one year in our time period, allowing us to isolate the contribution of the changing composition of our sample to differences in mobility computed using labor earnings, before-government income, and after-government income, respectively. This appendix contains tables analogous to tables 6.2 and 6.4–6.11 in the text (and numbered so as to facilitate direct comparison) containing estimated mobility rates using this sample.

Table 6B.2 *Labor earnings mobility, United States and Germany, individuals aged 25 to 55[a], restricted sample (%)*

Change in quintile		Transition period				
		$t+1$	$t+2$	$t+3$	$t+4$	$t+5$
Down 4	United States	1.0 [38]	1.4 [51]	2.1[***] [59]	2.7[***] [56]	2.8 [37]
	Germany	0.7 [27]	1.0 [34]	0.9 [24]	1.2 [16]	1.5 [8]
Down 3	United States	1.5 [146]	2.2 [180]	2.6 [163]	3.1 [133]	3.3 [88]
	Germany	1.3 [117]	1.9 [144]	2.4 [130]	2.8 [92]	3.4 [56]
Down 2	United States	3.0 [494]	4.3 [576]	5.1 [520]	5.7 [420]	6.2 [296]
	Germany	2.9 [420]	4.5 [472]	5.2 [372]	6.2 [272]	6.9 [134]
Down 1	United States	14.3[***] [3,423]	16.2[***] [3,076]	17.4[***] [2,532]	17.4[***] [1,824]	18.0[***] [1,171]
	Germany	12.9 [2,662]	13.3 [2,075]	14.2 [1,509]	14.2 [909]	13.3 [421]
No mobility	United States	69.3[***] [19,369]	62.9[***] [13,909]	58.3[***] [9,796]	55.8 [6,654]	52.6 [3,953]
	Germany	71.2 [16,483]	65.5 [11,247]	60.4 [7,383]	57.1 [4,364]	53.8 [1,907]

	United States	17.7[**]	20.5	22.9	24.1	25.7
		[4,038]	[3,640]	[3,030]	[2,241]	[1,511]
Up 1						
	Germany	16.5	19.6	22.7	24.4	27.4
		[3,338]	[2,992]	[2,367]	[1,594]	[835]
	United States	3.1	4.8	5.9	7.0	8.0
		[521]	[626]	[590]	[490]	[350]
Up 2						
	Germany	3.5	5.2	6.7	7.3	7.8
		[487]	[554]	[480]	[319]	[169]
	United States	1.3	2.3[*]	2.8	3.4[***]	4.1
		[127]	[178]	[169]	[151]	[114]
Up 3						
	Germany	1.6	2.8	3.3	5.2	5.4
		[127]	[169]	[153]	[141]	[80]
	United States	0.4[**]	1.0	1.2[**]	1.4[**]	1.6[***]
		[18]	[35]	[36]	[29]	[19]
Up 4						
	Germany	0.8	1.5	2.4	2.9	4.8
		[29]	[40]	[39]	[36]	[28]

Notes:

[a]   Each entry shows the number of individuals making the transition as a fraction of those eligible to make the transition (see text, p. 121). Column totals will *not* sum to 1 as a result.

[***] Indicates that the US and German rates are significantly different at the 1 percent level.

[**] Indicates that the US and German rates are significantly different at the 5 percent level.

[*]   Indicates that the US and German rates are significantly different at the 10 percent level.

Source: The 1989 Response–Nonresponse File of the PSID and the 1993 Syracuse University English Language Public Use File of the GSOEP.

Table 6B.4 *Before-government income mobility, United States and Germany, individuals aged 25 to 55[a], restricted sample (%)*

Change in quintile		Transition period				
		$t+1$	$t+2$	$t+3$	$t+4$	$t+5$
Down 4	United States	0.8 [34]	1.1** [42]	1.3*** [40]	1.5*** [31]	1.1*** [17]
	Germany	1.1 [45]	2.0 [54]	2.6 [54]	4.4 [45]	5.6 [28]
Down 3	United States	1.9 [247]	3.5 [318]	4.5 [294]	5.5 [246]	5.6 [159]
	Germany	1.8 [143]	3.4 [229]	4.8 [215]	4.5 [148]	4.5 [63]
Down 2	United States	4.3*** [753]	6.2*** [813]	7.6** [745]	8.6** [588]	9.4** [389]
	Germany	5.3 [721]	7.8 [811]	8.9 [662]	10.4 [471]	12.0 [246]
Down 1	United States	13.9*** [3,107]	15.3*** [2,730]	16.4*** [2,190]	16.4*** [1,547]	16.5 [973]
	Germany	17.8 [3,458]	18.6 [2,751]	19.2 [1,967]	18.9 [1,191]	17.8 [539]
No mobility	United States	67.7*** [19,106]	59.6*** [13,398]	53.1*** [9,170]	48.5*** [6,019]	44.7*** [3,508]
	Germany	61.5 [14,531]	53.7 [9,392]	48.0 [5,961]	44.0 [3,400]	41.5 [1,508]
Up 1	United States	17.4*** [3,816]	20.7*** [3,573]	23.5*** [3,054]	25.3*** [2,341]	26.8** [1,592]
	Germany	20.1 [3,889]	22.8 [3,390]	25.6 [2,615]	27.9 [1,745]	29.8 [858]
Up 2	United States	4.5*** [812]	7.5** [1,024]	9.7 [1,014]	12.0 [884]	14.0 [67]
	Germany	5.3 [707]	8.4 [831]	10.6 [749]	12.1 [566]	12.6 [285]

Up 3	United States	2.2**	3.5	4.6*	5.7**	6.6**
		[271]	[331]	[337]	[301]	[207]
	Germany	1.7	3.1	3.7	4.4	4.7
		[157]	[203]	[172]	[128]	[82]
Up 4	United States	0.5**	0.9***	1.4**	1.6**	1.8**
		[28]	[45]	[51]	[41]	[27]
	Germany	1.0	1.9	2.4	3.2	4.8
		[40]	[66]	[62]	[49]	[29]

Notes:
[a] Each entry shows the number of individuals making the transition as a fraction of those eligible to make the transition (see text, p. 121). Column totals will *not* sum to 1 as a result.
*** Indicates that the US and German rates are significantly different at the 1 percent level.
** Indicates that the US and German rates are significantly different at the 5 percent level.
* Indicates that the US and German rates are significantly different at the 10 percent level.
Source: The 1989 Response–Nonresponse File of the PSID and the 1993 Syracuse University English Language Public Use File of the GSOEP.

Table 6B.5 *After-government income mobility, United States and Germany, individuals aged 25 to 55[a], restricted sample (%)*

		Transition period				
Change in quintile		$t+1$	$t+2$	$t+3$	$t+4$	$t+5$
Down 4	United States	0.9** [41]	1.0** [41]	1.3*** [40]	1.6*** [34]	1.1*** [17]
	Germany	1.6 [67]	2.8 [70]	3.4 [62]	5.4 [58]	7.4 [33]
Down 3	United States	2.1** [283]	3.9 [353]	4.7 [313]	6.2 [267]	5.9 [163]
	Germany	2.8 [194]	3.8 [223]	4.8 [189]	5.2 [133]	5.3 [67]
Down 2	United States	4.2*** [760]	5.8*** [794]	7.3*** [744]	8.0** [564]	9.6 [397]
	Germany	5.0 [656]	7.5 [750]	9.1 [626]	9.5 [401]	9.0 [186]
Down 1	United States	13.4*** [3,038]	14.8*** [2,658]	15.6*** [2,097]	15.4*** [1,471]	15.2*** [899]
	Germany	18.7 [3,519]	19.4 [2,711]	19.1 [1,899]	18.7 [1,135]	19.3 [541]
No mobility	United States	68.0*** [19,043]	59.9*** [13,351]	52.6*** [9,161]	48.7*** [5,992]	44.4*** [3,486]
	Germany	59.0 [14,184]	51.7 [9,278]	46.6 [5,908]	43.9 [3,451]	40.8 [1,492]
Up 1	United States	17.3*** [3,846]	20.9*** [3,633]	23.5*** [3,085]	25.6 [2,375]	27.0 [1,600]
	Germany	21.2 [4,076]	23.7 [3,508]	26.7 [2,696]	26.8 [1,731]	28.7 [874]
Up 2	United States	4.4*** [812]	7.3*** [1,041]	9.6** [1,012]	12.1** [908]	14.9 [712]
	Germany	5.6 [765]	9.1 [899]	10.9 [827]	14.1 [651]	14.7 [337]

Up 3	United States	2.5	3.6	5.1**	6.3**	7.1
		[319]	[353]	[391]	[342]	[234]
	Germany	2.4	3.4	4.1	4.8	5.8
		[190]	[226]	[198]	[146]	[88]
Up 4	United States	0.5**	1.0**	1.4*	1.6	1.8*
		[32]	[50]	[52]	[45]	[31]
	Germany	1.1	2.0	2.2	2.3	3.4
		[40]	[62]	[52]	[37]	[20]

Notes:
a Each entry shows the number of individuals making the transition as a fraction of those eligible to make the transition (see text, p. 121). Column totals will *not* sum to 1 as a result.
*** Indicates that the US and German rates are significantly different at the 1 percent level.
** Indicates that the US and German rates are significantly different at the 5 percent level.
* Indicates that the US and German rates are significantly different at the 10 percent level.
Source: The 1989 Response–Nonresponse File of the PSID and the 1993 Syracuse University English Language Public Use File of the GSOEP.

Table 6B.6 *Labor earnings mobility, United States and Germany, men aged 25 to 55[a], restricted sample (%)*

		Transition period				
Change in quintile		$t+1$	$t+2$	$t+3$	$t+4$	$t+5$
Down 4	United States	1.4 [29]	2.4 [41]	3.1 [39]	3.2 [32]	4.3 [24]
	Germany	1.4 [33]	2.4 [43]	3.1 [33]	3.1 [19]	4.0 [10]
Down 3	United States	2.0 [86]	2.7 [96]	3.1[***] [83]	4.0 [74]	4.0 [55]
	Germany	2.0 [98]	2.3 [96]	1.7 [65]	3.0 [60]	4.5 [34]
Down 2	United States	3.8 [274]	4.8 [276]	5.7 [253]	6.0 [188]	6.4[*] [128]
	Germany	3.8 [339]	4.2 [289]	5.3 [250]	4.9 [159]	4.5 [90]
Down 1	United States	15.0 [1,545]	15.4 1,288]	15.9 [1,018]	15.3 [708]	14.9 [431]
	Germany	14.2 [1,747]	15.6 [1,431]	16.0 [1,017]	16.4 [637]	15.6 [270]
No mobility	United States	65.0 [8,457]	59.2 [6,083]	54.9 [4,267]	52.3 [2,868]	49.2 [1,704]
	Germany	66.2 [8,497]	59.9 [5,702]	55.3 [3,729]	51.1 [2,156]	47.8 [952]
Up 1	United States	20.0[**] [2,002]	23.5[***] [1,834]	25.4[**] [1,504]	27.7 [1,154]	29.1 [761]
	Germany	18.4 [2,142]	21.0 [1,799]	23.4 [1,380]	26.0 [940]	28.4 [474]
Up 2	United States	4.5 [330]	6.4[**] [370]	8.0[*] [353]	9.0 [283]	11.0 [215]
	Germany	5.2 [431]	7.7 [483]	9.5 [393]	9.9 [259]	11.3 [143]

Up 3	United States	1.8*	2.4***	3.1***	3.7***	4.6**
		[75]	[88]	[94]	[83]	[58]
	Germany	2.5	4.4	5.8	7.7	8.5
		[116]	[140]	[129]	[100]	[55]
Up 4	United States	1.0	2.1	3.1	3.0*	3.3**
		[27]	[39]	[42]	[29]	[23]
	Germany	1.5	2.4	3.2	5.6	7.7
		[32]	[40]	[40]	[41]	[27]

Notes:
a   Each entry shows the number of individuals making the transition as a fraction of those eligible to make the transition (see text, p. 121). Column totals will *not* sum to 1 as a result.
*** Indicates that the US and German rates are significantly different at the 1 percent level.
** Indicates that the US and German rates are significantly different at the 5 percent level.
* Indicates that the US and German rates are significantly different at the 10 percent level.
Source: The 1989 Response–Nonresponse File of the PSID and the 1993 Syracuse University English Language Public Use File of the GSOEP.

Table 6B.7 *Before-government income mobility, United States and Germany, men aged 25 to 55[a], restricted sample (%)*

Change in quintile		Transition period				
		$t+1$	$t+2$	$t+3$	$t+4$	$t+5$
Down 4	United States	1.0	1.5	1.6	1.8	1.9
		[23]	[25]	[21]	[17]	[11]
	Germany	0.7	1.3	1.8	2.3	3.4
		[19]	[27]	[26]	[20]	[13]
Down 3	United States	3.0***	4.6**	6.3*	7.5***	7.1
		[171]	[199]	[184]	[147]	[91]
	Germany	1.9	3.3	4.8	4.5	5.2
		[85]	[130]	[127]	[82]	[39]
Down 2	United States	4.5*	6.8	8.4	9.5	10.2
		[373]	[414]	[387]	[312]	[207]
	Germany	5.2	7.7	8.9	10.0	12.4
		[411]	[449]	[371]	[265]	[142]
Down 1	United States	14.6***	15.1***	16.2***	15.6***	16.1
		[1,521]	[1,273]	[992]	[668]	[423]
	Germany	18.4	19.1	19.1	19.7	18.4
		[2,002]	[1,618]	[1,131]	[699]	[317]
No mobility	United States	65.7***	58.3***	51.2**	47.2**	43.7
		[8,312]	[5,822]	[3,940]	[2,595]	[1,520]
	Germany	61.0	54.0	49.1	44.7	40.8
		[8,217]	[5,310]	[3,445]	[1,962]	[855]
Up 1	United States	17.6***	20.7*	23.5	25.0*	26.0**
		[1,815]	[1,675]	[1,425]	[1,071]	[708]
	Germany	20.0	22.1	24.4	27.1	29.9
		[2,187]	[1,874]	[1,398]	[942]	[478]
Up 2	United States	4.9	7.5	10.2	12.5	14.9
		[410]	[486]	[477]	[421]	[321]
	Germany	5.4	8.5	10.7	11.9	13.0
		[404]	[468]	[411]	[304]	[154]

	United States	3.1^{***}	4.5^{**}	5.8^{***}	7.2^{***}	7.3^{**}
		[180]	[193]	[197]	[169]	[105]
Up 3						
	Germany	1.8	3.3	3.7	4.5	4.5
		[87]	[110]	[90]	[68]	[42]
	United States	0.8	1.2	1.8	1.3^{**}	1.6^{*}
		[20]	[28]	[30]	[19]	[13]
Up 4						
	Germany	1.2	2.1	2.5	3.4	4.7
		[23]	[37]	[37]	[29]	[15]

Notes:

a   Each entry shows the number of individuals making the transition as a fraction of those eligible to make the transition (see text, p. 121). Column totals will *not* sum to 1 as a result.

*** Indicates that the US and German rates are significantly different at the 1 percent level.

** Indicates that the US and German rates are significantly different at the 5 percent level.

* Indicates that the US and German rates are significantly different at the 10 percent level.

Source: The 1989 Response–Nonresponse File of the PSID and the 1993 Syracuse University English Language Public Use File of the GSOEP.

Table 6B.8 *After-government income mobility, United States and Germany, men aged 25 to 55[a], restricted sample (%)*

Change in quintile		Transition period				
		$t+1$	$t+2$	$t+3$	$t+4$	$t+5$
Down 4	United States	1.1 [25]	1.3** [25]	1.4*** [19]	1.6*** [19]	1.3*** [10]
	Germany	1.3 [34]	2.7 [39]	3.5 [37]	4.8 [32]	6.4 [19]
Down 3	United States	3.1 [181]	5.5*** [224]	7.0*** [201]	8.4*** [159]	8.0* [97]
	Germany	2.8 [109]	3.7 [117]	4.7 [106]	4.4 [74]	5.3 [39]
Down 2	United States	4.3 [367]	5.8*** [382]	8.1 [388]	8.6 [292]	10.3 [207]
	Germany	4.9 [368]	7.5 [421]	8.8 [355]	9.9 [233]	9.3 [107]
Down 1	United States	14.1*** [1,487]	14.8*** [1,256]	15.4*** [949]	14.9*** [651]	15.3*** [411]
	Germany	18.7 [1,973]	19.4 [1,536]	19.4 [1,085]	18.6 [652]	20.0 [315]
No mobility	United States	66.6*** [8,357]	59.1*** [5,850]	51.7*** [3,958]	47.9** [2,605]	43.2 [1,496]
	Germany	59.7 [8,177]	52.4 [5,353]	47.6 [3,434]	44.7 [1,984]	41.6 [870]
Up 1	United States	17.2*** [1,787]	20.4*** [1,648]	23.2** [1,407]	24.8* [1,076]	26.4 [724]
	Germany	20.7 [2,212]	23.3 [1,905]	25.8 [1,437]	27.0 [948]	27.8 [472]
Up 2	United States	4.7** [407]	7.4** [493]	10.2 [492]	11.8 [403]	14.7 [317]
	Germany	5.7 [447]	8.8 [504]	10.8 [452]	13.1 [349]	13.9 [174]

	United States	3.2***	4.8***	6.4***	8.5***	8.8**
		[190]	[208]	[208]	[191]	[123]
Up 3						
	Germany	2.0	3.2	3.7	4.5	5.7
		[92]	[113]	[102]	[78]	[47]
	United States	1.0	1.3*	1.8	1.5	1.6
		[24]	[29]	[31]	[23]	[14]
Up 4						
	Germany	1.3	2.3	2.2	2.6	3.7
		[23]	[35]	[28]	[21]	[12]

Notes:
[a] Each entry shows the number of individuals making the transition as a fraction of those eligible to make the transition (see text, p. 121). Column totals will *not* sum to 1 as a result.
*** Indicates that the US and German rates are significantly different at the 1 percent level.
** Indicates that the US and German rates are significantly different at the 5 percent level.
* Indicates that the US and German rates are significantly different at the 10 percent level.
Source: The 1989 Response–Nonresponse File of the PSID and the 1993 Syracuse University English Language Public Use File of the GSOEP.

Table 6B.9 *Labor earnings mobility, United States and Germany, women aged 25 to 55[a], restricted sample (%)*

Change in quintile		Transition period				
		$t+1$	$t+2$	$t+3$	$t+4$	$t+5$
Down 4	United States	1.1 [24]	2.5 [45]	3.8 [54]	4.1[*] [43]	3.8[**] [22]
	Germany	1.7 [26]	3.7 [49]	5.3 [51]	6.8 [40]	8.8 [23]
Down 3	United States	1.9 [101]	2.9[***] [134]	4.1[***] [133]	5.6[*] [129]	7.6 [111]
	Germany	2.5 [102]	5.1 [162]	6.7 [149]	7.7 [108]	9.0 [56]
Down 2	United States	4.1[**] [381]	6.5 [468]	7.6 [432]	8.2[*] [342]	8.5 [229]
	Germany	5.2 [321]	6.7 [317]	8.2 [251]	10.0 [171]	8.8 [91]
Down 1	United States	16.0[***] [2,094]	18.4[***] [1,937]	19.5[***] [1,564]	21.0[***] [1,211]	20.8[***] [762]
	Germany	13.9 [1,169]	14.7 [911]	15.1 [661]	14.1 [394]	15.7 [189]
No mobility	United States	66.3 [10,080]	57.9[*] [6,968]	52.9 [4,864]	48.4 [3,163]	45.8 [1,898]
	Germany	66.9 [6,789]	59.5 [4,472]	52.8 [2,812]	49.8 [1,622]	44.6 [661]
Up 1	United States	18.2 [2,220]	20.6 [2,022]	22.5 [1,623]	23.5 [1,190]	24.1 [765]
	Germany	17.2 [1,465]	19.8 [1,298]	23.0 [1,028]	24.2 [693]	26.8 [375]
Up 2	United States	3.9[*] [349]	6.2[*] [426]	7.3[***] [393]	9.0[*] [343]	10.5[*] [237]
	Germany	4.7 [283]	7.2 [345]	9.7 [331]	11.1 [242]	13.7 [130]

Up 3	United States	1.3**	3.3	4.7	5.2	6.1
		[80]	[145]	[143]	[117]	[90]
	Germany	2.0	4.1	4.5	5.0	5.9
		[86]	[122]	[109]	[78]	[45]
Up 4	United States	0.7	1.5	2.0	3.2	3.7
		[20]	[34]	[36]	[41]	[26]
	Germany	1.1	1.6	2.6	3.4	2.2
		[15]	[28]	[29]	[24]	[13]

Notes:
[a] Each entry shows the number of individuals making the transition as a fraction of those eligible to make the transition (see text, p. 121). Column totals will *not* sum to 1 as a result.
*** Indicates that the US and German rates are significantly different at the 1 percent level.
** Indicates that the US and German rates are significantly different at the 5 percent level.
* Indicates that the US and German rates are significantly different at the 10 percent level.
Source: The 1989 Response–Nonresponse File of the PSID and the 1993 Syracuse University English Language Public Use File of the GSOEP.

Table 6B.10 *Before-government income mobility, United States and Germany, women aged 25 to 55[a], restricted sample (%)*

Change in quintile		Transition period				
		$t+1$	$t+2$	$t+3$	$t+4$	$t+5$
Down 4	United States	0.6**	0.9***	1.3***	1.7***	1.2***
		[14]	[18]	[22]	[16]	[8]
	Germany	1.6	2.6	3.6	7.0	7.7
		[24]	[27]	[26]	[24]	[13]
Down 3	United States	1.6	3.0	3.0**	4.0	4.2
		[106]	[140]	[115]	[105]	[67]
	Germany	1.5	3.7	4.9	5.1	4.8
		[57]	[101]	[97]	[67]	[28]
Down 2	United States	3.6***	5.2***	6.7***	7.0***	8.1**
		[344]	[384]	[359]	[263]	[182]
	Germany	5.6	8.0	9.2	10.1	11.2
		[319]	[363]	[292]	[203]	[104]
Down 1	United States	13.6***	15.6***	17.0	17.2	17.4
		[1,652]	[1,487]	[1,204]	[875]	[546]
	Germany	17.1	17.7	18.4	18.2	17.6
		[1,457]	[1,147]	[822]	[489]	[221]
No mobility	United States	69.1***	60.5***	54.4***	49.9***	45.8***
		[10,654]	[7,467]	[5,168]	[3,410]	[1,993]
	Germany	62.1	53.6	47.1	43.3	40.7
		[6,289]	[4,038]	[2,533]	[1,453]	[635]
Up 1	United States	17.2***	20.6***	23.3***	25.0***	26.2**
		[2,056]	[1,964]	[1,665]	[1,281]	[849]
	Germany	19.7	23.7	27.4	29.1	30.7
		[1,722]	[1,552]	[1,215]	[800]	[395]
Up 2	United States	4.2**	7.4	9.5	11.6	13.8
		[406]	[537]	[525]	[455]	[362]
	Germany	5.4	7.8	9.7	11.6	12.1
		[299]	[351]	[325]	[256]	[138]

	United States	1.6	2.8	3.9	4.9	6.3
		[107]	[144]	[161]	[149]	[113]
Up 3						
	Germany	1.6	3.3	4.2	4.7	5.5
		[72]	[95]	[87]	[62]	[36]
	United States	0.4	0.7**	1.1*	1.7	2.6
		[10]	[18]	[23]	[25]	[20]
Up 4						
	Germany	0.9	1.8	2.3	2.8	4.8
		[17]	[30]	[24]	[18]	[13]

Notes:
a   Each entry shows the number of individuals making the transition as a fraction of those eligible to make the transition (see text, p. 121). Column totals will *not* sum to 1 as a result.
***   Indicates that the US and German rates are significantly different at the 1 percent level.
**   Indicates that the US and German rates are significantly different at the 5 percent level.
*   Indicates that the US and German rates are significantly different at the 10 percent level.
Source: The 1989 Response–Nonresponse File of the PSID and the 1993 Syracuse University English Language Public Use File of the GSOEP.

Table 6B.11 *After-government income mobility, United States and Germany, women aged 25 to 55[a], restricted sample (%)*

Change in quintile		$t+1$	$t+2$	$t+3$	$t+4$	$t+5$
				Transition period		
Down 4	United States	0.6***	0.9***	1.3**	1.3***	1.6***
		[17]	[22]	[25]	[16]	[10]
	Germany	1.9	2.8	2.9	6.2	8.1
		[33]	[31]	[24]	[25]	[14]
Down 3	United States	1.7**	2.8*	3.2**	4.9	4.2
		[112]	[132]	[114]	[116]	[66]
	Germany	2.5	3.9	5.2	5.8	6.0
		[83]	[102]	[85]	[58]	[30]
Down 2	United States	3.5**	5.2***	6.4***	6.4***	7.7
		[333]	[391]	[357]	[251]	[173]
	Germany	5.3	8.0	8.9	9.3	8.6
		[297]	[333]	[256]	[174]	[75]
Down 1	United States	13.1***	14.8***	15.5***	15.8**	16.3
		[1,622]	[1,413]	[1,132]	[807]	[510]
	Germany	18.5	19.3	19.9	18.8	17.7
		[1,509]	[1,187]	[871]	[482]	[227]
No mobility	United States	69.6***	61.2***	55.5***	50.8***	45.6***
		[10,668]	[7,521]	[5,207]	[3,445]	[1,990]
	Germany	58.8	50.5	44.8	43.0	40.5
		[6,060]	[3,921]	[2,433]	[1,469]	[624]
Up 1	United States	17.1***	20.8***	23.3***	25.1	27.1
		[2,061]	[1,965]	[1,672]	[1,284]	[868]
	Germany	21.6	24.4	27.4	26.8	29.5
		[1,839]	[1,585]	[1,248]	[780]	[403]
Up 2	United States	4.1**	7.2***	9.4**	11.6**	14.4
		[404]	[537]	[534]	[464]	[382]
	Germany	5.3	9.5	11.4	14.6	15.6
		[320]	[403]	[382]	[297]	[160]

Up 3	United States	1.7***	2.9*	4.1	5.7	6.7
		[121]	[158]	[177]	[173]	[123]
	Germany	2.9	3.9	5.0	5.5	6.0
		[100]	[121]	[100]	[71]	[42]
Up 4	United States	0.4	0.8	1.1	1.3	2.0
		[11]	[20]	[24]	[23]	[18]
	Germany	0.8	1.3	1.9	1.9	2.9
		[15]	[21]	[22]	[16]	[8]

Notes:
a   Each entry shows the number of individuals making the transition as a fraction of those eligible to make the transition (see text, p. 121). Column totals will *not* sum to 1 as a result.
***   Indicates that the US and German rates are significantly different at the 1 percent level.
**   Indicates that the US and German rates are significantly different at the 5 percent level.
*   Indicates that the US and German rates are significantly different at the 10 percent level.
Source: The 1989 Response–Nonresponse File of the PSID and the 1993 Syracuse University English Language Public Use File of the GSOEP.

Notes

We are grateful to Martha Bonney, Esther Gray, and Ann Wicks for preparing the manuscript. Burkhauser's research was funded by the US National Institute on Aging, Program Project 1-PO1-AG09743-01, "The Well-Being of the Elderly in a Comparative Context." This program is the result of a collaborative effort between Syracuse University and Deutsches Institut für Wirtschaftsforschung, Berlin (DIW) to make the German Socio-Economic Panel available to English-speaking researchers.
1   As developed further below, in our discussions of labor earnings inequality or mobility, we look at individual labor earnings. In our discussion of income inequality or mobility we assume that household income is shared equally and assign each individual an equivalence scale-adjusted share of household income. In this discussion we use the generic term "income" for simplicity only.
2   See Moffitt and Gottschalk (1993) for a discussion of this point.
3   As with labor earnings, the GSOEP does not contain a detailed set of annual income measures. Burkhauser, Butrica and Daly (1995) discuss a constructed

annual household income measure created at Syracuse in conjunction with the DIW that enables researchers to compare annual household income in Germany with annual household income in the United States.

4   The tax burden for households in the GSOEP was computed using tax calculation routines created by Johannes Schwarze of the Deutsches Institut für Wirtschaftsforschung. A detailed discussion of the simulations is found in Schwarze (1995). For the United States we used the tax routine provided in the PSID data. Tax-adjusted values for both these data sets are available on the Syracuse University PSID and GSOEP Equivalent Data File. See Burkhauser, Butrica and Daly (1995) for a detailed discussion of these data.

5   We include food stamps, which are widely accepted as a "near-cash" transfer. We do not include the value of in-kind transfer (e.g. public health insurance) due to data limitations and because of the difficulties in determining their cash-equivalent value to recipients.

6   Jenkins (1991) makes a strong case for studying the within-family distribution of income. Lazear and Michael (1988) attempt to do so with respect to adults and children in a given family, but such an attempt is beyond the scope of this chapter. Finally, in both countries we determine household status and size on an annual basis: hence, while the composition of the household may change we are able to follow individuals as long as they remain in the sample. Unfortunately, in years in which the composition in the household changes we match only the income of those in the household at the time of the survey.

7   This is the most commonly used equivalence scale in the United States. It was originally based on food need standards adjusted for household composition. See Burkhauser et al. (1990) for a discussion of the sensitivity of US–German comparisons of economic well-being estimates.

8   The treatment of individuals who have zero labor earnings in a given year has varied in the literature. Lillard and Willis (1978) include only those individuals who report positive hours and earnings in each of the years they consider. Abowd and Card (1989) also delete individuals who did not have positive earnings and hours for each year under consideration.

9   The few negative values of household income we find in the data are set to zero.

10 Another sample issue is the inclusion or exclusion of the low income (Survey of Economic Opportunity) subsample in the PSID and the subsample of foreign workers in the GSOEP. In the text, we include both subsamples. We have reproduced our analyses excluding these workers, with little effect on the character of our conclusions.

11 As discussed above, we could further restrict the sample to only those individuals who appear in all years. To provide as broad a characterization of labor market dynamics as possible, we include all workers for each year, leading to different sample sizes in each year.

12 We restrict our sample to respondents and spouses in the PSID data because the PSID collects wage information only on these household members. The

GSOEP collects wage information on all household members aged 16 and over, but because we focus only on those aged 25 to 55 this difference in the surveys is not important.

13 In constructing these cross-sectional analyses, we weighted the data using the appropriate year-specific individual weight, making our samples representative of the working-age populations of the United States and Germany.

14 Because both the samples and the people in the quintiles are different, we are comparing quintile averages, not individuals in this table.

15 After-government income is based on actual income data from the PSID and the GSOEP. In contrast, before-government income is a "counterfactual" which makes the strong assumption that behavior does not change in the absence of government. This is clearly only an approximation of what would actually occur. Our before-government values are best thought of as a means of providing a baseline to show to whom current benefits go, given current government policy, rather than a measure of what would actually occur in the absence of government.

16 Because our main interest is in comparing mobility in the United States and Germany, we are limited to the years 1983 to 1988 for which the GSOEP data is available (and prior to the German reunification). Our goal in presenting cross-sectional results is to provide a familiar setting for our mobility analyses. The cross-sectional results will differ depending upon the specific time period and characteristics of the sample. It is now well established that labor earnings inequality in the United States has been growing since the 1970s. See Karoly (1993), Goldin and Margo (1992), and Burkhauser and Poupore (1997). Our cross-sectional results for labor earnings are similar to the ones found in Karoly (1993) for this period.

17 It is possible to compute transition probabilities that differ by year. Thus, one could identify, for example, changes in the one-year transition probabilities through time. Given our focus on cross-national features of mobility, we choose instead to concentrate on average transition probabilities computed using all the years available in our data.

18 In each example, macroeconomic shocks that are common to all individuals will have no impact on transition probabilities.

19 Another possible scheme is to group individuals on the basis of the percentage change in their labor earnings. Our desire to capture mobility between zero and non-zero earnings makes such a scheme impractical.

20 Appendix A contains a complete set of tables using this grouping scheme for each distribution in the text.

21 As displayed in appendix A, switching to our median income-based definition of "low," "medium," and "high" income individuals, measured immobility rises more in Germany than in the United States, with a corresponding increase in measured mobility in the United States. However, our conclusions with respect to the role of government are not affected; the patterns for before-government income and after-government income remain quite close to one another.

22 Appendix B contains a complete set of the results for the tables in the text using this restricted sample.
23 Burkhauser and Poupore (1997) reach the same conclusions using a parametric measure of the income distribution.

References

Abowd, J.M. and D. Card, 1989. "On the covariance structure of earnings and hours changes," *Econometrica*, 57, 411–45
Abraham, K. and S.N. Hauseman, 1993. *Job Security in America: Lessons from Germany*, Washington, DC: Brookings Institution
    1995. "Does employment protection inhibit labor market flexibility? Lessons from Germany, France, and Belgium," in R. Blank (ed.), *Social Protection versus Economic Flexibility*, Chicago: University of Chicago Press, 59–94
Atkinson, A., L. Rainwater and T.M. Smeeding, 1994. *Income Distribution in OECD Countries: The Evidence from the Luxembourg Income Study (LIS)*, Paris: OECD
Buhman, B., L. Rainwater, G. Schmaus and T.M. Smeeding, 1988. "Equivalence scales, well-being, inequality, and poverty: sensitivity estimates across ten countries using the Luxembourg Income Study (LIS) database," *Review of Income and Wealth*, 34, 115–42
Burkhauser, R.V. and J. Poupore, 1997. "A cross-national comparison of permanent inequality in the United States and Germany," *Review of Economics and Statistics*, 79, 10–17
Burkhauser, R.V., B.A. Butrica and M.C. Daly, 1995. "The Syracuse University PSID–GSOEP equivalent data file: a product of cross-national research," Cross-National Studies in Aging Program Policy Project paper 26, All-University Gerontology Center, The Maxwell School, Syracuse, NY: Syracuse University
Burkhauser, R.V., D. Holtz-Eakin and S.E. Rhody, 1995. "Labor earnings mobility and inequality in the United States and Germany during the 1980s," Syracuse University, mimeo
Burkhauser, R.V., G.J. Duncan, R. Hauser and R. Berntsen, 1990. "Economic burdens of marital disruptions: a comparison of the United States and the Federal Republic of Germany," *Review of Income and Wealth*, 36, 319–33
Duncan, G.J., T.M. Smeeding and W. Rogers, 1993. "W(h)ither the middle class: a dynamic view," in D. Papadimitriou and E. Wolff (eds.), *Economic Inequality at the Close of the 20th century*, New York: Macmillan, 240–71
Goldin, C. and R.A. Margo, 1992. "The current comparison: the wage structure in the United States at mid-century," *Quarterly Journal of Economics*, 107, 1–34
Gottschalk, P., 1993. "Changes in inequality of family income in seven industrialized countries," *American Economic Review, Papers and Proceedings*, 83, 136–42

Hill, M.S., 1992. *The Panel Study of Income Dynamics: A User's Guide*, Beverly Hills: Sage

Jenkins, S.P. 1991. "Poverty measurement and the within-household distribution: Agenda for Action," *Journal of Social Policy*, 20, 457–83

Karoly, L., 1993. "The trend in inequality among families, individuals, and workers in the United States: a twenty-five year perspective," in S. Danziger and P. Gottschalk (eds.), *Uneven Tides: Rising Inequality in America*, New York: Russell Sage Foundation, 19–98

Lazear, E.P. and R.T. Michael, 1988. *Allocation of Income within the Household*, Chicago and London: University of Chicago Press

Levy, F. and R.J. Murnane 1992. "US earnings levels and earnings inequality: a review of recent trends and proposed explanations," *Journal of Economic Literature*, 30, 1333–81

Lillard, L.A. and R.J. Willis, 1978. "Dynamic aspects of earning mobility," *Econometrica*, 46, 985–1012

Moffitt, R. and P. Gottschalk, 1993. "Trends in the covariance structure of earnings in the United States: 1969–1987," Department of Economics, Boston College, unpublished paper

Moon, M. and E. Smolensky (eds.), 1977. *Improving Measures of Economic Well-being*, New York: Academic Press

OECD, 1990. *Economic Outlook*, 48, Paris: OECD

Schwarze, J., 1995. "Simulating German income and social security tax payments using the GSOEP," Cross-National Studies in Aging Program Policy Project paper, 19, All-University Gerontology Center, The Maxwell School, Syracuse, NY: Syracuse University

Wagner, G.G., R.V. Burkhauser and F. Behringer, 1993. "The English language public use file of the German Socio-Economic Panel," *Journal of Human Resources*, 28, 413–15

Part II
Subjective approaches to welfare measurement

7 Poverty perceptions and the poverty line

Yoram Amiel and Frank Cowell

Introduction

This chapter is about the appropriateness or otherwise of assumptions that are commonly made in the field of poverty analysis. Much of the substantial literature on the topic – see Foster (1984), Hagenaars (1986), Ravallion (1994) and Seidl (1988) for surveys – assumes a given poverty line, although there are some important contributions that investigate the relationship between the line and measured poverty. This relationship is complicated because of the heterogeneity of the poor, because criteria for the determination of the poverty line – and for changes in the line – are a matter for debate and because the axioms that have been suggested for the purpose of poverty comparisons are varied and sometimes mutually contradictory (Kundu and Smith, 1983). This chapter investigates the effect of changing the poverty line upon perceptions of poverty and on poverty comparisons. We address issues such as whether poverty is related to individual perceptions of basic needs or to the general level of incomes in the community. To do this we use an application of techniques pioneered in the field of inequality analysis.

This is not an attempt to undermine the standard abstract approach to the ranking of income distributions by poverty, nor an attempt to provide a single "correct" answer to the difficult question of how poverty comparisons should be linked to the poverty line – if that were possible. Nor is it a test to examine which of a set of standard poverty measures people use when making judgments about income distributions. Rather, it is a suggestion for a systematic method of appraising the relative merits of formal axioms that give meaning to the concept of "poverty" in the presence of competing claims for attention of alternative intellectual approaches. It is also a first experiment to illustrate the extent to which views of non-specialist observers of poverty conform with assumptions about the structure of poverty comparisons. In many respects knowledge of the way in which poverty comparisons are perceived is a valuable adjunct to the analytical tools which economic theory has provided for the systematic study of poverty.

The issues

The poverty line obviously plays a central role in the definition of poverty. Sen (1979) has made the distinction between the "identification problem" and the "aggregation problem" as components of the general poverty measurement issue. The identification problem is that of determining a rule for labeling persons as "poor" or "non-poor"; the aggregation problem is that of using the information about those labeled as "poor" to derive an overall index of poverty. We might go further and subdivide the identification problem into two components, the partition problem and the observation problem. The partition problem is essentially the job for which the poverty line is introduced: a particular classification system according to some scalar is used to label persons or families as either "poor" or "non-poor" in principle; it encapsulates the question: "does the criterion for sorting of individuals into poor and non-poor make sense *in principle*?" The observation problem is that of determining whether or not a particular person or family meets the criterion.

Although the two principal components of poverty measurement – the identification problem and the aggregation problem – are logically distinct, there are obviously ways in which they interact. For example, increasing general prosperity may also affect the evaluation of rankings by poverty of the proportion of the population that falls below any given poverty line, or alternative poverty lines may be associated with different subjective views about the meaning of poverty, and therefore with different judgments about poverty comparisons. The present chapter focuses upon the interaction between these two main components of poverty analysis.

It is useful to categorize approaches to the poverty line and its relationship with the income distribution in two broad groups, the statistical and the absolutist. Each of these two broad categories has economically interesting subcategories which we shall not pursue in detail here. We assume that an individual's poverty status is completely determined by a well defined scalar x which we will call "income" (in practice, this could be a measure of consumption expenditure, or the quantity of some particular commodity), and that an individual is deemed to be in poverty if his or her income falls below a specified income level z.

The statistical approach to the poverty line can then be expressed as

$$z = \phi(F) \tag{7.1}$$

where ϕ is a functional and F is the distribution function of income. This concept can be further refined by specifying the distribution functions for different specific subgroups so as to generate different poverty lines z for each subgroup. This approach has been explicitly adopted by some governmental and statistical bodies (such as Eurostat) in the absence of a generally recognized poverty line introduced on the basis of external criteria, and it is implicit in some presentations of income distribution statistics (see, for example, DSS, 1992, 1993).

By contrast the absolutist approach can be represented as

$$z = \psi(u^*) \tag{7.2}$$

where u^* is a specified target level of individual welfare and ψ is an inverse utility function giving the money income required to attain a particular welfare level.

The distinction between the two approaches is not in terms of whether or not they take account of income growth: there is no reason to suppose that (7.2) yields poverty comparisons that are independent of scale transformations of income and, as Sen (1983) has pointed out, the absolutist approach does not imply fixity of the poverty line: the number u^* could be a function of all sorts of things that are correlated with mean living standards. It will be shown below that the distinction between the statistical and the absolutist approach is actually perceived to be quite a subtle one.

The approach

During 1992 we carried out a number of questionnaire studies on various issues concerning the measurement of poverty. For this chapter we employed a separate questionnaire from the one used for our companion study (Amiel and Cowell, 1994b) in which we investigated views about poverty conditional upon a fixed poverty line. However the general design of the two studies was similar and built upon the techniques outlined in Amiel and Cowell (1992) and used in the case of economic welfare in Amiel and Cowell (1994a). The questionnaire is reproduced in the appendix (p. 190), and the main features of the approach are as follows:

- 340 students from eight institutions[1] in six countries were asked to complete a short anonymous questionnaire that asked about their attitudes to poverty comparisons.
- The questionnaire was completed during class/lecture time so as to ensure a high response rate.

- The questionnaire consisted of two main sections which focused on the same issues: the first section presented these issues in the form of numerical examples, and the second in terms of verbal questions and lists of alternative replies from which the respondent was invited to select the view that corresponded most closely to his or her own.
- Respondents were also invited to indicate any desire to change their answers to the numerical problems once they had considered the verbal part of the questionnaire. This device is to offset the possibility that inappropriate answers to the numerical part were made through carelessness: no hints or clues were provided to the respondents about how a poverty line should be specified or about the way in which information about the poor might be aggregated into a poverty index.

Results

The presentation of the results follows the form of the questionnaire with which the respondents were presented. As in previous questionnaire studies we examined each issue both in terms of the respondents' assessments of simple numerical examples and of their answers to multiple-choice verbal questions, so we have matched the responses to the numerical and verbal questions on each issue and provided a cross-tabulation. The tables giving the results for each question in isolation have been broken down into subsamples by institution; the two-way tables cross-tabulating the responses to the verbal and numerical questions were in every case formed from the results for all students in the sample. Where appropriate, the results corresponding to the "standard" response have been highlighted in bold.

In Questions 1 and 4 respondents were asked to judge the two situations in which there was the same vector of personal incomes x, but two different "basic needs" income levels; the respondents were not prompted as to whether a specified basic needs level corresponds to a poverty line z. The left-hand side of table 7.1 (responses to Question 1) reveals that whilst a majority of respondents agrees that the higher basic needs level implies higher poverty there is a substantial dissenting minority who appear to think that changing the basic needs level should not affect measured poverty. The responses to Question 4 (right-hand side of table 7.1) throw some light on this: here, respondents were asked directly whether a higher basic needs income level implies, *ceteris paribus*, higher poverty. The Polish students seem to be sure that it does; the LSE and Ruppin respondents have substantial doubts. Where respondents had doubts they were expressed in terms of the "neither of the above"

Table 7.1 *Change (increase) of poverty line*

Institute	N	Numerical (Q1)			Verbal (Q4)		
		Agree: poverty increases (%)	Disagree 1: poverty decreases (%)	Disagree 2: poverty the same (%)	Agree: poverty increases (%)	Disagree 1: basic needs irrelevant (%)	Disagree 2: "neither" (%)
Alabama	80	**50**	10	39	**59**	15	26
LSE	34	**68**	3	27	**53**	21	26
Koblenz	31	**42**	6	52	**71**	13	16
Warsaw	34	**68**	6	26	**82**	9	9
SMU	19	**63**	11	26	**74**	16	10
TA Sociology	43	**61**	12	26	**70**	12	18
Ruppin	64	**72**	9	16	**55**	11	34
ANU	35	**60**	9	29	**66**	14	20
All	*340*	*60*	*9*	*30*	*64*	*13*	*23*

	Verbal (Q4)			
Numerical (Q1)	Agree (%)	Disagree 1 (%)	Disagree 2 (%)	All (%)
Agree	44	5	10	60
Disagree 1	4	1	4	9
Disagree 2	15	6	8	30
All	*64*	*13*	*23*	*100*

responses, which may indicate that more information would be required before an explicit judgment could be offered.[2]

The question arises as to why people might say that increasing the poverty line does not change poverty. Presumably the answer is that respondents are looking at poverty in some kind of absolutist or existentialist terms; in other words judgments on poverty are perceived as separate from the administration that happens to measure poverty and to announce the poverty line. According to this view, raising the poverty line is a mere artifact of official policy or of social convention that has little bearing upon the reality of the human condition. On this evidence alone it may be the case that some people view poverty in statistical terms, and they do not read poverty along the lines of the "basic needs" view;[3] but we have more to say on this below.

As a final point on the responses to the matched Questions 1 and 4, notice that there is little difference between the cross-section numerical and the verbal responses, although if we consider the responses together only 44 percent of the sample agree both numerically and verbally with the proposition that a higher basic needs level implies higher poverty.

Now consider what happens to poverty if all income values are scaled up. In Question 2 distribution B had an x-vector that was exactly double that of distribution A, and an implied z value that was also double that of A; Question 5 puts the issue in words. The results are reported in table 7.2.

In the numerical version of Question 2 (left-side of table 7.2) nearly half the respondents felt that a simple doubling of all incomes and the basic needs level left measured poverty unchanged; but there is a substantial minority view that poverty decreases (for the German, Polish, and Australian respondents, this view is in the majority). From the verbal responses to Question 5 in table 7.2 (right-hand side) it appears that the reported responses come more into line with what may be considered as the "conventional" view, in that the dissenting minority (those who think that doubling both incomes and basic needs will lead to a fall in poverty) becomes smaller when the issue is put in terms of words: see the breakdown at the bottom of table 7.2. However, note also from table 7.2 that "Disagree 3" (the view that whether poverty has gone up or not must depend on the income level) receives almost as much support as the dissenting minority view that poverty must fall.

Again, as with the results on Questions 1 and 4, it is tempting to characterize the majority view support for the "Eurostat" view of the poverty line, whereby poverty is viewed in terms of a relationship such as (7.1) but, as argued below, this conclusion may not be legitimate.

The final numerical experiment is to consider two income vectors and

Table 7.2 Double incomes and poverty line

		Numerical (Q2)			Verbal (Q5)			
Institute	N	Agree: poverty the same (%)	Disagree 1: poverty decreases (%)	Disagree 2: poverty increases (%)	(C) Agree: poverty the same (%)	(B) Disagree 1: poverty decreases (%)	(A) Disagree 2: poverty increases (%)	Disagree 3: depends (%)
Alabama	80	**43**	41	16	**71**	8	6	15
LSE	34	**53**	38	6	**71**	15	6	9
Koblenz	31	**32**	65	3	**55**	26	13	6
Warsaw	34	**29**	41	21	**53**	26	9	12
SMU	19	**47**	37	16	**74**	21	0	5
TA Sociology	43	**61**	28	9	**84**	2	5	9
Ruppin	64	**66**	17	16	**58**	19	12	11
ANU	35	**43**	51	6	**57**	9	3	31
All	*340*	**48**	*38*	*12*	**66**	*14*	*7*	*13*

Numerical (Q2)	Verbal (Q5)				
	Agree (%)	Disagree 1 (%)	Disagree 2 (%)	Disagree 3 (%)	All
Agree	36	4	2	6	48
Disagree 1	21	8	3	6	38
Disagree 2	7	2	1	1	12
All	*66*	*14*	*7*	*13*	*100*

basic needs levels that differ in terms of some absolute amount. Economic intuition does not provide an unambiguous suggestion as to the impact of such a shift on poverty: if $10 is added to basic needs and you give the $10 to each poor person, each poor person remains poor but has a higher percentage of total income; if the $10 were also given to each non-poor person this might be considered to be irrelevant from the point of view of the perception of poverty.

The issue addressed in Question 3 and in the two parts of Question 6 (call the second part Question 6') are related to the concept of monotonicity, which in its pure form is considered in the study reported in Amiel and Cowell (1994b). The verbal responses to Questions 6 and 6' are reassuringly consistent (table 7.3 and table 7.4); but they do not appear to be consistent with the corresponding numerical Question 3. In this case eleven respondents announced a change of mind about their response to the numerical Question 3, so it does not seem that misperception or misunderstanding of the question accounts for the discrepancy.

The discrepancy between the numerical responses to Question 2 and the verbal responses to the corresponding Question 5, and the discrepancy between Question 3 and the corresponding Questions 6 and 6' may be explained partly by the context of the questions. The numerical questions were expressed in terms of two regions, A and B with different basic needs levels, while the verbal questions spoke of income change. Other things being equal, a statistical view of poverty should have yielded broadly similar results to the two types of question, whereas an absolutist approach need not. For this reason the responses to our Question 7 reported in table 7.5 are particularly interesting. Here the agreement with the "basic needs" rather than the "statistical" approach to the poverty line appears persuasive – 72 percent; the response "relative to income distribution" (the "Eurostat" view) scores almost the same as the response "neither of the above."

Conclusions

In the introduction to her book *The Perception of Poverty* (1986), Aldi Hagenaars stated:

Poverty measurement is an important first step in a program aimed at reducing poverty; however the choice of the definition of poverty as a relative or an absolute concept may result in different measurement methods and hence different values of indices that measure the extent of poverty. A definition of poverty hence is essential for the results of poverty measurement. (1986, p. ix)

If economists are to offer advice on the measurement of poverty – let

Table 7.3 *Addition of fixed sum to incomes and poverty line*

Institute	N	Numerical (Q3)			Verbal (Q6)			
		Agree: poverty the same (%)	Disagree 1: poverty increases (%)	Disagree 2: poverty decreases (%)	Agree: poverty the same (%)	Disagree 1: poverty increases (%)	Disagree 2: poverty decreases (%)	Disagree 3: depends (%)
Alabama	80	**21**	26	53	**67**	10	14	9
LSE	34	**20**	15	65	**50**	18	18	15
Koblenz	31	**10**	19	71	**71**	0	26	3
Warsaw	34	**21**	18	53	**62**	15	15	6
SMU	19	**21**	11	63	**74**	0	10	0
TA Sociology	43	**16**	28	51	**67**	7	16	7
Ruppin	64	**19**	25	53	**53**	9	28	6
ANU	35	**6**	23	69	**60**	6	26	8
All	*340*	*17*	*22*	*58*	*62*	*9*	*19*	*7*

Table 7.4 *Subtraction of fixed sum from incomes and from poverty line*

Institute	N	Numerical (Q3)			Verbal (Q6')			
		Agree: poverty the same (%)	Disagree 1: poverty increases (%)	Disagree 2: poverty decreases (%)	Agree: poverty the same (%)	Disagree 1: poverty increases (%)	Disagree 2: poverty decreases (%)	Disagree 3: depends (%)
Alabama	80	**21**	53	26	**65**	22	5	6
LSE	34	**20**	65	15	**50**	23	12	15
Koblenz	31	**10**	71	19	**71**	23	0	6
Warsaw	34	**21**	53	18	**53**	23	12	12
SMU	19	**21**	63	11	**58**	11	11	0
TA Sociology	43	**16**	51	28	**67**	12	9	9
Ruppin	64	**19**	53	25	**52**	31	9	5
ANU	35	**6**	69	23	**54**	29	6	9
All	*340*	*17*	*58*	*22*	*60*	*22*	*8*	*8*

Table 7.5 *Definition of "poverty" (Q7)*

	N	Basic needs (%)	Relative to income distribution (%)	Neither (%)
Alabama	80	85	9	2
LSE	34	71	18	12
Koblenz	31	87	3	10
Warsaw	34	79	6	15
SMU	19	63	5	5
TA Sociology	43	56	26	12
Ruppin	64	61	13	13
ANU	35	71	6	20
All	*340*	*72*	*11*	*10*

alone practical help in quantifying it or in attempting to combat it – then it is as well that their theoretical and empirical constructs are informed by some understanding of the concept of poverty as it is generally perceived. One way of getting at this "general perception" is to ask people, and it seems reasonable to ask people who do not already have the preconceptions that professional economists bring to distributional comparisons.

In circumstances where an official or other independently specified poverty line is known and recognized the issues involved in poverty comparisons can be made considerably more straightforward. But there are many practical situations where this luxury is unavailable or ambiguous; the problem is particularly acute when making poverty comparisons between countries. In such cases, it might appear that the only thing to do is to take a simplified relativist approach to specifying the poverty, x percent of the mean or median, for example. However, apart from the practical problems of implementing this approach – it is often crucial what value x percent is and whether the median or mean is used – our results suggest that simple relativism may miss something essential in the underlying concept. People appear to perceive poverty and poverty comparisons in the abstract in a way that does not fit well into the x percent poverty line approach. This is evident both from the matched numerical exercises and verbal questions to our students, and particularly from the responses to our Question 7.

Of course we do not claim that asking students about poverty perceptions should be decisive in shaping theoretical and empirical work on the role of the poverty line in poverty comparisons. But we do think that an especially valuable step in this area would be to carry out further research on the way that ordinary people – be they students, social workers, policy makers, or people in the street – view changes in the income distribution and the poverty line. However, as Aldi Hagenaars commented, this is merely a first step to understanding a difficult and intractable problem.

Appendix: poverty questionnaire

This questionnaire concerns people's attitude to poverty. We would be interested in your views, based on some hypothetical situations. Because it is about attitudes there are no "right answers." Some of the suggested answers correspond to assumptions commonly made by economists, but these assumptions may not be good ones. Your responses will help to shed some light on this, and we would like to thank you for your participation. The questionnaire is anonymous.

In Alfaland there are two regions A and B. All the people of Alfaland are identical in every respect other than their incomes. The people of region A consider that the level of income which ensures a supply of basic needs in their region is 10 Alfa-dollars, and the people of region B consider that the basic needs income level in their region is 20 Alfa-dollars. Prices in A and in B are the same.

In each of the three following questions you are asked to compare two distributions of income – one for each region. Please indicate the region in which you consider poverty to be greater by circling A or B. If you consider that poverty is the same in the two regions then circle both A and B.

1     $A = (4,8,12,20,24,32,40)$ $B = (4,8,12,20,24,32,40)$
2     $A = (4,8,12,20,24,32,40)$ $B = (8,16,24,40,48,64,80)$
3     $A = (4,8,12,20,24,32,40)$ $B = (14,18,22,30,34,42,50)$

In each of the following questions you are presented with a hypothetical change and a several possible views about that change, labeled a, b, c . . . Please circle the letter alongside the view that corresponds most closely to your own. Feel free to add any comments which explain the reason for your choice.

4 Suppose two regions A and B have the same income distribution. Suppose the level of income which ensures a supply of basic needs is higher in region B.

    a It is clear that poverty in B *is greater than in* A.

    b The basic needs income level does not affect the level of poverty. So poverty is the same in A *and* B.

    c Neither of the above.

In the light of the above would you want to change your answer to Question 1? If so, please note your new response ("*A*" or "*B*" or "*A* and *B*") here:

5 Suppose the real income of each person and the basic needs income level are doubled.

    a Poverty increases.

    b Poverty decreases.

    c Poverty remains the same.

    d The direction of change of poverty depends on initial and final levels of real income.

In the light of the above, would you want to change your answer to Question 2? If so, please write your new response ("*A*" or "*B*" or "*A* and *B*") here:

6 Imagine a region in which some persons' incomes are less than the basic needs level. Suppose the real income of each person in the region is increased by the same fixed amount and that the basic needs income level is also increased by the same fixed amount.

    a Poverty increases.

    b Poverty decreases.

    c Poverty remains the same.

    d The direction of change of poverty depends on initial and final levels of real income.

Suppose instead that the real income of each person in the same region is decreased by the same fixed amount and that the basic needs income level is also decreased by the same fixed amount.

    a Poverty increases.

    b Poverty decreases.

    c Poverty remains the same.

    d The direction of change of poverty depends on initial and final levels of real income.

In the light of the above would you want to change your response to Question 3? If so, please note your new response ("*A*" or "*B*" or "*A* and *B*") here:

7 Poverty is a situation in which incomes are

   a *Not enough for a supply of basic needs.*
   b *Below a level which is relative to the income distribution (for example 50 percent of the median income).*
   c *Neither of the above.*

Notes

We would like to thank STICERD and the Ruppin Institute for facilitating our collaboration and the many colleagues who helped in running and processing the questionnaires, John Formby, Hanana Giladi, Anja Green, Boyd Hunter, Tomasz Panek, Wilhelm Pfähler, Moshe Semionov, Dan Slottje, and Harald Wiese. We are also grateful for the comments of two referees.

1   The institutions (and number of student respondents) were University of Alabama, USA (80), the London School of Economics, UK (34), Hochschule für Unternehmungsführung, Koblenz, Germany (31), University of Warsaw, Poland (34), Southern Methodist University, USA (19), Tel-Aviv (Sociology), Israel (43), the Ruppin Institute, Israel (64), Australian National University (72).
2   Elsewhere when the "Neither of the above" response was explicitly offered (Question 7) it did not receive such support.
3   We should also allow for the possibility that the "Disagree 1" on Question 1 may just be a numerical mistake. Note that it is the US universities and the Tel Aviv non-economists who appear to respond perversely, groups that have displayed a propensity for "unconventional" responses in previous, unrelated questionnaire studies – cf. Amiel and Cowell (1992, 1994a).

References

Amiel, Y. and F.A. Cowell, 1992. "Measurement of income inequality: experimental test by questionnaire," *Journal of Public Economics*, 47, 3–26
1994a. "Income inequality and social welfare," in J. Creedy (ed.), *Taxation, Poverty and Income Distribution*, Aldershot: Edward Elgar, 193–219
1994b. "The measurement of poverty: an experimental questionnaire investigation," London School of Economics, mimeo
Department of Social Security (DSS), 1992. *Households below Average Income: A Statistical Analysis 1979–1988/89*, London: HMSO
1993. *Households below Average Income: A Statistical Analysis 1979–1990/91*, London, HMSO
Foster, J.E., 1984. "On economic poverty: a survey of aggregate measures," in R.L. Basmann and G.F. Rhodes, Jr. (eds.), *Advances in Econometrics*, Greenwich, CN: JAI Press, 215–51
Hagenaars, A.J.M., 1986. *The Perception of Poverty*, Amsterdam: North-Holland
Kundu, A. and T.R. Smith, 1983. "An impossibility theorem on poverty indices," *International Economic Review*, 24, 423–34

Ravallion, M., 1994. *Poverty Comparisons: A Guide to Concepts and Methods*, Chur: Harwood Academic Publishers

Seidl, C., 1988. "Poverty measurement: a survey," in D. Bös, M. Rose and C. Seidl (eds.), *Welfare and Efficiency in Public Economics*, Berlin: Springer-Verlag, 71–148

Sen, A.K. 1976. "Poverty: an ordinal approach to measurement," *Econometrica*, 44, 219–31

1979. "Issues in the measurement of poverty," *Scandinavian Journal of Economics*, 91, 285–307

1983. "Poor, relatively speaking," *Oxford Economic Papers*, 35, 153–69

8 Using subjective information in microeconomic modeling: an application to vacation behavior

Peter Kooreman

Introduction

During the 1970s and early 1980s, the collection and analysis of subjective information was at the core of the research activities of economists at Leiden University, the university where Aldi Hagenaars obtained her PhD degree in 1985. Although at that time the use of subjective information was common in psychological and market research, the Leiden group was often considered an enclave within the economic profession. The faith its members professed, namely that utility could be measured on a cardinal scale, was initially at best received with scepticism; see Kapteyn (1985) for examples of the kind of objections raised by referees against papers using van Praag's direct cardinal measure of utility. Today, various examples in the literature show that economists have become less reluctant to use subjective information in microeconomics, and the Leiden project on the evaluation of income is likely to have contributed to this attitudinal change. Examples of types of subjective information used in microeconomic analysis, in addition to income evaluation questions, are (a) Cantril measures of well-being (e.g. Theeuwes and Woittiez, 1995); (b) job searchers' perception of the distribution of wage offers (e.g. van den Berg, 1990); (c) perception of taxes, liquidity constraints, and inflation (e.g. Wahlund, 1987; Bates and Gabor, 1986); (d) measures of consumer confidence (e.g. Acemoglu and Scott, 1994); (e) reservation wages of job searchers (e.g. Lancaster and Chesher, 1983); (f) measures of willingness to pay or accept (contingent valuation) (e.g. Cropper and Oates 1992); and (g) preferred working hours of individuals (e.g. Kapteyn, Kooreman and van Soest, 1990). The first four examples primarily reflect the individual's perception of the economic environment, while the last three describe intended behavior. As such, these reflect both preferences and the perception of the economic environment and constraints.

194

The use of subjective information in economics and a further integration of psychological and economic theories to increase our understanding of economic behavior was considered a fascinating challenge by Aldi Hagenaars (Hagenaars and Wunderink-van Veen, 1990 p. 257). The objective of this chapter is to investigate the usefulness of employing a particular type of subjective information on preferences in modeling an aspect of household behavior, choosing a vacation country. The subjective information consists of responses to a question in which respondents are asked whether they find particular aspects of a vacation unimportant, important, or very important. In the next section we discuss the nature and possible interpretations of our subjective information on preferences. The following section reports estimates of a sequence of ordered probit models which relate the subjective information to a set of "objective" household characteristics. Much of the variation in the subjective preference information appears to be independent of these characteristics. We then present estimates of a multinomial logit model with the choice of a vacation country as the dependent variables. Ample attention is paid to the likely endogeneity of the subjective information. When ignoring the endogeneity problem, the subjective information ostensibly increases the explanatory power of the logit model. The effect is mitigated once endogeneity is taken into account.

The data

The data are taken from the 1987 Fall Survey of the Dutch ANWB. The ANWB is an association that provides all kinds of services related to (car) travel and vacation to its members, including on-the-road assistance in case of vehicle breakdown and repatriation in case of accidents abroad. It also publishes magazines on (car) travel and tourism and organizes vacation trips. Almost half of all Dutch households are members of the ANWB. The 1987 Fall Survey is a sample of 1,036 members who were on vacation between October 1986 and September 1987. Sample statistics are presented in tables 8.1 and 8.2.

The vacation countries have been clustered into five groups: the Netherlands, Germany/Switzerland/Austria, France/Belgium, Spain/Portugal, and "other countries." In the category "other countries" Italy, Yugoslavia, and Greece had the largest shares with 5.3, 3.2, and 2.0 percent of the total sample, respectively. The data set does not provide information on vacation expenditures. Another weakness is that it does not contain direct information on income. Given the usually strong positive correlation between education and income, the

Table 8.1   *Sample statistics*

	Mean	St.dev.	Min	Max
Explanatory variables				
SEX	1.23	0.42	1	2
AGE	44.60	13.8	20	83
AGE2	21.80	13.3	4	68.89
FS	2.84	1.27	1	8
JOB	0.72	0.45	0	1
MBW	0.73	0.45	0	1
EDUC	4.84	2.46	1	9
CH05	0.21	0.56	0	3
CH612	0.30	0.67	0	4
CH1314	0.10	0.32	0	2
CH1519	0.21	0.50	0	3
CH20+	0.14	0.41	0	4
BIGCITY	0.11	0.32	0	1
CREDCARD	0.31	0.61	0	2
CAR	1.22	0.52	0	3
CARAV	0.22	0.43	0	2
TENT	0.45	0.58	0	2

No of obs.: 1,036

Explanation:

SEX	1 = male, 2 = female
AGE	age of respondent
AGE2	$AGE^2/100$
FS	size of respondent's family
JOB	1 if respondent has a paid job or is self-employed, 0 otherwise
MBW	1 if respondent is main breadwinner in the household, 0 otherwise
EDUC	education index ranging from 1 (lowest level) to 9 (highest level)
CH05	number of children between 0 and 5 years in respondent's household
CH612	number of children between 6 and 12 years
CH1314	number of children aged 13 or 14 years
CH1519	number of children between 15 and 19 years
CH20+	number of children aged 20 years or older
BIGCITY	1 if respondent lives in big city (Amsterdam, Rotterdam, The Hague), 0 otherwise
CREDCARD	number of credit cards owned by respondent
CAR	number of cars in respondent's household
CARAV	number of caravans (trailers) in respondent's household
TENT	number of tents in respondent's household

Vacation country[a]	%	Cumulative
Netherlands	26.4	26.4
France	21.6	48.0
Germany	10.1	58.1
Spain	7.6	65.7
Austria	6.8	72.5
Italy	5.3	77.8
Yugoslavia	3.2	81.0
Switzerland	3.0	84.0
Belgium	2.2	86.2
Greece	2.0	88.2
United Kingdom/Ireland	1.8	90.0
United States/Canada	1.8	91.8
Scandinavian countries	1.6	93.4
Portugal	1.4	94.8
Turkey	1.1	95.9
Rest Europe	*1.9*	*97.8*
Other	*2.2*	*100.0*

Note:

[a] Response to the question: "*In which country did you spend the largest part of this vacation?*"

estimated coefficients on the education variable may therefore primarily represent income effects. The same holds true for the variables on having a credit card and on having a paid job. The numbers of observations in table 8.2 differ since some respondents did not answer all items.

The distinguishing feature of the data set analyzed in this chapter is that much more information than usual is available on the utility the respondent attaches to particular aspects of a vacation, such as weather, pleasantness for children, type of food and drink, scenery, distance, etc.; see table 8.2. The exact phrasing of the questions is given in the note to table 8.2.

Interpreting the subjective information

Consider a household with preferences represented by the household utility function

$$U(c, w; \theta) \tag{8.1}$$

Table 8.2   *Subjective information on preferences^a: sample statistics*

	Unimportant (%)	Important (%)	Very important (%)	No of obs.
Inexpensive	29.5	55.2	15.4	964
Pleasant for children	46.0	11.3	42.7	892
Good weather is likely	12.8	33.1	54.2	964
Good place for hobbies and sports	49.2	32.1	18.7	953
Many possibilities for sightseeing	11.5	46.1	42.4	974
Good food and drink	30.4	41.2	28.4	960
Far away from home	77.4	19.4	3.2	947
Can be back home again quickly if necessary	54.5	31.7	13.8	965
Beautiful scenery	2.5	25.2	72.3	999
Trips organized by tour operators available	85.2	8.2	6.7	944
Many possibilities for tent/caravan	51.9	11.4	36.7	950
Easy to find places to spend the night	30.1	30.0	39.1	931

Note:
^{a} The phrasing of the question was as follows: "*Below you find a number of reasons that may have played a role in choosing your vacation. They refer to the country of destination. Please indicate for each of the reasons whether they have been very important, important or unimportant in choosing your vacation.*"

with $w = (w_1, \ldots, w_R)'$ being a vector of characteristics of a vacation and c representing all other commodities. θ is a vector of parameter that varies across households. (For notational simplicity we will suppress the subscript n until equation (8.4).) Examples of the vacation characteristics are given in table 8.2.

The respondent's perception of how well country k "produces" combinations of the various vacation characteristics is described the vector-valued subjective production functions

$$w = f_k(v_{1k}, \ldots, v_{Mk}; \Omega) \tag{8.2}$$

where $v_{mk}(m = 1, \ldots, M)$ are the quantities of input m used in country k Examples of inputs are transportation, accommodation, food and drink, etc. Thus each country k exhibits a different technology of transforming vacation inputs into a combination of vacation characteristics, and the perception of technologies varies across consumers. Thus Ω varies across households. Given that we know only the respondent's main vacation country, we assume that each household can choose only one destination. Since empirical results in van Soest and Kooreman (1987, 1989) show that vacations abroad require significant fixed costs, which induces most consumers to choose corner solutions, this assumption seems relatively innocent.

The utility function (8.1) is maximized subject to the restriction of choosing one vacation country only, and subject to the production functions (8.2) and the budget constraint $c + \sum_k \sum_m v_{mk} P_{mk} = y$. Here y is household income and p_{mk} is the price of input m in country k. (Note that when country k is chosen, $v_m = 0$ for $m = 1, \ldots, M$ and all $l \neq k$.) The optimization problem is solved in two stages. First, the optimal amounts of inputs are determined, given a particular destination. Thus for each k, the problem

$$\max \; U(c, f_k(v_{1k}, \ldots, v_{Mk}; \Omega) \; \text{s.t.} \; c + \sum_m v_{mk} p_{mk} = y \tag{8.3}$$

is solved. Let $\hat{v}_{mk}$ denote the optimal amount of input m used in a vacation in country k. In the second stage the utilities associated with a vacation in a particular country, given optimal inputs, are compared. Household n will spend its vacation in country k if and only if $\psi_{mk} > \psi_{nl}$ for all $l \neq k$, where

$$\psi_{nk} = U(y_n - \sum_{m=1}^{M} \hat{v}_{nmk} p_{nmk}, f_k(\hat{v}_{nlk}, \ldots, \hat{v}_{nMk}; \Omega_n); \theta_n) =$$

$$g(y_n, p_{mk}; \theta_n, \Omega_n) \tag{8.4}$$

with the household subscript n now made explicit. Within the context of the model described above, the subjective information reflects how the household weights the various vacation characteristics. Thus the responses contain direct information on preference heterogeneity in the utility functions. If this information were absent, preference heterogeneity in the econometric model would generally be allowed for by making some parameter(s) appearing in the utility function dependent on observed (objective) household characteristics and some random term(s) reflecting unobserved heterogeneity. In the presence of the subjective information it seems natural to treat it as additional observed household characteristics that can be used to parameterize the utility function.

An issue that requires careful consideration here is to what extent the information can be treated as exogenous. The main reason to suspect that this is not the case here is that the information is collected after the respondents had returned from their holidays. At that stage of the purchase process, people might be more likely to express opinions that are consonant with the choices they actually made. The experience of the vacation may have induced changes in the utility function (8.1) (how are vacation characteristics valued?) as well as in the subjective production functions (8.2) (how well does the country produce the various vacation characteristics?).

The empirical relationship between subjective preferences and objective household characteristics

Before discussing this issue further, it is interesting to investigate how the respondents' preferences for particular aspects of a vacation are related to a set of objective household characteristics. In particular, it is important to see to what extent the preference information constitutes an independent source of supplementary information and to what extent it is correlated with the objective variables. For example, if the correlation were high, including the preference information in explaining the choice of a vacation country would be unlikely to increase the explanatory power of the model.

Given the nature of the subjective information (possible responses are "unimportant," "important," or "very important") we estimate ordered probit models:

$$z_{nr}^* = x_n \gamma_r + \eta_{nr} \tag{8.5}$$

where the response is "very important" if $z_{nr}^* > c_{2r}$, "important" if $c_{1r} < z_{nr}^* < c_{2r}$, and "unimportant" if $z_{nr}^* < c_{1r}$. Here γ_r, c_{1r}, and c_{2r} are parameters to be estimated; the error term η_{nr} follows a normal distribution with mean zero and variance normalized to one.

The ordered probit estimates are reported in table 8.3. The results are interesting and plausible. People with a job and a high education (high income) find an inexpensive vacation unimportant. Especially for respondents with children between 6 and 14 years, the vacation should be pleasant for children. Good weather is less important if there are children younger than 6 years and more important if the family is large. The effect of age on finding hobbies and sports important is parabolic, with a maximum at age 29. Females find sightseeing more important than males, whereas the presence of children younger than 6 makes the respondent less interested in sightseeing. Good food and drink is most appreciated by people in their mid-thirties without children and with a credit card. People living in big cities prefer a vacation far away from home. Females appreciate organized trips and beautiful scenery more than males. People with a credit card seem to be uninterested in beautiful scenery (perhaps because they are more oriented toward a metropolitan type of vacation environment).

Many coefficients, on the other hand, are not significant and, as judged by the χ^2-values, much of the variation in the subjective preference information remains unexplained, in particular for "good weather," "sightseeing," "far away from home," and "easy to find a place to spend the night."

The choice of a vacation country

We now model the choice of a vacation country by means of a multi-nomial logit model. Given our focus on the role of subjective information we will not pursue the estimation of more flexible models in the present chapter. The multinomial logit model is usually motivated using a random utility argument. The utility ψ_{nk} respondent n attaches to a vacation in country k is decomposed in a deterministic and a random component:

$$\psi_{nk} = x_n\beta_k + z_n^*\delta_k + \varepsilon_{nk} \tag{8.6}$$

with $z_n^* = (z_{nl}^*, \ldots, z_{nR}^*)'$. Equation (8.6) is a reduced form transcription of (8.4), where some terms in (8.4) (income y_n, preference parameters θ_n) have been partly replaced by observed proxies (such as education, and the subjective preference information) and partly absorbed in the error terms; prices p_{mk} have been absorbed in the constant terms as they do not vary across consumers in a cross-section. The choice probabilities p_{nk} are defined as $p_{nk} = \Pr(\psi_{nk} > \psi_{nl}$ for all $l \neq k)$ which yields the multinomial logit model given specific assumptions on the error terms ε.

If only the objective information is available, the vector x_n will be confined to variables representing household composition, labor market status, and perhaps ownership of vacation-related consumer durables such as a tent or a caravan/trailer; cf. van Soest and

Table 8.3 *Estimation results ordered probits[a]*

	Inexpensive	Pleasant for children	Good weather is likely	Good place for hobbies and sports	Many possibilities for sightseeing	Good food and drink
SEX	−0.042	−0.261	−0.013	−0.118	0.273	−0.149
	(−0.3)	(−1.6)	(−0.1)	(−0.9)	(2.1)	(−1.1)
AGE	0.000	0.030	−0.01	0.041	0.033	0.039
	(0.0)	(1.0)	(−0.5)	(1.9)	(0.1)	(1.8)
AGE2	−0.007	−0.039	0.009	−0.071	−0.033	−0.058
	(−0.3)	(−1.2)	(0.4)	(−3.0)	(−1.5)	(−2.5)
FS	0.192	0.105	0.178	0.039	−0.013	0.048
	(2.0)	(1.1)	(2.0)	(0.4)	(−0.1)	(0.5)
JOB	−0.417	−0.216	0.071	−0.120	0.008	0.060
	(−3.8)	(−1.4)	(0.6)	(−1.0)	(0.1)	(0.5)
MBW	0.112	0.068	−0.112	−0.088	0.222	0.020
	(0.9)	(0.5)	(−0.8)	(−0.7)	(1.8)	(0.1)
EDUC	−0.075	−0.065	−0.001	−0.008	0.117	−0.018
	(−4.9)	(−3.1)	(−0.1)	(−0.5)	(0.8)	(−1.2)
CH05	−0.143	0.108	−0.490	−0.104	−0.306	−0.372
	(−1.1)	(8.3)	(−4.1)	(−0.8)	(−2.5)	(−3.1)
CH612	−0.061	0.846	−0.150	0.002	−0.135	−0.211
	(−0.5)	(7.2)	(−1.4)	(0.0)	(−1.1)	(−1.9)
CH1314	−0.064	0.830	−0.089	0.214	0.059	−0.279
	(−0.4)	(4.1)	(−0.5)	(1.4)	(0.4)	(−1.9)
CH1519	−0.128	0.446	−0.209	0.023	−0.120	−0.276
	(−1.0)	(3.4)	(−1.7)	(0.2)	(−1.0)	(−2.1)
CH20+	−0.048	0.051	−0.158	−0.252	−0.047	0.089
	(−0.3)	(0.4)	(−1.2)	(−1.8)	(−0.4)	(0.7)
BIGCITY	−0.044	−0.053	−0.014	−0.047	−0.033	0.125
	(−0.4)	(−0.3)	(−0.1)	(−0.4)	(−0.3)	(1.0)
CREDCARD	−0.052	0.017	−0.003	−0.023	0.016	0.129
	(−0.8)	(0.2)	(0.0)	(−0.4)	(0.3)	(2.1)
Constant1	−0.927	0.569	−1.208	−0.053	−0.012	−0.278
	(−1.7)	(0.9)	(−2.3)	(−0.1)	(−0.8)	(−0.5)
Constant2	0.709	1.031	−0.156	1.011	1.414	0.854
	(27.9)	(10.3)	(20.1)	(20.3)	(24.8)	(23.4)
No of obs.	964	892	964	953	974	960
Log likelihood	−905.7	−862.8	−913.9	−936.5	−925.6	−1007.0
$\chi^2(14)$[b]	69.9	500.5	24.7	84.6	37.3	69.1

Note: [a] *t*-values in parentheses.
[b] Null hypothesis: all slopes equal 0. The critical levels for 5 per cent and 1 per cent are 23.7 and 29.1, respectively

Table 8.3 (*cont.*)

	Far away from home	Can be back home again quickly	Beautiful scenery	Trips organized by tour operator	Many possibilities for tent/ caravan	Easy to find place to spend the night
SEX	−0.034	0.139	0.265	0.354	0.102	−0.000
	(−0.2)	(0.9)	(1.9)	(2.2)	(0.7)	(0.0)
AGE	−0.045	0.033	0.017	0.003	0.027	0.004
	(−1.8)	(1.5)	(0.7)	(0.1)	(1.1)	(0.2)
AGE2	0.046	−0.024	0.002	−0.003	−0.050	−0.002
	(1.7)	(−1.0)	(0.1)	(−0.1)	(−1.8)	(0.2)
FS	−0.027	−0.072	−0.038	0.037	0.215	0.087
	(−0.2)	(−0.7)	(−0.4)	(0.4)	(1.9)	(0.7)
JOB	0.073	−0.459	0.221	−0.249	−0.260	0.021
	(0.6)	(−4.0)	(1.8)	(−1.6)	(−2.1)	(0.2)
MBW	−0.069	0.250	0.121	0.185	0.047	0.019
	(−0.5)	(1.6)	(0.9)	(1.1)	(0.3)	(0.1)
EDUC	0.009	−0.115	0.021	−0.056	0.001	−0.061
	(0.5)	(−6.6)	(1.2)	(−2.5)	(0.1)	(−3.8)
CH05	−0.175	0.396	−0.030	−0.322	−0.170	−0.217
	(−1.0)	(2.8)	(−0.2)	(−2.0)	(−1.2)	(−1.5)
CH612	0.043	0.030	0.013	−0.239	−0.088	−0.180
	(0.3)	(0.2)	(0.1)	(−1.7)	(−0.6)	(−1.4)
CH1314	0.096	0.168	0.043	−0.399	0.116	−0.089
	(0.5)	(1.0)	(0.2)	(−1.7)	(0.6)	(−0.5)
CH1519	0.060	0.011	−0.108	0.017	−0.098	−0.241
	(0.3)	(0.1)	(−0.8)	(0.1)	(−0.7)	(−1.7)
CH20+	0.040	0.227	0.068	−0.043	−0.209	−0.021
	(0.3)	(1.5)	(0.5)	(−0.2)	(−1.3)	(−0.1)
BIGCITY	0.273	−0.000	−0.159	0.116	−0.207	−0.071
	(2.0)	(−0.0)	(−1.2)	(0.7)	(−1.5)	(−0.6)
CREDCARD	0.076	−0.125	−0.211	−0.044	−0.093	0.034
	(1.0)	(−1.9)	(−3.2)	(−0.5)	(−1.4)	(0.5)
constant1	−0.257	0.417	−0.736	1.167	0.620	−0.609
	(−0.4)	(−0.8)	(−1.2)	(1.6)	(1.0)	(1.0)
constant2	1.374	1.503	0.673	1.648	0.929	0.180
	(13.3)	(19.4)	(15.9)	(8.9)	(11.0)	(19.0)
# of obs.	947	965	999	944	950	931
Log-likelihood	−585.1	−863.1	−651.1	−472.3	−869.4	−1002.2
$\chi^2(14)^b$	15.4	142.3	45.3	40.7	76.6	27.5

[a] Null-hypothesis: all slopes equal 0. The critical levels for 5 per cent and 1 per cent are 23.7 and 29.1, respectvely.

Kooreman (1987, 1989). Here we add the subjective preference variables to the right-hand side of equation (8.1) in addition to the objective variables. Hence, we add the additional information as just other characteristics of the respondent which would otherwise be absorbed into the stochastic part of the model. Suppose the subjective information would have been collected before people went on holiday. Then exogeneity would require that the error terms in the ordered probit equations and ε_{nk} were independent. Consider an extreme example where one of the questions was whether the respondent finds it important to speak French during his vacation. In such a case the exogeneity assumption would not be tenable. In the present case, however, the items in the questions are of a general nature and no reference at all is made to any particular country.

As already noted, an additional problem here is that the information is collected after the respondents have returned from their holidays, which raises the possibility of rationalization in the responses. The possibilities to correct for this problem are quite limited. One might set up a simultaneous model consisting of (8.5) and (8.6) with vacation countries included as explanatory variables in (8.5). However, one would be confronted with the usual identification problems of simultaneous models. Given the large number of endogenous variables and the limited number of potential instruments, a large number of exclusion restrictions would be required, most of which would be difficult to justify. Moreover, a standard simultaneous model may not be appropriate conceptually because the *ex ante* and *ex post* values of z_n will not be equal. Explicit distinction between the two would only exacerbate identification problems.

Keeping in mind the qualifications with respect to a possible rationalization bias, the multinomial logit model with the vacation country as the dependent variable has been estimated (see table 8.4). Note that the coefficients on the subjective preference variables represent the respondents' average opinion on how good the country k is in producing the particular vacation characteristic. Many of the subjective preference variables that could not be explained satisfactorily on p. 201 are significant in this model. For example, someone who finds good weather very important has a significantly lower probability of going on vacation in the Netherlands or Germany/Switzerland/Austria, and a significantly higher probability of going to Spain/Portugal. People who find beautiful scenery important have a larger probability of going to Germany/Switzerland/Austria and France/Belgium and a lower probability of going to Spain/Portugal. France/Belgium is particularly popular among people who like camping. The estimates also indicate that the share of

Table 8.4 *Estimation results, multinomial logit[a]*

	Netherlands	Germany/ Switzerland Austria	France/ Belgium	Spain/ Portugal
Inexpensive[b]				
Important	0.546	0.172	0.008	0.991
	(1.5)	(0.6)	(0.0)	(2.1)
Very important	−0.193	−0.755	−0.979	0.470
	(−0.5)	(−1.7)	(−2.4)	(0.8)
Pleasant for children[b]				
Important	−0.039	0.142	0.186	0.944
	(−0.1)	(0.3)	(0.5)	(1.7)
Very important	0.537	0.710	0.351	0.899
	(1.3)	(1.8)	(1.0)	(1.8)
Good weather is likely[b]				
Important	−0.469	−2.160	0.440	0.378
	(−1.1)	(−0.5)	(1.0)	(0.3)
Very important	−2.33	−1.783	0.143	1.987
	(−5.4)	(−3.9)	(0.3)	(1.8)
Good place for hobbies and sports[b]				
Important	0.468	0.444	0.193	−0.329
	(1.5)	(1.4)	(0.7)	(−0.8)
Very important	0.765	−0.217	0.328	−0.447
	(2.0)	(−0.5)	(1.0)	(−0.9)
Many possibilities for sightseeing[b]				
Important	−0.683	−0.476	−0.431	0.120
	(−1.6)	(−1.0)	(−1.1)	(0.2)
Very important	−1.02	−0.526	−0.650	−0.672
	(−2.2)	(−1.1)	(−1.5)	(−1.1)
Good food and drinks[b]				
Important	−0.443	0.045	0.080	−0.232
	(−1.4)	(0.1)	(0.3)	(−0.5)
Very important	−0.378	0.102	0.432	1.111
	(−1.0)	(0.3)	(1.3)	(2.1)
Far away from home[c]				
Important or	−1.222	−0.675	−5.320	−0.636
very important	(−3.6)	(−2.2)	(−2.0)	(−1.7)
Can be back home again quickly[b]				
Important	0.600	0.441	0.047	−0.013
	(2.0)	(1.5)	(0.2)	(−0.0)
Very important	1.96	1.132	0.765	0.237
	(3.8)	(2.1)	(1.4)	(0.3)

Table 8.4 (*cont.*)

	Netherlands	Germany/ Switzerland Austria	France/ Belgium	Spain/ Portugal
Beautiful scenery[d]				
Very important	0.514	1.293	0.513	−0.782
	(1.7)	(3.7)	(1.9)	(−2.1)
Trips organized by tour operators[c]				
Important or	−0.658	−0.851	−1.43	0.508
Very important	(−1.7)	(−2.3)	(−3.4)	(1.3)
Many possibilities for tent/ caravan[b]				
Important	0.510	−0.232	0.585	−0.252
	(1.2)	(−0.5)	(1.6)	(−0.4)
Very important	0.650	0.188	1.38	−0.447
	(1.7)	(0.5)	(4.2)	(−0.9)
Easy to find place to spend the night[b]				
Important	−1.044	−0.997	−0.828	−0.783
	(−3.1)	(−2.7)	(−2.8)	(−1.6)
Very important	−0.306	0.076	−0.735	−0.335
	(−0.9)	(0.2)	(−2.3)	(−0.7)
SEX	−0.318	−0.201	−0.483	−0.470
	(−0.9)	(−0.6)	(−1.6)	(−1.0)
AGE	−0.023	0.020	0.057	0.163
	(−0.3)	(0.2)	(0.8)	(1.4)
AGE2	0.036	−0.004	−0.071	−0.237
	(0.4)	(−0.0)	(−0.9)	(−1.8)
FS	0.349	0.300	0.253	0.149
	(1.1)	(0.9)	(0.9)	(0.4)
JOB	−0.097	0.173	−0.277	−0.815
	(−0.2)	(0.4)	(−0.7)	(−1.5)
EDUC	−0.200	−0.278	0.021	−0.147
	(−3.5)	(−4.6)	(0.4)	(−1.9)
CH05	0.435	−0.487	0.154	−0.475
	(0.9)	(−0.9)	(0.3)	(−0.8)
CH612	−0.088	−0.195	−0.273	−0.798
	(−0.2)	(−0.4)	(−0.7)	(−1.6)
CH1319	−0.568	−0.322	−0.104	−0.343
	(−1.4)	(−0.7)	(−0.3)	(−0.7)
CH20+	−0.603	−0.439	−1.035	−0.544
	(−1.3)	(−0.9)	(−2.3)	(−1.0)
BIGCITY	−0.075	−1.339	−0.293	0.373
	(−0.2)	(−2.8)	(−0.8)	(0.8)

	Netherlands	Germany/ Switzerland Austria	France/ Belgium	Spain/ Portugal
CREDCARD	−0.369	−1.093	−0.216	0.433
	(−1.7)	(−3.8)	(−1.2)	(1.7)
TENT	−0.589	−0.611	−0.245	−0.690
	(−2.3)	(−2.4)	(−1.1)	(−2.0)
CARAV	−0.330	−0.138	−0.188	0.285
	(−0.9)	(−0.3)	(−0.6)	(0.6)
Constant	2.834	1.045	−0.499	−2.982
	(1.5)	(0.5)	(−0.3)	(−1.1)

Notes:
[a] *t*-values in parentheses.
[a] *Important* and *Very important* have been included as two distinct dummy variables.
[b] One dummy variable for *Important or Very important* has been included because of the small number of observations in each separate group (see table 8.2)
[c] Only a dummy variable for *Very important* has been included because of the small number of observations with response "unimportant" (see table 8.2).
No. of obs. 818 (number of respondents who answered all the questions on preferences).
Log likelihood: −922.9. The coefficients of "other countries" have been normalized to zero.
MBW has been excluded since it turned out insignificant in table 8.3 and preliminary estimates.

Germany/Switzerland/Austria and France/Belgium might increase if trips to these countries organized by tour operators were more widely available. France/Belgium is not attractive to people who find an inexpensive vacation very important, whereas Spain/Portugal is perceived as relatively inexpensive. The Iberian peninsula is also appreciated because of good food and drink.

Table 8.5 *Estimation results, multinomial logit: objective variables only*[a]

	Netherlands	Germany/ Switzerland Austria	France/ Belgium	Spain/ Portugal
SEX	−0.311	−0.246	−0.379	−0.756
	(−1.1)	(−0.8)	(−1.4)	(−1.9)
AGE	0.020	0.010	0.061	0.195
	(0.3)	(1.4)	(0.9)	(1.8)
AGE2	−0.020	−0.080	−0.083	−0.290
	(−0.3)	(−1.0)	(−1.1)	(−2.3)
FS	0.278	0.180	0.248	0.481
	(1.0)	(0.6)	(1.0)	(1.6)
JOB	−0.508	0.189	−0.193	−0.986
	(−1.5)	(0.5)	(−0.6)	(−2.2)
EDUC	−0.196	−0.244	0.033	−0.234
	(−4.0)	(−4.7)	(0.7)	(−3.6)
CH05	1.103	0.199	0.430	−0.218
	(2.6)	(0.4)	(1.1)	(−0.4)
CH612	0.070	0.071	−0.135	−0.814
	(0.2)	(0.2)	(−0.4)	(−2.0)
CH1319	−0.354	−0.144	−0.140	−0.540
	(−1.0)	(−0.4)	(−0.4)	(−1.4)
CH20+	−0.477	−0.277	−1.129	−0.588
	(−1.2)	(−0.7)	(−2.6)	(−1.3)
BIGCITY	−0.205	−1.335	−0.277	0.263
	(−0.6)	(−3.0)	(−0.8)	(0.7)
CREDCARD	−0.283	−0.955	−0.247	0.398
	(−1.5)	(−3.7)	(−1.5)	(1.9)
TENT	−0.433	−0.509	0.187	−0.881
	(−2.1)	(−2.3)	(1.0)	(−3.1)
CARAV	0.186	−0.082	0.711	0.280
	(0.7)	(−0.3)	(2.7)	(0.8)
Constant	0.771	−1.346	−0.989	−0.499
	(0.5)	(−0.8)	(−0.7)	(−0.3)

Notes: [a] *t*-values in parentheses
Log likelihood: −1129.3.

In addition to the model reported in table 8.4, two nested versions have been estimated, one excluding the 21 preference variables (table 8.5) and one excluding the 14 x-variables (results not reported). Both models are rejected against the general model, although the rejection of the model using x-variables only ($\chi^2(21) = 412.8$; critical value at 1 percent is 38.9) is more decisive than the rejection of the one with the preference variables only ($\chi^2(14) = 161.8$; critical value at 1 percent: 29.1). While the inclusion of the subjective preference variables substantially improves the explanatory power of the model, it hardly affects the size and significance of most of the coefficients of the objective variables. For example, the coefficients on education, big city, and tent in table 8.4 are very similar to the corresponding coefficients in table 8.5.

Finally, we compare the predictions per observation generated by the three models. The predicted country for an observation is defined as the country with the largest choice probability as implied by the estimated multinomial logit model. In the model with objective variables (x_n) only, the percentage of observations with correct predictions is 38. The model with preference variables only, however, does substantially better, with 49.4 percent correct predictions. In the general model, with both the objective and subjective preference variables, 52.7 percent of all individual choices are predicted correctly. Hence, it appears that the contribution of the subjective information to the explanatory power of the model is substantial. However, the size of the effect may be biased upward due to the endogeneity problem discussed above.

Concluding remarks

This chapter has investigated the potential role of subjective information on preferences in analyzing aspects of vacation behavior. It turns out that the variation in the preference information across households can be explained by objective household characteristics to a limited extent only. The subjective preference variables thus appear to be a largely independent source of supplementary information.

Including the subjective preference information as additional explanatory variables substantially increases the explanatory power of the model of choosing a vacation country. However, the size of the effect may be biased upward due to the possible endogeneity of the subjective information. The estimation results also shed light on which countries are thought to be good in producing the various desired aspects of a vacation.

Acknowledgements

I thank W. Fred van Raaij, Stephen Jenkins, and an anonymous referee for helpful comments.

References

Acemoglu, D. and A. Scott, 1994. "Consumer confidence and rational expectations: are agents' beliefs consistent with the theory?," *Economic Journal*, 104, 11–19

Bates, J.M. and A. Gabor, 1986. "Price perception in creeping inflation: report on an enquiry," *Journal of Economic Psychology*, 7, 291–314

Berg, G. van den, 1990. "Nonstationarity in job search theory," *Review of Economic Studies*, 57, 255–77

Cropper, M.L. and W.E. Oates, 1992. "Environmental economics: a survey," *Journal of Economic Literature*, 30, 675–740

Hagenaars, A.J.M. and S.R. Wunderink-van Veen, 1990. *Soo Gewonne, soo Verteert: Economie van de Huishoudelijke Sector* (Easy Won, Easy Gone: Economics of the Household Sector) Leiden and Antwerp: Stenfert Kroese Uitgevers

Kapteyn, A., 1985. "Utility and economics," *De Economist*, 133, 1–20

Kapteyn, A., P. Kooreman and A. van Soest, 1990. "Quantity rationing and concavity in a flexible household labor supply model," *Review of Economics and Statistics*, 57, 55–62

Lancaster, T. and A. Chesher, 1983. "An econometric analysis of reservation wages'," *Econometrica*, 51, 1661–76

Woittiez, I. and J. Theeuwes, 1995. "Well-being and labour market status," chapter 9 in this volume

Van Praag, B.M.S., 1968. *Individual Welfare Functions and Consumer Behavior*, Amsterdam: North-Holland

Van Soest, A. and P. Kooreman, 1987. "A microeconometric analysis of vacation behavior," *Journal of Applied Econometrics*, 2, 215–26

1989. "Vakantiebestemming en -bestedingen," *Maandschrift Economie*, 53, 43–51

Wahlund, R., 1987. "Does lowering the marginal taxes rates matter?," *Working Paper*, Department of Economic Psychology, Stockholm School of Economics

9   Well-being and labor market status

Isolde Wottiez and Jules Theeuwes

Introduction

The main issue in this chapter is measuring the effect of labor market status on well-being. Are the unemployed less happy than the employed? And what about early retirees or the disabled? Why is it important to know the effect of labor market state on well-being? The answer is twofold – it ties in with the measurement of utility differences in economic theory and it affects economic policy. Let us concentrate first on economic theory. Utility differences between the employed and the unemployed are a key component in job search models. Utility differences between employment and unemployment are mostly motivated by income differences, but clearly also non-pecuniary aspects of employment status play a role. One could argue that well-being which is dependent on both pecuniary and non-pecuniary aspects of one's employment status is a more comprehensive measure of the utility difference. Second, when looking for economic policies to alleviate unemployment a crucial question to be answered is whether individuals are voluntary or involuntary unemployed. If the answer is that unemployment is predominantly voluntary, then one might wish to reduce the attractiveness of being without work. If the answer is that unemployment is predominantly involuntary, one must perhaps consider policies to raise the number of jobs. Few studies attempt to evaluate directly whether unemployment is voluntary or not. Economists are often worried about the notion that utility can be measured.

In this chapter we will study the welfare distribution with the help of the Cantril scale (Cantril, 1965). This is a scale that ranks satisfaction with life in general on a scale from 1 to 10, with 1 being the pits and 10 being bliss. In this report we are joining a growing group of scholars using direct measures of well-being to analyze interpersonal differences in utility, leaving behind the traditional school of economists who view interpersonal comparison of utility and cardinalization of utility as inadmissible. Aldi Hagenaars, to whose memory this volume is dedicated, opens her dissertation (1986) with a chapter on the poverty concept in which she develops the Leiden poverty line definition based on measurement of interpersonal utility. In the theoretical background of this chapter, two areas are relevant: the behaviorist approaches to measure interpersonal comparable utility levels, and the relation between well-being and labor market status.

Interpersonal comparison of utility

The issue of interpersonal comparison of utility is a hard one in economics and the relationship between the Cantril scale and individual utility or well-being is an open question. We could avoid it by claiming we are measuring the distribution of Cantril scale results among Dutch elderly and nothing more.

Hammond (1991) discusses alternative behaviorist approaches to measuring interpersonal comparable utility levels which have been suggested in the literature. The most common suggestion for cardinalization of individual utility functions before comparing their differences interpersonally is to use von Neumann–Morgenstern utility functions. Another approach starts from an indicator of well-being (such as the Cantril scale) which is individually measured and related to the determinants of the utility function. The indicator is seen as a proxy for utility. This approach was used among others by Clark and Oswald (1993, 1994), Korpi (1994), Morawetz *et al.* (1977), Plug and van Praag (1993), Simon (1974), and Tomes (1986). The Leiden approach of van Praag and his associates (including Kapteyn and Hagenaars) involves constructing an interpersonal comparable relative indicator of well-being. The construction is ingeniously based on the intervals of net family income levels that each individual in a sample reports as being necessary to achieve an income that is "excellent," or "good," or "barely sufficient," or "bad," etc.

Well-being and labor market status

The relation between well-being and labor market status is a much discussed item in psychology. Typical in the psychological theories as to why unemployment may have an effect on well-being is the distinction between individual and environmental factors. Theories focusing on individuals highlight their ability to cope with different situations. We will measure these effects by level of education and age. Environmental theories focus on the situation the individual finds himself or herself in, such as opportunity for skill use, opportunity for interpersonal contact, and status. Unemployment is assumed to score lower than employment on these features, and is consequently associated with a lower level of well-being. These effects are measured indirectly by labor market state, since we have no direct measurement of opportunities and status. The disadvantages of employment such as stress, fatigue, restricted leisure, and commuting are also obvious (van Raaij and Antonides, 1991).

It has been recognized that there could exist an health effect which works through the employment status. Health problems may be the reason for becoming unemployed or may make it more difficult to find new employment. Consequently a low feeling of well-being may be the cause rather than the effect of joblessness. To control for this we should check for selectivity bias. In this chapter we rely on evidence from the psychological literature that there are no (strong) effects from health on labor market state and proceed.

In comparison with previous studies in this area we provide an extension by distinguishing between different non-work states, instead of combining them all into one state. Moreover, our data allow us to extend the number of explanatory variables. As a result we are able to disentangle the various effects embedded in the labor market state effect on well-being. Finally, we are able to give some indication on the issue of involuntariness of being in a specific labor market state.

In the next section we discuss the determinants of well-being. We then present the data. The model is then given, the estimation results are shown and discussed, and some conclusions drawn.

The determinants of well-being

In the literature on the determinants of individual well-being, labor market status, income, personal characteristics such as education, age, and sex are frequently encountered explanatory variables. As additional determinants we use housing variables, variables referring to the partner, labor market history, and all kinds of subjective labor market-related variables proxying preferences for work. We will briefly discuss each of these.

Labor market status

These are the central explanatory variables in our analysis. In a previous chapter (Woittiez, Lindeboom and Theeuwes, 1994) we studied the exit routes out of the labor force of Dutch elderly and found that alternative income flows were an important determinant of the choice of exit into the disability scheme, the unemployment program, or early retirement. Using Moffitt's (1983) model on welfare stigma we found that individuals in early retirement appreciate their benefit income more than others, closely followed by individuals drawing a disability allowance. Appreciation of wage income by workers is somewhat lower, while appreciation of unemployment benefit by the unemployed is far lower. In this chapter we are generalizing these appreciation aspects of our (1994) chapter analyzing the effects of these labor market states on the level of well-being.

Compared with being employed, being unemployed is usually found to have a significant negative effect on well-being (Clark and Oswald 1994). The same goes for being on strike or laid off (Tomes, 1986). Korpi (1994) finds that employment is evaluated higher than participating in a governmental labor market program, which in turn is better than being unemployed.

Income

The effect of income on well-being is a much researched relationship in the behaviorist approaches to measuring individual utility. First of all one expects the own income level to have a (non-linear) relationship to reflect the commonly assumed diminishing marginal utility of income. Partner's income should have a positive coefficient (less than the coefficient on own income) if one is altruistic. The sign of the coefficient on other people's income depends on envy or altruism (Tomes, 1986). Income distribution measures also depend on envy or altruism (Tomes, 1986; Morawetz et al., 1977). The effect of comparison income is quite important. "Comparison income" is the level of income that comparable individuals (peer groups) would have (Kapteyn, 1985) or the income that one should earn given personal and labor market characteristics (i.e. income predicted from a standard income equation, Clark and Oswald, 1993).

Personal characteristics and health

It is commonly found that women have a higher level of well-being than men and that satisfaction with life diminishes with higher levels of education. Being divorced or having children is also associated with less contentment (Clark and Oswald, 1993). Age usually has a non-linear U-shaped relation with well-being (Clark, Oswald and Warr, 1994). In the literature good health is found to have a positive effect on well-being. (For a good overview see Korpi, 1994.)

Other determinants

One would expect that better housing situations lead to a higher well-being. A healthier partner would also probably lead to a higher well-being of the respondent. Clark and Oswald (1994) provide evidence that previous unemployment experiences have a negative effect on one's well-being, suggesting that the effect of the unemployment spells on well-being is permanent, while a study by Björklund (1985) found no effects of current or previous unemployment. Preferences for work measure directly (but also subjectively) the voluntariness of being in a particular labor market status.

Data

Data were obtained from a survey which was held by the Centre for Economic Research on Retirement and Aging (CERRA) of the University of Leiden in the Netherlands in October 1993 among 4,700 heads of households who were between 43 and 63 years old. Although there are quite a number of retrospective questions in the survey, our analysis is cross-sectional. These CERRA data contain information on labor market characteristics, personal characteristics, health, and income, and to some extent wealth situation and debts. We also asked the respondents to rank their present satisfaction with life in general on a scale from 1 to 10, with 1 being the lowest and 10 being the highest level. This scale is borrowed from the psychological literature where it is known as the Cantril scale. In this chapter we study welfare distribution with the help of this scale. The question referring to the Cantril scale is as follows:

Below you find 3 ladders, each with 10 steps. They represent the "life ladder." The bottom of this ladder represents the worst possible life. If you ascend you will reach the top of the ladder; this represents the best possible life. Could you please mark on which step you stand at this moment, in your own view. Would you please mark next on which step you were situated 2 years ago, and finally on which step you think you will be in 2 years from now.

In the data we observed the distribution of the self-reported ranking of present happiness on the Cantril scale at the time of the interview shown in table 9.1. There is some bunching around 8 (almost 38 percent), and almost 8 percent of the respondents are perfectly happy. At the lower end there is much less happening. In view of this we decided to aggregate levels 1–4 into one level. Hence, in the empirical analysis in table 9.2 our adjusted Cantril scale has only seven levels, ranging from 0 to 6.

Our main emphasis is on the effect of labor market status on well-being. In our data we distinguish between eight labor market states:

Table 9.1   *Distribution of self-reported present happiness (Cantril scale ranking)*

	Value	Frequency	%
	1.00	13	0.4
	2.00	9	0.3
	3.00	33	0.9
	4.00	62	1.7
	5.00	185	5.2
	6.00	362	10.1
	7.00	908	25.4
	8.00	1,335	37.4
	9.00	383	10.7
	10.00	280	7.8
Total		*3,570*	*100.0*

working in salaried employment, *self-employed, disabled, early retirees* receiving retirement benefits, *pensioners* receiving pension benefits, non-working who regard themselves as pensioned but do not receive pension benefit (*non-working/pensioner*), *unemployed*, and other non-working, not looking for a job (*non-working/other*). As this is a sample of elderly the percentage of working in salaried employment is small. Starting at age 50 we see a decline in the number working from 70 percent to less than 20 percent when they reach 60. From 62 onwards it remains constant at about 10 percent. The number of early retirees increases dramatically from less than 5 percent at age 55 to about 45 percent from age 60 onwards. The number of disabled first rises from age 50 (8 percent) until age 60 (23 percent), after which it decreases to about 17 percent. Table 9.2 shows the average scores on the Cantril scale of well-being per labor market status, and compares this with the ranking of several other possible measures of well-being.

Column (1) shows that disabled score particularly low with 2.76 average. The unemployed and non-working/other follow with a score around 3. Pensioners are quite a bit happier with a score of 3.5. The workers, both in salaried employment and self-employed score high, with 3.7. The high score for the non-working/pensioner is surprising. They score as high as the working. Top of the bill, finally, are early retirees, with an average of 4. At first glance, the data seem to reveal evidence of involuntariness of being in the disability or unemployment scheme. We have also included several other indicators of well-being, and their rankings based on average scores. Columns (2)–(4) give the

Table 9.2 *Ranking of labor market states*

	Well-being[a] (= Cantril) (1)	HSCL total (2)	HSCL psych. (3)	HSCL somatic (4)	Subjective health (5)	Relative health (6)
Disabled	2.76 1	1	1	1	1	1
Non-working/other	2.98 2	2	2	2	2	2
Unemployed	3.03 3	3	5	3	3	6
Pensioner	3.45 4	4	3	4	4	3
Self-employed	3.67 5	7	7	7	6	5
Working	3.70 6	6	6	6	7	4
Non-working/pensioner	3.71 7	5	4	5	5	7
Early retirees	4.00 8	8	8	8	8	8

Notes:
[a] This column presents the average of the adjusted Cantril scale (from 0–6) per labor market status and the ranking based on these averages.
HSCL: Hopkins Symptoms Checklist:
  total: average total score on scale for psychic and somatic health
  psych: average score on scale for psychic health
  somatic: average score on scale for somatic health
  Subjective health: average score on subjective individual health evaluation question
  Relative health: average score on question subjectively comparing individual health with others.

ranking of the total, psychic and somatic health score on the Hopkins Symptoms Checklist (HSCL). This list contains 58 questions related to physical and psychological symptoms. The questions are divided into 17 psychical items, 8 somatic and 33 other items, all 58 together give a total score. Examples of such questions are: "*Will you please indicate if you were troubled by the following disorders last week: headache, nervousness, dizziness, felt lonely, felt hurt, and so on.*" The list is especially good for measuring psychological well-being and could, like the Cantril scale, be used for measuring overall well-being. Column (5) and (6) refer to subjective health questions. The subjective health question is: "*How is your health in general?*" The answer can vary between very good, good, rather good, sometimes bad and sometimes good, and bad. The relative health question is: "*How is your health compared to other people of your age?*" The answer can vary between much better and much worse.

Table 9.2 shows that for all indicators disability always ranks the lowest, non-working/other are also low and early retirement always

Table 9.3   *Average absolute change in Cantril scale and change in labor market status, 1991 and 1993*

1991 \ 1993	Working	Self-employed	Disabled	Early retiree	Unemployed	Non-working
Working	0.26 (1823)		0.16 (45)	0.38 (243)	−0.23 (30)	0.60 (43)
Self-employed		0.36 (172)				0.43 (7)
Disabled			0.35 (555)		−0.62 (8)	0.37 (19)
Early retiree				0.32 (212)		−0.18 (22)
Unemployed	1.36 (14)				−0.08 (59)	0.80 (15)
Non-working	1.14 (7)		0.86 (7)	1.09 (11)	0.61 (23)	0.42 (289)

Notes: Blank entries: fewer than seven observations.
        Number of observations (transitions) in parentheses.

ranks the highest. In between the ranking is fairly stable over the different indicators, which gives some confidence in the Cantril measure of well-being.

The mean difference of the Cantril score of 1.24 between the disabled and the early retirees on a scale from 0 to 6 seems to say that the disabled have a substantially lower well-being than the early retirees. Later we will present a number of regression results to explain further the pattern found in table 9.2.

The pattern in table 9.2 is confirmed by table 9.3 in which we look at the relation between the average change in the Cantril scale in 1991 and 1993 and the change in labor market status in the same period. To retain enough observations we have aggregated non-working/other, pensioners, and non-working/pensioners into one group: the non-working.

Table 9.3 tells us that remaining in the same labor market situation (diagonal terms) would lead to an increase in well-being, with only one exception: unemployment. Changing from unemployment in 1991 to employment in 1993 increases welfare substantially. Similar improvements for exiting the non-working situation can also be seen. The transition from employment in 1991 to unemployment in 1993 reduces well-being whereas the movement to early retirement or even disability increases well-being.

The model

We assume that c_i^* is a measure of well-being in the following way:

$$c_i^* = U[(x_{i1}, \ldots, x_{ik}),\ z_{i1}, \ldots, z_{in},\ \eta_i] + \varepsilon_i$$

U is a transformation of the variables x and z and the random term η on the Cantril scale and is seen as a measure of well-being. Ideally, U should have a subscript i allowing the utility function to be different for different individuals. Unfortunately, this would create insoluable empirical problems. The xs are the observed arguments of utility, which describe characteristics pertaining to the labor market situation, the z-variables capture other influences such as income, health, family composition, age, and so on. The η is a random term which captures unobserved influences. For example, an optimistic individual could have a high η and thus a high score c_i^*, whereas a pessimistic individual, with the same characteristics and in the same circumstances and with the same utility function scores lower on the happiness scale. With panel data η could be estimated as a fixed effect. Finally, ε is a random term that captures measurement errors such as might arise if one was just having a bad day at the time of interview. In the estimation model both error terms are added into one composite random term.

Implicitly we assume that all respondents interpret the personal well-being question in exactly the same way and evaluate scale differences in well-being in such a way that the individual responses measure the same comparable level of utility. This is the maintained hypothesis. Personal evaluation of well-being can be very much influenced by adjustment and acceptance. Respondents in very dissimilar situations (one being poor, living alone, in a squalid environment, the other being rich, living among caring people, and in a beautiful beach house) can still respond with the same level of well-being having adjusted to their situation. This point was stressed by Sen (1992) and earlier by Easterlin (1973, 1974) and Layard (1980).

In our approach current self-reported happiness is explained by current exogenous variables. For simplicity, utility is assumed to be linear in its arguments: $c_i^* = \beta x_i + \zeta_i$. The self-reported ranking of happiness (c_i) is a number on a seven-point adjusted Cantril scale ranking from 0 (= lowest possible position on the happiness scale) to 6 (highest possible ranking) and is modelled stochastically as an ordered probit:

$$
\begin{aligned}
c_i &= 0 \quad \text{if} \quad \quad c_i^* \leq 0 \\
c_i &= 1 \quad \text{if} \quad 0 < c_i^* \leq \alpha_1 \\
&\;\;\vdots \\
c_i &= 6 \quad \text{if} \quad \alpha_5 < c_i^*
\end{aligned}
$$

where, $0 < \alpha_1 < \alpha_2 < \ldots \alpha_5$.

The estimation results for this model estimated over the whole sample are presented in the next section.

Estimation results

We have estimated a number of ordered probit equations in which individuals' well-being levels, measured by the Cantril scale, are regressed on a set of variables. These variables can be divided into personal characteristics, housing characteristics, health characteristics, labor market status, and other labor market-related variables, income variables, and finally variables containing information about the partner if present. We will build up from a restricted to an extended specification by gradual addition of regressors. Results are shown in table 9.4. As one can see, the effect of labor market status (column (1)) on well-being is fairly stable over the various specifications. The first specification is the simplest, with only labor market status variables on the right-hand side. Workers are the reference group. The results correspond with the ranking in table 9.2. The ordered probit threshold levels are denoted α_1 to α_5. The coefficients suggest that being in the disability scheme instead of working in salaried employment decreases an individual's well-being with 0.73. This decrease is large enough to drop from welfare level 2 to 1 (the difference between α_2 to α_1 is 0.52).

In column (2) we added personal characteristics as regressors. Although the coefficients of pensioner and early retiree change, the ranking remains the same. Well-being first decreases with age, and later from 50 years onwards, increases with age. Other results show that this age effect is picked up by the early retiree dummy and pensioner dummy in the first specification. In other words early retirees are not happier than workers just because they are in the early retirement program, but because they are in general older than workers, and older people are happier than younger ones. Having children at home is associated with less contentment. Being married or living together significantly increases one's well-being, being divorced or widowed decreases it, but this is not significantly different from being alone. Dutch are happier, as are women and "persons with a religion," but the effects are insignificant. No significant effects are found for education.

Adding housing variables in column (3), shows that well-being does not depend on the type of house one is living in (a single family dwelling, or a rental house). When they have difficulties with paying housing costs people really get worried, which leads to a lower feeling of well-being. Part of the negative effect of being disabled, unemployed, or non-working/other arises from the problems with paying housing costs. But even after correcting for this there seems to be an inherent negative feeling correlated with being in one of these states.

Adding objective health variables such as medical visits, hospitalization,

Table 9.4 *Ordered probit results*

	(1)	(2)	(3)	(4)	(5)	(6)	(7)	(8)	(9)
Labor market status									
Disabled	−0.73	−0.81	−0.74	−0.51	−0.48	−0.48	−0.46	−0.48	−0.40
	(0.05)	(0.05)	(0.05)	(0.06)	(0.06)	(0.06)	(0.06)	(0.06)	(0.07)
Non-working/ other	−0.55	−0.42	−0.30	−0.24	−0.21	−0.18	−0.17	−0.27	−0.23
	(0.06)	(0.09)	(0.09)	(0.09)	(0.09)	(0.09)	(0.09)	(0.10)	(0.11)
Unemployed	−0.54	−0.44	−0.31	−0.29	−0.24	−0.22	−0.20	−0.28	−0.17
	(0.09)	(0.09)	(0.10)	(0.10)	(0.10)	(0.10)	(0.10)	(0.11)	(0.13)
Pensioner	−0.19	−0.40	−0.38	−0.36	−0.36	−0.36	−0.33	−0.42	−0.38
	(0.11)	(0.12)	(0.12)	(0.12)	(0.12)	(0.12)	(0.12)	(0.13)	(0.14)
Self-employed	−0.02	0.00	−0.02	−0.04	−0.07	−0.07	−0.08	−0.12	−0.13
	(0.08)	(0.08)	(0.08)	(0.08)	(0.08)	(0.08)	(0.08)	(0.08)	(0.08)
Non-working/ pensioner	0.03	−0.13	−0.07	−0.05	−0.03	−0.04	−0.01	−0.11	−0.05
	(0.13)	(0.13)	(0.13)	(0.14)	(0.14)	(0.14)	(0.14)	(0.15)	(0.16)
Early retiree	0.25	0.01	0.02	0.00	0.01	0.00	0.03	−0.00	0.02
	(0.05)	(0.06)	(0.06)	(0.07)	(0.07)	(0.07)	(0.07)	(0.07)	(0.07)
Personal characteristics									
Family size		0.09	0.11	0.12	0.07	0.07	−0.06	0.07	0.08
		(0.11)	(0.12)	(0.11)	(0.12)	(0.11)	(0.11)	(0.11)	(0.11)
Children at home		−0.22	−0.22	−0.25	−0.23	−0.23	−0.23	−0.23	−0.24
		(0.08)	(0.08)	(0.08)	(0.08)	(0.08)	(0.08)	(0.08)	(0.08)
Children left home		0.01	0.02	0.01	0.00				
		(0.05)	(0.05)	(0.05)	(0.05)				
Married		0.30	0.29	0.30	0.33	0.32	0.28	0.27	0.27
		(0.12)	(0.12)	(0.12)	(0.12)	(0.11)	(0.12)	(0.12)	(0.12)
Living together		0.23	0.23	0.29	0.32				
		(0.17)	(0.17)	(0.17)	(0.18)				
Divorced		−0.18	−0.11	−0.11	−0.12	−0.10	−0.09	−0.10	−0.10
		(0.10)	(0.10)	(0.10)	(0.10)	(0.08)	(0.08)	(0.08)	(0.08)
Widow(er)		0.02	−0.01	−0.04	−0.05				
		(0.10)	(0.10)	(0.10)	(0.11)				
Dutch		0.18	0.16	0.13	0.14	0.13	0.13	0.13	0.12
		(0.07)	(0.07)	(0.07)	(0.07)	(0.07)	(0.07)	(0.07)	(0.07)
Female		0.04	0.08	0.13	0.16	0.16	0.17	0.17	0.17
		(0.07)	(0.07)	(0.07)	(0.07)	(0.07)	(0.07)	(0.07)	(0.07)
Religious		0.04	0.03	0.04	0.04	0.04	0.05	0.05	0.04
		(0.04)	(0.04)	(0.04)	(0.04)	(0.04)	(0.04)	(0.04)	(0.04)
Education level:									
Lower general		−0.04	−0.05	−0.08	−0.05	−0.09	−0.09	−0.09	−0.09
		(0.10)	(0.10)	(0.10)	(0.10)	(0.09)	(0.09)	(0.10)	(0.10)

(*cont.*)

Table 9.4 (*cont.*)

	(1)	(2)	(3)	(4)	(5)	(6)	(7)	(8)	(9)
Lower vocational		−0.08	−0.10	−0.14	−0.11				
		(0.10)	(0.10)	(0.10)	(0.10)				
Secondary general		0.01	−0.03	−0.07	−0.07	−0.08	−0.09	−0.09	−0.09
		(0.10)	(0.10)	(0.10)	(0.10)	(0.10)	(0.10)	(0.10)	(0.10)
Secondary vocational		−0.00	−0.04	−0.09	−0.08				
		(0.11)	(0.10)	(0.10)	(0.10)				
Higher general		0.09	0.01	−0.06	−0.08	−0.05	−0.06	−0.06	−0.05
		(0.14)	(0.14)	(0.14)	(0.14)	(0.10)	(0.10)	(0.10)	(0.10)
Higher vocational		0.13	0.06	−0.01	−0.03				
		(0.10)	(0.10)	(0.10)	(0.10)				
Academic		−0.04	−0.11	−0.18	−0.25	−0.26	−0.28	−0.27	−0.26
		(0.12)	(0.12)	(0.12)	(0.12)	(0.12)	(0.12)	(0.12)	(0.12)
Age		−0.10	−0.10	−0.08	−0.08	−0.08	−0.08	−0.07	−0.07
		(0.07)	(0.07)	(0.07)	(0.07)	(0.06)	(0.06)	(0.06)	(0.06)
Age squared		0.001	0.001	0.001	0.001	0.001	0.001	0.001	0.0009
		(0.0006)	(0.0006)	(0.0006)	(0.0006)	(0.0006)	(0.0006)	(0.0006)	(0.0006)
Housing									
Single family dwelling		−0.00	−0.01	−0.01					
		(0.05)	(0.05)	(0.05)					
Rented house		−0.03	−0.03	−0.01					
		(0.04)	(0.04)	(0.04)					
Difficulties with paying housing costs			−0.54	−0.47	−0.47	−0.46	−0.46	−0.47	−0.45
			(0.06)	(0.06)	(0.06)	(0.06)	(0.06)	(0.06)	(0.06)
Health									
Visited general practioner				−0.09	−0.09	−0.09	−0.09	−0.07	−0.08
				(0.04)	(0.04)	(0.05)	(0.04)	(0.06)	(0.04)
Visited medical specialist				−0.08	−0.08	−0.08	−0.08	−0.08	−0.08
				(0.04)	(0.04)	(0.04)	(0.04)	(0.04)	(0.04)
Been hospitalized				−0.21	−0.20	−0.20	−0.22	−0.21	−0.19
				(0.10)	(0.10)	(0.10)	(0.10)	(0.10)	(0.10)
Undergone surgery				0.21	0.21	0.21	0.22	0.22	0.21
				(0.12)	(0.12)	(0.12)	(0.12)	(0.12)	(0.11)
Visited physical therapist				−0.10	−0.10	−0.10	−0.10	−0.10	−0.11
				(0.05)	(0.05)	(0.05)	(0.05)	(0.05)	(0.05)
No problems with daily routine				0.26	0.26	0.26	0.26	0.26	0.26
				(0.05)	(0.05)	(0.05)	(0.05)	(0.05)	(0.05)
No problems with daily activities				0.13	0.12	0.13	0.13	0.12	0.13
				(0.04)	(0.04)	(0.05)	(0.04)	(0.04)	(0.04)
No disorders				0.13	0.13	0.13	0.12	0.12	0.12
				(0.05)	(0.05)	(0.05)	(0.05)	(0.05)	(0.05)
Income									
Own income					0.29	0.28	0.28	0.28	0.26
					(0.11)	(0.11)	(0.11)	(0.11)	(0.11)
Partner income					−0.01	−0.02	0.21	0.20	0.18
					(0.46)	(0.46)	(0.46)	(0.46)	(0.47)

	(1)	(2)	(3)	(4)	(5)	(6)	(7)	(8)	(9)
Non-labor income					0.52	0.52	0.51	0.51	0.57
					(0.19)	(0.18)	(0.19)	(0.19)	(0.20)
Labor market history									
Duration of previous						−0.003	−0.003	−0.003	−0.003
unemployment spell						(0.001)	(0.001)	(0.001)	(0.001)
Duration of current labor						−0.20	−0.22	−0.22	−0.24
market situation						(0.14)	(0.14)	(0.14)	(0.14)
Partner variables									
Both partners work							0.09	0.09	0.08
							(0.06)	(0.06)	(0.06)
Partner visited general							−0.08	−0.08	−0.09
practioner							(0.05)	(0.05)	(0.05)
Partner has no problems							0.11	0.11	0.11
with daily routine							(0.05)	(0.05)	(0.05)
Comparison income									
Predicted income								−0.25	−0.25
								(0.14)	(0.14)
Subjective labor market-related variables									
If working, prefers to									−0.40
stop working									(0.12)
If non-working, prefers to									−0.24
have a paid job									(0.06)
If working, looking for a job									−0.36
									(0.12)
If non-working, looking for									0.04
a job									(0.12)
Threshold levels									
α_1	0.50	0.52	0.53	0.54	0.54	0.54	0.54	0.54	0.55
	(0.03)	(0.04)	(0.04)	(0.04)	(0.04)	(0.04)	(0.04)	(0.04)	(0.04)
α_2	1.02	1.05	1.08	1.11	1.11	1.11	1.11	1.11	1.12
	(0.04)	(0.04)	(0.04)	(0.04)	(0.04)	(0.04)	(0.05)	(0.04)	(0.04)
α_3	1.82	1.87	1.91	1.96	1.96	1.97	1.97	1.97	1.98
	(0.04)	(0.05)	(0.05)	(0.05)	(0.05)	(0.05)	(0.05)	(0.05)	(0.05)
α_4	2.91	2.99	3.03	3.10	3.11	3.11	3.12	3.12	3.14
	(0.05)	(0.05)	(0.05)	(0.05)	(0.05)	(0.05)	(0.05)	(0.05)	(0.05)
α_5	3.44	3.52	3.56	3.65	3.66	3.66	3.67	3.67	3.69
	(0.05)	(0.05)	(0.05)	(0.05)	(0.06)	(0.06)	(0.06)	(0.06)	(0.06)
Constant	2.10	3.95	4.11	3.37	3.28	3.30	3.14	3.25	3.21
	(0.05)	(1.76)	(1.77)	(1.77)	(1.77)	(1.71)	(1.71)	(1.72)	(1.73)
Log likelihood	−5731.9	−5658.9	−5619.9	−5544.0	−5534.1	−5529.8	−5524.2	−5522.4	−5503.5

Note: Standard errors in parentheses.

and surgery, etc. (column (4)) changes the coefficients of the disabled and other non-working. Evidently part of the negative feeling of being on disability is the result of ill-health, which can be seen by comparison of columns (3) and (4). But more surprisingly this also holds for the non-working/other, while their health is not worse than the health of early retirees. Maybe bad health bothers the non-workers/other more than the early retirees. The health variables we used are dummies for having visited a general practitioner last year; a medical specialist; been hospitalized; undergone surgery; visited a physical therapist; having no problems with daily routine, such as going up and downstairs, getting dressed, sitting down and getting up from a chair; no problems with daily activities, the so called ADL-list, like lifting, kneeling, walking, reading, doing sums, and having had no disorders, like high blood pressure, bronchitis, etc. All variables have the expected sign, so that well-being is higher among the healthy. Having had surgery also has a positive effect, possibly relating to the success of the operation. We have tried to use the more objective health measures, but still some endogeneity problems in the relation between health and labor market status might be bothering us here.

Adding income variables hardly changes the effects of labor market status on well-being (column (5)). We could interpret the coefficients of labor market states in columns (1)–(4) as total effects (pecuniary and non-pecuniary), while coefficients of labor market states in column (5) represent only the non-pecuniary effect on well-being. The income effect is taken up by the income variable. In contrast with Clark and Oswald (1994), we found robust income effects, always with the expected sign that more income leads to higher well-being. The partner's income has no significant influence on one's well-being, just as with most other partner variables, as we will see later. Non-labor income has a positive effect. This could be seen as a proxy for the wealth effect. We did not include wealth since there were quite a number of missing data on this variable. Adding income results in a negative effect of academic education. The positive effect through higher income for academic educated people reduces the higher education effect.

In column (6) we added labor market history variables such as previous unemployment duration over the working life and the duration of the current labor market situation. We find hardly any changes in the coefficients of the labor market states. The coefficient on previous unemployment experience has a negative effect on one's well-being, suggesting that the negative effect of unemployment is permanent. This is comparable with a study by Clark and Oswald (1994). Other studies such as Korpi (1994) found no effect of previous unemployment spells, or of current unemployment status (Björklund, 1985). There are a number of possible explanations for these differences in results: different measures of well-being or the different sample composition. In our sample, the vast majority is male, while the results of the other studies were based on females only, or on a sample with an equal proportion of men and women. There are indications that women have less trouble coping with unemployment. Including the duration of the current labor market situation, we try to measure a sort of persistence effect. The negative coefficient implies that a longer duration in a certain labor market state leads to lower well-being. In other words: variety is the spice of life.

The small effect of partner variables was somewhat surprising (column (7)). If the partner has no problems with daily routine the respondent's well-being increases, and there is a small negative effect of the partner having visited the family doctor. A working partner has a positive effect on the well-being of working heads of households.

In column (8) we have added a comparison or reference level of income proxying a level of income against which an individual compares himself or herself. The notion behind this, well known in psychology but seldom used in economics, is that well-being depends on relative income. Comparison income has been imputed as the predicted value from an income regression equation. Comparison income has a significant negative effect. As we expected, the higher your own income relative to the income of comparable persons, the higher your well-being.[1] As we can see, adding comparison income enlarges the differences in the coefficients of the labor market states. A possible explanation of this could be the difference in income equality within labor market states. The unemployed and disabled have lower income inequality than workers and thus fewer grounds for envy. This could mitigate the effects of labor market states on well-being. If we disentangle the envy effect from the pure labor market states effect, the latter would increase, as is the case.

Column (9) adds subjective, labor market-related variables. Adding these subjective labor market variables we try to distinguish the involuntary character of the labor market state from a "pure" state effect. For workers, we add a variable which measures whether the respondent prefers to stop working, for non-workers whether they would like to have a paid job or not. For both we add a variable which measures whether they are looking for a job. A non-worker who prefers to have a paid job might have been laid off, while a non-worker who does not prefer to have a paid job might have chosen to stop working voluntarily. The involuntary character of either working or not working clearly decreases well-being. Working respondents, looking for another job, are less happy, whereas looking for a job by non-workers is not relevant for well-being. Comparison of column (9) with column (8) shows that a large part of the negative unemployment effect is related to the involuntary character of being unemployed.

Even after controlling for all these effects, there remains a dominant negative effect of being in the disability program. The negative effect of being unemployed has gradually decreased, and is at the end barely significant at the 10 percent level. Academic education has a significant negative effect. This is a well known result in the literature, perhaps caused by unrealistic aspirations. In our age group, 43–63, older people are happier than younger people. Clark, Oswald and Warr (1994) find that happiness is lowest in the mid-thirties' age group. Well-being is higher among the healthy. In contrast with other studies, income has a robust positive effect on well-being, and comparison income has a negative effect. Previous unemployment lowers well-being. Duration of the current spell in the same labor market status also reduces well-being. A healthy partner increases well-being and being involuntarily in the current labor market state decreases well-being.

Conclusions

We studied the relation between labor market status and well-being. We analyzed elderly persons in the Netherlands who have many routes to retire early. They are often the first to be laid off during reorganizations and shut-downs. For all these reasons, it is interesting to know the effect on well-being of being out of work.

We found that after correcting for health and housing characteristics, and preferences for work, there still remains a negative effect on welfare of being in one of the non-working states. The negative effect of non-working is strongest for disabled and pensioners, and slightly less for the non-working and unemployed. The effect of being early retired is not significantly different from the effect of being a worker. One should be cautious with the finding that disabled are less happy than workers, since the coefficient for disabled could be biased due to simultaneity problems. The overall picture that emerges is that the older non-working individual has a lower well-being than a similar but working individual, maybe because he or she feels pushed out. The negative effect of being a pensioner on well-being is remarkable and is not as might be expected.

We do not find evidence that individuals with a better ability to cope with different situations (such as higher education and/or being older) have a higher well-being. The effect might be suppressed by the effect that the higher educated have higher aspiration levels and thus are more easily frustrated.

Higher income leads to a higher level of well-being and the higher income is relative to others, the higher the well-being. We found a clear income comparison effect. Better health, being female and better housing conditions also increase well-being.

The negative effect of unemployment on well-being can be explained for a large part by the involuntary nature of being unemployed. The large drop in the well-being coefficient of unemployment when a measure of involuntariness is added to the specification sustains the view that unemployment is predominantly involuntary.

Appendix: data, means and frequencies

Table 9A.1 *Means and frequencies of variables*

Means

			Mean	Min.	Max.
Own income	=	yearly wage and/or benefit income of head of household in Dutch guilders	39,537	1,020	248,000
Partner income	=	yearly wage and/or benefit income of partner in Dutch guilders	1,022	0	45,864
Non-labor income	=	yearly child allowance + separation allowance + interest in Dutch guilders	1,937	0	2,000,000
Family size (log)			0.79	0	2.30
Age			55	43	65
Duration of current labor market situation (months)			322	0	540
Duration of previous unemployment spell			3	0	240
Expected income			38,716	11,423	93,685

Frequencies

Well-being, transformed Cantril scale	1991	1993
0 = Very unhappy	231	117
1	280	185
2	464	362
3	881	908
4	1,087	1,335
5	372	383
6 = Very happy	239	280

(*cont.*)

Table 9A.1 (*cont.*)

Well-being, transformed Cantril scale		1991	1993
Dummies		**1**	**0**
Disabled		581	2,989
Non-working/other		217	3,353
Unemployed		117	3,453
Pensioner		95	3,475
Self-employed		172	3,398
Working in salaried employment		1,791	779
Non-working/pensioner		48	3,522
Early retiree		549	3,021
Children at home		1,500	2,070
Children left home		2,542	1,028
Married		2,654	1,028
Living together		82	3,488
Divorced		363	3,207
Widow(er)		257	3,313
Dutch		3,388	182
Female		601	1,384
Religious		2,186	1,384
Education level:	Lower general	633	2,937
	Lower vocational	780	2,790
	Secondary general	502	3,068
	Secondary vocational	550	3,020
	Higher general	159	3,411
	Higher vocational	659	2,911
	Academic	198	3,372
Single family dwelling		2,748	822
Rented house		1,515	2,055
Difficulties with paying housing costs		356	3,214
Visited general practioner, last year		2,504	1,066
Visited medical specialist, last year		1,442	2,128
Been hospitalized last year		373	3,197
Undergone surgery last year		240	3,330
Visited physical therapist last year		796	2,774
No problems with daily routine		2,740	830
No problems with daily activities		1,186	2,384
No disorders		1,373	2,197
Both partners work		644	2,926
Partner visited general practioner		1,916	1,654
Partner has no problems with daily routine		2,062	1,508
Respondent works and prefers to stop working		86	3,483
Respondent does not work and prefers to have a paid job		604	2,966
Respondent works and is looking for a job		84	3,486
Respondent does not work and is looking for a job		100	3,470

Notes

Research for this chapter was financed by a grant from NESTOR, the Dutch Stimulation Program for Aging Research, and from the University of Leiden Speerpunten Program. We thank Peter van Wijck and two anonymous referees for helpful comments on an earlier draft.
1   Writing y for own income and $\hat{y}$ for comparison income we estimated the combined income effects as $\alpha_1 y + \alpha_2(y - \hat{y})$ or $(\alpha_1 + \alpha_2)y - \alpha_2 \hat{y}$. We expected $\alpha_2 > 0$ or in our specification $-\alpha_2 < 0$.

References

Björklund, A., 1985. "Unemployment and mental health: some evidence from panel data," *Journal of Human Resources*, 20, 469–83
Cantril, H., 1965. *The Pattern of Human Concern*, New Brunswick, NJ.: Rutgers University Press
Clark A.E. and A.J. Oswald, 1993. "Satisfaction and comparison income," *Working Paper*, 367, London School of Economics
1994. "Unhappiness and unemployment," *Economic Journal*, 104, 648–59
Clark A.E., A.J. Oswald and P.B. Warr, 1994. "Is job satisfaction unshaped in age?," *CEPREMAP Research Memorandum*, 940
Easterlin, R.A., 1973. "Does money buy happiness?," *Public Interest*, 30, 3–10
1974. "Does economic growth improve the human lot? Some empirical evidence," in P.A. David and M.W. Reder (eds.), *Nations and Households in Economic Growth*, New York: Academic Press
Hagenaars, A.J.M., 1986. *The Perception of Poverty*, Amsterdam: North-Holland
Hammond, P., 1991. "Interpersonal comparison of utility: why and how they are and should be made," in J. Elster and J.E. Roemer (eds.), *Interpersonal Comparisons of Well-being*, Cambridge: Cambridge University Press, 200–54
Kapteyn, A., 1985. "Utility and economics," *De Economist*, 133, 1–20
Korpi, T., 1994. "Is well-being related to employment status?: Unemployment, labor market policies and psychological well-being of youth," *Discussion Paper*, Stockholm University
Layard, R., 1980. "Human satisfactions and public policy," *Economic Journal*, 90, 737–50
Moffitt, R., 1993. "An economic model of welfare stigma," *American Economic Review*, 73, 1023–35
Morawetz, D., E. Atia, G. Bin-Nun, L. Felous, Y. Gariplerden, E. Harris, S. Soustiel, G. Tombros and Y. Zarfaty, 1977. "Income distribution and self-rated happiness," *Economic Journal*, 87, 511–22
Plug, E.J.S. and B.M.S. van Praag, 1993. "Family equivalence scales within a narrow and broad welfare context," *Discussion Paper*, University of Amsterdam
Raaij, W.F. van and G. Antonides, 1991. "Costs and benefits of unemployment and employment," *Journal of Economic Psychology*, 12, 667–87
Sen, A., 1992. *Inequality Reexamined*, Oxford: Clarendon Press

Simon, J.L., 1974. "Interpersonal welfare comparisons can be made and used for redistribution decisions," *Kyklos*, 27, 63–97

1978. "Interpersonal welfare comparisons: a reply," *Kyklos*, 31, 315–17

Tomes, N., 1986. "Income distribution, happiness and satisfaction: a direct test of the interdependent preferences model," *Journal of Economic Psychology*, 7, 425–46

Woittiez, I., M. Lindeboom and J. Theeuwes, 1994. "Labour force exit routes of the Dutch elderly, a discrete choice model," in A.L. Bovenberg (ed.), *The Economics of Pensions: The Case of The Netherlands*, OCFEB, Research Centre for Economic Policy, Erasmus University, Rotterdam, 1–23

Part III
Summarizing welfare

10 Do inequality measures measure inequality?

Gary Fields

Introduction

I first met Aldi Hagenaars at the World Econometric Society Congress in Cambridge, Massachusetts in 1985. At that time, we had a long discussion about the question posed in the title of this chapter. The driving force behind Aldi's research program became clear to me then: a profound concern with people's feelings about their economic well-being accompanied by the quest to devise measures that reflect those underlying feelings.

This chapter follows that tradition. My own research program has dealt with the twin questions of who benefits how much from economic growth and why. Before answering these questions, it is necessary to decide what measure to take to the data to determine if economic growth is welfare-enhancing. For many people, one component of a social welfare judgment is the extent of income inequality.

There is no shortage of inequality measures (Gini coefficient, Theil index, Atkinson index, etc.). The task is to decide what we mean by "inequality" and then to determine which, if any, of the available measures behave as "inequality" does.

The literature offers two principal ways of relating social welfare to the inequality of income.[1] One, due to Kolm (1966) and Atkinson (1970), first constructs a social welfare function defined on the space of incomes

$$W = W(y_1, y_2, \ldots, y_n) \tag{10.1}$$

then defines the equally distributed income as the amount of income which, if equally distributed would yield the same social welfare as the actual distribution, and finally measures inequality as the gap between the actual mean income $\bar{y}$ and the equally distributed income y^*

$$I = I - (y^*/\bar{y})$$

Another way of taking the level of national income and the inequality of its distribution into account in welfare judgments is to rank income distributions in terms of the mean income level $\bar{Y}$, income inequality I and perhaps other things:

$$W = f(\bar{Y}, I, \ldots), \quad \partial W/\partial \bar{Y} > 0, \quad \partial W/\partial I < 0$$

Ranking income distributions in terms of income level and income inequality is common practice in a whole host of empirical studies of "growth and equity." This practice receives abundant theoretical support, for instance, in Sen (1973), Blackorby and Donaldson (1977, 1984), Fields (1979), Ebert (1987), and Lambert (1989). Schur-concave social welfare functions provide one justification for this practice; another is diminishing marginal utility of identical interpersonally comparable utility functions.

To be able to rank income distributions in this way, we must determine how the inequality of one distribution compares to that of another, which means that the primitive concept of "inequality" must be made precise. Amartya Sen (1973, pp. 2, 3) has written:

> there are some advantages in . . . try[ing] to catch the extent of inequality in some *objective* sense . . . so that one can distinguish between (a) *"seeing"* more or less inequality, and (b) *"valuing"* it more or less in ethical terms . . . There is, obviously, an objective element in this notion: a fifty-fifty division of a cake between two persons is clearly more equal in some straightforward sense than giving all to one and none to the other. [First emphasis Sen's, second and third emphases mine.]

It is precisely this objective sense of "seeing" what inequality is which I shall adopt in this chapter in the context of inequality comparisons.

In the literature, much attention has been paid to a number of aspects of inequality including the distinction between relative and absolute inequality, axiomatization of inequality, the Lorenz criterion for inequality comparisons, properties of various inequality measures, and inequality decomposition. In no way do I wish to argue with the main results derived in these areas. Rather, my purpose here is to add to the theory of inequality measurement by dealing with one aspect of inequality which has been largely ignored by economists[2] and by others.[3] This is the question of how inequality changes – in particular, whether it increases, decreases, or remains unchanged – when income grows in specified ways.[4]

The balance of this chapter deals with two distinct conceptual entities, "inequality" and "inequality measures." The next section analyzes how "inequality" might be said to change under various types of economic growth and explores the foundations for alternative views. One approach in terms of "elitism of the rich" and "isolation of the poor" is then described. The following section looks into the behavior of "inequality measures" and the relationship between "inequality measures" and "inequality," and a final section draws some conclusions.

How does inequality change with economic growth?

In this chapter, inequality is analyzed on the space of "incomes" among "persons," ruling out multiple goods and problems of aggregation. The analysis proceeds axiomatically, following a long tradition which dates back at least to Pigou (1912) and Dalton (1920) and has been accepted by many others ever since.[5] It holds that whenever a transfer of income is made from a person[6] who is relatively poor to another who is relatively rich, inequality increases. Notice two things about this way of conceptualizing the primitive concept "inequality." First it is in terms of *conditional* "if . . . then" statements. Second, the answer to the question "what is inequality?" is sought by looking at inequality *orderings* on pairs of distributions, addressing the related question "when is one distribution more equal than another?" I shall follow this practice and seek to clarify the meaning of "inequality" by formulating a series of conditional statements on binary comparisons.

Let the economy consist of n "persons," total population being assumed fixed. Let Φ be the share of persons having income y_H and $1 - \Phi$ the share having income $y_L(< y_H)$. Analyzing this restricted domain is helpful in forming precise views on the meaning of inequality before moving on to analyze inequality on the more general domain of incomes, a task left for the future.

Throughout the rest of this chapter, we shall use the notation $\Phi = nH/n$ and $\Theta = Y_H/Y_L$ whenever $\Phi \in (0,1)$.[7] The term "increase in Θ" shall be understood as signifying an increase in Y_H/Y_L $\forall \Phi \in (0,1)$.

In the two-income world, income growth can take place by increasing Y_H, Y_L, or Φ, or by some combination of these. A simple example shows why inequality rankings are sometimes difficult to make when incomes are growing, even in so simple a world.

Consider an economy consisting of six individuals with an initial distribution of income [1,1,1,1,1,6]. Now suppose the economy experiences income growth of $5. The change in inequality depends on how that $5 is distributed.

First let the entire $5 go to the rich person. We have little difficulty in ranking the new distribution [1,1,1,1,1,11] as *more unequal* than the old.

Suppose instead that the $5 of income growth is divided equally among all the low income persons, resulting in a new distribution [2,2,2,2,2,6]. Once again, the ranking is likely to be uncontroversial: the new distribution may be said to be *more equal* than the old.

Consider a third possibility: that the $5 of income growth produces an income gain for *just one* of the low income persons.[8] Compare the two income distributions

$$Y_1 = [1,1,1,1,1,6]$$

and

$$Y_2 = [1,1,1,1,6,6]$$

Which is more equal, Y_1 or Y_2?[9] The rest of this chapter seeks an answer.

A natural starting point would be Lorenz curve comparisons. One income distribution is said to *Lorenz-dominate* another if the first distribution's Lorenz curve is somewhere above and nowhere below that of the second. The *Lorenz criteria for relating the inequality of two distributions* consist of several parts:

(i)   If two distributions $X, Y \in Z$ have the same Lorenz curves L_x and L_y, then they are equally unequal ($=_L$) by the Lorenz criterion, i.e.

$$L_X = L_Y \Rightarrow X =_L Y$$

(ii) If distribution X Lorenz dominates distribution Y, then X is more equal than Y by the Lorenz criterion (L):

$$L_X \succeq L_Y \Rightarrow X \succ_L Y$$

(iii) If the Lorenz curves of X and Y cross, then the inequality of the two distributions cannot be compared using the Lorenz criterion alone.

Together, these are termed ranking $\succeq_L$.[10]

When economic growth causes the income distribution to change from $Y_1 = [1,1,1,1,1,6]$ to $Y_2 = [1,1,1,1,6,6]$, we may calculate the cumulative income shares Cum $Y_1 = [1/11, 2/11, 3/11, 4/11, 5/11, 1]$ and Cum $Y_2 = [1/16, 2/16, 3/16, 4/16, 8/16, 1]$ and note that their Lorenz curves cross. Therefore the two distributions' relative inequalities cannot be ranked on the basis of the Lorenz properties alone. Likewise, in a sequence of income distributions whereby an economy progresses from $Y_1 = [1,1,1,1,1,6]$ to $Y_2 = [1,1,1,1,6,6]$ to $Y_3 = [1,1,1,6,6,6]$ to $Y_4 = [1,1,6,6,6,6]$ to $Y_5 = [1,6,6,6,6,6]$, *all* of the associated Lorenz curves cross each other. If we want to say how the inequalities of the different distributions compare, we must go beyond the Lorenz criteria considered thus far and appeal to additional properties.

One way of sharpening our views about what inequality *is* is to look at the sequence of distributions from Y_1 through Y_5 and see what we "see."[11] From simple eyeballing of the sequence Y_1 through Y_5, many different patterns emerge as plausible possibilities. It might be said that inequality decreases monotonically, increases monotonically, follows a U-shaped path, follows an inverted U-shaped path, or even remains unchanged. This does not exhaust the possible patterns.

Experimental evidence confirms the diversity of views for a similar thought experiment. Amiel and Cowell (1992) asked more than 1,000 university students to compare the inequality of two distributions

$$A = [5, 5, 5, 10]$$

and

$$B = [5, 5, 10, 10]$$

40 percent judged A as more unequal, 56 percent judged B as more unequal, and 4 percent judged them equally unequal. When asked to compare

$$B = [5, 5, 10, 10]$$

with

$$C = [5, 10, 10, 10]$$

57 percent judged B as more unequal, 40 percent judged C as more unequal, and 3 percent judged them equally unequal. Furthermore, in three-way comparisons, by far the most common judgment was to deem [5, 5, 10, 10] as less unequal than *both* [5, 5, 5, 10] and [5,10,10,10], a view consistent with the U-shaped pattern.

In addition, Amiel and Cowell's respondents were asked about their views on what I have here called the high income sector-enlargement process. Specifically, the question asked was:

Suppose there is a society consisting of n people. There is one rich person and n − 1 identical poor people. One by one, some of those who were poor acquire the same income as the rich person, so that eventually there are n − 1 (identical) rich people and just one poor person. Please circle the appropriate response:

Inequality increases continuously.	(7.5%)
Inequality decreases continuously.	(20.5%)
Inequality at first increases and then decreases.	(19.9%)
Inequality at first decreases and then increases.	(36.7%)

Inequality remains the same throughout.   (11.2%)

None of the above.   (4.1%)

(The frequency distribution of valid responses is given in brackets).

Here, as well, the U-shaped pattern is the most common.

At this point, I would invite the reader to consider his or her own rankings of the inequality of Y_1 versus Y_2 versus Y_3 versus Y_4 versus Y_5, of A versus B versus C, and of the high income sector-enlargement process described in the previous paragraph.

Justifying alternative patterns in terms of "elitism of the rich" and "isolation of the poor"

If you had trouble making the inequality comparisons asked for above, it may be because you lack a framework for moving beyond Lorenz comparisons. This section may help in that regard.

A philosopher, Temkin (1986), has analyzed essentially the same process, different only in that he has total income falling rather than rising. Temkin's analysis is in terms of individual complaints – how serious the inequality in a situation is from the standpoint of particular individuals in that situation. Alternative principles (additive, weighted additive, and maximin) and referents (relative to the average, relative to the best-off person, and relative to all those better off) lead plausibly, in his view, to most of the various patterns raised above.

In an earlier paper (Fields, 1987), I adopted a different approach, which I also take here. Rather than weighing "individual complaints," I look at the question from a societal point of view. The specific way in which I now prefer to do this is with reference to two concepts – "elitism of the rich" and "isolation of the poor" – which are developed formally in Fields (1993).

Briefly put, *elitism of the rich* (ER) is the following idea. When one person has a high income ($\$y_H$) and everybody else has a low income ($\$y_L$ each), the one rich person may be thought to have a very elite position. In this case the economy may be said to have a high degree of elitism of the rich. Now let a second person acquire a high income, all others' incomes remaining the same (Φ increases). Because each of the rich now has to share his elitist position with someone else, the two rich persons together might be regarded as less elite than one person was when he alone was rich. Thus, elitism of the rich falls. If a third person is enriched, elitism of the rich might be thought to fall further, but not by

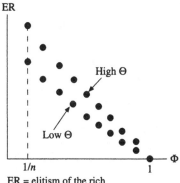

ER = elitism of the rich

Figure 10.1 Elitism of the rich

as much as when the second person was enriched. In general, the larger the fraction rich, the smaller is elitism of the rich and the smaller is the change in elitism of the rich for a given increase in size of the high income group. When everybody is rich, there no longer is any elitism of the rich.

Elitism of the rich also varies with the ratio of high incomes to low incomes (Θ). Holding the number of persons in the two income groups constant, if the amount received by each high income person increases or if the amount received by each low income person decreases, elitism of the rich should increase.

Figure 10.1 summarizes how elitism of the rich varies with Φ and Θ.

Isolation of the poor (IP) may be defined as a reciprocal notion to elitism of the rich. When everyone in an economy is equally poor, there is no isolation of the poor, because there are no rich from whom to be isolated. When one person escapes poverty, isolation of the poor is created. As the number with high incomes increases, those who are left behind may be regarded, as a group, as increasingly isolated. For this reason, isolation of the poor may be viewed as increasing at an increasing rate as the high income group expands. Finally, when just one person is poor, it can be argued that that one person is *very* isolated from everyone else, at which point isolation of the poor attains a maximum. Now, holding the numbers in the two groups constant any increase in the ratio between high and low incomes (Θ) should increase isolation of the poor. These properties of isolation of the poor are shown in Figure 10.2.

From these concepts of elitism of the rich and isolation of the poor, we may derive various inequality patterns. Those observers who wish to view inequality solely in terms of elitism of the rich would see inequality

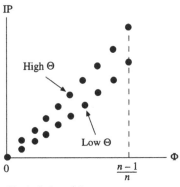

IP = isolation of the poor

Figure 10.2 Isolation of the poor

as *falling* continuously on the interval $\Phi \in (0,1)$ for any given Θ. The higher is Θ, the higher is inequality. This class, shown in figure 10.3, will be termed the I class.

Others may wish to view inequality solely in terms of isolation of the poor. These observers would see inequality as *rising* continuously on the interval $\Phi \in (0,1)$ for any given Θ. A higher Θ implies more inequality. Figure 10.4 depicts this class, denoted the I_+ class.

Many observers hold the view that inequality consists of *both* elitism of the rich and isolation of the poor. How might these notions be combined on their common domain, the open interval (0,1)?

Elitism of the rich and isolation of the poor need to be expressed in comparable units, which may be done by postulating that for any Φ, $ER(\Phi) = IP(1 - \Phi)$.

Next, elitism of the rich and isolation of the poor need to be combined in some plausible way. Suppose equal weight is given to each. The simplest such mixing function, defined on the open interval (0,1), the common domain of $ER(\cdot)$ and $IP(\cdot)$, is

$$I(\Phi, \Theta) = (ER + IP)/2$$

Alternatively, unequal weights may be posited by using a linear mixing function:

$$\bar{I}(\cdot) = w \, ER(\cdot) + (1 - w) \, IP(\cdot), \quad w > 0, \quad w \neq 1 - w$$

Define the I_{min} *class* to be those $I(\cdot)$ rankings which are U-shaped as Φ varies on the open interval (0,1) for a given Θ, and which lie on higher contours for higher Θ, as shown in figure 10.5; denote those which also are symmetric with a unique minimum at $\Theta = 1/2$ as the symmetric I_{min}

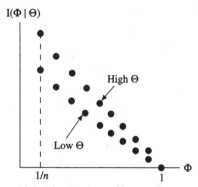

Figure 10.3 The I_- class of inequality rankings

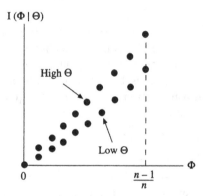

Figure 10.4 The I_+ class of inequality rankings

class. Fields (1993) proves that the preceding properties with *equal* weights generate the symmetric I_{min} class and these properties with *unequal* weights generate a ranking which is a member of the I_{min} class but not the symmetric I_{min} class.

Note two things. First, given $I(\cdot) = w\ ER(\cdot) + (1+w)IP(\cdot)$, for $w = 1$, we have the I_- pattern shown in figure 10.3, and for $w = 0$, the I_+ pattern shown in figure 10.4, which may be attractive to some observers. Second, these are the *only* patterns consistent with the preceding axioms. In particular, the inverted-U pattern *cannot* be generated from the preceding properties.

It remains to extend the inequality ordering to the end-points $\Phi = 0$ and $\Phi = 1$. If we adopt the Lorenz axioms, we obtain two additional restrictions on the inequality orderings. One restriction, arising from the transfer principle, is that a situation in which everyone has the same income must be regarded as more equal than any situation in which

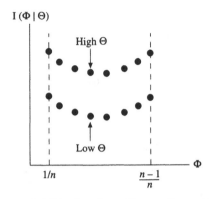

Figure 10.5 The I_{min} class of inequality rankings

incomes differ. Accordingly, the Lorenz properties require that a situation of equally distributed incomes be deemed a "most equal point." The other restriction, arising from the income homogeneity principle, is that all equally distributed incomes be deemed "most equal points." If we adopt a natural normalization – that most equal points have *no* inequality – we then have

$$I(Y/n, Y/n, \ldots Y/n) = 0$$

for all total income amounts Y.

The concept of a most equal point accords with the notions introduced earlier of elitism of the rich and isolation of the poor. Suppose that two incomes are possible but that everybody has one of those incomes and nobody has the other. In one case, there is no elitism of the rich, because there are no rich; and in the other case, there is no

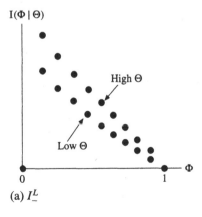

(a) I^L_-

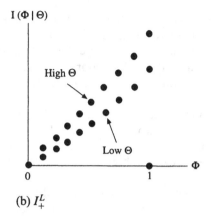

(b) I_+^L

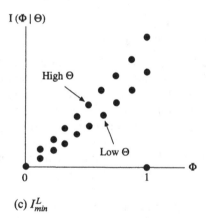

(c) I_{min}^L

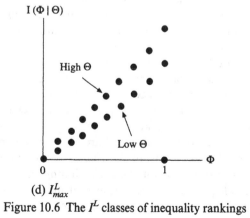

(d) I_{max}^L

Figure 10.6 The I^L classes of inequality rankings

isolation of the poor, because there are no poor. One would be inclined to say that a situation where all are equally rich or equally poor is more equal than a situation where some are rich and some are poor and that the two situations ("all rich" and "all poor") have the same inequality as one another. Inequality notions in the I_-^L, I_+^L, and I_{min}^L classes make these judgments.

Combining these judgments with the alternative enlargement patterns as depicted in figures 10.3 through 10.5, we obtain the three inequality orderings I_-^L, I_+^L, and I_{min}^L shown in figures 10.6a–6c respectively. All are Lorenz consistent, yet they treat high income sector enlargement in very different ways.

Note, too, that the familiar inverted U-shaped pattern shown in figure 10.6d *cannot* be generated from the preceding axioms. A different justification is needed. I shall not pursue that here.

Inequality measures and inequality

Any relative inequality relation such as those considered on p. 236 determines which of two income vectors X, $Y \in Z$ is more equal than the other. An inequality function $I(\cdot)$ which assigns a real number r to X and Y representing the inequality of that vector such that $I(X)$ and $I(Y)$ are ordered by the usual greater than or equal to relation $\geq$ is said to be an *inequality measure* (alternatively, a "numerical inequality measure" or an "inequality index"). A *relative inequality measure* has the additional property that an equiproportionate change in everyone's income leaves inequality unchanged.

Some relative inequality measures are Lorenz consistent (meaning that they make precisely those judgments specified by the Lorenz properties whenever Lorenz comparisons can be made) and some are not, either because they are only weakly Lorenz consistent (meaning that if one Lorenz curve lies partly above but not below another, the measure may rank the two distributions as equally unequal) or because they are Lorenz inconsistent (meaning that there may be a case in which one distribution Lorenz dominates another and yet the measure deems the first distribution to be more unequal than the second). Among those known to be Lorenz consistent are the Gini coefficient, Theil's two measures, Atkinson's index, and the coefficient of variation. Among those known not to be Lorenz consistent are some which are only weakly Lorenz consistent (income share of the richest $X\%$ or poorest $Y\%$) and others which are Lorenz inconsistent (including the mean absolute deviation and the logarithm of the variance of incomes). Lorenz consistent inequality measures are emphasized hereafter.

It will be said that *an inequality measure measures inequality*, or equivalently, that the *inequality measure is consistent with a specified ranking*, when the ordinal ranking assigned by the inequality measure matches the ordinal ranking of inequality assigned by the observer. All that can be hoped for is agreement on conditional statements of the type: "For all those whose inequality notions are of such and such type, such and such inequality measures measure inequality (and such and such other inequality measures do not)."

Consider now the process of high income sector enlargement on the domain of two incomes, as analyzed on pp. 235–44. It was shown in Fields (1993), building on the work of Anand and Kanbur (1993), that each of six commonly used inequality measures (Theil's entropy index, Theil's second measure, CV^2, Atkinson index, Gini coefficient, non-overlapping case, and log variance) starts at zero, increases continuously to an interior maximum at Φ^*, and then decreases to zero.[12]

Thus, Theil's entropy index, Theil's second measure, the CV^2, the Atkinson index, and the Gini coefficient (non-overlapping case) are Lorenz consistent and follow an inverted U-shaped pattern in high income sector-enlargement growth.[13] These commonly used measures therefore go beyond the Lorenz ordering in a way that produces a similar *pattern* of rankings (the inverted U-pattern).[14]

Turning now to the question of symmetry, it is sometimes said that on the two-income domain, inequality should reach a turning point when half the population is in the high income group and half in the low income group, i.e. at $\Phi^* = 1/2$. Do the five Lorenz consistent inequality measures considered above have this property? It can be shown by numerical example that the answer is "no." Those who believe that inequality *should* increase until half the population is in the high income group and decrease thereafter might find this result disturbing.

There is, though, an inequality measure that follows the inverted U-shaped pattern and *does* turn at $\Phi = 1/2$, namely, the log variance. It, however, is not Lorenz consistent.

These five commonly used inequality measures (excluding the log variance, which is not Lorenz consistent) all belong to the *same* subclass, namely, the $I^L_{\max}$ subclass depicted in figure 10.6d. Is it possible to construct Lorenz consistent inequality measures possessing the $I^L_{\min}$ pattern depicted in figure 10.6c? The answer is "yes." An example of such a measure is:

$$I = (\Theta - 1)^\alpha \, (K + 1/4 - \Phi(1 - \Phi))^{1-\alpha}$$

where

$$\Theta = y_H/y_L, \quad \Phi \in (0,1)$$
$$= 1, \quad \Theta = 0, 1$$
$$0 < \alpha < 1$$

and

$$K > 0.^{15}$$

This index is but one example of a real-valued function with the desired properties. There are many other possible representations, e.g. $I' = (\Theta^2 - 1)^\alpha (K + 1/4 - \Phi(1 - \Phi))^{1-\alpha}$. It remains to explore the properties of various alternatives and determine their relative merits.

Conclusion: do inequality measures measure inequality?

This chapter has set out different views which prescribe how inequality rankings "ought" to behave in certain circumstances. The Lorenz axioms have been unchallenged. The contribution of this chapter has been to analyze inequality orderings when Lorenz curves cross.

The findings in this chapter raise two conceptual problems for empirical researchers. One problem confronts those who use these measures in empirical applications but who have not yet decided which enlargement pattern they favor. Use of the standard measures implicitly imposes an ordering. Before using one of these measures, the researcher should ask whether the ordering imposed (the I_{max}^L ordering) is the one he or she wishes to impose.

A different problem arises for those of us who believe that inequality "should" be highest when most people are in one income group and few are in the other. For such observers, the standard measures do not do what they "should" do.

The most important task for future work is to expand the domain to allow for intra-group inequality, and for more than two groups.

Notes

This research was carried out at Cornell University, DELTA in Paris, France and at the Suntory-Toyota International Centre for Economics and Related Disciplines, London School of Economics. I am grateful for those institutions' support of this work. I thank Tony Atkinson, François Bourguignon, Frank Cowell, James Foster, Aldi Hagenaars, Bob Hutchens, George Jakubson, Peter Lambert, Pierre Pestieau, Debraj Ray, Amartya Sen, Tony Shorrocks, Nick Stern, Amos Witztum, Manny Yaari, and an anonymous referee for helpful comments and discussion.

1 Use of the term "income" is purely for verbal convenience. Inequality of consumption or of anything else could be treated identically.
2 But see Fields (1987, 1993).
3 But see Temkin (1986).
4 Attention here is limited to the ordinal aspects of the problem.
   To avoid possible misunderstanding of the purpose of this chapter, let me state explicitly that it is *not* about the question of when one distribution is *better* than another. Possible criteria for such judgments include comparisons of income level and income inequality, the Pareto criterion on the space of incomes, the Rawlsian maximin criterion, comparisons of generalized Lorenz curves, Kolm's criteria for optimal justice, and various dominance criteria. These criteria from welfare economics, as well as others from ethics and political philosophy, are reviewed and developed by Sen (forthcoming). But all of these criteria are for *welfare* rankings and this chapter is about *inequality* rankings, on which Sen's earlier work (Sen, 1973) is a classic.
5 See, for instance, Sen (1973), Atkinson (1983), Foster (1985), and the references cited therein.
6 "Person" stands for whatever recipient unit is relevant, which may be an individual, a family, or *per capita*.
7 When $\Phi = 0$ or $1, \Theta = 1$.
8 Analysis of this process is of more than academic interest: Simon Kuznets won a Nobel Prize in part for showing that the gradual shift of economic activity from low income to high income sectors is the essence of modern economic growth and for analyzing inequality change under such a process (Kuznets, 1955, 1966).
9 Again please remember that the question is "which is more equal?", *not* "which is better?" The great majority of observers rank Y_2 as *better* than Y_1.
10 Ranking inequalities using $\succeq_L$ is equivalent to making inequality comparisons using four basic properties: anonymity, income homogeneity, population homogeneity, and the Pigou–Dalton transfer principle. For details, see Dasgupta, Sen and Starrett (1973), Rothschild and Stiglitz (1973), and Fields and Fei (1978). Contrary to these relative approaches, Kolm (1976) and Eichhorn and Gehrig (1982) are among those who have adopted more absolute perspectives on inequality comparisons. For a review of the literature on non-relative views, see Ebert (1987).
11 Aldi Hagenaars liked this approach; we had a long, fruitful talk about it.
12 Such a result was already known for the Gini coefficient from the work of Knight (1976) and Fields (1979) and was implied by work on the coefficient of variation by Swamy (1967), on the log variance by Robinson (1976), and on the generalized entropy class, the Atkinson index, and the income share of the poorest p percent by Kakwani (1988).
13 The log variance, although not Lorenz consistent, also follows an inverted U-shaped pattern.
14 A higher value of Atkinson's inequality aversion parameter ε produces a smaller value of Φ^*. As $\varepsilon \to \infty$, the Atkinson index produces peak inequality

at $\Phi = 1/n$, thus representing the I^L-ordering. I am grateful to Tony Atkinson for pointing this out to me.
15 $L > 0$ guarantees that $I > 0$ for all Φ, in particular, at the interior minimum. The necessity of including such a parameter was first pointed out to me by Aldi Hagenaars and James Foster.

References

Amiel, Y. and F. Cowell, 1992. "Measurement of income inequality: experimental test by questionnaire," *Journal of Public Economics*, 47, 3–26
Anand, S. and R. Kanbur, 1993. "The Kuznets process and the inequality-development relationship," *Journal of Development Economics*, 40, 25–52
Atkinson, A.B., 1970. "On the measurement of inequality," *Journal of Economic Theory*, 2, 244–63
    1983. *Social Justice and Public Policy*, Cambridge, MA: MIT Press
Blackorby, C. and D. Donaldson, 1977. "Utility vs. equity: some plausible quasi-orderings," *Journal of Public Economics*, 7, 365–81
    1984. "Ethically significant ordinal indexes of relative inequality," *Advances in Econometrics*, 3, 131–47
Dalton, H., 1920. "The measurement of the inequality of incomes," *Economic Journal*, 3, 348–61
Dasgupta, P., A. Sen and D. Starrett, 1973, "Notes on the measurement of inequality," *Journal of Economic Theory*, 6, 180–7
Ebert, U., 1987. "Size and distribution of incomes as determinants of social welfare," *Journal of Economic Theory*, 41, 23–33
Eichhorn, W. and W. Gehrig, 1982. "Measurement of inequality in economics," in B. Korte (ed.), *Modern Applied Mathematics*, Amsterdam: North-Holland
Fields, G.S., 1979. "A welfare economic analysis of growth and distribution in the dual economy," *Quarterly Journal of Economics*, 93, 325–53
    1987. "Measuring inequality change in an economy with income growth," *Journal of Development Economics*, 26, 357–74
    1993. "Inequality in dual economy models," *Economic Journal*, 103, 1228–1235
Fields, G.S. and J.E.H. Fei, 1978. "On inequality comparisons," *Econometrica*, 46, 303–16
Foster, J., 1985. "Inequality measurement," in H. Peyton Young (ed.), *Fair Allocation*, Providence, RI: American Mathematical Society
Kakwani, N., 1988. "Income inequality, welfare and poverty in a developing economy with applications to Sri Lanka," in W. Gaertner and P.K. Pattanaik (eds.), *Distributive Justice and Inequality*, New York: Springer-Verlag
Knight, J.B., 1976. "Explaining income distribution in less developed countries: a framework and an agenda," *Bulletin of the Oxford Institute of Economics and Statistics*, 58, 161–77
Kolm, S.C., 1966. "The optimal production of social justice," in H. Guitton and J. Margolis (eds.), *Public Economics*, London: Macmillan

1976. "Unequal inequalities," *Journal of Economic Theory*, 12, 416–42.

Kuznets, S., 1955. "Economic growth and income inequality," *American Economic Review*, 45, 1–28

1966. *Modern Economic Growth*, New Haven: Yale University Press

Lambert, P., 1989. *The Distribution and Redistribution of Income*, Cambridge, MA: Blackwell

Robinson, S., 1976. "A note on the U hypothesis relating income inequality and economic development," *American Economic Review*, 66, 437–40

Rothschild, M. and J. Stiglitz, 1973. "Equilibrium in competitive insurance markets: an essay on the economics of imperfect information," *Quarterly Journal of Economics*, 90, 629–50

Sen, A.K., 1973. *On Economic Inequality*, Oxford: Oxford University Press

1982. *Choice, Welfare and Measurement*, Oxford: Basil Blackwell

(forthcoming). *Equality and Diversity*

Shorrocks, A. and J. Foster, 1987. "Transfer sensitive inequality measures," *Review of Economic Studies*, 54, 485–97

Swamy, S., 1967. "Structural changes and the distribution of income by size: the case of India," *Review of Income and Wealth*, 13, 155–74

Temkin, L.S., 1986. "Inequality," *Philosophy and Public Affairs*, 15, 99–121

11 Deprivation profiles and deprivation indices

Anthony Shorrocks

Introduction

The use of simple diagrams to represent and evaluate information on distributions yields considerable benefits, particularly to non-specialist audiences. In the context of inequality analysis, the value of Lorenz curves has long been recognized, and they are now regarded as an indispensable tool. Generalized Lorenz curves, as formulated by Shorrocks (1983), serve a similar function when welfare, rather than inequality, is the object of attention. However, neither of these constructs is ideally suited to the analysis of variables which are "bads" rather than "goods." In such cases, a different kind of diagram is required.

A series of recent papers on seemingly unrelated topics has revealed the form that this diagram should take. In their study of poverty, Spencer and Fisher (1992) call it the "absolute rotated Lorenz curve," while Jenkins' (1994) article on wage discrimination refers to the "inverse generalized Lorenz curve." A similar graph in Shorrocks (1993) is named the (unemployment) "duration profile." The aim of this chapter is to provide a general framework in which to describe and explore certain important features of this diagram. To this end, it is referred to here as the "deprivation profile," a label designed to reflect the generic nature of the construction and to allow "deprivation" to be given a more precise interpretation in specific applications. Maximum generality is also achieved by initially framing the analysis in terms of cumulative distribution functions rather than the equally weighted samples of observations used in earlier work.

Later in the chapter, deprivation is identified with absolute or normalized poverty gaps along the lines set out by Spencer and Fisher (1992), and Jenkins and Lambert (1993, 1994). Other applications of deprivation profiles have associated deprivation with wage differentials due to discrimination (Jenkins, 1994), the duration of unemployment (Shorrocks,

1993), and the length of time spent in poverty (Blanke and Shorrocks, 1994). In each of these applications, deprivation is a "bad" rather than a "good," so a rise in individual deprivation leads to a reduction in aggregate welfare. Another characteristic in common is the presumption that aggregate welfare decreases when deprivation is distributed more unequally. It is these two properties which comprise the core components of this chapter, and which necessitate the development of a framework different to that applied to distributions of "goods."

The chapter begins by explaining how data on individual deprivation may be captured in the form of deprivation profiles, and by outlining the main features of this method of representation. The ordering of distributions based on non-intersecting deprivation profiles is termed "deprivation dominance" and, in theorem 1, provided with an equivalent characterization in terms of elementary transformations applied to the distribution of deprivation. On pp. 254–7 we consider various numerical measures of deprivation and identify the class of indices which are consistent with deprivation dominance. Theorem 2 shows that unanimity among this class is both necessary and sufficient for deprivation dominance, thereby offering another equivalent characterization of the deprivation dominance ordering.

Poverty analysis is likely to provide the most fertile ground for the application of deprivation profiles. We examine the link between conventional poverty indices and the deprivation profile constructed for poverty gaps, covering territory similar to that of Spencer and Fisher (1992) and Jenkins and Lambert (1993). This connection is explored further on pp. 261–4, where it is shown that members of the class of "Daltonian" indices proposed by Hagenaars (1986) may be interpreted as weighted areas beneath the poverty gap profile. The Hagenaars–Dalton index which corresponds to the (unweighted) area below the poverty gap profile has a particularly simple geometric interpretation which, together with other properties, makes it an attractive candidate for a poverty index.

Deprivation profiles

Consider some measure of individual deprivation, distributed across the population according to the cumulative distribution function F, and define the *deprivation profile* $D(F; \cdot)$ for F by

$$D(F;p) = \int_{F^{-1}(1-p)}^{\infty} x \, dF(x) = \int_{1-p}^{1} F^{-1}(q) \, dq, \quad p \in [0, 1] \quad (11.1)$$

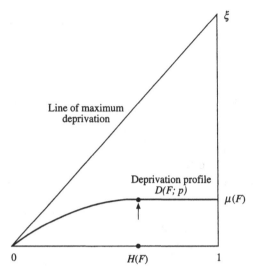

Figure 11.1 Deprivation profiles

In effect, $D(F; \cdot)$ is constructed by successively cumulating the deprivation values of the most disadvantaged members of society.[1] Since

$$\frac{\partial D(F; p)}{\partial p} = F^{-1}(1 - p) \tag{11.2}$$

deprivation profiles are seen to provide an equivalent representation of the distribution of deprivation, in the sense that $F(\cdot)$ can be recovered whenever $D(F; \cdot)$ is known. As illustrated in figure 11.1, $D(F; \cdot)$ has a continuous, concave graph which begins at the origin and rises continuously over the interval $[0, H(F)]$, where

$$H(F) = F(0) \tag{11.3}$$

denotes the "headcount ratio" or, in other words, the fraction of the population with positive deprivation.

If individual deprivation is non-negative, as typically will be the case, the graph of $D(F; p)$ becomes horizontal at the point $p = H(F)$, with its maximum height determined by the mean deprivation value

$$\mu(F) = \int_0^1 F^{-1}(q)dq \tag{11.4}$$

Deprivation profiles are similar in nature to Lorenz curves and generalized Lorenz curves, and a simple relationship exists between these different types of graphs. From the definition of the Lorenz curve,

$$L(F;p) = \frac{1}{\mu(F)} \int_0^p F^{-1}(q)dq, \ p \in [0,1] \qquad (11.5)$$

it follows that

$$D(F;p) = \mu(F)[1 - L(F; 1 - p)], \ p \in [0,1] \qquad (11.6)$$

Alternatively, the deprivation profile may be expressed in terms of the generalized Lorenz curve $GL(F; \cdot) \equiv \mu(F)L(F; \cdot)$ by writing

$$D(F;p) = \mu(F) - GL(F; 1 - p), \ p \in [0,1] \qquad (11.7)$$

The similarity between deprivation profiles and standard Lorenz curve diagrams becomes even more apparent if there is an upper bound ξ on individual deprivation. For then the distribution function

$$F^*(x) = \begin{cases} 0 & x < \xi \\ 1 & x \geq \xi \end{cases} \qquad (11.8)$$

represents the worst possible outcome, and its deprivation profile

$$D(F^*;p) = \xi p, \ p \in [0,1] \qquad (11.9)$$

may be portrayed, as in figure 11.1, as the "line of maximum deprivation."[2]

Bearing in mind that lower deprivation values are preferred, the distribution F_1 will be said to *deprivation dominate* F_2 if

$$F_1 \not\equiv F_2 \text{ and } D(F_1;p) \leq D(F_2;p) \text{ for all } p \in [0,1] \qquad (11.10)$$

It may be seen from (11.1) that the deprivation profile shifts upwards if one or more of the deprivation values increases, while (11.6) shows that the profile moves downwards if individual deprivation becomes more equally distributed. These features may be captured formally by saying that the distribution F_1 is obtained from F_2 by *decrements* if

$$F_1 \not\equiv F_2 \text{ and } F_1(s) \geq F_2(s) \text{ for all } s \geq 0 \qquad (11.11)$$

and that F_1 is obtained from F_2 by a (mean-preserving) equalization if

$$F_1 \not\equiv F_2; \ \mu(F_1) = \mu(F_2); \text{ and}$$
$$L(F_1; p) \geq L(F_2; p) \text{ for all } p \in [0, 1] \tag{11.12}$$

Since (11.11) is equivalent to the statement

$$F_1 \not\equiv F_2 \text{ and } F_1^{-1}(p) \leq F_2^{-1}(p) \text{ for all } p \in [0, 1] \tag{11.13}$$

it follows from (11.1) and (11.6) that F_1 deprivation dominates F_2 whenever F_1 is obtained from F_2 by a sequence of decrements and/or equalizations. Furthermore, Proposition 1 of Shorrocks (1993) shows that the converse also holds.[3] It is therefore possible to establish:

> *Theorem 1   The distribution F_1 deprivation dominates F_2 if and only if F_1 can be obtained from F_2 by a sequence of decrements and/or equalizations.*

Thus we have an equivalent characterization of deprivation dominance in terms of simple transformations of distributions, analogous to the well known results for Lorenz dominance and generalized Lorenz dominance.

Deprivation indices

This section considers a variety of deprivation indices $\Delta(F)$ which can be expressed in terms of the deprivation distribution F or, equivalently, in terms of the deprivation profile $D(F; \cdot)$. Two properties of social indices are implicit in the decision to make $\Delta(\cdot)$ a function of F, rather than a function of a sample $\{x_1, x_2, \ldots, x_n\}$ of deprivation values. As the distribution function disregards information on the characteristics of individuals associated with any given deprivation value, $\Delta(F)$ will automatically satisfy the standard symmetry (or anonymity) condition. In addition, as the distribution function is unchanged when two or more identical samples are pooled, the replication invariance property will also hold.[4] In effect, this implies that the index value will be independent of the sample size.

To ensure that deprivation indices are consistent with deprivation dominance, two further requirements are needed. First, the index value must rise whenever individual deprivation values increase: in other words, $\Delta(\cdot)$ must be strictly monotonic:

Definition The deprivation index $\Delta(\cdot)$ is *strictly monotonic* if $\Delta(F_1) < \Delta(F_2)$ whenever F_1 is obtained from F_2 by decrements.

Second, the index value must also rise when the distribution of deprivation becomes relatively more unequal. This requirement is captured by the equality preference condition, defined as follows:

Definition The deprivation index $\Delta(\cdot)$ is *equality preferring* if $\Delta(F_1) < \Delta(F_2)$ whenever F_1 is obtained from F_2 by a (mean-preserving) equalization.

Now denote by Δ^* the subset of deprivation indices $\Delta(\cdot)$ which are strictly monotonic and equality-preferring. The following result establishes the link between deprivation dominance and the index set Δ^*, and makes precise the sense in which an unambiguously higher level of deprivation is associated with a higher deprivation profile.

Theorem 2 For any deprivation distributions F_1 and F_2,

F_1 deprivation dominates F_2 (11.14a)

if and only if

$\Delta(F_1) < \Delta(F_2)$ for all $\Delta(\cdot) \in \Delta^*$ [5] (11.14b)

Proof Assume first that (11.14a) holds. Then, by Theorem 1, F_1 can be obtained from F_2 by a sequence of decrements and/or equalizations, each of which reduces the value of all indices in the set $\Delta(\cdot)$. Hence (11.14b) must also be true.

For the converse, consider the class of indices that may be expressed in the form

$$\Delta_\theta(F) = \int_0^1 \theta(p)D(F;p)dp, \quad \theta(p) > 0 \text{ for all } p \in [0,1] \text{ (11.15)}$$

These indices are clearly consistent with deprivation dominance. Each is therefore strictly monotonic and equality-preferring, and hence a member of the set Δ^*.

Now suppose that (11.14a) is false. Then there is some q such that $D(F_1;q) > D(F_2;q)$, and hence, by continuity of $D(F;\cdot)$, some open interval $Q \subseteq [0,1]$ such that $D(F_1;q) > D(F_2;q)$

for all $q \in Q$. By setting $\theta(q) = \bar{\theta} > 0$ for $q \notin Q$, and $\theta(q) = k\bar{\theta}$ for $q \notin Q$, we deduce that $\Delta_\theta(F_1) > \Delta_\theta(F_2)$ for sufficiently large k. Thus (11.14b) cannot hold if (11.14a) is false, and the converse is established. ∎

A number of obvious candidates for deprivation indices do not meet the requirements for membership of Δ^*. For example, the headcount ratio $H(F)$ is not strictly monotonic, and mean deprivation $\mu(F)$ is not equality-preferring. However, the counterparts of the Foster, Greer and Thorbecke (1984) class of poverty indices

$$\Delta_\alpha(F) = \int_{-\infty}^{\infty} x^\alpha \, dF(x) \tag{11.16}$$

belong to Δ^* when $\alpha > 1$, as do members of the more general class of decomposable deprivation indices

$$\Delta_\phi(F) = \int_{-\infty}^{\infty} \phi(x) \, dF(x) \tag{11.17}$$

when $\phi(\cdot)$ is strictly increasing and strictly convex.

Other attractive candidates are provided by indices of the form given in (11.15), which may be interpreted as weighted areas beneath the deprivation profile. Assuming that individual deprivation has an upper bound ξ these may be normalized to take values in the interval [0,1] by setting

$$\bar{\Delta}_\theta(F) = \frac{\int_0^1 \theta(p)D(F;p)dp}{\int_0^1 \theta(p)\xi \, pdp}, \quad \theta(p) > 0 \text{ for all } p \in [0,1] \tag{11.18}$$

The case corresponding to $\theta(p) \equiv 1$ is of special interest. For the index then becomes

$$\begin{aligned}\bar{\Delta}(F) &= \frac{\int_0^1 D(F;p)dp}{\int_0^1 \xi \, pdp} \\ &= \frac{\text{Area below } D(F;\cdot)}{\text{Area below the line of maximum deprivation}}\end{aligned} \tag{11.19}$$

and may be interpreted in a similar way to the Gini coefficient. Using (11.6), this index may also be written

$$\bar{\Delta}(F) = \frac{2}{\xi} \int_0^1 D(F;p)dp = \frac{2\mu(F)}{\xi} \int_0^1 [1 - L(F; 1 - p)]dp$$

$$= \frac{\mu(F)}{\xi} \left[1 + 2 \int_0^1 [p - L(F;p)]dp \right] = \frac{\mu(F)}{\xi} [1 + G(F)] \tag{11.20}$$

where $G(F)$ denotes the Gini value for distribution F. The link with the Gini coefficient means that $\bar{\Delta}(F)$ is neither decomposable nor "subgroup consistent."[6] But it is an ideal index of deprivation in other respects.

For most of the specific applications mentioned in the Introduction, the framework developed above provides all the basic tools required to portray and analyze data on deprivation, variously interpreted. However, the traditional (cross-section) study of poverty requires further consideration, since there already exists a well established literature on poverty indices. It is therefore necessary to spell out in detail the relationship between deprivation profile analysis and conventional poverty analysis, as Spencer and Fisher (1992) and Jenkins and Lambert (1993) attempt to do. The next section shows how some of the central results of these papers flow directly from theorem 2, once "deprivation" is suitably defined.

An application to poverty analysis

To explore the connection between deprivation profiles and the traditional (cross-section) study of poverty, we revert to the familiar notation of poverty analysis by considering a poverty line $z > 0$ and a n-person vector $y = (y_1, y_2, \ldots, y_n)$ of non-negative incomes, arranged in increasing order of magnitude. The deprivation x_i of person i may be taken to be either the absolute poverty gap

$$x_i^a(y, z) \equiv \max\{z - y_i, 0\} \tag{11.21}$$

which measures the income shortfall from the poverty line, or else the normalized poverty gap

$$x_i^r(y, z) \equiv \max\{\frac{z - y_i}{z}, 0\} \tag{11.22}$$

There is little to choose between these two alternatives when z is fixed. However, (11.22) is likely to be preferred when the poverty line is allowed to vary, and it has the additional merit of being dimension-free. To avoid repetition, therefore, the deprivation distribution $x = x(y, z)$ is taken to refer to normalized poverty gaps (11.22) unless stated otherwise.

It should be noted that poverty gap values do not discriminate between those on the poverty line and those with incomes greater than z. As a consequence, it is possible to recover the headcount ratio from the distribution of poverty gaps if z is taken to be the minimum income of the non-poor, but not if the poverty line is defined as the maximum income of the poor. This distinction is immaterial to most poverty indices, including all those which are continuous functions of individual incomes. But it does suggest that the set of poor persons is best defined as $Q = \{i \mid y_i < z\}$ whenever the analysis is based on poverty gaps. This is the convention adopted here. The number of poor persons is therefore given by

$$q = \#\{i \mid y_i < z\} = \#\{i \mid x_i > 0\} \tag{11.23}$$

and the headcount ratio by

$$H \equiv \frac{q}{n} = \frac{\#\{i \mid y_i < z\}}{n} \tag{11.24}$$

Deprivation profiles for normalized poverty gaps – for brevity, called poverty gap profiles – are illustrated in figure 11.2. They have the same increasing, concave shape as figure 11.1, leveling out at the headcount value H, at which point the height of the graph is given by the normalized *per capita* poverty gap

$$\mu(x) \equiv \frac{1}{n} \sum_{i=1}^{q} \frac{z - y_i}{z} = HI \tag{11.25}$$

where

$$I \equiv \frac{1}{q} \sum_{i=1}^{q} \frac{z - y_i}{z} \tag{11.26}$$

is Sen's (1976) "income gap ratio." Since incomes have been taken to be non-negative, normalized poverty gaps are bounded above by 1, and the "line of maximum poverty" has a unit slope, mirroring exactly the line of complete equality in the Lorenz diagram. Replacing normalized poverty gaps (11.22) with absolute poverty gaps (11.21) yields a similar

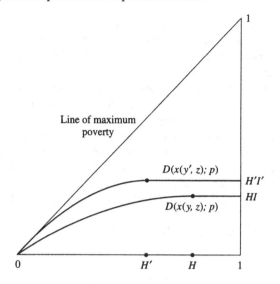

Figure 11.2 Poverty gap profiles

graph, the only difference being that the deprivation profiles and the line of maximum poverty are both scaled up by the factor z.[7]

Poverty indices are usually expressed in the form $P(y; z)$. However, they can always be reformulated in terms of the distribution of poverty gaps, given the so called "focus axiom" and the decision to regard z as the minimum income of the non-poor (rather than the maximum income of the poor). The focus axiom requires $P(\cdot)$ to be insensitive to changes in the incomes of the non-poor, so the overall poverty level remains unchanged when the incomes y_i are replaced by their censored values

$$y_i^z = \min \{y_i, z\} = z(1 - x_i(y, z)) \tag{11.27}$$

Denoting the unit vector by $e = (1, 1, \ldots, 1)$, it follows that

$$P(y; z) = P(z(e - x); z) = \bar{\bar{\Pi}}(x(y, z); z)^8 \tag{11.28}$$

for some function $\bar{\bar{\Pi}}(\cdot)$. This may be simplified further if $P(\cdot)$ is a relative index of poverty, in the sense that $P(y; z)$ is homogeneous of degree zero in y and z. For then

$$P(y; z) = P(y/z; 1) = \bar{\Pi}(x(y/z, 1); 1) = \bar{\bar{\Pi}}(x(y, z); 1)$$
$$= \Pi(x(y, z)), \text{ say} \tag{11.29}$$

The advantage of reformulating poverty indices in this way is that $\Pi(\cdot)$ can be interpreted as a deprivation index of the type described on pp. 254–7. Furthermore, the other restrictions typically imposed on poverty indices correspond exactly to the conditions required for membership of the deprivation index set Δ^*. The symmetry and replication invariance properties of $P(\cdot)$ impose identical constraints on $\Pi(\cdot)$, and are both necessary and sufficient for $\Pi(x)$ to depend only on the distribution function for x; while the monotonicity and transfer axioms postulated by Sen (1976) are equivalent to the requirements that $\Pi(\cdot)$ be strictly monotonic and equality-preferring. So if P^* denotes the set of relative poverty indices which satisfy symmetry, replication invariance, strict monotonicity, and the focus and transfer axioms,[9] we have

$$P(y; z) < P(y'; z') \text{ for all } P(\cdot) \in P^* \tag{11.30}$$

if and only if

$$\Pi(x(y, z)) < \Pi(x(y', z')) \text{ for all } \Pi(\cdot) \in \Delta^* \tag{11.31}$$

which, by theorem 2, is equivalent to the statement

$$x(y, z) \text{ deprivation dominates } x(y', z') \tag{11.32}$$

Thus the poverty gap profile for $x(y, z)$ lies nowhere above, and somewhere below, the profile for $x(y', z')$ if and only if all indices in P^* agree that the level of poverty associated with the income distribution y and the poverty line z is less than the level associated with the distribution y' and the poverty line z'.[10]

The significance of this result is that poverty gap profiles provide not only a convenient means of representing data on poverty, but also a simple way of checking whether poverty comparisons are sensitive to the choice of index from among the set P^*. Figure 11.2, for instance, depicts a situation in which the income distribution y has unambiguously less poverty than y', given the shared poverty line z. It also illustrates an interesting implication of deprivation profile analysis. For the fact that y has a larger headcount ratio than y' means that a higher value of H can be neither necessary nor sufficient for unambiguously greater poverty. Few people will be startled by the observation that a lower headcount ratio does not necessarily imply less poverty. But many will be surprised to discover that an unambiguous reduction in poverty can be accompanied by a *rise* in the fraction of the population below the poverty line.[11]

The Hagenaars–Dalton class of poverty indices

In her discussion of poverty measurement, Hagenaars (1986) used the properties of the set P^* to place constraints on general classes of poverty indices. Of special interest are those she termed the "Dalton indices based on social welfare functions of the weighted income type," which may be written

$$P(y;z) = \frac{\sum_{i=1}^{n} w(i,n) \max\left\{\frac{z-y_i}{z}, 0\right\}}{\sum_{i=1}^{n} w(i,n)} \tag{11.33}$$

where the weights $w(i,n)$ are positive, decreasing in i, and chosen to ensure that $P(\cdot;z)$ is replication invariant (Hagenaars, 1986, pp. 134–36). Hagenaars noted that none of the well known poverty indices satisfies these conditions. Yet the indices given by (11.33) – referred to here as the Hagenaars–Dalton class – have many attractive properties. In particular, the family contains all the poverty indices which are counterparts of the deprivation indices given in (11.18), and which may therefore be interpreted as the weighted area under the poverty gap profile, suitably normalized.

To see why this is so, consider any (non-normalized) index $\Delta_\theta(\cdot)$ satisfying (11.15) and let

$$\omega(p) = \int_p^1 \theta(s)ds \tag{11.34}$$

so that

$$\Delta_\theta(F) = \int_0^1 \theta(p)D(F;p)dp = -\int_0^1 \frac{d\omega(p)}{dp}D(F;p)dp$$
$$= \int_0^1 \omega(p)F^{-1}(1-p)dp \tag{11.35}$$

using integration by parts and (11.2). Applying (11.35) to the n-person distribution x yields the deprivation index

$$\Delta_\theta = \sum_{i=1}^{n} \int_{(i-1)/n}^{i/n} \omega(p)x_i dp = \sum_{i=1}^{n} w(i,n)x_i \tag{11.36}$$

where

$$w(i,n) = \int_{(i-1)/n}^{i/n} \omega(p)dp \qquad (11.37)$$

The normalized deprivation index corresponding to (11.18) is therefore given by

$$\bar{\Delta}_\theta = \frac{\displaystyle\sum_{i=1}^{n} w(i,n)x_i}{\displaystyle\sum_{i=1}^{n} w(i,n)\xi} \qquad (11.38)$$

which translates into the poverty index (11.33) when x is taken to be either the distribution of normalized poverty gaps with upper bound $\xi = 1$, or the distribution of absolute poverty gaps with upper bound $\xi = z$. Since $\omega(p)$ is positive and decreasing for $p \in [0,1]$, the weights $w(i,n)$ given by (11.37) meet all the requirements of the Hagenaars–Dalton class.

One interesting implication of this result is that poverty gap profiles cannot intersect when all members of the Hagenaars–Dalton class (11.33) agree on their ranking. For the proof of theorem 2 shows that unanimity among the set of normalized deprivation indices (11.18) is sufficient to ensure a dominance relation between deprivation profiles,[12] so unanimity among their poverty index counterparts in the Hagenaars–Dalton class must ensure a similar dominance relation between poverty gap profiles. Since the index family (11.33) is a subset of P^*, it follows, using the link from (11.32) to (11.30), that a unanimous verdict by all Hagenaars–Dalton indices is both necessary and sufficient for non-intersecting poverty gap profiles.

The special index $\bar{\Delta}(F)$ given in (11.19) is obtained by setting $\theta(p) \equiv 1$. In this case, (11.34) and (11.37) imply

$$w(i,n) = \int_{(i-1)/n}^{i/n} 2(1-p)dp = \frac{1}{n^2}(2n - 2i + 1) \qquad (11.39)$$

so $\bar{\Delta}(F)$ becomes

$$\bar{\Delta} = \frac{1}{n^2} \sum_{i=1}^{n} (2n - 2i + 1) \frac{x_i}{\xi} = \frac{1}{n^2} \sum_{i=1}^{q} (2n - 2i + 1) \frac{z - y_i}{z} \qquad (11.40)$$

This poverty index is a member of both P^* and the Hagenaars–Dalton class (11.33). It is also continuous in individual incomes, and normalized to take values in the interval [0,1]. Furthermore, the value of $\bar{\Delta}$ corresponds to the area under the poverty gap profile relative to the area under the line of maximum poverty, when individual deprivation is measured by either the normalized poverty gap (11.21) (as in figure 11.2) or the absolute poverty gap (11.22).

Despite these appealing features, $\bar{\Delta}$ is not one of the well known poverty indices. Its nearest relative is the Thon (1979) index

$$P(y; z) = \frac{1}{n(n + 1)} \sum_{i=1}^{q} (2n - 2i + 2) \frac{z - y_i}{z} \qquad (11.41)$$

since (11.41) will converge to (11.40) as the distribution y is successively replicated: in effect, (11.40) is the replication-invariant version of the "asymptotic" Thon index.[13] The proposal by Takayama (1979),

$$P(y; z) = \frac{1}{n^2} \sum_{i=1}^{q} (2n - 2i + 1) \frac{z - y_i}{\mu(x)} = \frac{z}{\mu(x)} \bar{\Delta} \qquad (11.42)$$

is also closely related to (11.40). But the fact that (11.42) is not monotonic (see Takayama, 1979, p. 758) makes it an unsatisfactory measure of poverty.

From (11.25) and (11.40), it follows that

$$\bar{\Delta} = HI[1 + G(x)] \qquad (11.43)$$

where

$$G(x) = \frac{1}{n^2 \mu(x)} \sum_{i=1}^{n} (n + 1 - 2i) x_i \qquad (11.44)$$

is the Gini coefficient for the distribution x of poverty gap values.[14] Alternatively, $\bar{\Delta}$ may be expressed in terms of the Gini value $G_p(y)$ for income inequality among the poor by rewriting (11.40) as

$$\bar{\Delta}=\frac{1}{n^2}\sum_{i=1}^{q}(2n-q)\frac{z-y_i}{z}+\frac{1}{n^2}\sum_{i=1}^{q}(q+1-2i)-\frac{1}{n^2}\sum_{i=1}^{q}(q+1-2i)\frac{y_i}{z}$$

$$=(2-H)HI+0+H^2(1-I)\frac{1}{q^2(1-I)z}\sum_{i=1}^{q}(2i-q-1)y_i$$

$$=(2-H)HI+H^2(1-I)G_p(y) \tag{11.45}$$

This formulation is more complex than (11.43), but has the merit in common with the original Sen index, or more accurately its "asymptotic version"

$$S=H[I+(1-I)G_p(y)] \tag{11.46}$$

of expressing poverty in terms of the headcount ratio, the income gap ratio, and income inequality among the poor. In fact, as Shorrocks (1995) demonstrates, $\bar{\Delta}$ has more in common with the Sen index than may be immediately apparent. For the two indices coincide when the headcount ratio is one. If the Sen index is chosen when everyone is poor, and if the poverty level is a continuous function of all incomes, then $\bar{\Delta}$ rather than S emerges as the appropriate index form.

Summary and conclusions

This chapter has shown how data on poverty and other forms of deprivation may be usefully represented by deprivation profiles. These profiles offer not only a method of displaying important aspects of the pattern of deprivation, such as the headcount ratio and the *per capita* deprivation value, but also a simple procedure for checking whether one distribution exhibits unambiguously greater deprivation. For, as demonstrated in theorem 2, all strictly monotonic and equality-preferring indices agree on the ranking of a given pair of distributions if and only if the corresponding deprivation profiles do not intersect.

Although deprivation may be defined in many different ways, the interpretation in terms of absolute or normalized poverty gaps is likely to be the most fruitful. The proliferation of alternative poverty indices prompted by Sen (1976) has encouraged the idea that poverty comparisons will often depend on the particular index selected. Poverty gap profiles provide an antidote to this, frequently incorrect, impression, by indicating when unanimous agreement will be reached among the set of poverty indices which satisfy the properties most commonly invoked.

The chapter has also revealed an interesting link between deprivation profiles and the Hagenaars–Dalton class of poverty indices, which contains all the indices corresponding to normalized versions of the weighted area under the poverty gap profile. The index obtained by taking the area below the poverty gap profile relative to that below the "line of maximum poverty" has a particularly appealing interpretation. Although not decomposable across population subgroups, it is an ideal poverty index in all other respects.

Notes

This study has been supported by a grant from the ESRC for a project on the theory and application of social index numbers. Stephen Jenkins, Kuan Xu, and two referees provided helpful comments.

1 This is best seen by supposing that F corresponds to an equally weighted sample of n individual deprivation values x_i arranged in *decreasing* order, so that $x_i \geq x_2 \ldots \geq x_n$. The deprivation profile will then have a piecewise linear graph characterized by the points

$$D(F; \frac{k}{n}) = \sum_{i=1}^{k} x_i \text{ for } k = 0, 1, \ldots, n$$

2 If individual deprivation is unbounded above, there is still likely to be a natural reference level which can be used to provide a suitable value for ξ. For example, if deprivation is interpreted as the poverty gap value, as on p. 257 below, and if income can be negative, then there is no upper bound on individual deprivation. In this case, the deprivation level associated with zero income provides an obvious candidate for the value of ξ. The corresponding deprivation profile (11.9) no longer represents *maximum* deprivation, although it may still be used for the purposes of normalization, as on p. 262 below.

3 Strictly speaking, the proof in Shorrocks (1993) applies only when $F(\cdot)$ corresponds to an equally weighted sample of observations. However, the result can be extended to more general forms of distributions.

4 The index properties discussed in this section are closely related to the restrictions frequently imposed on poverty indices. As a consequence, the analysis here draws heavily on the literature on poverty measurement developed by Sen (1976, 1979), Thon (1979), Clark, Hemming and Ulph (1981), Chakravarty (1983), Foster, Greer and Thorbecke (1984), Hagenaars (1987), and Foster and Shorrocks (1991), among others, and reviewed by Foster (1984), Hagenaars (1986), and Seidl (1988). Formal definitions of symmetry and replication invariance are given in Foster and Shorrocks (1991).

5 In the context of discrete distributions, rather than cumulative distribution functions, this result appears as proposition 2 of Shorrocks (1993) and theorem 1A of Jenkins and Lambert (1993).

6   For a discussion of decomposability and subgroup consistency in the context of poverty indices, see Foster and Shorrocks (1991).

7   The deprivation profile for absolute poverty gaps may be interpreted as the *per capita* cost of eliminating the most severe cases of poverty. For example, if monetary units are denominated in dollars and the profile value is 25 when $p = 0.1$, then an expenditure of $25 per head of the population is sufficient to eradicate poverty among the lowest income decile. Profile values for normalized poverty gaps may be interpreted in a similar manner, although the *per capita* cost is now expressed not in monetary units, but as a proportion of the poverty line figure.

8   When the set of poor persons is defined more conventionally as $Q = (i \mid y_i \leq z)$, this result still holds if $P(y; z)$ is continuous in each income y_i.

9   While each of these properties is satisfied by the majority of poverty indices, many indices do not meet all the requirements. For instance, a surprising number are not replication invariant, including the original Sen (1976) index and the subsequent suggestions by Thon (1979) and Kakwani (1980). Yet violation of replication invariance causes many practical difficulties, not least the fact that the relevant population size is far from evident when faced with a typical weighted sample of income observations. For this reason alone, the property is highly desirable, if not absolutely essential.

10   When the poverty line z is fixed, it is no longer necessary to require $P(\cdot)$ to be a relative index of poverty: see Jenkins and Lambert (1993), theorem 2. Spencer and Fisher (1992) use an additional separability property in the statement of their similar result, due to Yitzhaki (1990). Atkinson (1987) was the first to explore systematically the circumstances in which sets of poverty indices agree on their ranking, although Foster (1984, pp. 242–3) also touches briefly on this issue.

11   This result is, of course, a consequence of the fact that the headcount index $H(\cdot)$ does not belong to the set P^*. Note that an unambiguous decrease in poverty cannot be accompanied by a rise in the product of H and I, since HI determines the maximum height of the poverty gap profile.

12   This result requires $\bar{\theta}$ to be chosen to satisfy $\xi \int_0^1 p\theta(p)dp = 1$ in the proof of theorem 2.

13   The relationship between the Thon index and the area under the poverty gap profile has also been noted by Jenkins and Lambert (1993).

14   Recall here that x is arranged in *decreasing* order.

References

Atkinson, A.B., 1987. "On the measurement of poverty," *Econometrica*, 55, 749–64

Blanke, L. and A.F. Shorrocks, 1994. "A longitudinal approach to the measurement of poverty," paper presented to the AEA Meetings in Boston

Chakravarty, S.R., 1983. "Ethically flexible measures of poverty," *Canadian Journal of Economics*, 16, 74–85

Clark, S., R. Hemming and D. Ulph, 1981. "On indices for the measurement of poverty," *Economic Journal*, 91, 515–26

Foster, J.E., 1984. "On economic poverty: a survey of aggregate measures," in R.L. Basmann and G.F. Rhodes, Jr. (eds.), *Advances in Econometrics*, 3, Greenwich, CN: JAI Press

Foster, J.E. and A.F. Shorrocks, 1991. "Subgroup consistent poverty indices," *Econometrica*, 59, 687–709

Foster, J.E., J. Greer and E. Thorbecke, 1984. "A class of decomposable poverty indices," *Econometrica*, 52, 761–6

Hagenaars, A.J.M., 1986. *The Perception of Poverty*, Amsterdam: North-Holland

1987. "A class of poverty indices," *International Economic Review*, 28, 583–607

Jenkins, S.P., 1994. "Earnings discrimination measurement: a distributional approach," *Journal of Econometrics*, 61, 81–102

Jenkins, S.P., and P.J. Lambert, 1993. "Poverty orderings, poverty gaps, and poverty lines," *Discussion Paper*, 93–07, Economics Department, University College of Swansea

1994. "Ranking poverty gap distributions," *Discussion Paper*, 94–09, Economics Department, University College of Swansea

Kakwani, N., 1980. "On a class of poverty measures," *Econometrica*, 48, 431–6

Seidl, C., 1988. "Poverty measurement: a survey," in D. Bös, M. Rose and C. Seidl (eds.), *Welfare and Efficiency in Public Economics*, Berlin: Springer-Verlag

Sen, A.K., 1976. "Poverty: an ordinal approach to measurement," *Econometrica*, 44, 219–31

1979. "Issues in the measurement of poverty," *Scandinavian Journal of Economics*, 81, 285–307

Shorrocks, A.F., 1983. "Ranking income distributions," *Economica*, 50, 3–17

1993. "On the measurement of unemployment," *Discussion Paper*, 418, Economics Department, University of Essex

1995. "Revisiting the Sen Poverty Index," *Econometrica*, 63, 1225–30

Spencer, B.D. and S. Fisher, 1992. "On comparing distributions of poverty gaps," *Sankyā: The Indian Journal of Statistics*, series B, 54, 114–26

Takayama, N., 1979. "Poverty, income inequality, and their measures: Professor Sen's axiomatic approach reconsidered," *Econometrica*, 47, 747–59

Thon, D., 1979. "On measuring poverty," *Review of Income and Wealth*, 25, 429–39

Yitzhaki, S., 1990. "Necessary and sufficient conditions for dominance of concave and convex functions using absolute Lorenz curves," Hebrew University, Jerusalem, mimeo

12 Poverty orderings for the Dalton utility-gap measures

James Foster and Yong Jin

Introduction

Much of the recent theoretical work on poverty measurement has focused on ways of "robustifying" its two key steps, namely, the *identification step* in which the poverty standard is fixed and the *aggregation step* in which a specific measure of poverty is chosen. Foster and Shorrocks (1988a, 1988b) presented a first attempt to deal with the inherent arbitrariness in setting the poverty line.[1] The main tool is the variable-line "poverty ordering" or dominance ranking of distributions obtained when one distribution has a higher level of poverty than another for a whole range of poverty lines. They restrict attention to the Foster, Greer and Thorbecke (1984) or FGT family of measures, widely used because of its decomposition and other attractive properties,[2] and find that the variable-line poverty orderings associated with three key members of this family are linked to the well known stochastic dominance relations. A number of other papers have followed this general approach to robust poverty analysis.[3]

The second robustness question – on variations in the choice of poverty measures for a fixed poverty line – was discussed by Foster (1984), who derived the "unanimity" ranking for poverty measures satisfying a set of basic axioms including Sen's (1976, 1981) monotonicity and transfer axioms. It was shown that for distributions having the same population size and number of poor, unanimously lower poverty (for all such poverty measures) entails an unambiguously higher generalized Lorenz curve for the distribution of income among the poor.[4] It is not difficult to extend this result to arbitrary distributions: for example, one can show that the poverty ordering associated with the set of continuous measures satisfying the basic axioms is just generalized Lorenz dominance evaluated over the "censored distribution" – the distribution in which each non-poor income is replaced with the poverty line.[5]

268

Atkinson (1987) provided innovative results which effectively combine the two types of poverty orderings – for both a variable range of poverty lines and a class of poverty measures. Among other results, Atkinson shows that (i) first degree stochastic dominance up to a highest poverty line ensures that all continuous poverty measures in a class of "monotonic" indices will agree on the poverty judgment irrespective of the poverty line, while (ii) second degree stochastic dominance over this range ensures unanimous judgment at all poverty lines in the range for all continuous and monotonic indices satisfying the transfer axiom.[6]

Ravallion (1994) has suggested that to implement this approach in making actual comparisons, one should graph the "poverty curves" associated with the first three FGT measures over a reasonable range of poverty lines. The first curve, which he calls the "poverty incidence curve," plots the headcount ratio at the various poverty lines and gives information on potential unanimity rankings for monotonic indices. The second curve, which he calls the "poverty deficit curve," plots the poverty gap – the average shortfall from the poverty line – at various poverty lines. This poverty curve can be used to make comparisons that hold for all monotonic indices satisfying the transfer principle. The third curve is related to the well known distribution-sensitive index P_2 from the FGT family. This "poverty severity curve," as it is called by Ravallion, offers a view of poverty that places greater emphasis on incomes at the lowest part of the distribution. The FGT indices and their accompanying poverty orderings and curves are useful tools for evaluating poverty.

Apart from the FGT measures, little is known about the variable-line poverty orderings obtained from specific poverty indices. Of course, the easiest way to apply the approach for a specific measure is to graph poverty curves associated with the measure over the range of lines of interest, and make comparisons directly. However a theoretical study and characterization of specific measures' poverty orderings may offer new insights into what a particular index is actually measuring, and reveal unexpected relationships between measures – analogous to the results obtained earlier for the FGT measures. This is the point of departure for this chapter.

Our focus is a class of measures which might be called the *Dalton utility-gap* indices following the suggestion of Hagenaars (1986, 1987) and Chakravarty (1983b). Suppose that an individual i has an income level x_i at or below the poverty line z. Then i's deprivation might be measured by the utility shortfall $u(z) - u(x_i)$ for some utility function u. A Dalton index P^u is one which takes overall poverty to be the average "utility-gap" deprivation in the population (where a non-poor person's deprivation is assumed to be 0). Examples include the single-parameter family of Clark, Hemming and Ulph (1981) or CHU measures, which contains Chakravarty's (1983b) decomposable class of poverty measures as well as the pioneering distribution-sensitive measure of Watts (1968).[7]

Our main result characterizes the variable-line poverty orderings for the Dalton utility-gap measures. It is shown that distribution x has more poverty than distribution y at some poverty line, and no less at all poverty lines, if the *utility* distribution associated with y dominates the utility distribution of x according to the generalized Lorenz criterion. In other words, the variable-line poverty ordering is the converse of second degree stochastic dominance over utility – rather than income – distributions. So, for example, the poverty ordering associated with the Watts index is reflected in the generalized Lorenz criterion applied to the *natural log* of incomes, which is broader in its coverage than the standard generalized Lorenz ranking over incomes. The proof follows directly from the results of Foster and Shorrocks (1988a, 1988b) for the poverty gap measure.

We also show that the Dalton variable-line poverty orderings are nested: if v is more risk averse than u, then the poverty ordering associated with P^v is an extension of the poverty ordering of P^u, and hence it is more complete. Consequently, we may interpret the poverty ordering for a Dalton measure P^u as a unanimity poverty ordering as well, since it indicates when all Dalton measures P^v with v more risk averse than u would agree on the poverty judgment.

Most poverty measures in common use satisfy a "scale invariance" property, which requires that a simultaneous doubling of the poverty line and all incomes leaves the poverty value unchanged. We verify that the CHU measures are the only Dalton utility-gap measures to satisfy this additional property, and then reinterpret our main results for this specific family of measures. In particular, since the CHU parameter measures the (relative) risk aversion of the associated utility, the CHU poverty orderings are nested and become more complete as the parameter falls. Finally we note that our new poverty orderings are essentially Meyer's (1977) "second degree stochastic dominance with respect to a function u," and discuss some possible implications.

Poverty indices

This section presents the framework for poverty measurement, some basic properties, and several of the measures in common use. Let D_n be the set of all positive income distributions $x = (x_1, \ldots, x_n)$ of length $n \geq 1$, and let D be the union of all D_n. The population size of an arbitrary distribution x will be denoted by $n = n(x)$. Given a poverty line income z in D_1, it is often useful to consider the *censored* distribution $x^* = x^*(z)$ associated with x, defined by $x_i^* = x_i$ if $x_i \leq z$, and $x_i^* = z$ if $x_i > z$. The *ordered version* $\hat{x}$ of x is a permutation of x such that $\hat{x}_1 \leq \hat{x}_2 \leq \ldots \leq \hat{x}_{n(x)}$. The *generalized Lorenz curve* of x is found by linking the points

$$(0,0), \quad \left(\frac{1}{n}, \frac{\hat{x}_1}{n}\right), \ldots, \left(\frac{k}{n}, \frac{\hat{x}_1 + \hat{x}_2 + \ldots + \hat{x}_k}{n}\right), \ldots, (1, \mu(x))$$

where $\mu(x) = \frac{\hat{x}_1 + \hat{x}_2 + \ldots + \hat{x}_n}{n}$ is the mean of x. Distribution x is said to *generalized Lorenz dominate* y, written x **GL** y, if the generalized Lorenz curve of x is no lower than the generalized Lorenz curve of y, and somewhere it is strictly higher. For distributions having the same population size, x **GL** y is equivalent to a "partial sum" condition:

$$\sum_{i=1}^{k} \hat{y}_i \geq \sum_{i=1}^{k} \hat{x}_i \text{ for all } k = 1, \ldots, n \text{ with } > \text{ for some } k.$$

A *poverty measure* is a function $P(x;z)$ mapping each distribution x in D and poverty line z in D_1 to a real number $P(x;z)$ indicating the level of poverty in x given z. Denote the number of poor in x given z by $q = q(x;z)$.[8] The *headcount ratio* $H(x;z) = q(x;z)/n(x)$ is the share of the population that is poor. The *(per capita) poverty gap*

$$G(x;z) = \frac{1}{n} \sum_{i=1}^{q} (z - \hat{x}_i)$$

indicates the average distance incomes lie below the poverty line.

There are five basic axioms for poverty measures to satisfy. The first two are standard symmetry and replication invariance axioms. The third is a focus axiom, which requires the incomes of the poor to be the focus of the measure. The final axioms, called the monotonicity and transfer axioms, give the proper orientation to the measure. In particular, they ensure that the measure reflects the frequency, intensity, and distribution of poverty – in descending order of importance.[9] All share the same general form of requiring the measure to react appropriately to a given change in the distribution. We say that x is obtained from y: by a *permutation* if $\hat{x} = \hat{y}$; by a *replication* if $x = (y, y, \ldots, y)$; by an *increment among the non-poor (poor)* if $x_j > y_j$ for some j and $x_i = y_i$ for all $i \neq j$, where $y_j > z$ (resp. $y_j \leq z$); by a *decrement among the non-poor (poor)* if $x_j < y_j$ for some j and $x_i = y_i$ for all $i \neq j$, where $y_j > z$ (resp. $y_j \leq z$); by a *progressive transfer* among the poor if $x_i + x_j = y_i + y_j$ and $x_k = y_k$ for all $k \neq i,j$, where $y_i < x_i \leq x_j < y_j \leq z$.

Where x and y range over all distributions and z can be any poverty line in D_1, the basic axioms for poverty measures are defined as follows:

- *Symmetry* If x is obtained from y by a permutation, then $P(x;z) = P(y;z)$
- *Replication invariance* If x is obtained from y by a replication, then $P(x;z) = P(y;z)$
- *Focus* If x is obtained from y by an increment to a non-poor person, then $P(x;z) = P(y;z)$
- *Monotonicity* If x is obtained from y by an increment to a poor person, then $P(x;z) \leq P(y;z)$; if x is obtained from y by a decrement to a poor person, then $P(x;z) > P(y;z)$
- *Transfer* If x is obtained from y by a progressive transfer among the poor, then $P(x;z) < P(y;z)$

The final two axioms are often expressed as weak inequalities, which has the effect of including "partial" measures of poverty like the headcount ratio and poverty gap. Sometimes a stronger transfer axiom is defined, which requires a regressive transfer to increase (or not lower) poverty, even though the headcount ratio may fall. It is not clear that this stronger property is so compelling. But in any event, it follows directly from the basic axioms if the poverty measure $P(x;z)$ is *continuous* in x.[10]

There are numerous examples of poverty measures in the literature, including the FGT family

$$P_\alpha(x;z) = \frac{1}{n(x)} \sum_{i=1}^{q(x;z)} \left(1 - \frac{\hat{x}_i}{z} \right)^\alpha, \qquad \text{where } \alpha \geq 0$$

and the transformed CHU family

$$C_\beta(x;z) = \frac{1}{\beta} \frac{1}{n(x)} \sum_{i=1}^{q(x;z)} \left(1 - \left(\frac{\hat{x}_i}{z} \right)^\beta \right), \qquad \text{where } \beta < 1 \text{ and } \beta \neq 0$$

P_0 is the headcount ratio $H = q(x;z)/n(x)$, a measure that violates the transfer and monotonicity axioms, and allows discontinuous jumps as incomes cross the poverty line. The remaining measures in both families are monotonic and continuous. The next FGT index

$$P_1 = \frac{1}{n} \sum_{i=1}^{q} \left(\frac{z - \hat{x}_i}{z} \right)$$

is a normalized version of the *per capita* poverty gap G and hence it violates the transfer axiom. The P_α indices beyond $\alpha > 1$, including the commonly used measure

$$P_2 = \frac{1}{n}\sum_{i=1}^{q}\left(\frac{z - \hat{x}_i}{z}\right)^2$$

satisfy the five basic axioms as do all members of the CHU family. Notice that as β tends to 0, the measure C_β tends to the *Watts* index.[11]

$$C_0(x;z) = \frac{1}{n(x)}\sum_{i=1}^{q(x;z)}(\ln(z) - \ln(\hat{x}_i))$$

Each of these measures is also *decomposable* in the sense that regional poverty levels $P^1, \dots, P^m$ can be linked to overall poverty P by the formula

$$P = \frac{n_1}{n}P^1 + \dots + \frac{n_m}{n}P^m$$

where n_j/n is the population share in region j. Note that both P_α and C_β can be expressed as an "average deprivation" index

$$P^d(x;z) = \frac{1}{n(x)}\sum_{i=1}^{q(x;z)}d(\hat{x}_i;z) \tag{12.1}$$

where d is interpreted as an "individual deprivation" function. It is not difficult to verify that every average deprivation index is decomposable. Foster and Shorrocks (1991) showed the converse to be true as well.

Variable-line poverty orderings

We now define the poverty orderings obtained when poverty lines are varied and state the characterization results for the FGT indices. Let P be any poverty index and let x and y be any two distributions of income. If $P(x;z) > P(y;z)$ at a given poverty line z, this provides some evidence that x may indeed have greater poverty than y. To check the robustness of this result, one can see whether the original inequality is reversed at some other reasonable poverty line. Following Foster and Shorrocks (1988a, 1988b) we consider the widest possible robustness requirement as incorporated in the following definition.

> *Definition* Distribution x is said to have *unambiguously more poverty than y according to P*, written x **P** y, if and only if $P(x;z) \geq P(y;z)$ for all $z > 0$ with $>$ for some z.

Any such poverty ordering is clearly transitive but not necessarily complete.[12]

The poverty orderings $\mathbf{P}_\alpha$ associated with the FGT indices P_α for $\alpha = 0, 1, 2$, were the subject of Foster and Shorrocks (1988a, 1988b). They observed that the poverty ordering $\mathbf{P}_0$ for the headcount ratio is (the converse of) first degree stochastic dominance.[13] For discrete distributions x and y with the same population size, $x\ \mathbf{P}_0\ y$ translates to the requirement that $\hat{y}$ vector dominates $\hat{x}$. For the normalized *per capita* poverty gap measure P_1, the poverty ordering $\mathbf{P}_1$ is generalized Lorenz dominance or, equivalently, second degree stochastic dominance as characterized by the well known "integral condition." For same-sized discrete distributions, $x\ \mathbf{P}_1\ y$ reduces to

$$\sum_{i=1}^{k} \hat{y}_i \geq \sum_{i=1}^{k} \hat{x}_i$$

for all $k = 1, \ldots, n$ (with $>$ for some k) – the partial sum restatement of the generalized Lorenz condition. Clearly $\mathbf{P}_1$ is more complete than $\mathbf{P}_0$ and includes the latter as a subrelation. Finally, the poverty ordering $\mathbf{P}_2$ for the distribution-sensitive index P_2 is the converse of third degree stochastic dominance, which can make even more comparisons than $\mathbf{P}_1$ and $\mathbf{P}_0$, and includes them both as subrelations.

In what follows it will be helpful to note an extension of the second degree result to cases where incomes and cut-offs may be negative. Generalized Lorenz dominance (or the integral condition) can be applied to this setting without any change. However, the normalized *per capita* poverty gap P_1 is not applicable because of its $1/z$ normalization factor. Instead, the *per capita* poverty gap measure G furnishes the appropriate equivalent condition:[14] If x and y are real vectors of arbitrary dimensions, then $y\ \mathbf{GL}\ x$ is equivalent to $G(x;z) \geq G(y;z)$ for all $z \in R$ with $>$ for some z.

The Dalton utility-gap indices

Consider the class of poverty indices of the form

$$P^u(x;z) = A(z) \frac{1}{n(x)} \sum_{i=1}^{n(x)} [u(z) - u(x_i^*)] \qquad (12.2)$$

where $u: D_1 \to R$ is a utility function, $A: D_1 \to R_{++}$ is a normalization factor, and x_i^* is the ith income from the censored distribution $x^* = x^*(z)$.[15] Each of these measures can be viewed as an "average deprivation" index (12.1), where individual deprivation is based on the utility shortfall $u(z) - u(x_i)$ for all $x_i \leq z$. Following Hagenaars (1986, 1987) and Chakravarty (1983b) we call this class the *Dalton utility-gap measures*. It is clear that each P^u satisfies symmetry, replication invariance, and the focus axiom by construction. Moreover, P^u satisfies the monotonicity axiom if u is strictly increasing, the transfer axiom if u is strictly concave, and continuity in each x_i if u is continuous.

Given a utility function u, the poverty measure P^u has the nice interpretation as the (normalized) average utility loss due to poverty, where u is restricted to depend only on i's income. This rules out the Thon (1979) index which is additive, but has utility depending on the rank of an individual – hence on the entire distribution. It also excludes the FGT indices whose individual deprivation functions, if expressed in utility-gap form, would force utility to depend on the poverty line. And it dismisses the Sen measure for both of these reasons. In contrast, each CHU index has the Dalton form (12.2) with the utility functions

$$u_\beta(s) = \begin{cases} s^\beta/\beta & \beta \neq 0 \text{ and } \beta < 1 \\ \ln s & \beta = 0 \end{cases}$$

Notice that each $u_\beta(s)$ is strictly concave with a constant risk aversion parameter $1 - \beta$ that increases as β falls.

Other measures are not themselves in the P^u class, but are expressible as monotonic transformations of Dalton utility-gap indices. Consider, for example, the class of "ethical indices" described by Chakravarty (1983a): $E(x;z) = (z - e(x^*))/z$, where $e(x^*)$ is the "representative income" of the censored distribution $x^* = x^*(z)$ for a given welfare function $W(x)$. If W has the additive form

$$W(x) = \frac{1}{n} \sum_{i=1}^{n(x)} u(x_i)$$

then it is easy to show that E is a monotonic transformation of P^u. Since monotonic transformations rank distributions in precisely the same way, any characterization of poverty orderings for the utility-gap measures will also describe the poverty orderings for these related indices.

The Dalton utility-gap poverty orderings

We now offer a characterization of the variable-line poverty orderings for the Dalton utility-gap poverty measures. Denote the poverty ordering associated with the Dalton measure P^u by $\mathbf{P}^u$, and let

$u^x = (u(x_1), \ldots, u(x_n))$ be the *utility distribution* of x given u. We can show that the poverty ordering for a Dalton measure is the converse of the generalized Lorenz ranking taken over the associated utility distributions.

> **Theorem 1** *Let u be strictly increasing and continuous, and let x and y be arbitrary distributions. Then $x\,\mathbf{P}^u\,y$ if and only if $u^y\,\mathbf{GL}\,u^x$.*
>
> **Proof** Setting $z' = u(z)$ we see that $P^u(x;z) = A(z)G(u^x;z')$. Consequently, $x\,\mathbf{P}^u\,y$ is equivalent to
>
> $$G(u^x;z') \geq G(u^y;z') \;\forall\; z' \text{ in } u(D_1), \text{ with } > \text{ for some } z' \quad (12.3)$$
>
> If the interval $u(D_1)$ is the entire reals, then according to the second degree result noted on p. 274, this is equivalent to $u^y\,\mathbf{GL}\,u^x$, and we are done. Alternatively, suppose that the interval $u(D_1)$ is a strict subset of the reals. Then for any z' below $u(D_1)$, we have $G(u^x;z') = G(u^y;z') = 0$ since no one is poor in this case. For z' above $u(D_1)$, everyone is poor and so $G(u^x;z') - G(u^y;z') = G(u^x;z'') - G(u^y;z'')$ where $z'' \in u(D_1)$ is the highest utility level from u^x and u^y. Hence (12.3) is identical to
>
> $$G(u^u;z') \geq G(u^y;z') \text{ for all } z' \text{ in } R, \text{ with } > \text{ for some } z' \quad (12.4)$$
>
> which renders $x\,\mathbf{P}^u\,y$ equivalent to $u^y\,\mathbf{GL}\,u^x$. $\blacksquare$

To determine whether two distributions are ranked by the poverty ordering $\mathbf{P}^u$, one converts the income distributions into utility distributions and checks whether the generalized Lorenz condition (or, equivalently, the integral condition) is applicable. For example, consider the two distributions $x = (1,3,5)$ and $y = (2,2,4)$ which, incidently, are not ranked by $\mathbf{GL}$, and let $u(s) = \ln s$ as in the Watts measure. Then the associated utility (or log income) distributions are approximately $u^x = (0, 1.10, 1.61)$ and $u^y = (0.69, 0.69, 1.39)$, from which we readily see that $u^y\,\mathbf{GL}\,u^x$. Clearly x has unambiguously more poverty than y according to the Watts measure.[16]

Now what is the relationship between $\mathbf{P}^u$ and $\mathbf{P}^v$ for two different utility-gap measures? It turns out that when utility functions are ranked by risk aversion, there is a straightforward relationship between poverty orderings.

> **Theorem 2** *Let u and v be strictly increasing and continuous, and let x and y be arbitrary distributions. If v is more risk averse[17] than u, then $x\,\mathbf{P}^u\,y$ implies $x\,\mathbf{P}^v\,y$.*

Proof Assume that $u(s)$ is more risk averse than $v(s)$, so that there exists a concave function f such that $u(s) = f(v(s))$. Let $x\ \mathbf{P}^u\ y$. Since P^u is replication-invariant, we may assume without loss of generality that x and y have the same dimension n. Consequently, by theorem 2 and the partial sum criterion for generalized Lorenz dominance, we have

$$\sum_{i=1}^{k} u(\hat{y}_i) \geq \sum_{i=1}^{k} u(\hat{x}_i)\ \forall\ k = 1, \ldots, n \text{ with } > \text{ for some } k$$

Since f is strictly increasing and concave, it follows from Marshall and Olkin (1979) that

$$\sum_{i=1}^{k} f(u(\hat{y}_i)) \geq \sum_{i=1}^{k} f(u(\hat{x}_i))\ \forall\ k = 1, \ldots, n \text{ with } > \text{ for some } k$$

and hence

$$\sum_{i=1}^{k} v(\hat{y}_i) \geq \sum_{i=1}^{k} v(\hat{x}_i)\ \forall\ k = 1, \ldots, n \text{ with } > \text{ for some } k$$

which yields $x\ \mathbf{P}^v\ y$. ∎

The knowledge that $\mathbf{P}^u$ can rank two distributions thus gives information about judgments for all P^v with v having greater risk aversion than u. For example, if u is risk neutral, then $\mathbf{P}^u$ (or $\mathbf{GL}$) ensures that $\mathbf{P}^v$ holds for all risk averse v. Conversely, if P^v is inapplicable for some v that is more risk averse than a given u, then $\mathbf{P}^u$ also cannot apply. In this sense, we can view P^u as a variable-measure poverty ordering as well: it indicates when all partial orderings in the class $\{\mathbf{P}^v : v$ is more risk averse than $u\}$ agree that one distribution has unambiguously more poverty than another.

Note that the above analysis holds for arbitrary continuous and increasing u, including functions that are concave, convex, or neither. One interesting implication of this is that measures with convex u, which would not ordinarily be considered reasonable due to a violation of the transfer axiom, are potentially useful in the context of poverty orderings. For if P^u with, say, $u(s) = s^2$ concludes that one distribution has unambiguously more poverty than another, the same must be true for P^v with concave $v(s)$ (and, indeed, any continuous poverty measure satisfying the five basic axioms). The ordering $\mathbf{P}^u$ is a subrelation of the more complete ordering $\mathbf{P}^v$; it cannot make as many comparisons as $\mathbf{P}^v$, but when it does make a judgment, $\mathbf{P}^v$ must agree with it. The nested property of the Dalton utility-gap orderings is noteworthy, and potentially quite useful.

The CHU poverty indices

We now turn to the CHU family of indices C_β obtained when the utility u_β has the special "isoelastic" form $u_\beta(s)$ presented on p. 275 above. The CHU measures, like the FGT indices and most other poverty measures in common use, have the property that a simultaneous doubling of the poverty line and all incomes leaves poverty unchanged. More precisely, we say that $(x;z)$ is obtained from $(x';z')$ by a *proportional change* if $(x;z) = (\alpha x';\alpha z')$ for some $\alpha > 0$. A poverty measure P is said to be *scale-invariant* if $P(x;z) = P(x';z')$ whenever $(x;z)$ is obtained from $(x';z')$ by a proportional change. While all of the CHU measures, including the Watts measure, satisfy scale invariance, the Dalton utility-gap measures, in general, need not do so.[18] The next result, which is closely related to Chakravarty (1983b) and Zheng (1993b), shows that this property effectively characterizes the CHU indices among the Dalton class.

Theorem 3   *Let u be strictly increasing and continuous. Then $P^u(x;z)$ satisfies the scale invariance and transfer axioms if and only if it is (a positive multiple of) a CHU index.*

Proof   Without loss of generality, we may assume that $u(1) = 0$ and $A(1) = 1$ (otherwise we could use $A^o(r) = A(r)/A(1)$ and $u^o(r) = A(1)[u(r) - u(1)]$ for $r \in R$). By definition (12.2) and scale invariance,

$$P^u(x;z) = P^u(x^*;z) = P^u\left(\frac{x^*}{z};1\right) = \frac{-1}{n(x)}\sum_{i=1}^{n} u(x_i^*/z)$$

Hence, we need only determine the form of $u(r)$ over the interval $(0,1)$ to determine $P(x;z)$ for arbitrary x and z. Note that $A(r) > 0$ and $u(r) < 0$ for all $r \in (0,1)$.

Let s and t be any real numbers in $(0,1)$. By scale invariance, $P^u(st,\ldots,st;t) = P^u(s,\ldots,s;1)$, hence by definition (12.2) we have

$$A(t)[u(t) - u(st)] = -u(s)$$

A simple manipulation yields

$$u(t) + u(s)/A(t) = u(st) \tag{12.5}$$

while a similar argument leads to its symmetric restatement

$$u(s) + u(t)/A(s) = u(st) \tag{12.6}$$

Equating (12.5) and (12.6) yields

$$\frac{1}{u(t)}\left(1 - \frac{1}{A(t)}\right) = \frac{1}{u(s)}\left(1 - \frac{1}{A(s)}\right) \text{ for all } s,t \in (0,1)$$

hence

$$\frac{1}{u(r)}\left(1 - \frac{1}{A(r)}\right) = c \text{ for all } r \in (0,1)$$

for some constant $c \in R$. Clearly, then,

$$cu(r) = 1 - \frac{1}{A(r)}$$

for each $r \in (0,1)$, which implies that $A(r)$ is continuous on $(0,1)$. Now multiplying (12.5) by c (and substituting

$$1 - \frac{1}{A(r)}$$

for each $cu(r)$) yields the functional equation $A(s)A(t) = A(st)$ for all $s,t \in (0,1)$. This is a Cauchy equation which, given $A(1) = 1$, has continuous solution[19]

$$A(r) = r^{-\beta} \quad \text{for some } \beta \in R$$

Consider first the case $\beta = 0$. Then $A(r) = 1$ for all $r \in (0,1)$ and (12.5) reduces to the functional equation $u(t) + u(s) = u(st)$. This is another Cauchy equation with continuous solution[20]

$$u(r) = k \ln r, \text{ for some } k \in R$$

where $k > 0$ by the fact that u is strictly increasing. Therefore,

$$P^u(x;z) = \frac{-k}{n(x)}\sum_{i=1}^{n(x)} \ln\left(\frac{x_i^*}{z}\right)$$
$$= kC_0(x;z) \text{ for some } k > 0$$

Now consider the case $\beta \neq 0$, which implies $c \neq 0$ and hence $u(r) = (1 - r^\beta)/c$. Setting $k = -\beta/c$, we obtain $u(r) = k(r^\beta - 1)/\beta$ for some non-zero reals k and β, where $k > 0$ by the fact that u is strictly increasing. Consequently,

$$P^u(x;z) = \frac{k}{n(x)} \sum_{i=1}^{n(x)} \left[1 - \left(\frac{x_i^*}{z} \right)^\beta \right] / \beta$$

Note further that β must be less than 1 in order for P^u to satisfy the transfer axiom, and hence we conclude that

$$P^u(x;z) = kC_\beta(x;z) \text{ for some } k > 0 \text{ and } \beta < 1. \blacksquare$$

Thus the CHU measures are the only Dalton utility gap indices that are consistent with the scale invariance and transfer axioms. It should be noted that the role of the transfer axiom in the above proof is merely to restrict the parameter values to the range $\beta < 1$. Without this assumption, admissible functional forms would include all C_β with values $\beta \geq 1$ – which have convex utility functions – and in particular, the risk neutral case $\beta = 1$ which produces the poverty gap measure P_1.

The CHU poverty orderings

We will now reexamine the conclusions of theorems 1 and 2 applied to the C_β measures. First, we note that since $u_\beta(r)$ for $\beta < 1$ is more risk averse than $u_1(r)$, it follows from theorem 2 that all the CHU poverty orderings are consistent with second degree stochastic dominance or, equivalently, the usual generalized Lorenz ranking over income distributions. Now how far beyond second degree dominance does C_β take us? To get an idea of this, let us apply theorem 1 to the case where x and y have the same population size n. Then for $\beta < 1$ and $\beta \neq 0$ the statement $x \, \mathbf{C_\beta} \, y$ reduces to

$$\sum_{i=1}^{k} \frac{\hat{y}_i^\beta}{\beta} \geq \sum_{i=1}^{k} \frac{\hat{x}_i^\beta}{\beta} \quad \forall \, k \text{ with } > \text{ for some } k \tag{12.7a}$$

while for $\beta = 0$ it becomes

$$\sum_{i=1}^{k} \ln \hat{y}_i \geq \sum_{i=1}^{k} \ln \hat{x}_i \quad \forall \, k \text{ with } > \text{ for some } k \tag{12.7b}$$

Condition (12.7) is the partial sum definition of the generalized Lorenz ranking applied to utility distributions. Since utility is a strictly concave function of income, this expands the possibilities for comparisons beyond the usual generalized Lorenz ranking. For example, consider the distributions $x = (1,9,16)$ and $y = (4,4,16)$, which are not comparable under the generalized Lorenz criterion. Clearly, $x \, \mathbf{C_\beta} \, y$ holds for $\beta = 1/2$, as $2 > 1$, $2 + 2 \geq 1 + 3$, and $2 + 2 + 4 \geq 1 + 3 + 4$. The concavity of $u_{0.5}(s) = 2\sqrt{s}$ de-emphasizes the differences at the top of the distributions and makes the transformed distributions comparable under the generalized Lorenz criterion.

A similar series of comparisons shows that $x\ \mathbf{C}_\beta\ y$ holds for $\beta = -1/2$, or, indeed, for *any* β less than 1/2. Indeed, theorem 2 ensures that, for any $x,y \in D$, we have $x\ \mathbf{C}_\beta\ y$ implies $x\ \mathbf{C}_\gamma\ y$ whenever $\gamma < \beta$. The CHU poverty orderings are nested, with $\mathbf{C}_\beta$ becoming more complete as β is lowered. Exactly what kind of judgments are added as β falls and, in particular, how this compares to way that the nested P_α orderings expand as α rises is an open question.

Concluding remarks

We have derived the poverty orderings for the Dalton utility-gap measures and, in particular, the indices of Clark, Hemming and Ulph (CHU) (1981) and Watts (1968). We concluded that these rankings are conceptually related to second degree stochastic dominance or, equivalently, to generalized Lorenz dominance. This link is not surprising since virtually every major theorem or concept in distribution analysis has an analogue in the theory of risk measurement. But in the present case the link turns out to be particularly strong. In an interesting paper, Meyer (1977) introduced a form of stochastic dominance he called "second degree stochastic dominance with respect to a function." His main characterization result entails an altered integral condition with the integration taken with respect to the given function. It turns out that when this function is $u(s)$, his new form of stochastic dominance is the converse of $\mathbf{P}^u$. In other words, the Dalton poverty ordering $\mathbf{P}^u$ is essentially Meyer's second degree stochastic dominance with respect to u.

Meyer presents a number of results which may well provide additional insight into these poverty orderings. For example, his theorem 3 applied to discrete distributions x and y establishes the existence of Dalton index such that $\mathbf{P}^u$ can unambiguously rank x and y. It also shows that once a pair has been so ranked, no other $\mathbf{P}^v$ can rank distributions in the opposite direction: unambiguous judgments cannot be reversed by switching to a different utility function. It would be useful to explore this direction further.

Meyer's ranking is called "second degree dominance with respect to u" since it uses second degree dominance – or in our context, poverty gap dominance – over the utility distribution. One might naturally enquire whether first or third degree dominance, as delivered up by the headcount ratio P_0 and the FGT index P_2, might be the basis of interesting poverty orderings. In other words, following the analogy of $P^v(x;z) = P_1(u^x;u^z)$, where $u^z = u(z)$, we might evaluate the measures $P_0(u^x;u^z)$ and $P_2(u^x;u^z)$ and their respective poverty orderings. The answer for the first of these measures is straightforward. Since $P_0(u^x;u^z) = P_0(x;z)$ for all x and z, the resulting poverty ordering is the same as $\mathbf{P_0}$, the converse of first degree stochastic dominance. Put differently, if x dominates y by first degree stochastic dominance and one transforms the income variable by some increasing function u, then u^x will first degree dominate u^y as well. In contrast, the transformation clearly affects second degree dominance, so it will undoubtedly alter third degree dominance as well. Whether and in what context this might prove useful is a topic for future work.

Notes

The authors would like to thank the editors for their patience and encouragement, the referees for refining our presentation and arguments, and especially Tony Shorrocks for his help in delivering the paper at the conference and in providing the key arguments leading to theorem 3.

1 See also Foster (1984) who previews the results of Foster and Shorrocks (1988a, 1988b).

2 See for example Kanbur (1987), Besley and Kanbur (1988), and Ravallion (1994).

3 For example, see Atkinson (1987), Howes (1993a, 1993b), Jenkins and Lambert (1993), and Zheng (1993a).

4 The generalized Lorenz curve is obtained by scaling up the Lorenz curve by the distribution mean. See Shorrocks (1983) or p. 271 below.

5 The comparable result for non-continuous indices entails an additional condition involving the headcount ratio (or percentage of the population that is poor) evaluated at the poverty line. See Foster and Sen (1994) for the proof of these extensions. These results are related to Atkinson (1987) and Howes (1993b) when their poverty line range is degenerate.

6 Since Atkinson's results are limited to continuous poverty measures, they exclude measures like the well known Sen (1976) index. Howes (1993b) extends Atkinson's second degree result to allow measures that may experience a jump when incomes cross the poverty line, by adding to second degree dominance a limited form of first degree dominance – a condition that is also present in Zheng's (1993a) partial characterization of the poverty ordering for Sen's measure.

7 What we call the CIIU indices are actually the decomposable transformations used by Atkinson (1987), which more closely resemble Chakravarty's (1983b) decomposable family than the original CHU indices. The associated utility functions are the same isoelastic (or constant relative risk aversion) functions used by Atkinson (1970) to obtain his family of inequality measures.

8   This chapter uses the strong definition of the poor: i is poor if and only if $x_i \leq z$.

9   See Foster and Sen (1994) for this interpretation.

10 A verification is given in Foster and Sen (1994). Note that every continuous and focused poverty measure satisfies $P(x;z) = P(x^*;z)$ where x^* is the censored distribution.

11 Clearly

$$\lim_{\beta \to 0} \left(1 - \left(\frac{\hat{x}_i}{z} \right)^{\beta} \right) / \beta = \lim_{\beta \to 0} - \left(\frac{\hat{x}_i}{z} \right)^{\beta} \ln \left(\frac{\hat{x}_i}{z} \right) = \ln(z) - \ln(\hat{x}_i)$$

12 The precise term for such rankings that are transitive, irreflexive, and possibly incomplete, is *partial ordering*. We will use the generic term "poverty ordering" in lieu of the more precise term "poverty partial ordering."

13 We shall often omit the parenthetical phrase in the rest of the chapter. For the general definitions of the three degrees of stochastic dominance see, for example, Bawa (1975) or Foster and Shorrocks (1988a, 1988b).

14 Note that both sides of the equivalence are unchanged when a constant is added to all incomes; so this follows from the above results where incomes are all non-negative.

15 This class was first defined by Chakravarty (1983b) as part of his derivation of his CHU-based family of measures. Zheng (1993a) considers a related class in his derivation of the Watts index. Hagenaars (1986, 1987) assumes the special form $A(z) = 1/u(z)$ in her definition of the Dalton indices. However, this may lead to difficulties if the utility function takes on negative values (e.g. the CHU indices). Hagenaars also considers rank order utility functions, which we have ruled out by the requirement that u be a function of i's income alone. This more general class of Dalton indices is studied by Shorrocks (1994).

16 Tests for restricted ranges of poverty lines can be also derived following the approaches of Foster and Shorrocks (1988a, 1988b) and Atkinson (1987), among others.

17 A twice differentiable utility function u is more risk averse than another v if $R_u(s) \geq R_v(s) \,\forall\, s$, where $R_u(s) = -su''(s)/u'(s)$ is the Arrow–Pratt measure of relative risk aversion (or, equivalently, the elasticity of marginal utility). Pratt (1964) notes that this condition implies the existence of a concave f such that $u(s) = f(v(s)) \,\forall\, s$. Since we do not require differentiability, we use this as our general definition of "more risk averse."

18 Many Dalton indices would satisfy the analogous property in utility terms: if the change in incomes and the poverty line doubles each of the corresponding utility levels, then the measure should be unchanged. For $u(s) > 0$, this can be accomplished by using the normalization factor $A(z) = 1/u(z)$. See Hagenaars (1986, 1987).

19 See Aczel (1966, p. 41). To be precise, we can account for the restricted domain of s and t by making the substitutions $s = e^{-a}$ and $t = e^{-b}$ to obtain

$f(a) = A(e^{-a})$ and $f(b) = A(e^{-b})$ and the functional equation $f(a + b) = f(a)f(b)$ for $a,b > 0$. The solution (1966, p. 38) is $f(a) = e^{\beta a}$ for some $\beta > 0$, hence $A(s) = s^{-\beta}$.

20 See Aczel (1966, p. 41). Once again the restricted domain forces us to transform s and t as in n. 19 above, with $f(a) = u(e^{-a})$ and $f(b) = u(e^{-b})$ yielding $f(a + b) = f(a) + f(b)$ for $a,b > 0$. The solution (1966, p. 34) can be written as $f(a) = -ka$ for some $k \in R$, hence $u(s) = k\ln s$.

References

Aczel, J., 1966. *Lectures on Functional Equations and their Applications*, New York: Academic Press
Atkinson, A.B., 1970. "On the measurement of inequality," *Journal of Economic Theory*, 2, 244–63
1987. "On the measurement of poverty," *Econometrica*, 55, 749–64
Bawa, V., 1975. "Optimal rules for ordering uncertain prospects," *Journal of Financial Economics*, 2, 95–121
Besley, T. and R. Kanbur, 1988. "Food subsidies and poverty reduction," *Economic Journal*, 98, 701–19
Chakravarty, S.R., 1983a. "Ethically flexible measures of poverty," *Canadian Journal of Economics*, 16, 74–85
1983b. "A new index of poverty," *Mathematical Social Sciences*, 6, 307–13
1990. *Ethical Social Index Numbers*, Berlin: Springer-Verlag
Clark, S., R. Hemming and D. Ulph, 1981. "On indices for the measurement of poverty," *Economic Journal*, 91, 515–26
Dalton, H., 1920. "The measurement of the inequality of incomes," *Economic Journal*, 30, 348–61
Foster, J.E., 1984. "On economic poverty: a survey of aggregate measures," in R.L. Basmann and G.F. Rhodes, Jr. (eds.), *Advances in Econometrics, volume 3*, Greenwich, CN: JAI Press, 215–51
Foster, J.E. and A.K. Sen, 1994. "Inequality and poverty," Vanderbilt University, mimeo
Foster, J.E. and A.F. Shorrocks, 1988a. "Poverty orderings," *Econometrica*, 52, 761–6
1988b. "Poverty orderings and welfare dominance," *Social Choice and Welfare*, 5, 179–98
1991. "Subgroup consistent poverty indices," *Econometrica*, 59, 687–709
Foster, J.E., J. Greer and E. Thorbecke, 1984. "A class of decomposable poverty indices," *Econometrica*, 52, 761–6
Hagenaars, A.J.M., 1986. *The Perception of Poverty*, Amsterdam: North-Holland
1987. "A class of poverty measures," *International Economic Review*, 28, 583–607
Howes, S., 1993a. "Mixed dominance: a new criterion for poverty analysis," Distributional Analysis Research Programme, 3, London School of Economics
1993b. "Robust distributional analysis," London School of Economics, mimeo

Jenkins, S. and P. Lambert, 1993. "Poverty orderings, poverty gaps, and poverty lines," *Discussion Paper*, 93–07, Economics Department, University College of Swansea

Kanbur, S.M.R., 1987. "Structural adjustment, macroeconomic adjustment and poverty: a methodology for analysis," *World Development*, 15, 1515–27

Marshall, A.W. and I. Olkin, 1979. *Inequalities: Theory of Majorization and its Applications*, New York: Academic Press

Meyer, J., 1977. "Second degree stochastic dominance with respect to a function," *International Economic Review*, 18, 477–87

Pratt, J., 1964. "Risk aversion in the small and the large," *Econometrica*, 32, 122–36

Ravallion, M., 1994. *Poverty Comparisons: A Guide to Concepts and Methods*, Chur: Harwood Academic Publishers

Sen, A.K., 1976. "Poverty: an ordinal approach to measurement," *Econometrica*, 46, 437–46

　1981. *Poverty and Famines: An Essay on Entitlement and Deprivation*, Oxford: Oxford University Press

Shorrocks, A.F., 1983. "Ranking income distributions," *Economica*, 50, 3–17

　1994. "Deprivation profiles and deprivation indices," chapter 11 of this volume

Thon, D., 1979. "On measuring poverty," *Review of Income and Wealth*, 25, 429–39

Watts, H.W., 1968. "An economic definition of poverty," in D.P. Moynihan (ed.), *On Understanding Poverty*, New York: Basic Books, 316–29

Zheng, B., 1993a. *Poverty Measurement, Statistical Inference, and an Application to the United States*, PhD dissertation, West Virginia University

　1993b. "An axiomatic characterization of the Watts poverty index," *Economics Letters*, 42, 81–6

13 Changing welfare in a changing world?: income and expenditure inequalities in the Czech and Slovak republics

Thesia Garner

Introduction

The year 1989 marked a major turning point for Czechoslovakia, as it did for many other transition countries in east central Europe. In late 1989 the totalitarian system was rejected, and a new government established. With this new government came political and economic changes to transform Czechoslovakia from an economy based on central planning and rule into a pluralist, market-based democracy. However, within the two republics of Czechoslovakia, differences in opinion concerning the approaches to accomplish the transition emerged. Leaders in the Czech republic promoted a rapid but phased introduction of the market. In contrast, a more interventionist, less harsh economic reform was preferred in the Slovak republic (also referred to as Slovakia). Differences between the republics eventually lead to a new name for the country in April 1990, the Czech and Slovak Federal Republic, and then to a split into two separate countries on January 1, 1993. Although both republics supported strong social policies, their differences were translated into variations in social policy implementation in 1990 and 1991. However, by 1992, reforms regarding unemployment and other social programs including pensions, were harmonized in the two republics. The implementation of privatization reforms, however, continue to diverge.

The purpose of this chapter is to examine, from a standard economic perspective, how households living in the two republics have responded to, and have been affected by, the changing economy and reforms introduced during the early years of the transition period. Such an approach presupposes that welfare, interpreted here as economic well-being, is our ultimate concern. The response of, and impact on, households is especially important to study because the success or failure of the reforms is greatly dependent upon households. Neglecting the situation of households can lead to social unease and distrust of the government making the reforms. The periods 1989 and 1992 serve as a basis for the analysis, since 1989 is the last year central planning dominated the economy and 1992 is the last year the republics formed one country.

"Economic well-being" is assessed in terms of inequality in both household *per capita* income and expenditures, because it is not clear *a priori* which is a better measure of this concept. By examining inequality, the focus is on relative rather than absolute economic well-being. Although income is the traditional resource used by researchers to assess economic well-being, expenditures are likely to become more valuable for this measurement as the shadow economy gains in importance and income reporting in household surveys decreases. Several inequality measures are used to examine differences overall. Aggregate inequality is examined further by decomposing it by sources. Comparisons are made across the republics and across time. Micro level household data from the Family Budget Surveys (FBS) from each republic are used for the analysis. FBSs have been conducted annually since the 1950s. Although not entirely representative of the total population by 1992, the FBS data set was chosen for the analysis because it is the only source which includes information on both income and expenditures. Microcensus surveys are used to collect income data from a more representative sample of the population; however these data are collected only once every four or five years, limiting their usefulness in assessing welfare during a rapidly changing transitional period.

This research is different from the work of others studying the transition in the Czech and Slovak republics in three ways: (1) adjustments are made in the data to make the FBS sample more representative of the total population; (2) the same samples are used to assess welfare using both income and expenditures from the FBS; and (3) the inequalities in income and expenditures are decomposed into factor components and changes over time are identified. Although other researchers (see, for example, Atkinson and Mickelwright, 1992; Dlouhy, 1991; Garner, Lubyova and Terrell, 1995; Hirsl, 1993; Jilek *et al.*, 1995; Kucharova, 1993; Milanovic, 1992a, 1992b; UNICEF, 1993; Vavrejnova, 1993; Vavrejnova and Moravcikova, 1995; Vecernik, 1995) have examined the incomes and/or expenditures of households in the Czech and Slovak republics, none has followed an approach such as the one employed here.

It must be emphasized that this chapter focuses on distributional concerns without focusing specifically on equality of opportunity, the gap between rich and poor, or levels of welfare. Some individuals have been more able to take advantage of greater opportunities while others have not. Some have become richer and others poorer. Focusing on these opportunities and the gap between rich and poor reflects other major objectives of welfare which analyses such as this one do not address.

The remainder of this chapter is organized into four sections. The next section provides a brief description of the economy in the two republics and outlines the economic changes and reforms which are likely to have influenced households' incomes and expenditures during the early years of the transition period. We then present the methodology and data, including the results and discussion of the major findings. The final section summarizes some ideas concerning the changes in equality.

Institutional background and potential relationship to inequality

Economic background

In 1948 Czechoslovakia became part of the Soviet bloc; democracy was replaced by a totalitarian regime and central planning was introduced. A deliberate equalization policy was applied to wages, incomes, and retirement pensions by this regime, with differences in family size accommodated by generous family benefits. Based on this strategy, small differences among different strata of the population resulted. In terms of industrial structure, the private non-agricultural sector was virtually eliminated during 1948–53. By the mid-1970s, agriculture became highly collectivized with agro-industrial enterprises combining farms and processing, and by 1985, collective agriculture accounted for 90 percent of gross farm output (Jeffries, 1993). From 1948 through 1989, official unemployment did not exist. In the 1980s Czechoslovak economy stagnated and there was an underlying deterioration in key aspects of economic performance.

The decline in economic performance continued through 1992 (see Dyba and Svejnar, 1995). From 1989 to 1992, real industrial and agricultural output fell in both republics. Decreases in average employment and the productivity of labor also resulted, however labor hoarding was expected. In terms of purchasing power, through 1991, increases in the average wage and money incomes did not keep pace with inflation; however, by 1992, they did. Through 1991, annual increases in money income were greater than those for wages; this suggests that people were finding other ways to supplement their incomes. In general, economic performance, as measured by the factors mentioned above, was quite similar in the two republics from 1989 to 1992. However, differences emerged in terms of unemployment. From the beginning, Slovakia experienced greater unemployment than did the Czech republic, primarily due to its historically greater dependence on heavy industry and armaments. By 1992 unemployment in the Czech republic was only 2.6

percent while in Slovakia it was 10.3 percent. Durations of unemployment were also longer in Slovakia than in the Czech republic.

Reforms

With the transition to the market and dismantling of the previous regime, the government introduced reforms to promote privatization and reduce subsidies, while at the same time revising social policies and activating a new social safety net. Reforms were introduced which led to changes in industrial and employment structure, income taxes, and transfer benefits. Each of these would be expected to affect the distribution of income. Factors likely to affect expenditures include changes in policies related to commodity taxes and prices, and the quantity and quality of commodities available.

Reforms related to industrial structure and employment
The primary change in industrial and employment structure was due to government policies promoting extensive privatization. Unlike in Poland and Hungary, Czechoslovakia started its transformation process from a position of virtually complete state ownership of the economy; only 1.2 percent of the labor force belonged to the private sector in 1989 (Dyba and Svejnar, 1995). However, by 1992, the private sector was providing jobs to about 50 percent of the labor force in the Czech republic (OECD, 1994); the rate was somewhat lower for Slovakia. In both 1991 and 1992, employment in the traditional state and cooperative sector fell by more in the Czech republic than in Slovakia (European Commission, 1993a). These differences would be expected to lead to greater wage inequality in the Czech republic. Privatization also prompted the transfer of state property to private hands through restitution and voucher distributions, bringing windfall gains to some owners. Owners could use this "new" property to generate additional income.

The structure of employment changed in other ways also, for example by branch and gender. During this time period employment in agriculture and industry steadily declined; however, employment in the service sector increased (OECD, 1994; European Commission, 1995). In 1989, the proportion of persons employed in industry was fairly comparable across the republics, while the proportion employed in agriculture was slightly greater in Slovakia than in the Czech republic. However, by 1992, major shifts in employment had occurred, impacting the republics differently. Employment in agriculture fell by a third in the Czech republic but only by about half that in Slovakia from 1989 to 1992. The share of employment in industry fell by 10 percent in Slovakia against only 5 percent in the Czech republic (European Commission, 1993b).

Under the previous regime, a high rate of labor force participation was stimulated by a social policy predicated on the model of a two-earner family and the collective upbringing of children. Thus, high rates of labor force activity existed for both men and women; in 1989 male activity rates were 95 percent in the Czech republic and 92 percent in Slovakia; female rates were 90 percent and 80 percent, respectively, for the two republics. By 1992, labor force participation rates had declined for males by about 3 percentage points, the decline for females was 10–12 points (European Commission, 1995).

As part of the country's comprehensive stabilization program, relatively strict wage controls, were introduced in 1991 and 1992. Enterprises, primarily those with majority state or municipal ownership, were taxed heavily if they allowed their wage bill to rise above a certain percentage. By 1992, wage growth was tied to firm productivity; however, wages were expected to remain fairly compressed.

Because of the decreased demand for industrial goods and state sector production, policies were introduced to reduce labor supply. Compared to other countries in transition in the region, "a much larger component of employment reduction in the Czech republic has been accompanied by pushing people out of the labor force rather than into unemployment" (OECD, 1994, p. 4). In Slovakia, redundant workers have been more likely to be pushed into unemployment (European Commission, 1993b).

Policies to reduce labor supply included the introduction of retirement schemes to encourage older workers to leave the work force. For example, in 1991 a high personal income tax rate for those working above the retirement age was introduced, forcing many working pensioners to retire and rely primarily on their pensions. A concurrent payment of pensions and wages was no longer favored.[1] It has been suggested that such a policy was followed more strictly in the Czech republic than in Slovakia, however (Papaj, 1994), and this difference in implementation could lead to differences in income inequality for the two republics.

Persons retiring because of "old age" as well as disability increased over the period. Pension authorities attribute the increase in disability retirement to collusion between employees and employers as they selected the most attractive retirement package for redundant workers. A World Bank report (1994) notes that employees more than two years away from retirement age were economically significantly better off with disability pensions than with unemployment benefits. Between 1991 and 1992, pensioners improved their income position relative to that of the working-age population over the previous years.

Changing the maternal allowance to a parental allowance and extending benefits to cover the first three years of a child's life were other measures introduced to reduce the supply of persons seeking employment outside of the home. In Slovakia, the average number of monthly claimants for these benefits doubled between 1990 and 1992 (World Bank, 1994). During this period parental benefits were more generous than were unemployment benefits.

Income taxes and transfer benefits
Under the previous regime, direct taxes played almost no role in redistribution. They were relatively small and only mildly progressive. Most taxation was borne by enterprises (in the form of profit or payroll taxes), although wage earners were required to pay taxes on their earnings. In January 1992, new tax laws came into effect. Personal income taxes were made more progressive and a new law was introduced for individuals to pay personal income tax on private non-wage income (Heady, Rajah and Smith, 1994).

Social security has had a long tradition in these republics. However, the role of transfer benefits began to change during the early years of the transition in response to downturns in the economy and to price increases; unemployment and poverty became grave realities. To soften the loss of income for some and to boost it for others, several new social policies were introduced. Indexation of old age pensions was begun in 1990 to dampen the fall in pensioners' purchasing power. Cash benefits for the unemployed were also introduced in this year. A transfer benefit was introduced in 1990 and continued through 1992 to compensate individuals for the social consequences originating from a rise in prices, first for food (the benefit was the same for all persons), and second for energy (the benefit was increased for pensioners and children only). In 1991, a social safety net was introduced for the first time in the Czech and Slovakian republics, to act as the state's guarantee of minimum assistance for citizens in difficulty. Specific subsistence cash benefits were introduced for those on low incomes as a part of this program, although marginal supplementary social assistance to needy individuals and families had existed previously. By 1992, family and child allowances were still primarily universal for households with children, even though means-testing principles were being introduced.

Commodity taxes and prices
The major exogenous shocks on consumer expenditures during the period were due to changes in commodity tax policies and to price liberalization. The first interim step in tax reform by the Czechoslovak

government was the removal of the negative turnover tax rates or retail price subsidies on food in July 1990. Large-scale price liberalization was launched on January 1, 1991 and served as the second stage. The negative turnover tax rates on most non-food commodities were removed (without a compensation benefit), and the number of turnover tax rates was reduced. By the middle of 1992 all price ceilings, except those on rents, were lifted. Prices rose considerably from 1989 to 1992 in the two republics, but more so in Slovakia (96 percent) than in the Czech republic (91 percent); prices for some commodities, such as those for energy, doubled. Compared to other countries in the region, these two republics experienced relative price stability. Price increases were anticipated, and this anticipation too affected consumer spending. Jilek *et al.* (1995) note that there was an exaggeration of purchases of goods that took place in the second half of 1990. A similar anticipation was expected to exert an influence on consumer expenditures in late 1992, since a 23 percent value added tax (applicable to a large percentage of commodities) was introduced on January 1, 1993.

Consumer goods
Vavrejnova (1993) reports that under the previous regime, the consumer market was characterized by low quality goods (especially non-food products such as metal products, tools, appliances for the household and garden, and some textiles) which required frequent repairs and replacement. Thus, with better quality goods (needing less repair and replacement) entering the market, only marginal changes in expenditures were expected for certain non-food goods.

Potential relationship to inequality
The reforms introduced and economic performance resulting are likely to have impacted the distributions of income and expenditures. For this study, it was expected that overall income and expenditure inequality would increase from 1989 to 1992, but only marginally (see Garner, Lubyova and Terrell, 1995). Greater unemployment and more private sector employment is expected to lead to increases in aggregate income inequality. The increase is expected to be only marginal, however, because of the remaining dominant state sector and a cultural and historical tradition of equality (Jilek *et al.*, 1995; Teichova, 1988; Vecernik, 1994). Controlled wages, more targeted social transfer benefits, and the indexation of pensions are expected to have equalizing effects on income inequality. Incomes are expected to be more equally distributed in Slovakia than in the Czech republic. This hypothesis is based on the expectation that social transfers, including pensions, will be more

important as a part of total household income in Slovakia due to greater industrial restructuring and differences in social policy implementation.

Changes in commodity taxes, price liberalization, and greater access to a variety of commodities, may lead to increases in expenditures for all households with little change in the distributions. However, due to the elimination of, or reductions in subsidies for necessities, households are likely to have allocated a greater share of their total budget to these commodities and away from luxuries. Such a shift is likely to result in a decrease in expenditure inequality.

It is expected that income inequality will be lower than expenditure inequality. This is based on the fact that income, particularly wage income, was significantly compressed in these republics through 1992.

Methodology and data

Measures of inequality

The measures of inequality used for this analysis include the decile ratio, the Robin Hood Index[2] (Atkinson and Micklewright, 1992), the Gini coefficient, and three generalized entropy measures (see Coulter, Cowell and Jenkins, 1992). Each of the measures differs in its sensitivity to income or expenditure variations at different levels of the distribution. The Lerman and Yitzhaki (1985, 1989, 1994) source decomposition method of the Gini coefficient is used to determine the share of aggregate inequality which is due to each component of income or expenditures, and the contribution of each to changes in aggregate inequality from 1989 to 1992.

Variables of interest

Since economic well-being cannot directly be observed, two related proxies are considered in this study: income and consumption expenditures. Each proxy has its advantages and disadvantages (see Blundell and Preston, 1991). Not accounted for in either proxy are subsidies for goods and services provided by the state, the leisure time of household members, or non-agricultural home production. The level of economic well-being is likely to be affected by this omission; however, inequality may not be.

Income

Income is the most often used measure of economic well-being in inequality studies. It reflects one's potential control over economic resources, and can be viewed as an indication of one's ability to sustain a flow of consumption and thus to enjoy a certain level of living. For this study, flow income is the concept used and is defined as the sum of net monetary income (income from wages, agriculture production, pensions, benefits, welfare, and additional monetary income *minus* wage and other taxes paid by the household), the value of in-kind consumption, and the income flow from the owner occupancy of housing. In-kind consumption is evaluated by the Czech and Slovakia Statistical Offices (SOs) at current prices which exist in the area in which the household lives. In-kind expenditures include those for food and beverages, rent in-kind, and other products and services. The values of agricultural production for home consumption and gifts received from persons outside the household are included in this latter group. The estimated value of the flow of services from the ownership of a home or cooperative is imputed from an hedonic rental equation.[3]

Consumption expenditures

Consumption expenditures reflect one's exercise of control over economic resources, and are often considered a better approximation to life cycle income than is current income when households base their spending plans on their expected lifetime income. Consumption expenditures in this study are defined as the sum of household monetary expenditures (including commodity taxes) for goods and services *plus* the value of in-kind consumption (as defined previously), *minus* the value of goods and services given to persons outside the household as gifts.[4] Also included is the value of imputed rent for home owners. The full purchase price of durables is included in the total, since adequate information is not available to estimate the flow of services from these commodities.

Observation unit and treatment of household size

The observation unit for this study is the household, and is defined by the SO as a group of individuals who live together and share expenditures for food, housekeeping, home maintenance, and other commodities. To account for differences in household size, I divided each household's income and expenditures by the number of persons in the household, thus producing household *per capita* values.

Since the focus of this research is the economic well-being of individuals, household *per capita* income and expenditures are allocated to each member in the household. This weighting results in the individual distribution rather than household distribution of resources.

Data description

Data are from the 1989 and 1992 Family Budget Surveys (FBSs) of the Czech and Slovak republics, and are collected by the central SO in each republic. Data are collected monthly using a diary completed by households and a survey instrument which is completed by an interviewer. In 1989, households maintained diaries for approximately 11.6 months and in 1992 for 11.3 months. For this analysis I annualized the income and expenditure data. The 1989 Czech sample includes 3,978 households[5] and the sample for 1992 includes 3,336. The Slovak sample for 1989 includes 1,702 households and for 1992, 1,695. The 1992 samples are from the primary files only (see Garner, Lubyova and Terrell, 1995).

Households are selected by the SOs for inclusion in the sample following an intentional quota design. The quota design or plan accounts for region of residence and several household characteristics. The primary household characteristic is the social group of the head of household. Four social groups are defined: manual workers, employees, persons working in agriculture, and pensioner households without economically active members. Using the quota design, within a region, households are included in the sample mainly based on their characteristics, not their exact addresses. Thus, if a visited household does not fit into one of the quota categories, other households are visited until the quota is met within a region. There is no adjustment to account for refusals to participate in the survey. Because of the quota procedure, response rates are not computed.

Changes in the sample design have been introduced since 1989 which could affect the inequality results. By 1992 (but not after 1993), if the head of the household became a private non-agricultural entrepreneur, the household would be excluded from the sample and a replacement household would be added. However by 1992, household heads who were private entrepreneurs working in agriculture, as well as all others working in agriculture, were included in the redefined agriculture social group; in 1989, the agriculture group included only cooperative farmers. In 1989 a household headed by a private entrepreneur would not be included in any of the social groups. Another change in the sample design is that if the household head became unemployed for more than three months, the household would be excluded in 1989; however, by 1992, the household would remain in the sample, in the social group as originally identified.

The SOs do not produce weights to combine households from the quota sampled FBS so that they are representative of Czech and Slovak households. Thus, for this analysis, I created household weights using data from the 1988 and 1992 Microcensus.[6] The weights are based on the distribution of households in each of the republics defined in terms of social group, region, and family size. Based on the 1988 Microcensus, about 95.4 percent of all households in the Czech republic and 94.4 percent of all households in Slovakia are represented by the FBS samples. By 1992 the four social groups in the FBS represent about 90 percent of Czech households, and 84.2 percent of households in Slovakia. Not included in the 1989 FBS are households headed by private entrepreneurs who represented about 0.2 percent of households in the Czech republic and 0.1 percent in Slovakia; in 1989 agricultural private entrepreneur-headed households represented about 0.01 percent of Czech households and 0.04 percent of Slovak households. By 1992, private non-agricultural entrepreneur households, not accounted for in the FBS, represented 5.7 percent of all Czech households and 3.5 percent of Slovak households. Also not included in the FBS samples are pensioner households with economically active members. In 1989 this group accounted for approximately 4 percent of all households in the Czech republic, and 5 percent in Slovakia; however, by 1992, 5.1 percent of Czech households and 8.2 percent of Slovak households were in this group. Other households not included in the four FBS social groups are those headed by students and non-working persons not receiving a pension or wage, for example.[7]

The distribution of persons by social group in the combined re-weighted samples differs somewhat from 1989 to 1992.[8] Persons in pensioner households represent 13 percent of all persons in the Czech 1989 FBS sample and 18 percent in the 1992 sample; the data for Slovakia reflect a large increase as well, from 11 to 20 percent of all persons. Employee households account for 37 percent of all persons in the Czech sample in 1989 and 35 percent in the Slovak sample. By 1992, the percentage of persons in the employee households drops to about 30 percent in the two republics. Worker households account for about 44 percent of persons in the Czech and Slovak FBS samples, while persons in agricultural households account for 10 percent or less of the total each year.

Reliability of family budget survey data

There may be some concern that income and expenditures from the FBSs may not be reliable for distributional analyses. According to individuals with the SOs, the expenditure data are considered to be fairly accurate, as is income from non-private entrepreneurial activites. However, it is likely that incomes from the shadow economy are poorly reported, as they are in other household surveys. Shadow economy incomes include, for example, those from unregistered activities of cross-border workers in Austria and Germany, and incomes connected with tourism, namely those from renting private accommodation to foreigners. The importance of incomes associated with tourism increased largely in the first years of the transition period, particularly in the Czech republic (Jilek *et al.*, 1995). The omission or under-reporting of these incomes is likely to result in under-estimates of the true change in income and inequality during this early transitional period.

Another factor which could affect the data is that there is no explicit design feature to rotate households in and out of the sample. Kalmus (1994) reports that for the Czech republic, about 50 percent of the same households are in both the 1989 and 1992 samples. The impact of this time in sample feature cannot be examined with the 1989 and 1992 data because household identifiers were not retained in the 1989 data file.

Perhaps the greatest potential problem for distributional analysis is that income and expenditures from the FBS may not adequately reflect the resources for households at the extreme ends of the distributions (Blagonavova *et al.*, 1992). If this is true, the inequality results using these data will under-estimate the inequality of economic well-being for the total population.

Results and discussion

Overall inequality

Table 13.1 includes the results for the measures of aggregate inequality.[9] The lower the inequality index value, the more equal the distribution. The indices consistently show that inequality in consumption expenditures decreased in the Czech republic from 1989 to 1992. Decreases in inequality are also revealed by the decile ratio, the Robin Hood Index, the Gini coefficient, and the mean log deviation measures for both income and expenditures for the two republics, with one exception. The exception is for flow income in Slovakia; here income inequality appears to increase over time when using the mean log deviation index. The trend toward decreasing income inequality is in contrast to that hypothesized. Potential reasons for the decline in inequality over the time period are likely to be related to changes in industrial and employment structure, income taxes, and transfer bvenefits, as noted earlier. However, the small changes in income inequality may also indicate that income disparities in the private and informal sectors have not been as great as were expected, or that there has been a decrease in the quality of income reports.

Table 13.1 Indices of inequality for household per capita flow income and consumption expenditures, 1989 and 1992

| | Flow income | | | | | | Consumption expenditures | | | | | |
| | Czech republic | | | Slovak Republic | | | Czech republic | | | Slovak Republic | | |
	1989	1992	% change[a]	1989	1992	% change[a]	1989	1992	% change[a]	1989	1992	% change[a]
Decile ratio/1000	0.224	0.214	−4.61	0.218	0.213	−2.31	0.242	0.224	−7.74	0.241	0.232	−3.80
Robin Hood index	0.131	0.127	−3.05	0.124	0.122	−1.61	0.144	0.134	−6.94	0.147	0.135	−8.16
Gini	0.182	0.179	−1.65	0.174	0.174	−0.39	0.203	0.190	−6.26	0.206	0.197	−3.97
Mean log deviation	0.052	0.052	−0.54	0.048	0.049	−2.23	0.066	0.059	−10.16	0.068	0.066	−2.87
CV²/2	0.062	0.065	−4.51	0.058	0.065	−11.43	0.083	0.078	−5.79	0.085	0.105	−23.47
Theil entropy	0.055	0.056	−1.28	0.052	0.054	−4.89	0.071	0.064	−9.43	0.073	0.075	−3.42

Note:
[a] % change may differ from values obtained using indices presented in tables due to rounding.

The general pattern found in this research follows the continuing decline in monetary income inequality reported by Atkinson and Mickle-wright (1992) for Czechoslovakia from 1958 to 1988. For another transition country, the Ukraine, Kakwani (1995) also reported declining income inequality from 1980 to 1991 using FBS data (a marginal increase was found for 1992, however).

A different pattern in the change in inequality over time is exhibited by the measures which are more sensitive to variations at the top of the distribution, $CV^2/2$ and the Theil measure, with the exception of Czech expenditures noted previously. Using these two measures, inequality increases in both income and expenditures from 1989 to 1992, with the greatest increases for Slovakia. These results suggest that those at the top, compared to those at the bottom, are perhaps better able to take advantage of greater opportunities in employment and in the consumer market present in 1992.

The results presented in table 13.1 show that incomes are more equally distributed than are consumption expenditures across the repub-lics and time period, as hypothesized. Incomes are more equally distributed in Slovakia than in the Czech republic, while expenditures are more equally distributed in the Czech republic than in Slovakia. The difference in income inequality between the two may be a reflection of greater private sector employment in the Czech republic. As alluded to above, a reason why incomes are more equally distributed than are expenditures may be because most wages were still being set by the state in 1992 and were designed to be fairly equal; equality of expenditures was not a direct aim of government policy, though equal access to basic commodities was. The income–expenditure inequality relationship found here differs from that reported for developed western economies (e.g. Garner, 1989; Kakwani, 1986); in these countries, consumption expenditures are found to be more equally distributed across the population than are incomes.

The general trend toward equality in income shown by these results is in contrast to those reported by researchers using the Microcensus data. For example, Vecernik (1995) reports increasing income inequality with Gini indices of 0.20 in 1988 and 0.22 in 1992 for the Czech republic and 0.19 and 0.20 for Slovakia in the two years, respectively, using household *per capita* net monetary income. Thus one might conclude that the FBS data under-estimate income inequality for the total population.

Regardless of the data source used, the Czech and Slovak republics have exhibited the most equal income distributions compared to other countries in the region during these early transition years. They also had the most equal distributions during the previous regime. Since 1989, Gini coefficients have been produced for other countries in the region of 0.217 or higher (Milanovic, 1992a; Kakwani, 1995). However, for the states representing the former German Democratic Republic, Hauser *et al.* (1992) report a Gini index of 0.199 using income data collected nine months after the reunification with the western German state. Gini indices for incomes in Western countries have been reported to be in the range of 0.262 to 0.330 (see Smeeding, 1991).

Decomposition by factor components

Decomposing the Gini coefficient provides a way of measuring how much a particular component contributes to aggregate inequality, and how changes in the components of income and expenditures have affected aggregate inequality over time. The basic ingredients needed are the share of each component, each component's correlation with the total income or expenditure, and each factor's own Gini. Using these, the percentage of total inequality[10] and the percentage change in source contribution[11] can be derived. Decomposition results are presented in tables 13.2 and 13.3 for income and tables 13.4 and 13.5 for expenditures. Because my interest is net income and consumption expenditures, wage and related taxes, and the value of gifts given enter the decompositions as negative values. Results in the tables show that there were marked changes in income packaging over the time period, and that expenditure patterns also changed. The overall impact on aggregate inequality of these changes is greater for expenditures than for income, and the impacts are greater for the Czech republic than they are for Slovakia.

Flow income

Gross wages of the head account for the largest percentage of total flow income inequality in both years for the two republics; however, the percentage of inequality due to this source is greater in 1992 than in 1989. This increase appears to be related to increasing inequality within head's wages,[12] and decreases in the share of persons allocated these wages. Wife's gross wages are the second largest contributor to aggregate income inequality each year, and there is also a decrease in the percentage of persons with these wages in both republics. However, in the Czech republic, the share of total income from wife's wages increases from 1989 to 1992. In contrast, in Slovakia, the share of total income from wife's wages decreases over the period. These results reveal that, as a separate source of income, wife's wages have become more important during the transition in the Czech republic and less in important in Slovakia.[13]

The percentage change in the source contribution can be used to identify which factors had the greatest influence on the change in aggregate inequality over time. The larger the percentage change, the greater the influence. The sum of the percentage changes equals the percentage change in aggregate inequality. Percentage change impacts can be produced only for components which are identifiable for both 1989 and 1992. Thus, in the case of income, the sum of the changes will not equal the percentage change in aggregate inequality.

Among those sources of income identifiable in both years in the Czech republic, changes in wife's wages produces the greatest influence on changing aggregate inequality; however, these changes had a disequalizing effect. The next largest percentage change source contribution is for wage taxes, leading to reductions in inequality, followed by changes in wife's pension, and head's agricultural income.

As for the Czech republic, in Slovakia, the sign of the factor with the greatest influence on aggregate income inequality is positive. Changes in the head's pension produces a disequalizing effect. Equality is enhanced by changes in head's agricultural income and wife's wages.

Changes in agricultural income appear to have led to greater equality in both republics, but the changes were more equalizing for Slovakia. Changes in taxes played a minor role in reducing inequality in Slovakia, unlike in the Czech republic. Although pensions became more important in total income from 1989 to 1992, the net effect of changes in pension income contributed to reductions in inequality in the Czech republic but increases in Slovakia. This difference may be due to variations in program implementation related to retirement schemes and indexation. In 1989 and 1992, transfer benefits accounted for slightly greater shares of total income, with the share greater in Slovakia. In both republics, the introduction of unemployment, subsistence, and compensation benefits is likely to have contributed significantly to decreasing income inequality.

Gini elasticities[14] are also presented in tables 13.2 and 13.3. Negative elasticities are an indication that sources of income are more directed at the lower end of the income distribution. For 1989 these sources include head's pensions, child allowances, other benefits, and welfare payments (which include those paid by non-government charities). By 1992 monetary benefits for unemployment, subsistence, and compensation have this distinction.

Table 13.2 *Gini index decomposition: flow income in the Czech republic, 1989 and 1992*

	1989						1992						
	%≠0	Household per capita income / Share of total income	Std. dev. / Correlation	Gini coeff. / Factor Gini	Std. err. / % of total inequality	Gini elasticity	%≠0	Household per capita income / Share of total income	Std. dev. / Correlation	Gini coeff. / Factor Gini	Std. err. / % of total inequality	Gini elasticity	% change in source contribution
Flow income (crowns)		25,096.69	8,871.64	0.182	0.002			36,325.99	13,128.09	0.179	0.003		−1.65
Head's gross wage	0.797	0.468	0.550	0.394	0.558	1.191	0.740	0.427	0.528	0.457	0.575	1.346	0.78
Wife's wage	0.618	0.213	0.469	0.566	0.310	1.457	0.562	0.220	0.480	0.613	0.361	1.642	4.48
Other's wage	0.090	0.023	0.497	0.945	0.061	2.578	0.090	0.023	0.499	0.944	0.061	2.630	−0.05
Temporary job income	0.994	0.028	0.407	0.467	0.029	1.043	0.975	0.030	0.514	0.524	0.045	1.503	1.47
Head's agricult. income	0.075	0.035	0.292	0.942	0.053	1.509	0.080	0.031	0.163	0.941	0.026	0.857	−2.66
Wife's agricult. income	0.059	0.018	0.328	0.955	0.030	1.720	0.053	0.014	0.277	0.964	0.021	1.492	−1.02
Other's agricult. income	0.007	0.002	0.748	0.996	0.007	4.089	0.005	0.001	0.316	0.997	0.001	1.755	−0.60
Other agricult. income	0.013	0.001	0.674	0.996	0.002	3.682	0.012	0.000	0.204	0.995	0.000	1.134	−0.17
Head's pension	0.178	0.088	−0.047	0.867	−0.020	−0.224	0.239	0.102	−0.006	0.833	−0.003	−0.026	−1.71
Wife's pension	0.127	0.034	0.196	0.903	0.033	0.969	0.154	0.040	0.026	0.877	0.005	0.126	−2.83
Other's pension	0.025	0.006	0.273	0.984	0.009	1.474	0.023	0.005	0.259	0.985	0.007	1.423	−0.23
Child allowance	0.692	0.050	−0.495	0.476	−0.065	−1.294	0.659	0.033	−0.490	0.507	−0.046	−1.387	2.04
Sickness benefits	0.558	0.023	0.225	0.777	0.022	0.958	0.490	0.017	0.248	0.800	0.019	1.107	−0.38

Other benefits	0.143	0.006	−0.391	0.913	−0.011	−1.961	0.162	0.012	−0.302	0.887	−0.018	−1.496	−0.63
Unemployment benefits							0.043	0.002	−0.112	0.979	−0.001	−0.614	
Subsistence benefits							0.011	0.000	−0.661	0.994	−0.001	−3.664	
Compensation benefit							0.896	0.040	−0.429	0.305	−0.029	−0.730	
Welfare payments	0.021	0.001	0.288	0.989	−0.002	−1.564	0.035	0.001	−0.279	0.989	−0.002	−1.530	−0.04
Income/agricult. sales	0.142	0.004	0.426	0.958	0.010	2.241	0.126	0.003	0.472	0.966	0.008	2.545	−0.19
Income/insurance	0.142	0.005	0.437	0.957	0.011	2.297	0.141	0.005	0.466	0.963	0.013	2.506	0.17
Stock and bond yields							0.031	0.002	0.525	0.987	0.007	2.893	
Indep. farmer income							0.003	0.001	0.673	0.999	0.002	3.749	
Indep. non-farmer income							0.029	0.004	0.429	0.990	0.009	0.372	
Other monetary income	0.688	0.047	0.476	0.768	0.095	0.008	0.685	0.042	0.528	0.785	0.097	2.315	−0.01
In-kind consumption	0.924	0.060	0.357	0.526	0.062	1.032	0.894	0.064	0.366	0.529	0.069	1.080	0.64
Imputed owner's rent	0.587	0.018	0.227	0.540	0.013	0.691	0.610	0.021	0.254	0.539	0.016	0.765	0.31
Wage tax	0.828	−0.127	0.657	0.439	−0.202	1.583	0.782	−0.134	0.639	0.493	−0.236	1.756	−3.05
Other tax	0.592	0.003	0.350	0.770	−0.005	1.483	0.482	−0.003	0.379	0.847	−0.005	1.793	−0.06

Table 13.3 *Gini index decomposition: flow income in the Slovak republic, 1989 and 1992*

	1989						1992						% change in source contribution
Household per capita income	223,349.61						312,272.12						
Std. dev.	7,642.03						11,287.98						
Gini coeff.	0.174						0.174						
Std. err.	0.004						0.005						-0.39
Flow income (crowns)	%≠0	Share of total income	Correla-tion	Factor Gini	% of total in-equality	Gini elast-icity	%≠0	Share of total income	Correla-tion	Factor Gini	% of total in-equality	Gini elast-icity	
Head's gross wage	0.790	0.449	0.502	0.392	0.508	1.131	0.733	0.401	0.481	0.470	0.521	1.304	1.29
Wife's wage	0.635	0.228	0.499	0.533	0.348	1.526	0.565	0.218	0.413	0.591	0.306	1.404	-4.19
Other's wage	0.101	0.026	0.465	0.941	0.066	2.508	0.069	0.022	0.466	0.958	0.055	2.571	-1.12
Temporary job income	0.976	0.028	0.493	0.507	0.040	1.433	0.966	0.026	0.502	0.499	0.038	1.443	-0.24
Head's agricult. income	0.103	0.053	0.350	0.919	0.098	1.846	0.077	0.031	0.220	0.943	0.037	0.195	-6.04
Wife's agricult. income	0.072	0.021	0.359	0.946	0.041	1.948	0.059	0.013	0.207	0.960	0.015	1.145	-2.60
Other's agricult. income	0.004	0.002	0.758	0.997	0.007	4.335	0.005	0.001	0.826	0.998	0.006	4.748	-0.12
Other agricult. income	0.018	0.001	0.438	0.994	0.001	2.497	0.010	0.000	0.763	0.999	0.001	4.389	-0.08
Head's pension	0.127	0.066	-0.125	0.902	-0.043	-0.647	0.216	0.107	-0.084	0.834	0.043	0.403	8.59
Wife's pension	0.091	0.022	0.152	0.936	0.018	0.814	0.150	0.038	0.137	0.877	0.026	0.700	0.82
Other's pension	0.055	0.012	0.324	0.961	0.021	1.784	0.046	0.010	0.377	0.968	0.021	2.100	0.06
Child allowance	0.764	0.070	-0.523	0.419	-0.088	-1.259	0.725	0.048	-0.495	0.446	-0.061	-1.273	2.71
Sickness benefits	0.475	0.017	0.173	0.785	0.013	0.778	0.442	0.015	0.286	0.812	0.021	1.339	0.71

Other benefits	0.118	0.006	-0.451	0.920	-0.015	-2.381	0.132	0.011	-0.301	0.910	-0.018	-1.580	-0.43
Unemployment benefits							0.063	0.002	-0.325	0.966	-0.004	-1.810	
Subsistence benefits							0.027	0.001	-0.536	0.985	-0.003	-3.041	
Compensation benefit							0.895	0.045	-3.019	0.282	-0.023	-0.519	
Welfare payments	0.024	0.001	-0.306	0.987	-0.002	-1.734	0.028	0.001	0.217	0.989	0.001	1.237	0.26
Income/agricult. sales	0.135	0.005	0.476	0.950	0.013	2.592	0.101	0.003	0.467	0.965	0.008	2.599	-0.53
Income/insurance	0.073	0.002	0.555	0.977	0.007	3.109	0.079	0.003	0.404	0.970	0.006	2.257	-0.05
Stock and bond yields							0.005	0.000	0.170	0.997	0.000	0.978	
Indep. farmer incomes							0.014	0.004	0.473	0.994	0.010	2.712	
Indep. non-farmers income							0.003	0.000	0.585	0.999	0.000	3.368	
Other monetary income	0.656	0.042	0.444	0.775	0.084	1.977	0.664	0.037	0.523	0.782	0.086	2.354	0.19
In-kind consumption	0.894	0.055	0.387	0.559	0.068	1.241	0.887	0.060	0.455	0.561	0.089	1.472	2.04
Imputed owner's rent	0.659	0.022	0.217	0.521	0.014	0.649	0.704	0.031	0.291	0.500	0.026	0.839	1.18
Wage tax	0.834	-0.126	0.640	0.428	-0.198	1.575	0.762	-0.128	0.571	0.491	-0.206	1.616	-0.75
Other tax	0.333	-0.002	0.266	0.866	-0.002	1.320	0.245	-0.002	0.304	0.926	-0.003	1.621	-0.08

Table 13.4 *Gini index decomposition: consumption expenditure in the Czech republic, 1989 and 1992*

Consumption expenditures (crowns)	1989									1992									
	%≠0	Household per capita expenditure / Share of total expenditures	Std. dev.	Gini correlation	Factor Gini	Gini coeff.	Std. err.	% of total inequality	Gini elasticity	%≠0	Household per capita expenditure / Share of total expenditure	Std. dev.	Gini correlation	Factor Gini	Gini coeff.	Std. err.	% of total inequality	Gini elasticity	% change in source contribution
Consumption expenditures (crowns)		22,886.48	9,341.27			0.203	0.003				33,780.38	13,382.76			0.190	0.004			-6.26
Food	1.000	0.228		0.434	0.212			0.103	0.454	1.000	0.244		0.423	0.208			0.113	1.462	0.24
Non-alcoholic beverages	1.000	0.027		0.421	0.291			0.016	0.603	1.000	0.022		0.444	0.282			0.015	1.660	-0.30
Alcoholic beverages	0.993	0.032		0.439	0.409			0.028	0.885	0.993	0.028		0.460	0.422			0.029	2.020	-1.14
Restaurants	0.953	0.041		0.396	0.402			0.032	0.784	0.944	0.039		0.358	0.436			0.032	1.821	-0.23
Textiles/clothing	0.999	0.112		0.580	0.298			0.095	0.852	0.997	0.095		0.569	0.328			0.093	0.981	-0.80
Personal goods	1.000	0.028		0.502	0.259			0.018	0.642	1.000	0.030		0.510	0.275			0.022	0.738	0.28
Medical goods	0.849	0.002		0.256	0.689			0.001	0.871	0.881	0.004		0.330	0.650			0.004	1.129	0.27
Furnishing/equipment	0.990	0.058		0.559	0.606			0.097	1.671	0.984	0.058		0.622	0.624			0.119	2.041	1.42
Private transportation	0.799	0.083		0.704	0.606			0.097	1.671	0.984	0.058		0.622	0.624			0.119	2.041	1.42
Cultural goods	0.999	0.068		0.567	0.501			0.095	1.401	1.000	0.063		0.618	0.480			0.099	1.562	-0.28
Tobacco products	0.811	0.013		0.229	0.755			0.011	0.855	0.781	0.014		0.241	0.763			-0.013	0.969	0.14
Fuel/conn struct. mats.	0.637	0.019		0.463	0.805			0.035	1.838	0.618	0.019		0.361	0.796			0.029	1.511	-0.79

Rent	0.987	0.033	0.325	0.295	0.016	0.473	0.986	0.035	0.365	0.282	0.019	0.541	0.19
Electricity/gas	0.992	0.030	0.259	0.358	0.014	0.457	0.996	0.037	0.258	0.382	0.019	0.518	0.44
Water/other utilities	0.832	0.014	0.182	0.639	0.008	0.573	0.908	0.037	0.183	0.583	0.021	0.560	1.11
Public transport	0.942	0.014	0.433	0.537	0.016	1.146	0.936	0.015	0.433	0.513	0.018	1.167	0.04
Telephone	0.996	0.014	0.349	0.442	0.011	0.761	0.996	0.016	0.382	0.400	0.013	0.803	0.09
Repairs	0.945	0.021	0.541	0.666	0.037	1.777	0.938	0.024	0.522	0.667	0.044	1.833	0.36
Personal services	0.991	0.018	0.412	0.477	0.018	0.970	0.989	0.017	0.482	0.469	0.020	1.188	0.06
Education/cultural services	0.899	0.008	0.241	0.531	0.005	0.631	0.861	0.010	0.262	0.624	0.008	0.861	0.31
Recreation	0.658	0.022	0.438	0.755	0.035	1.630	0.542	0.018	0.431	0.790	0.033	1.790	-0.49
Medical services	0.855	0.001	0.297	0.862	0.002	1.261	0.745	0.001	0.300	0.834	0.002	1.319	0.02
Child care	0.234	0.003	-0.289	0.850	-0.003	-1.212	0.201	0.003	-0.219	0.872	-0.003	-1.005	0.08
Other services	0.503	0.002	0.350	0.871	0.004	1.502	0.512	0.003	0.306	0.859	0.005	1.382	0.07
Insurance	0.921	0.027	0.229	0.466	0.014	0.526	0.920	0.021	0.226	0.478	0.012	0.569	-0.30
Other expenditures	0.992	0.054	0.594	0.567	0.089	1.661	0.987	0.051	0.575	0.590	0.090	1.781	-0.49
In-kind consumption	0.924	0.065	0.350	0.526	0.059	0.908	0.894	0.069	0.349	0.529	0.067	0.970	0.31
In-kind giving	0.834	-0.039	0.456	0.687	-0.060	1.544	0.784	-0.035	0.422	0.708	-0.055	1.572	0.86

Table 13.5 *Gini index decomposition: consumption expenditure in the Slovak republic, 1989 and 1992*

Consumption expenditures (crowns)	1989						1992						
	%≠0	Share of total expenditures / Household per capita expenditure	Gini correlation / Std. dev.	Factor Gini / Gini coeff.	% of total inequality / Std. err.	Gini elasticity	%≠0	Share of total expenditures / Household per capita expenditure	Gini correlation / Std. dev.	Factor Gini / Gini coeff.	% of total inequality / Std. err.	Gini elasticity	% change in source contribution
(summary)		20,226.03	8,332.91	0.206	0.005			29,784.06	13,635.17	0.197	0.006		−3.97
Food	1.000	0.238	0.464	0.197	0.105	0.444	1.000	0.256	0.504	0.203	0.133	0.518	2.18
Non-alcoholic beverages	1.000	0.026	0.491	0.278	0.017	0.665	0.999	0.020	0.507	0.287	0.015	0.738	−0.30
Alcoholic beverages	0.995	0.038	0.455	0.390	0.033	0.862	0.994	0.030	0.424	0.400	0.026	0.860	−0.81
Restaurants	0.916	0.041	0.425	0.422	0.036	0.873	0.879	0.037	0.341	0.479	0.031	0.827	−0.68
Textiles/clothing	1.000	0.131	0.646	0.295	0.122	0.928	0.999	0.111	0.567	0.339	0.109	0.975	−1.76
Personal goods	1.000	0.028	0.559	0.262	0.020	0.713	1.000	0.029	0.554	0.275	0.023	0.773	0.14
Medical goods	0.760	0.001	0.301	0.717	0.002	1.048	0.710	0.002	0.327	0.731	0.003	1.212	0.12
Furnishing/equipment	0.964	0.050	0.576	0.645	0.091	1.806	0.951	0.050	0.551	0.657	0.092	1.835	−0.24
Private transportation	0.693	0.065	0.680	0.722	0.155	2.391	0.680	0.050	0.574	0.697	0.102	2.026	−5.68
Cultural goods	0.998	0.056	0.595	0.539	0.086	1.558	1.000	0.050	0.585	0.493	0.073	1.461	−1.62
Tobacco products	0.800	0.012	0.167	0.722	0.007	0.586	0.747	0.013	0.167	0.750	0.008	0.634	0.06
Fuel/conn struct. mats.	0.473	0.019	0.449	0.853	0.035	1.863	0.431	0.017	0.278	0.832	0.020	1.172	−1.58

Rent	0.991	0.036	0.318	0.289	0.016	0.446	0.987	0.044	0.385	0.322	0.028	0.627	1.06
Electricity/gas	0.995	0.031	0.342	0.369	0.019	0.614	0.996	0.039	0.315	0.441	0.027	0.703	0.73
Water/other utilities	0.709	0.019	0.200	0.602	0.011	0.586	0.780	0.036	0.209	0.586	0.022	0.622	1.01
Public transport	0.897	0.013	0.457	0.554	0.016	1.232	0.903	0.014	0.415	0.519	0.015	1.090	−0.19
Telephone	0.987	0.015	0.386	0.468	0.013	0.879	0.996	0.018	0.462	0.409	0.017	0.956	0.29
Repairs	0.875	0.016	0.589	0.700	0.033	2.007	0.871	0.019	0.526	0.721	0.036	1.922	0.17
Personal services	0.980	0.018	0.586	0.515	0.026	1.466	0.979	0.015	0.496	0.480	0.018	1.206	−0.92
Education/cultural services	0.777	0.006	0.037	0.637	0.006	0.951	0.752	0.008	0.303	0.697	0.008	1.069	0.23
Recreation	0.455	0.011	0.482	0.839	0.022	1.965	0.342	0.002	0.422	0.881	0.003	1.833	−1.92
Medical services	0.750	0.001	0.299	0.869	−0.003	1.262	0.689	0.002	0.413	0.877	0.003	1.835	0.13
Child care	0.271	0.003	−0.204	0.821	0.003	−0.814	0.214	0.003	−0.135	0.862	−0.001	−0.588	0.12
Other services	0.266	0.002	0.319	0.927	0.010	1.439	0.375	0.003	0.284	0.896	0.004	1.290	0.08
Insurance	0.894	0.027	0.168	0.428	0.014	0.350	0.861	0.019	0.132	0.452	0.006	0.302	−0.40
Other expenditures	0.981	0.052	0.588	0.558	0.082	1.595	0.983	0.059	0.646	0.608	0.117	1.990	2.94
In-kind consumption	0.894	0.061	0.386	0.559	0.063	1.048	0.887	0.063	0.419	0.561	0.076	1.191	0.89
In-kind giving	0.573	−0.018	0.441	0.800	−0.030	1.717	0.476	−0.014	0.382	0.834	−0.023	1.614	0.81

Consumption expenditures
The results of the Gini decomposition by detailed expenditure groups are presented in tables 13.4 and 13.5. The commodity which accounts for the largest share of inequality in total expenditures in the Czech republic is private transportation in 1989 and 1992. Second in importance, in terms of accounting for inequality in each year, is food in 1989, followed by furnishings and equipment; by 1992, the ranking of the two commodity groups is reversed. Changes in private transportation expenditures account for the greatest change in aggregate expenditure inequality over the time period, producing an equalizing influence. The influence of changes in commodities other than private transportation were quite small and fairly similar for the Czech republic.

Private transportation also accounted for the greatest share of aggregate expenditure inequality in Slovakia in 1989, followed by textiles and clothing, then food. However, by 1992, food expenditures accounted for the largest share of aggregate expenditure inequality, textiles and clothing was second, and private transportation was third. Aggregate expenditure inequality over the time period was most influenced by changes in private transportation expenditures, followed by those for "other expenditures" and food.

In 1990 and 1991, subsidies for food and energy, commodities with lower elasticities, were removed. In 1991 and 1992, higher tax rates were applied to commodities with relatively higher elasticities, such as private transportation (Kamenichova, 1993). One might predict that the removal of such subsidies would increase aggregate inequality, while the application of the taxes on commodities like private transportation would probably lead to reductions. For these commodities, such changes appear to have offset each other in terms of impacting relative expenditure distributions.

In addition to general changes in commodity taxes and prices and the availability of commodities previously discussed, differential changes in the cost-of-living for different subgroups of the population are also likely to have affected aggregate expenditure inequality (see Garner, Lubyova and Terrell, 1995). For example, pensioner households (compared to those headed by manual workers, employees, and those working in agriculture) experienced the greatest relative price increases for non-food commodities and services versus those for food and beverages from 1989 to 1992. With necessities like food and utilities becoming relatively more expensive, households shifted their spending away from commodities like private transportation, on average. However, the combination of the shift to necessities and the increase in the proportion of persons in pensioner-headed households is likely to have produced counteracting impacts on inequality. The effect of such demographic shifts on aggregate inequality will be explored in future analysis. The expenditure results could also be driven by decreases in real income,[15] another issue for future study.

Summary and conclusions

The focus of this chapter has been changing welfare in a changing world, with emphasis on the Czech and Slovak republics during the early years of the transition to a pluralistic, market-based democracy. Welfare, based on an economic perspective, is examined in terms of inequality in the distribution of income and expenditures across individuals. Using data from the Family Budget Surveys (FBSs), I found that aggregate inequality decreased or changed very little, on average, during the early years of the transition from centrally planned to more market oriented economies. Compared to incomes in the Czech republic, those in Slovakia were more equally distributed; this is probably not surprising given the latter republic's preference for greater government participation in the economy and less harsh economic reforms. Consumption expenditures were slightly more unequally distributed than were incomes in the two republics over the two years. As with flow income, consumption expenditure inequality decreased from 1989 to 1992 in the two republics, with decreases greater for the Czech republic. The decile ratio, the Robin Hood Index, and mean log deviation measures also reveal a trend towards inequality in both resources. However, the other two entropy indices suggest that inequality actually increased from 1989 to 1992. For expenditures, increases in equality are also revealed for Slovakia but there is a decrease for the Czech republic. This difference in trend is probably a reflection of the sensitivity of the inequality measures to variations in different parts of the distribution.

In addition to the factors discussed in previous sections, the trend toward greater equality in income and expenditures may also be related to the methodology and data. First, the results may be sensitive to the weighting scheme used to combine the FBSs, as well as to sample representativeness. Pensioner households, and thus smaller households, may be weighted more heavily than they should be. Giving pensioner households less weight would be expected to increase aggregate inequality. Jilek *et al.* (1995) report an increase in *per capita* net monetary income for all social groups except pensioners from 1988 to 1992 in the Czech Republic, using Microcensus data, but an increase in income inequality overall. The decrease in income inequality experienced by pensioners may be counteracting the increase in inequality accounted for by households in the other social groups. Second, the FBS samples, upon which this analysis is based, probably do not adequately account for persons with resources at the extremes of the distribution, as noted earlier, resulting in under-estimates of total population inequality.

The sensitivity of some of the methodological and data problems on future trends can be tested using more recently collected FBS data. However, a more direct way to deal with these potential problems is to eliminate them or to reduce the possibility for their occurrence. I strongly recommend that the sample design of the FBS be changed so that the entire population in each of the new countries is represented. Sample rotation would also be desirable so that "self-selection time-in-sample" biases could be reduced. Changes such as these are necessary as expenditures gain in importance as a complementary measure to income in assessing the economic well-being of individuals living in these emerging market economies. Including a broader set of economic measures (e.g. assets and liabilities) would increase the usefulness of the FBS as well.

In this study I assumed a relative welfare concept by concentrating on inequality and changes in inequality. However, such an analysis provides no information concerning levels of income and expenditures, and therefore provides little information concerning whether welfare actually improved over the time period; greater equality does not necessarily translate into welfare improvement. To address this issue I needed information about both levels and distributions. Using such information, I plotted generalized Lorenz curves (not shown) and found that changes in real income and expenditures from 1989 to 1992 for the two republics were not welfare-improving. Thus, I must conclude that the general trend towards equality did not compensate for decreases in real income and expenditures during this transitional period.

What might the future hold in terms of inequality and welfare in general? Continuing changes are expected for several years as the economy continues to change and as current policies are revised, old ones discarded, and new ones introduced. One change to be expected is a reverse in the relationship between income and expenditure inequality. With fewer controls by the state and improvements in the economy, it is quite likely that incomes will become more unequal than expenditures, exhibiting the same pattern found in western economies. Differences in reported inequality for the republics are likely to continue with the split of the Czech and Slovak federal republic into two separate countries, and their decision to pursue different paths to balance the relationship between state and market. The potential dislocations in the market which may result from reductions in labor hoarding and the removal of rent subsidies are not discussed in this chapter. Whether these will translate into greater or less inequality depends upon the performance of the economy and government policies. Changes in inequality and welfare are also expected as the population becomes more accustomed to the market, with different opportunities in employment and ways to meet consumer demand.

Even with these expected future changes, the distribution of economic resources may remain fairly equal across the populations in the "new" Czech republic and Slovakia. This may reflect societies' preference for equality and social peace more than changes in the economic situation or welfare policies. Whether this preference will continue into the next chapter of history is a question which remains to be answered.

Although inequality may change little, we can hope that welfare will increase, reflecting the realization of dreams and renewed freedoms. To account for increased opportunities – those being experienced by the current generation and those being established for future generations – for changes in attitudes and a sense of freedom to pursue one's dreams, and for the costs of this pursuit, an expanded set of methods is needed, in addition to a broader measure of welfare. The result of such an endeavor would be a more complete picture of the impact of the transition on both individuals and households.

Notes

Many individuals provided assistance to me while I conducted this research. I particularly want to thank those in the Czech and Slovak Statistical Offices and Institute of Sociology–Czech Academy of Sciences for help with the data. I also gratefully acknowledge the comments provided by colleagues at the BLS, the University of Pittsburgh, and CERGE-EI in Prague. I am especially indebted to Sarah Jarvis, Stephen Jenkins, Jan Ritzema, Kathy Terrell and Panos Tsakloglou for their reviews and comments. Special technical assistance was provided by Shlomo Yitzhaki, John Bishop, David Johnson, Mike Fratantoni, and Steve Verdon.

This research is dedicated to the memory of Aldi Hagenaars – friend, colleague, and guiding light.

1 In 1992, the existing legislation enabled an individual to receive an unlimited old-age pension simultaneously with income from paid work for one year.
2 The Robin Hood Index is based on data grouped by deciles; it is an approximation of the share of total income or expenditures which has to be taken from those above the mean, and transferred to those below the mean in order to achieve equality.
3 Details are available from the author.
4 Cash gifts given to persons outside the household could not be identified in the 1989 file; therefore, these are included in "other expenditures" in 1989.

For consistency, they are also included in "other expenditures" in 1992 as well.

5 One household was dropped from the original sample because total consumption expenditures were less than zero.

6 Response rates for the Microcensus in 1988 were 95.8 percent in the Czech republic and 98.4 percent in Slovakia (Atkinson and Micklewright, 1992). For 1992, the response rate was approximately 84 percent for the Czech republic and 93 percent for Slovakia (LIS, 1995).

7 Percentage distributions for the Microcensus are based on the author's own calculations.

8 Although pensioner households with economically active members were not included in the FBS quota samples, their distributions from the Microcensus were used in the creation of weights to combine the FBS samples. This procedure was followed due to the Microcensus data made available to the author and the coding of variables provided by the SFOs. Following this procedure, the share of pensioner households with economically active members was allocated to the worker group for the Czech sample in 1992 and to the pensioners without economically active members group for the Slovak sample. In the 1992 Microcensus household data files, the agriculture social group, as defined by the SOs, includes only households headed by cooperative farmers in Slovakia; however, for the Czech republic, any household head working in agriculture is included in this social group.

9 Inequality indices were also produced for a reduced sample which only included households who participated in the survey for a full twelve months. The indices are only slightly lower than for the analysis sample, the difference being in the third digit to the right of the decimal point for almost all cases.

10 The percentage of total inequality due to a source is obtained by dividing the product of the share of total income (or expenditures), Gini correlation, and factor Gini by the overall Gini coefficient.

11 The percentage change in the source's contribution to aggregate inequality is obtained by multiplying, for each source, the percentage of total inequality attributed to the source (times 100) in the base period by the percentage change in the absolute contribution (see Jenkins, 1995).

12 The Gini coefficient for persons with non-zero values can be calculated using the following equation:

$$G = (1 - P) + PG^*$$

where G is the factor Gini as presented in tables 13.2–13.5, P is percentage of non-zero values, and G^* is the factor Gini for distribution with no zeroes (Yitzhaki, 1990).

13 In tables 13.2 and 13.3, wages are before taxes while total income is net of taxes. Therefore, to determine the amount of total after tax income inequality due to wages, the percentage of total inequality due to wage taxes must be subtracted from the percentage for total gross wages (those of the head, wife, and other).

14 The income elasticities presented are with respect to after-tax income and thus are typically higher than elasticities with respect to before-tax income. The after-tax elasticities could be transformed into before-tax elasticities by multiplying each of the former by the elasticity of after-tax income with respect to gross income (see Lerman and Yitzhaki, 1994).

15 Real expenditures for utilities increased from 1989 to 1992, while those for other commodities decreased, as did real income. Real decreases in food expenditure were less than real decreases in income.

References

Atkinson, A.B. and J. Micklewright, 1992. *Economic Transformation in Eastern Europe and the Distribution of Income*, Cambridge: Cambridge University Press

Blagonravova, Z., J. Dlouhy, J. Kux, M. Hirsl, D. Rydl and J. Vecernik, 1992. "Social policy and a vulnerable population: recent changes and new research in Czechoslovakia," country paper for the LIS–AID East–West Project Workshop, LIS, Luxembourg

Blundell, R. and I. Preston, 1991. "The distinction between income and consumption in measuring the distribution of household welfare," *Discussion Paper*, 92–01, University College London

Coulter, F.A.E., F.A. Cowell and S.P. Jenkins, 1992. "Differences in needs and assessment of income distribution," *Bulletin of Economic Research*, 44, 77–124.

Dlouhy, J., 1991. "The impact of social transfers on income distribution in the Czech and Slovak Federal Republic," Socialist Economies Reform Unit, Country Economics Department, *Research Paper Series*, 4, Washington, DC: World Bank

Dyba, K. and J. Svejnar, 1995. "A comparative view of economic developments in the Czech republic," in J. Svejnar (ed.), *The Czech Republic and Economic Transition in Eastern Europe*, San Diego: Academic Press, 21–45

European Commission, 1993a. "Main features of the Czech and Slovak republics," *Employment Observatory, Central & Eastern Europe, Employment Trends and Developments*, 4

1993b. "Structural changes in employment in the transition," *Employment Observatory, Central & Eastern Europe, Employment Trends and Developments*, 5

1995. "Systems of unemployment compensation in Central and Eastern Europe" and "Statistical tables 1989–95," *Employment Observatory, Central & Eastern Europe, Employment Trends and Developments*, 7

Garner, T.I., 1989. "Consumer expenditures and inequality: an analysis using the Gini coefficient," *BLS Working Paper*, 197, Office of Prices and Living Conditions, Bureau of Labor Statistics, US Department of Labor

Garner, T.I., M. Lubyova and K. Terrell, 1995. "Changes in expenditures and income inequality: an examination of the micro data (1989 vs 1992)," in

J. Svejnar (ed.), *The Czech Republic and Economic Transition in Eastern Europe*, San Diego: Academic Press, 331–75

Hauser, R., K. Muller, G. Wagner and J. Frick, 1992. "Inequality in income and satisfaction – a comparison of East and West Germans before and after unification," Deutsches Institut für Wirtschaftsforschung, Berlin, unpublished manuscript

Heady, C., N. Rajah and S. Smith, 1994. "Tax reform and economic transition in the Czech Republic," *Fiscal Studies*, 15, 64–80

Hirsl, M., 1993. "Social development and policy in the Czech Republic in transition period," Prague, unpublished manuscript

Jeffries, I., 1993. *Socialist Economies and the Transition to the Market: A Guide*, London: Routledge

Jenkins, S.P., 1995. "Accounting for inequality trends: decomposition analyses for the UK, 1971–86," *Economica*, 62, 29–63

Jilek, J., J. Friedlander, J. Moravova and D. Bilkova, 1995. "Household incomes, expenditures and their changes in the last years," *Prague Economic Papers*, 1, 41–64

Kakwani, N., 1986. *Analyzing Redistribution Policies: A Study using Australian Data*, Cambridge: Cambridge University Press

    "Income inequality, welfare, and poverty: an illustration using Ukrainian data," *Policy Research Working Paper*, 1411, Washington, DC: World Bank

Kalmus, J. 1994. Fax communication, Czech Statistical Office, Prague, Czech republic (April 19)

Kamenichova, V., 1993. Letter to Colin Lawson, University of Bath, concerning tax policies in the Czech republic

Kucharova, V., 1993. "Impacts of economic and social transformation on households' incomes and consumption in the Czech Republic," Research Institute of Labor and Social Affairs, Prague, unpublished manuscript

Lerman, R.I. and S. Yitzhaki, 1985. "Income inequality effects by income sources: a new approach and applications to the US," *Review of Economics and Statistics*, 67, 151–6

    1989. "Improving the accuracy of estimates of Gini coefficients," *Journal of Econometrics*, 42, 43–7

    1994. "The effect of marginal changes in income sources on US income inequality," *Public Finance Quarterly*, 22, 403–17

Luxembourg Income Study (LIS), 1995. "Questionnaires on survey content and procedures – Czech Republic and Slovak Republic," personal communication with Debra Bailey, LIS Project, Syracuse University, New York

Milanovic, B., 1992a. "Income distribution in late socialism: Poland, Hungry, Czechoslovakia, Yugoslavia, and Bulgaria compared," Socialist Economies Reform Unit, Country Economics Department, *Research Paper Series*, 1, Washington, DC: World Bank

    1992b. "Distributional impact of cash and in-kind transfers in Eastern Europe and Czechoslovakia," Socialist Economies Reform Unit, Country Economics Department, *Research Paper Series*, 9, Washington, DC: World Bank

Organization for Economic Co-operation and Development (OECD), 1994. *Review of the Labour Market in the Czech Republic*, Directorate for Education, Employment, Labor and Social Affairs, Employment, Labor and Social Affairs Committee, report presented in Prague (December)

Papaj, K., 1994. Slovak Statistical Office, personal communication (September)

Smeeding, T.M., 1991. "Cross-national comparisons of inequality and poverty position," in L. Osberg (ed.), *Economic Inequality and Poverty: International Perspectives*, Armonk, NY: M.E. Sharpe, 39–59.

Teichova, A., 1988. *The Czechoslovak Economy, 1918–1980*, London: Routledge

UNICEF International Child Development Centre, 1993. "Central and Eastern Europe in transition: public policy and social conditions," *Regional Monitoring Report*, 1

Vavrejnova, M., 1993. "Czech households in transition period: incomes, expenditures, and savings," CERGE-EL, Charles University, Prague, unpublished manuscript

Vavrejnova, M. and I. Moravcikova, 1995. "The Czech household sector in the transition," in J. Svejnar (ed.), *The Czech Republic and Economic Transition in Eastern Europe*, San Diego: Academic Press, 317–29

Vecernik, J., 1994. "Economic inequalities old and new: the Czech case," paper presented at the OECD Conference on Rural Unemployment in Central and Eastern Europe, Vienna (November)

   1995. "Incomes in Central Europe: distributions, patterns, and perceptions," paper presented at the LIS Summer Workshop for Russian and Eastern European Students, Luxembourg

World Bank, 1994. *Slovakia: Restructuring for Recovery*, Washington, DC: World Bank

Yitzhaki, S., 1990. "On the progressivity of commodity taxation," *Working Paper*, 187, Department of Economics, Hebrew University, Jerusalem

Part IV
The household, income, and welfare

14 The distribution of income, wealth, and economic security: the impact of unemployment insurance reforms in Canada

Lars Osberg, Sadettin Erksoy and Shelley Phipps

Introduction

> The development of the modern welfare states can only be explained by some general aversion to risk ... if a society, by free choice and democratic procedure, introduces a welfare state, risk aversion must in some way dominate the decision process. (Borch, 1968, p. 74)[1]

Most of the debate on reform of the welfare state has focused on the size of income transfers to and from various groups in society and the possible incentive effects of social welfare programs on labor market behavior. However, very little attention has been paid to the role which potential social transfers also play in reducing economic insecurity for all members of society, although reducing economic insecurity is one of the fundamental reasons for the existence of the welfare state. Insecurity and economic inequality are linked, since the value of the increased security produced by social insurance programs is very different at different points in the income distribution. Changes to the social insurance role of the welfare state therefore affect the overall distribution of economic well-being both directly, by changing the expected transfer income of different groups in society, and indirectly, by altering the economic security and the labor market behavior of individuals.

Since unemployment insurance is the largest single Canadian social insurance program,[2] this chapter focuses on the change in the distribution of economic well-being in Canada implied by changes in unemployment insurance. Over the last two decades, benefit/wage replacement rates have been reduced, entrance requirements have been tightened, and benefit durations reduced. For some workers (e.g. a tenured professor), the impact of these changes has been very small. People who have (1) nil risk of unemployment; or (2) relatively high income (hence relatively small marginal utility of income changes); or (3) sufficient assets and/or

321

access to credit to maintain consumption during spells of low earnings, do not need unemployment insurance to provide income security – hence they lose little by its reduction.

However, low income workers (e.g. research assistants) typically do not have these characteristics. In general, the value of the security which unemployment insurance provides depends on the probability of an individual becoming unemployed, their ability to smooth consumption by borrowing or dissaving, and the change in utility implied by changes in consumption. Since low income individuals have a tendency to (1) face a relatively high probability of unemployment, (2) have a high marginal utility of income, and (3) have low assets and/or poor access to credit, the determinants of the security value of unemployment insurance are correlated. Individuals also differ in the degree to which they can change their labor market behavior in response to changes in unemployment insurance parameters. Given the correlation of these factors, the objective of this chapter is to assess the impact on the distribution of economic well-being of changes in the level of unemployment insurance, as an example of the more general issue of the impact of the welfare state on the distribution of economic well-being.

The next section outlines our theoretical framework for discussion of income risk, and the reasons why we believe it is appropriate to measure the income value of the change in expected utility associated with changes in unemployment insurance regimes, rather than the change in expected income associated with social policy reform. We then discuss the empirical calculations, which have two major steps. We first use a micro-simulation model to estimate, for a representative sample of individuals, the fluctuations in labor earnings and unemployment insurance receipts associated with alternative Canadian unemployment insurance regimes (those in place in 1971 and 1994). The model incorporates individual behavioral responses, such as changes in the incidence and duration of unemployment, which may result from changes in unemployment insurance legislation. Given estimated changes in labor earnings and unemployment insurance transfers, we then use a Stone–Geary utility function to calculate the present discounted values of individual utility associated with each unemployment insurance regime. These are used to calculate the implied certainty equivalent income value of the change in expected utility associated with decreased protection from income loss due to unemployment. We then discuss the distribution of these changes in economic well-being within the Canadian income distribution, and finally draw some conclusions.

Theoretical perspective

In the market for private insurance against such risks as fire, automobile theft, or loss of life, individuals can be observed voluntarily paying premiums which exceed the expected value of their insurance claims (due to administration costs and profits within the insurance industry). Although the marginal individual may be indifferent between purchasing or not purchasing insurance, infra-marginal individuals with greater risk aversion receive net gains in their utility from the existence of the option to decrease risk. Although the net expected income of insurance buyers is on average lower than in the absence of insurance (by the amount of the administration costs and profits of the insurance industry), the average utility of insurance buyers is increased by their ability to avoid risk. In private insurance markets, one can use the demand for insurance at different premium levels to estimate willingness to pay for insurance protection and the implied social benefits of the existence of the option to insure against particular risks.

Unemployment insurance (UI) also provides insurance against the risk of income loss, but evaluation of UI presents a range of difficulties not present in the private insurance example. Private markets for UI are not feasible, partly because private insurers would face huge losses in recessionary times, due to the correlation of unemployment outcomes across individuals. Individuals with private knowledge of their greater risk of personal unemployment could also be expected to self-select for the purchase of UI, at any given premium rate.[3] UI is not, therefore, voluntarily purchased.[4]

Furthermore, since UI, like other social insurance programs, embodies ideas of *social* fairness, not *actuarial* fairness, one can expect to observe systematic differences across individuals in the ratio of expected UI benefits to UI premiums.[5] Nonetheless, UI retains an insurance function – since UI reduces the risk of income loss due to unemployment, risk averse individuals can be expected to be willing to pay some amount, which differs according to individual circumstance, for the reduction in income risk which UI provides.

To fix ideas, figure 14.1 outlines the position of a risk averse individual (decreasing marginal utility of income) who faces some risk of income loss. It contrasts the situation of the individual in a regime with high UI benefits for high premiums (aa') and a regime with low UI benefits and low premiums (bb'). If the individual remains fully employed, a net income of Y'_b is received, when the low benefit UI scheme is in operation. However, since higher UI benefits require higher UI premiums, Y'_a is the

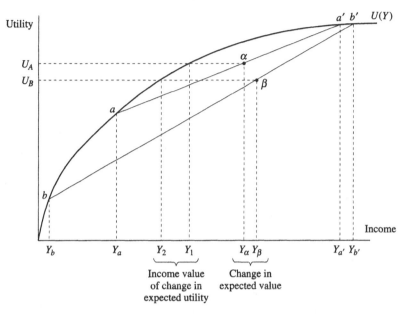

Figure 14.1 The impact on utility of alternative unemployment insurance regimes

individual's income in the absence of unemployment when the high benefit UI scheme is in operation. If the individual experiences unemployment, total income from labor earnings and UI benefits is Y_a if the high benefit UI scheme is in operation, and Y_b under the low benefit UI regime.

The expected income of each individual is determined by their relative probability of unemployment. In figure 14.1 Y_α is the expected income under regime A, where point α defined by $Y_\alpha Y_{a'}/Y_a Y_{a'}$ is the probability of unemployment. Similarly, $Y_\beta Y_{b'}/Y_b Y_{b'}$ is the probability of unemployment under regime B. Usually, $Y_\beta Y_{b'}/Y_b Y_{b'} \neq Y_\alpha Y_{a'}/Y_a Y_{a'}$. Although it is this change in the probability of unemployment that is the focus of most of the literature on UI, one can argue that the focus *should* be the impact of UI on individual well-being $(U_A - U_B)$.

There is no reason to believe that individuals face the same probability of unemployment under different UI regimes – indeed most of the literature on UI is about the possible impacts of the implicit incentives of UI on the probability of unemployment (for example, see Atkinson and Micklewright, 1991). The simulation model which we discuss on p. 337 is built up from a series of estimated behavioral equations which embodies the responses of individuals to changes in the specific parameters of UI in

Canada – hence changes in UI regimes affect individual probabilities of unemployment.

Given these behavioral responses, the relative probability of unemployment corresponding to each UI scheme implies that the expected value of income under the low benefit UI scheme is Y_β and under the high benefit scheme Y_α. The levels of utility associated with these uncertain income streams are graphed on the vertical axis as U_A and U_B. Individuals who are averse to risk get the same level of utility from a certain income as they would get from an uncertain lottery with higher expected value. In figure 14.1, Y_1 is the certainty equivalent income which produces the same level of utility as the expected value of income (Y_α) which the individual would receive under the higher benefit UI scheme. In figure 14.1, Y_α minus Y_1 represents the risk premium – the amount which the individual would be willing to pay to rid themselves entirely of the income risk of unemployment (i.e. receive a certain income rather than the uncertain prospect of income Y'_a if no unemployment and Y_a if unemployed). Similarly, Y_2 is the certain income which would generate the utility level U_B, the same level of utility as generated by the uncertain prospect of Y'_b if not unemployed and Y_b if unemployed under the less generous UI scheme. The change in utility associated with the change in UI regimes is $U_A - U_B$ and the money equivalent of that loss in utility (the change in certainty equivalent income) is $Y_1 - Y_2$.

Note that the change in certainty equivalent income has arisen from changes in *both* the level *and* the riskiness of income flows. The change in level of income arises both from changed behavior (hence changes in earnings) and changes in UI transfers. The impact of changes in unemployment insurance legislation on the distribution of economic well-being may not be captured by simple calculation of changes in the expected value of income. In figure 14.1, shifting from a high benefit/high premium to a low benefit/low premium UI scheme *increases* the expected value of income (from Y_α to Y_β). However, the decrease in income security which this entails produces a *decrease* in net utility (from U_A to U_B), the income value of which is given by $Y_1 - Y_2$.[6]

The contrast in figure 14.1 between social insurance revisions which produce a *gain* in expected income and a *loss* in certainty equivalent income deserves some emphasis. Much of the literature on social policy reform (including some of our own work – Erksoy, Osberg and Phipps, 1994a, 1994c) has calculated the change in realized income flows associated with social policy changes and ignored the value of income security. The lesson of figure 14.1 is that even those who realize increases in expected income may experience losses in utility.

Empirical calculations

Micro-simulation of income and labor market outcomes under the 1971 and 1994 UI regimes

The rationale underlying micro-simulation is the idea that if we are to understand how the economy would have functioned under a different set of incentives (such as those embodied in different UI regimes), we have to take full account of the heterogeneity of individual character-istics, the interdependence of economic processes, and the endogeneity of individual characteristics over time. The origins of micro-simulation lie in the work of Guy Orcutt and his colleagues (Orcutt, 1957; Orcutt, Merz and Quinke, 1986). The basic idea is to take microdata on a representa-tive panel sample of individuals and simulate the impact over time of alternative policy scenarios on *each* individual member of the panel. The aggregate implications of changes in policy are, therefore, built up from explicit calculation of its impacts on each and every individual. One of the major advantages of micro-simulation modeling is that it allows the simultaneous consideration of policy impacts on a number of different behaviors (e.g. the impacts of UI on both unemployment and labor force participation) which imposing consistency of predicted impacts (e.g. weeks unemployed *plus* weeks employed *plus* weeks not in the labor force must sum to 52).

In a series of papers and reports (Erksoy, Osberg and Phipps, 1994a, 1994b, 1994c), we have outlined the methodology of our micro-simula-tion model, presented explicitly the estimated behavioral equations which drive the model and demonstrated its sensitivity to alternative assump-tions (e.g. the importance of past labor market outcomes). We present an abbreviated description of the model in appendix B (p. 337) and refer interested readers to our other work for additional detail.

For present purposes, the key thing about our microsimulation model is that it generates, for each of the 19,488 respondents to Statistics Canada's 1984 Survey of Assets and Debts, a predicted vector of labor earnings, UI receipts, weeks unemployed, weeks employed, and weeks not in the labor force for each year of the business cycle. We run the model with two alternative policy frameworks – Canadian 1971 UI legislation and 1944 UI legislation – and compare the results.

The impact of revisions to UI on well-being

If changes to social insurance have only small impacts on income riskiness, and produce the same expected value of income flows, then the

Arrow–Pratt risk premium can be estimated directly from data on absolute risk aversion, without explicit representation of the underlying utility function of individuals. However, the Canadian revisions to UI between 1971 and 1994 are not like that. When policy revisions have relatively large impacts on both income riskiness *and* the expected value of some individuals' incomes, calculation of the impact of those policy changes on certainty equivalent income requires the specification of some underlying utility function.

Economists typically use the idea of utility maximization to drive their theories of individual behavior, and most find it easy to agree on general characteristics – e.g. individual utility is a positive function of income, but there is declining marginal utility of income and wealth. Beyond that, there is little consensus. Indeed, although empirical economists have estimated many models of individual behavior (such as labor supply) whose empirical specification also implies an underlying individual utility function, the characteristics of these implicit utility functions have often not been carefully examined (as Stern, 1986, has emphasized).

In this chapter, we use estimates of Canadian labor supply behavior based on the Stone–Geary utility function to estimate the utility value of income flows associated with 1971 and 1994 UI regimes, over the 1981–89 business cycle. In each case, we calculate the present discounted value of yearly flows of utility over the entire period, using a discount rate of $5\frac{1}{2}$ percent per annum (the average real interest rate on home mortgage indebtedness in Canada from 1981 to 1989). The change in well-being attributable to UI revisions is the difference between the present discounted value of utility under the alternative UI regimes. To put a money value on this change in utility, we calculate the certainty equivalent income which corresponds to the average annual level of utility under each UI regime, at average annual levels of labor supply.

In calculating the change in certainty equivalent income for individuals which correspond to a change in policy regimes we are, in essence, asking each individual: *"If you knew in advance how you would fare under each policy regime, what sum of money (positive or negative) would make you equally well off in one policy regime, compared to the other?"* This chapter asks specifically: *"If you knew in advance how you would have fared, over a business cycle such as that of 1981 to 1989, under the 1994 rules of Canadian UI legislation compared to the 1971 rules, what sum of money per year would make you equally well off with 1994, compared to 1971 UI legislation?"* This can be seen as performing an *ex ante* evaluation of the realized (*ex post*) outcomes of policy reform – in a sense we are asking what fully informed individuals would think would be the implications of policy reform (which may perhaps be a somewhat idealistic type of policy evaluation).

In table 14.1, the Y_{71}^* is the certainty equivalent annual income corresponding to the 1971 UI regime and Y_{94}^* is the certainty equivalent annual income corresponding to the 1994 UI regime. More specifically, define:

Y_{it} = income from earnings and UI under 1971 legislation

Y'_{it} = income from earnings and UI under 1994 legislation

L_{it} = weeks of non-labour time under 1971 legislation

L'_{it} = weeks of non-labour time under 1994 legislation

i = individual

t = year (1981–9)

$$\bar{L}_i = \sum_{t=0}^{8} L_{it}/9$$

U_{it} $= U(Y_{it}, L_{it})$

U'_{it} $= U(Y'_{it}, L'_{it})$

$\hat{U}_i$ $= \displaystyle\sum_{t=0}^{8} \frac{U_{it}}{(1 + 0.055)^t}$ = present value of utility of individual i under 1971 legislation

$\hat{U}'_i$ $= \displaystyle\sum_{t=0}^{8} \frac{U'_{it}}{(1 + 0.055)^t}$ = present value of utility of individual i in period t under 1994 legislation

Y_{71}^* $= U^{-1}(\hat{U}_i/9 \mid L_{it} = \bar{L}_i)$

Y_{94}^* $= U^{-1}(\hat{U}'_i/9 \mid L_{it} = \bar{L}_i)$

In evaluating the labor supply responses of Canadian households to UI reforms, Phipps (1990, 1991a, 1991b) used the Stone–Geary functional form

$$U_{it} = B[Y_{it} - \gamma_0]^{1-\theta}[L_{it} - \gamma_1]^{\theta}$$

where Y_{it} is earnings *plus* UI transfers received by individual i in period t and L_{it} is weeks of non-labor time.

The Stone–Geary functional form has the convenient feature that Phipps (1990, 1991a, 1991b) has already provided estimates of its

Table 14.1 *Impact of 1971–94 UI revisions on average annual "income,"
by deciles, ages 16 to 65*[*]

	Males			Females		
	Certainty equivalent income			Certainty equivalent income		
Decile	Y^*_{71}	Y^*_{94}	$\Delta Y^*\%$	Y^*_{71}	Y^*_{94}	$\Delta Y^*\%$
1	619	280	54.8	598	565	5.5
2	2,917	1,874	35.8	1,751	1,679	4.1
3	7,015	6,059	13.6	2,893	2,767	4.4
4	10,435	9,602	8.0	3,534	3,404	3.7
5	14,226	13,251	6.9	4,083	3,967	2.8
6	17,759	16,899	4.8	5,772	5,479	5.1
7	21,232	20,317	4.3	8,557	8,140	4.9
8	25,193	24,266	3.7	12,024	11,515	4.2
9	30,612	29,708	3.0	16,468	15,915	3.4
10	45,390	44,487	2.0	26,510	25,932	2.2
Overall	17,539	16,674	13.7	8,219	7,936	4.0
Gini	0.42003	0.43923	−4.6	0.494	0.498	−0.8
Theil	0.30919	0.34073	−10.6	0.411	0.417	−1.5
CV	0.7850	0.8210	−4.6	0.996	1.010	−1.4
Atkinson						
$r = 0.5$	0.17377	0.19662	−13.1	0.205	0.207	−0.9
$r = -0.5$	0.70162	0.77475	−10.4	0.633	0.633	0.0
$r = -1.0$	0.91471	0.93762	−2.5	0.859	0.862	−0.3

Note: Labor earnings and UI receipts only, 1981$, for 1981 labor market
participants.

parameters in the explicit context of the influence of UI on labor supply.[7]
Its disadvantages include the fact that all goods must be substitutes,
Engel curves are constrained to be linear and the labor supply function is
constrained to be monotonic with respect to wages.[8] Another feature of
the Stone–Geary functional form (which we dislike) is that is assumes
that all non-labor time has positive utility value. An alternative perspective (dominant in social psychology and sociology) sees unemployment in
a more negative light, as something which is psychologically harmful,
which people typically do not like (see Hayes and Nutman, 1981; Jahoda,
1979 and Kelvin and Jarrett, 1985). In the economics literature, Narendranathan and Nickell (1985) found a negative valuation on unemployment time, while Clark and Oswald (1994, p. 658) use survey evidence to

argue strongly that "unemployed people in Great Britain in 1991 have much lower levels of mental well-being than those in work." In future research, we hope to devise a way of distinguishing the relative utility of time spent unemployed, time spent in leisure, and time engaged in unpaid work. However, since our focus in this chapter is on *income* security, we proceed with the Stone–Geary specification.

Distributional impact of social insurance revisions

Table 14.1 presents the average annual certainty equivalent income[9] for men and women and for each decile of the income distribution under the 1971 and 1994 regimes, as evaluated over the business cycle from 1981 to 1989. Although the dollar value of the average income change associated with the 1971 to 1994 revisions to UI is roughly comparable across many of the deciles of the male distribution, this income loss is a much larger fraction of the annual income of poorer deciles than of richer. For males, there is thus a very significant decrease in income associated with UI cutbacks, which is unambiguously much larger, in percentage terms, for the poorer deciles of the income distribution. For females, it is clear that the 1971–94 revisions to UI in Canada increase the inequality of the distribution of economic well-being – but the distributional impacts are smaller and less clearly concentrated on poorer deciles of the income distribution.[10]

Several caveats are, however, in order. First, since the income concept used in this chapter is that of annual labor earnings *plus* annual receipts of unemployment insurance payments, capital income and (more importantly) pension income and social assistance receipts are excluded. The relatively low annual earnings and unemployment insurance receipts of poorer deciles reflects in part a tendency of those with long duration unemployment spells to withdraw entirely from labor force participation – a tendency which is particularly important for older cohorts and for women. Since our objective is to model the distributional impacts of a particular social insurance program (UI), we do not build in any assumptions of automatic receipt of social assistance by individuals with low annual income or automatic receipt of pension income by retirees. Clearly, however, UI is part of the larger welfare state of public and private social transfers, and the extent to which other transfers will kick in to offset cutbacks in UI is a crucially important issue.

Furthermore, one must emphasize that table 14.1 refers to the population of individuals who participated in the labor market in 1981 (some of whom may have withdrawn from the labor force from 1982–9). Table 14.1 contains no consideration of household income or household size.

Table 14.2   *Males, 16 to 65: Stone–Geary utility functions, percentage gains/losses from UI revisions, by decile of income under 1971 scheme*

	Loss			Nil	Gain		
	More than 50% loss (1)	26%– 50% loss (2)	6%– 25% loss (3)	No change ± 5% (4)	6%– 25% gain (5)	26%– 50% gain (6)	More than 50% gain (7)
Decile							
1	47.02	14.14	5.90	21.65	1.48	1.40	8.41
2	34.53	11.59	14.20	28.58	2.10	0.99	8.02
3	10.45	8.64	18.21	56.60	2.66	1.40	2.04
4	4.95	6.53	18.28	67.70	1.08	0.82	0.64
5	3.82	4.74	14.80	75.35	0.53	0.21	0.56
6	1.84	3.91	15.27	78.27	0.47	0.00	0.23
7	2.11	1.39	14.68	81.55	0.27	0.00	0.00
8	1.18	1.60	11.28	85.87	0.00	0.00	0.07
9	1.31	1.96	12.39	84.31	0.00	0.03	0.00
10	0.43	1.18	6.85	91.35	0.12	0.00	0.07

The Stone–Geary utility function underlying the calculations of certainty equivalent annual income is that for single males and females. Evaluating the distribution of utility across households raises complex issues of equivalence of incomes (see Phipps, 1997) and of the division of resources within households (see Phipps and Burton, 1995) which we hope to address more fully in future work.

Table 14.1 is based on deciles of incomes, as ordered by 1971 and 1994 income, respectively. Since UI revisions imply that some individuals experience gains, while others experience losses, the individuals in each decile of 1971 and 1994 income are not all the same. To illustrate the dispersion in impacts within income deciles, tables 14.2 and 14.3 illustrate the distribution of the percentage change in income, by decile of original income under the 1971 UI regime. All these tables tell essentially the same story (although much stronger for males than for females). The percentage of individuals which is essentially unaffected by revisions to unemployment insurance rises with income – over 90 percent of the top income decile are essentially unaffected by unemployment insurance revisions, while only 20 percent of the males (60 percent of the females) in the bottom income decile are similarly unaffected. Within the lower deciles of the income distribution, there is a very significant minority who experience very large percentage losses in annual income, and a very much smaller proportion who experience gains.

Table 14.3   *Females, 16 to 65: Stone–Geary utility functions, percentage gains/losses from UI revisions, by decile of income under 1971 scheme*

	Loss			Nil	Gain		
	More than 50% loss (1)	26%– 50% loss (2)	6%– 25% loss (3)	No change ± 5% (4)	6%– 25% gain (5)	26%– 50% gain (6)	More than 50% gain (7)
1	3.50	4.32	15.07	62.66	9.57	1.50	3.38
2	1.47	4.41	16.66	70.00	5.52	0.93	1.00
3	1.86	2.02	14.19	79.16	1.67	0.55	0.56
4	0.59	0.39	12.34	86.32	0.37	0.00	0.00
5	0.67	3.76	14.85	80.57	0.14	0.00	0.00
6	0.36	1.48	17.96	79.09	0.98	0.09	0.04
7	0.64	2.54	19.87	75.95	0.77	0.23	0.00
8	0.19	1.69	14.41	83.64	0.00	0.00	0.00
9	0.53	1.07	11.57	86.51	0.32	0.00	0.00
10	0.10	0.65	6.03	93.03	0.19	0.00	0.00

So far, this chapter has focused on the utility gains and losses associated with the risk of *income* fluctuations, but economists normally think of utility as being derived not from *income*, but from the *consumption* which income permits. However, in order to go from a discussion of variations in income flows to an analysis of consumption flows, one needs to discuss saving and dissaving behavior. Up to this point, intertemporal utility maximization has been based on a time separable utility function and a discount rate of 5.5 percent, but savings behavior depends on more than that. The issue we are concerned with in this chapter is income insecurity, and to the degree that income flows are more uncertain, choices between more and less liquid forms of saving (bank accounts and term deposits versus home ownership, automobiles, durables, pensions) will shift toward the liquid assets available to smooth consumption during a spell of unemployment, rather than the illiquid assets which are not. Changes in social insurance legislation are therefore likely to alter both the level and the composition of personal savings.

A full resolution of these issues lies beyond the scope of this chapter. Furthermore, Canada does not now have[11] longitudinal panel data which would enable one to assess directly the impact of income fluctuations over time on individual consumption and savings patterns. Table 14.4 therefore simply asks what percentage of the population in fact has enough assets to smooth consumption to any significant degree – i.e. we use cross-sectional evidence on net household assets to assess the relative

Table 14.4   *Income deciles and net liquid assets* [a]

	Males		Females	
Deciles	Net liquid assets (1)	Available home equity (2)	Net liquid assets (3)	Available home equity (4)
Poorest 10%	46.43	76.84	33.80	65.92
11–20	32.15	61.86	31.89	58.51
21–30	21.21	44.70	27.11	56.20
31–40	21.74	49.88	30.58	64.08
41–50	24.04	54.75	32.90	60.56
51–60	26.57	58.52	30.07	60.95
61–70	29.17	65.15	31.14	57.30
71–80	34.88	70.01	28.71	59.22
81–90	38.00	76.00	32.89	61.46
Top 10%	47.00	81.88	38.35	67.15
Overall average	*32.12*	*63.96*	*31.74*	*61.14*

Note:
[a] Percentage with greater than $3,020, 16 to 64 years; $3,020 = 1981 single person poverty line for 21.6 weeks (the average uninterrupted duration of a spell of unemployment in 1984).

importance of liquidity constraints (i.e. the percentage of individuals who are members of households whose assets or access to credit are insufficient to smooth consumption, so that $Y_{it} \simeq C_{it}$ necessarily). Columns (1) and (3) of table 14.4 present the percentage of persons within each 1981 income decile living in households where liquid assets are greater than $3,020[12] while columns (2) and (4) add to those liquid assets the credit limit on available home equity loans.[13]

Conclusions

The innovation of this chapter is its attempt to evaluate the impacts on the distribution of economic well-being of revisions to the social insurance role of the welfare state by combining micro-simulation of behavioral responses to policy changes with an explicit specification of the utility functions of individuals. We have argued that reforms to the welfare state can be expected to alter individual labor market behaviors and that individuals care about both the expected value of their income and the riskiness of that income – hence it is necessary to evaluate jointly the expected value of future income, the uncertainty of income flows, and the behavioral responses of individuals.

Since our micro-simulation model incorporates behavioral response to changes in UI parameters, it explicitly takes account of "moral hazard" in UI induced changes in labor market behavior. Moreover, incorporating behavioral response in a logically consistent model structure implies that we consider the implications of changes in *both* labor force participation and unemployment. Part of the "moral hazard" story about Canadian UI is the argument that easier entrance requirements after 1971 increased the labor supply of some "marginal" workers, who entered the labor force in order to qualify for UI benefits (see Card and Riddell, 1993) – the implication is that when UI qualification becomes more difficult, as in 1994, such workers will decrease their labor supply, thereby decreasing total earnings. Even though the unemployment rate falls when there is a change to a more restrictive UI program, this produces a drop in labor force participation which means that average total incomes also fall.

In doing all this, we are well aware that calculation of the value of a Stone–Geary utility function under alternative UI and unemployment scenarios is a rather bloodless exercise. In the real world, people stay up late at night worrying about how they are going to make ends meet and what they will do if they lose their jobs. Economic anxiety makes real people tense and irritable and they may lash out at their families or try to drown their anxieties in alcohol or drugs. Our model does not capture the sense of anxiety and powerlessness that comes from the increasing withdrawal of the Canadian state from its social insurance role and its denial of responsibility for macroeconomic outcomes.[14]

Much more needs to be done to improve our analysis. We are in the process of revising our micro-simulation model to incorporate demographic transitions and some consideration of household influences on labor market behavior. We need to know more about savings/dissavings and the ability of households to smooth consumption flows over time, despite variations in income flows. We want to experiment further with alternative specifications of the functional form of utility functions and the appropriate specification of utility for individuals within households, and we want to investigate the sensitivity of the importance of income risk to alternative parameter values for individual utility functions.

We have two major concerns with the Stone–Geary specification – that it may not exhibit enough risk aversion to income change and that it imposes a common (positive) valuation on all non-labor time. For the Stone–Geary utility function, evaluated for males at an income of $30,000 and two weeks' leisure, the Arrow–Pratt coefficient of relative risk aversion is 0.28 – far below other estimates of risk aversion. The logarithmic utility function is popular in the financial literature (see Rubinstein, 1977) and is somewhat more consistent than the Stone–Geary specification with observed risk aversion behavior in financial portfolios, but the Arrow–Pratt coefficient of relative risk aversion is still only 1 – Friend and Blume (1975) concluded that the coefficient of relative risk aversion is at least 2.

Even when unemployment is relatively high (e.g. 10 percent), the vast majority of the labor force (90 percent) are employed – hence the majority of people have relatively little non-labor time, and it seems reasonable that they derive positive utility from it. However, the pleasures of another day with nothing to do decline rapidly as the days add up. Unemployment, particularly long duration unemployment, is very different from "leisure," and we are convinced by such authors as Clark and Oswald (1994) that unemployment generally reduces utility. In future work we hope to experiment with functional forms which allow the utility value of non-labor time to vary with its duration and nature.

Meanwhile, since the current Stone–Geary specification implies that increased non-labor time partly "balances" lower money income and since we suspect that our current results under-state the importance of income risk, a more satisfactory treatment of these two issues would very probably strengthen the conclusions of this chapter.

Although there are many technically complex steps to our argument, the basic conclusion is fairly direct. The 1971–94 revisions to UI in Canada substantially decreased the level of benefits paid by the Canadian UI system, and produced decreases in economic well-being for all deciles of the income distribution. Since declines in economic well-being were especially large, in percentage terms, for the poorest deciles of the distribution, UI revisions increased the inequality of the distribution of economic well-being, in addition to decreasing average economic well-being. And, as we have noted in other work (Erksoy, Osberg and Phipps, 1994c), UI revisions have the same qualitative impact on the distribution of income, whether measured by annual income or the present value of income over the business cycle.

Furthermore, since we get essentially the same result from examination of the distribution of certainty equivalent income, the present value of income flows over the business cycle, or annual money incomes, our hunch is that our results are fairly robust. And we also think that the Canadian public knows that reducing the social insurance role of the modern welfare state increases inequality and decreases economic well-being – when asked in March 1994 whether they approved or disapproved of reducing the level of UI benefits, 61 percent of Canadians replied that they disapproved – and the percentage was significantly higher among low income Canadians than among those with higher incomes.[15] Nevertheless, a major revision to UI in Canada was legislated in 1996, altering many plan parameters and changing the name to "Employment Insurance." When fully phased in, benefits payable are expected to decline by 11 percent nationally and up to 19 percent in provinces with high unemployment (HRDC, 1996).

Appendix A: key features of the 1971 and 1994 UI regimes

	Simulation 1981–9, based on 1971 UI system	Simulation 1981–9, based on 1994 UI system
Benefit wage ratio	(a) 75% of insured earnings for claimants with less than or equal to 1/3 maximum insurable earnings and with dependents	(a) 60% of insured earnings for claimants with less than or equal to 1/2 of maximum insurable earnings and with dependents
	(b) 66% for all other claimants	(b) 55% for all other claimants
Maximum insurable earnings	From $315/week in 1981 to $460/week in 1989	From $315/week in 1981 to $460/week in 1989
Minimum insurable earnings	20% of maximum insurable earnings	20% of maximum insurable earnings
Minimum employment weeks to qualify	8 weeks	from 12 weeks to 20 weeks depending on regional unemployment rates
Maximum annual benefit period	50 weeks	50 weeks
Benefit period determination	(1) Up to 15 weeks of benefits for the first 20 weeks of work	(1) Up to 20 weeks of benefits, based on 1 week of benefits for every 2 weeks of work for the first 40 insured weeks of work
	(2) Additional 10 weeks for the unemployed at the end of phase 1	(2) Up to 12 weeks of benefits, based on 1 week of benefits for each week of work beyond the first 40 weeks

(3) Up to 18 weeks of extended benefits for insurable employment beyond 20 weeks	(3) Up to 26 weeks, based on 2 weeks of benefits for every percentage point by which the regional unemployment rate is above 4%
(4) If national unemployment rate is 4–5% then an additional 4 weeks of benefits; if the national unemployment rate is above 5% then an additional 8 weeks of benefits	

Appendix B: model structure

All equations are estimated using microdata from the 1986/87 Statistics Canada Labor Market Activities Survey.

Complete labor force withdrawal

In any simulation year over the cycle the model starts by computing for each individual the probability of being outside of the labor force for all 52 weeks of the year. The underlying regression is a logit model. Individuals are then ordered in descending order of the probability of being out of the labor force for 52 weeks. Those with highest probability of complete labor force withdrawal are assigned 52 weeks of non-participation weeks until the total number of such individuals reaches the exact proportion of the population with complete labor force withdrawal in that year. For those who are assigned 52 weeks of not being in the labor force, no further calculations of labor market behavior are made for that year. They may still collect UI benefits as a continuation of a claim whose duration has not yet expired from the previous year but they cannot establish a new UI claim in that year. However, they are retained in the model, since they may re-enter the labor force in a subsequent year.

Some weeks of labor force withdrawal

Given the remaining proportion of the population with some labor force participation, the model assigns each individual some weeks out of the labor force based on a Tobit model of weeks of non-labor force participation. Given that each individual has been assigned an estimate of their desired labor supply, the next step is to determine whether or not they can get employment for the weeks in which they are willing to participate in the labor market.

Weeks of unemployment

In this stage the model first computes for each individual a probability of unemployment experience using a logit specification. All individuals are then ordered in descending probability of unemployment. For each individual, unemployment weeks are calculated based on an accelerated failure time model. If an individual's unemployment experience this year is predicted to be greater than that of last year, the person faces no constraint in increasing the weeks of unemployment. If, however, the individual's unemployment weeks are less than that of last year, this person must locate additional employment weeks. Therefore, for all individuals with an expected decrease in unemployment the model computes the probability of being constrained in getting an additional week of work. The individual is assigned one more week of employment (one less week of unemployment) if a random number drawn from a uniform distribution exceeds the estimated probability of constraint. Those who want to increase their labor supply by more than one week of work, given that they have been successful in obtaining one additional week of employment, face a certain probability of being able to get the second additional week of work, etc. We proceed in this way until the individual has either reached the expected additional employment or encountered a constraint in obtaining an additional week of work. Together the duration model and the under-employment model determine for each person the expected weeks of unemployment, if they experience any unemployment.

Since individuals are ordered in descending order of probability of unemployment in a given year, unemployment is assigned to those with the highest probability of experiencing unemployment up to the point where the total number of assigned unemployment weeks equals aggregate unemployment weeks for the year. Aggregate unemployment weeks are given by the product of the total number of labor force weeks and the aggregate unemployment rate in that year.

Alternative scenarios

In each situation run, two scenarios are compared: the "base" and the "shock" scenario. The base and shock scenario differ in the assumed structure of unemployment insurance legislation, but have identical estimated behavioral response to unemployment insurance parameters, and the influence of personal characteristics.

Stochastic component

In order to preserve the underlying stochastic element in labor market behavior, in each estimated equation random error terms drawn from a distribution with variance consistent with the observed unexplained variance are added to the conditional expectations. Furthermore, we assume that in the real world the underlying stochastic element consists of permanent and temporary features. The former is regarded as the persistent part of the total unobserved heterogeneity which remains constant in each year and represents 30 percent of the individual random error term in each equation. It is generated once and kept constant in each year. The temporary component which corresponds to the remaining 70 percent of the error term is generated separately in each year. Therefore, in a given year the sum total of the permanent and temporary components gives the total stochastic element in each behavioral equation. Further note that random error terms are initially generated for each individual in all behavioral equations and in all years. These random error terms are then retained and used in alternative policy simulations which conveniently allows us to compare alternative policy scenarios directly since we have the same distribution of the stochastic element in all simulations.

The effect of alternative UI systems on the aggregate unemployment rate

The model is embedded within a changing macroeconomic environment by allowing the aggregate unemployment rate to change over time and calculating the associated aggregate weeks of unemployment. The impact of unemployment insurance on aggregate unemployment is a hotly contested empirical issue in Canada. Myatt (1996) presents a summary of fourteen published studies on the impact of the liberalization of UI in 1971. As he notes: "Of these studies, seven found a significant positive effect [of UI on aggregate unemployment], five found no significant effect and two found no significant effect in seven out of ten provinces (it is worth noting that these latter studies disagree on which three provinces have the significant positive effect . . .). A more evenly divided result could not be imagined."

In this chapter, we assume that reductions in the generosity of UI coincide with reductions in aggregate unemployment. These adjustments are based on the presumption that there was a 0.6 percent increase in the unemployment rate due to the introduction of more generous UI regulations by the Unemployment Insurance Act in 1971 (see Grubel, Maki and Sax, 1975). The 1971 Act reduced the minimum employment weeks to qualify for UI benefits from 30 weeks over the previous 104-week qualifying period to 8 weeks in the previous 52-week period, increased the waiting period from one week to two weeks, and raised the replacement rate from 50 percent to 66 percent. In order to be able to extrapolate the effects of changes in the UI system on the aggregate unemployment rate we look at the behavior of an hypothetical individual who follows a repeated cycle of working the minimum required weeks in order to collect the maximum benefits under alternative UI systems. This individual could obtain 2.4 (=(51–15)/15) benefit weeks per week of employment in the pre-1971 period (assuming the 30-week entrance requirement is satisfied in the qualifying period), and 5.25 (=(50–8)/8) benefit weeks per week of employment in the post-1971 period. Therefore, the change in the UI generosity in the post-1971 period compared to the pre-1971 period is about 192 percent (=(3.5–1.2)/1.2). If then one assumes that 192 percent increase in the benefits leads to 0.6 percent increase in the unemployment rate due to the response of our hypothetical individual, one can calculate the effects of UI policy changes on the unemployment rate (U) as follows:

$$\% \text{ change in } U = (a/b \times 0.6\%)$$

where a is the \$ change in UI benefits for a given change in the regulations, and b is the \$ increase in UI benefits in the post-1971 period, which is 192 percent.

Overall, the changes in the UI system in place by 1994 represented a -44.5 percent change in generosity (compared to 1971) for the marginal individual, implying a -0.14 percent change in the aggregate unemployment rate.

Appendix C: Model equations[a]

$$(\Pr(WKSNLF_{it} < 52) = \hat{F}_1(X_{it}, WKSUN_{i,t-1}, LM_t) + \varepsilon_{2i} \tag{1}$$

$$WK\hat{S}NLF_{it} = \hat{F}_1(X_{it}, WKSUN_{i,t-1}, LM_t, UI_t) + \varepsilon_{2i} \tag{2}$$

$$\Pr(U_{it} \mid 0 \leq WKSNLF < 52) = F_3(X_{it}, WKSUN_{i,t-1}, LM_t) + \varepsilon_{3i} \tag{3}$$

$$(WKS\hat{U}N_{it} \mid \hat{U}_{it} = 1) = \hat{F}_4(X_{it}, WKSUN_{i,t-1}, LM_t, UI_t) + \varepsilon_{4i} \tag{4}$$

$$WKS\hat{E}MP_{it} = 52 - WKS\hat{N}LF_{it} - WK\hat{S}UN_{it} \tag{5}$$

$DESIRED_{it}[WKSUNEMP_i \mid UI'_t]$ (6)

$IF\ DESIRED_{it} < WKS_{it}\ THEN\ \text{Prob}\ [WKSUN'_{it} = WKS\hat{U}N_{it} - 1]$ (7)
$= 1 - \text{Pr}(CONS)$
$\text{Pr}(CONS) = \hat{F}_5(X_{it}, WKSUN'_{it}, LM_t, UI'_t) + \varepsilon_{5i}$ model iterates

$\hat{F}_1, \hat{F}_2, \hat{F}_3, \hat{F}_4, \hat{F}_5$	estimated structural relationships (probit, tobit, logit, Weibull, and logit respectively) using the 1986/87 Statistics Canada Labor Market Activities Survey
$\varepsilon_{1i}, \varepsilon_{2i}, \varepsilon_{3i}, \varepsilon_{4i}, \varepsilon_{5i}$	random error term from corresponding structural equation
	i = individual
	$t, t-1$ = period
X_{it}	personal characteristics
$WKSUN_{it}$	weeks unemployed
$WKSNLK_{it}$	weeks not in labor force
U_{it}	experience of some unemployment during year
$CONS$	constrained in obtaining additional weeks work
UI_t	parameters of UI system (UI'_t denotes changed UI parameters)
LM_t	local labor market condition
$WKSEMP_{it}$	weeks employed

Note:
[a] See Erksoy, Osberg and Phipps (1994a) for details.

Notes

We would like to thank the Social Sciences and Humanities Research Council of Canada, the Natural Sciences and Engineering Research Council of Canada, and Human Resource Development Canada for their financial support, and Audri Mukhopadhyay, Lynn Lethbridge, and Tom McGuire for their excellent work as research assistants on this project. Brian MacLean and an anonymous reviewer provided useful comments, but any errors remaining are our sole responsibility.

1 Borch goes on to argue that there may be a minority of risk lovers who would prefer a society with greater risks, and that this may explain some of the dissatisfaction with the welfare state.

2 In 1993, UI benefits of $18.3 billion were paid to 3.4 million Canadians. Appendix A summarizes the key features of the 1971 and 1994 UI regimes.

3 The problem of self-selection has been recognized for a long time. Atkinson (1991, p. 117) quotes Winston Churchill speaking in the British House of Commons in 1911: "Voluntary schemes of unemployment insurance . . . have always failed because those men likely to be unemployed resorted to

them, and, consequently, there was a preponderance of bad risks . . . which must be fatal to the success of the scheme" (*Hansard*, 1911, vol. 26, col. 495).

4 Given that governments make decisions on macroeconomic policy which may imply an increase in unemployment (e.g. a restrictive monetary policy to combat inflation), it has often been argued that society as a whole should compensate those individuals who are affected. In the 1970s, Canadian UI legislation embodied a recognition of social responsibility for unemployment by requiring the government to pay from general revenues the costs of claims in excess of those associated with 4 percent unemployment (amended in 1976 to unemployment exceeding an eight-year moving average). In the 1980s, denial of macroeconomic responsibility produced legislative amendments which shifted UI funding entirely to premiums.

5 Due to the difference in claims experience, it is normal for insurance companies to charge young male drivers substantially higher premiums for automobile insurance, but although there are similar differences by age and gender in UI claims' experience, such discrimination in UI premiums or claims eligibility is socially unacceptable.

6 Similarly, a legislative change which deprived individuals of protection against financial loss due to home burglary by prohibiting the sale of such insurance could be expected to decrease the incidence of home burglary (as individuals purchased burglar alarms, etc. to decrease the risk of burglary), and would increase the net cash income of individuals, in aggregate (since premiums paid to burglary insurers exceed claims paid out by the amount of administration expenses and industry profits), *but* such a change would decrease the utility of all those who previously purchased insurance. (Figure 14.1 is really a generic diagram of the implications, in general, of higher or lower levels of insurance coverage.)

7 In Phipps (1990, 1991a, 1991b) individual utility is dependent on consumption of goods *plus* non-labor time. These estimates allow for the possibility that time spent unemployed was not a utility maximizing choice – that some unemployed individuals faced demand-side constraints (see also Osberg, 1988). Implicitly, writing utility as a function of income assumes that individuals are liquidity constrained (i.e. consumption equals income) (see table 14.3, p. 332).

8 In practice, annual hours of female labor supply in Canada are a positive function of the wage for low wage workers but a negative function of the wage (i.e. the "income effect" dominates the "substitution effect") for above average wages – see Osberg and Phipps (1993). The calculations reported in tables 14.1 and 14.2 use the parameter values of the Stone–Geary specification reported in Phipps (1991b, p. 202).

9 We also carried out the same analysis using expected incomes. Results were qualitatively very similar, as might be expected given the choice of the fairly restrictive Stone–Geary utility function.

10 Notice that to be affected by changes in UI, one must have been covered by UI in the first place. We conjecture that many women in the lower deciles,

while having had positive earnings and UI in 1981, did not maintain eligibility for UI (which requires achievement of threshold weeks per year as well as hours or earnings per week) throughout the 1981–9 period.

11 Statistics Canada is now pre-testing the Survey of Labor and Income Dynamics, which will, when completed and available, provide a six-year panel of income and labor dynamics. The Labor Market Activity Survey of 1986/87 and 1988/90 is now available but contains no consumption information.

12 The Labor Force Survey (LFS) of 1984 recorded the average (uninterrupted) duration of an unemployment spell at 21.6 weeks, and the single person (1978 Base) Statistics Canada, Low Income Cutoff in 1981 dollars was $7,268 per year – hence $3,020 is the cash required to finance an average duration unemployment spell, at a poverty line standard of living.

13 A survey of local banks provided the following rule-of-thumb formula for second mortgage credit limits: credit limit = 75 percent of market value of house – balance outstanding on first mortgage.

14 Economic anxiety in Canada is, in fact, much more widespread than the issue of unemployment–unemployment insurance. In October 1993, 34 percent of Canadians agreed with the statement: "It is quite possible that I or someone in my household will seek benefits under the Unemployment Insurance Program over the next year or two." (Another 10 percent were uncertain.) A larger number (52 percent of respondents) agreed with the statement: "I feel I have lost all control over my economic future" (see EKOS Research Associates, 1993).

15 73 percent of Canadians with a household income less than $15,000 disapproved of reducing the level of UI benefits, while only 53 percent of those with household incomes in excess of $50,000 disapproved (see Environics Research Group, 1994).

References

Atkinson, A.B., 1991. "Social insurance: the 15th annual lecture of the Geneva Association," *The Geneva Papers on Risk and Insurance Theory*, 16, 113–32, Boston: Kluwer Academic

Atkinson, A.B. and J. Micklewright, 1991. "Unemployment compensation and labour market transitions: a critical review," *Journal of Economic Literature*, 29, 1679–1727

Betson, D. and J. van der Gaag, 1985. "Measuring the benefits of income maintenance programs," chapter 7 in M. David and T. Smeeding (eds.), *Horizontal Equity, Uncertainty and Economic Well-being*, NBER, *Studies in Income and Wealth, vol. 50*, Chicago: University of Chicago Press, 215–38

Bird, E.J., 1993. "An exploratory comparison of income risk in Germany and the United States," Department of Economics, University of Rochester, mimeo

Borch, K.H., 1968. *The Economics of Uncertainty*, Princeton, NJ: Princeton University Press

344   Lars Osberg, Sadettin Erksoy and Shelley Phipps

Card, D. and C.W. Riddell, 1993. "A comparative analysis of unemployment in
    Canada and the United States," in D. Card and R. Freeman (eds.), *Small
    Differences that Matter: Labor Market and Income Maintenance in the
    United States and Canada*, Chicago: University of Chicago Press, 149–89
Clark, A.E. and A.J. Oswald, 1994. "Unhappiness and unemployment,"
    Economic Journal, 104, 648–59
EKOS Research Associates, 1993. "A mid-campaign report: the EKOS election
    1993 analysis," Ottawa: EKOS Research Associates
Environics Research Group Limited, 1994. *The Focus Canada Report 1994–1*,
    Toronto: Environics Research Group Limited (March)
Erksoy, S., L. Osberg and S. Phipps, 1994a. "The distributional implications of
    unemployment insurance – a microsimulation analysis," report prepared for
    Human Resource Development and Labor, Department of Economics,
    Dalhousie University, mimeo
    1994b. "Panel data and policy analysis," paper presented to the 1994 Meetings
    of the Canadian Economics Association, Calgary, Department of
    Economics, Dalhousie University, mimeo
    1994c. "The distributional implications of unemployment insurance – revi-
    sions," paper presented to the 1994 Meetings of the Canadian Economics
    Association, Calgary, Department of Economics, Dalhousie University,
    mimeo
Friend, I. and M.E. Blume, 1975. "The demand for risky assets," *American
    Economic Review*, 65, 900–22
Grubel, H.G., D. Maki and S. Sax, 1975. "Real and insurance induced
    unemployment in Canada," *Canadian Journal of Economics*, 8, 174–91
Hansard (1911), *Parliamentary Debates*, 26, col. 995, London: Reuter's
Hayes, J. and P. Nutman, 1981. *Understanding the Unemployed: The Psychologi-
    cal Effects of Unemployment*, London and New York: Tavistock Publica-
    tions
HRDC, 1996. "Employment insurance: impacts of reform," Human Resources
    Development Canada, 1, Ottawa (January)
Jahoda, M., 1979. "The psychological meanings of unemployment," *New
    Society*, 492–5
Kelvin, P. and J.E. Jarrett, 1985. *Unemployment: Its Social Psychological Effects*,
    Cambridge: Cambridge University Press
Myatt, T., 1996. "Why do we know so little about unemployment determination
    and the effects of unemployment insurance?" in L. Osberg and B. MacLean
    (eds.), *The Unemployment Crisis: All for Naught*, Kingston and Montreal:
    McGill and Queen's University Press, 107–28
Narendranathan, W. and S. Nickell, 1985. "Modeling the process of job search,"
    Journal of Econometrics, 28, 29–49
Orcutt, G., 1957. "A new type of socio-economic system," *Review of Economics
    and Statistics*, 58, 773–97
Orcutt, G., H.J. Merz and H. Quinke (eds.), 1986. *Microanalytic Simulation
    Models to Support Social and Financial Policy*, Amsterdam: North-Holland

Osberg, L., 1988. "The 'disappearance' of involuntary unemployment," *Journal of Economic Issues*, 22, 707–27

Osberg, L. and S. Phipps, 1993. "Labour supply with quantity constraints: estimates from a large sample of Canadian workers," *Oxford Economic Papers*, 45, 269–91

Phipps, S., 1990. "Quantity constrained household responses to unemployment insurance reform," *Economic Journal*, 100, 124–40

1991a. "Behavioural response to UI reform in constrained and unconstrained models of labour supply," *Canadian Journal of Economics*, 14, 34–54

1991b. "Equity and efficiency consequences of unemployment insurance reform in Canada: the importance of sensitivity analyses," *Economica*, 58, 199–214

(1997). "What is the income cost of a child? Exact equivalence scales for Canadian two parent families," *Review of Economics and Statistics*, forthcoming

Phipps, S. and P. Burton, 1995. "Sharing within families: implications for the measurement of poverty," *Canadian Journal of Economics*, 28, 177–204

Rubinstein, M., 1977. "The strong care for the generalized logarithmic utility model as the premier model of financial markets," in H. Levy and M. Sarrot (eds.), *Financial Decision Making under Uncertainty*, New York: Academic Press, 11–65

Stern, N., 1986. "On the specification of labour supply functions," in R. Blundell and I. Walker (eds.), *Unemployment, Search and Labour Supply*, Cambridge: Cambridge University Press, 143–89

15 A structural model of the determinants of educational success

Robert Haveman, Kathryn Wilson and Barbara Wolfe

Introduction

Education has long been viewed as the primary key to socio-economic success. Persons with more education have higher wage rates and labor market earnings, obtain larger fringe benefits associated with employment, and are less likely to be unemployed. Hence, inequality in the distribution of earnings is a reflection of variation in the distribution of educational attainments. Moreover, the gains from education go beyond the labor market – *ceteris paribus*, schooling is positively related to occupational prestige, health status, efficiency in consumption, marriage and fertility choices, and offspring quality.[1] For these reasons, and others, identifying those factors that determine individuals' level of education is of substantial interest.

In this chapter, we attempt to identify the factors that underlie the schooling choices of US youth. We present estimates from a structural model of children's choice regarding whether or not to graduate from high school, in which both expected utilities (incomes) in alternative states of educational attainment and family/neighborhood factors can influence the choices made. In the next section, we discuss the potential determinants of educational choices, after providing some background information on trends in educational attainment in the United States. We then describe our data. We then present a structural model that reflects the view that educational choices are rational responses to the economic returns associated with various levels of schooling attainments, and describes our procedure in estimating the model. We then present the results from our estimation of this model, and draw some conclusions.

The determinants of educational attainment

Over the post-war period, the level of education attained by the average US person has steadily increased. In 1950, for example, the average US person 25 or older had 9.3 years of education; by 1990, this had increased to 12.7 years. This increase in the average level of education in the US population is reflected in an increased rate of high school completion. In the cohort aged 25 to 29 in 1960, nearly 40 percent failed to graduate high school; by 1993, the proportion of high school drop outs in this age cohort had fallen to 12 percent. While the median years of schooling of whites still exceeds that of non-whites (12.9 years for whites compared to 12.7 years for non-whites in 1993 for adults 25 and over), this gap has narrowed significantly over the past three decades.

Numerous factors have contributed to the changing pattern of educational attainment, and the economic status that is associated with it. In addition to a wide variety of "background factors" (e.g. parental education and values, race, gender, and ability), these involve decisions made by governments (e.g. school quality, neighborhood attributes), and by parents (e.g. parental nurturing and monitoring, family structure, parental work and earnings, family moves). Children's schooling outcomes also depend on the choices made by children themselves in response to the structure of economic and other opportunities associated with alternative education attainments.

Our analysis builds on work by prior researchers who have sought to measure the effects of a variety of these determinants of educational success.[2] Most of these studies employ information on individual children and their families, and emphasize the potential role of parental characteristics and choices. Our review of this work reveals a variety of factors that have been found to be consistently related to the schooling attainments of children – parental education, family income, number of parents in the child's family, and parental expectations are among the more important.[3]

Our study differs in several ways from prior research on the family-based determinants of educational attainment. First, the model that we estimate reflects our view that a child's ultimate educational attainment is the result of conscious and rational decisions made by society (e.g. the community environment in which the child lives), the child's parents, and the individual himself or herself. For example, beyond the minimum number of years of education mandated by the state, the individual is viewed as processing information on the gains and losses associated with specific educational options so as to make choices that will maximize well-being; these choices determine when the individual ceases school attendance, and hence the number of years of completed schooling.

Second, we view these direct schooling choices as nested in an environment which is created by the choices of other decision makers – the society (or, more particularly, the government) and the child's parents. Decisions made by communities and parents also influence choices regarding the amount of education attained. The quality of the schooling provided for young children, for example, is likely to affect their tastes for schooling, and their perception of their success at the education enterprise. Similarly, the parental monitoring of school performance or expressions of expectations regarding schooling are likely to influence a child's ultimate evaluations of the gains and costs of incremental schooling.

Third, as already implied, we leaven an economic perspective on the determinants of education with the insights from other social sciences – sociology and developmental psychology – regarding the determinants of children's educational attainment. Hence, we introduce parental decisions that may create stress during the child's formative years (e.g. location changes) or alter the child's values regarding economic attainment (e.g. parental welfare receipt).

Data on children, their families, and their neighborhoods

Our analysis is based on a large longitudinal data set constructed from observations of a national stratified sample of families, the Michigan Panel Study of Income Dynamics (PSID).[4] The PSID data provides longitudinal information on 6,000 families beginning in 1968. As of 1994, 21 years of information were available – from 1968 to 1988. We selected children who were ages 0 to 6 in the beginning year of the survey, and follow them for the full 21 years. For each child, these data include information on family status, income and source of income, parental education, neighborhood characteristics, and background characteristics such as race, religion, and location. They also include information on a variety of children's attainments. By 1988, the children are young adults, ranging in age from 21 to 27 years.

Only those individuals who remained in the survey for each year until 1988 are included in the sample. In 1968, there were 3,120 children aged 0 to 6 in the PSID. During the subsequent 21 years, 1,370 children were lost from the sample due to one or another reason for sample attrition over such a long period. With the exception of race, those who attrited do not appear to differ from the remaining sample. However, as with other studies employing panel data, it is possible that some of our coefficient estimates are biased because of sample attrition.

In order to analyze the influence of various family and community decisions and characteristics while children were young on their educational choices, we transformed the time-varying data elements of either the children or their parents into an age-indexed data set. That is, rather than have the data defined by year of its occurrence (1968 or 1974, for example), we converted the data so that it is assigned to the child by the child's age (age 6 or 9, for example). Thus, for two children, one aged 2 and the other aged 6 in 1968, comparable information for each from ages 6 to 18 is obtained using data from 1972 to 1984 for the first child and data from 1968 to 1980 for the second child.

Transforming the data in this way enables age-specific comparisons of individuals with different birth years, and allows us to analyze whether the *timing* of particular events – whether an event or circumstance occurs when the child is young or an adolescent – has a differential influence on the ultimate attainment of the child. To compare income and other monetary values over time, all dollar values from the PSID are expressed in 1976 prices using the Consumer Price Index (CPI) for all items.

Because a number of important aspects of family and social investments in children are not included in the information contained in the PSID, we merged two additional types of information onto our basic data. First, we added neighborhood information constructed by matching small area data from the 1970 and 1980 Censuses to the location of the children in our sample.[5] The merged neighborhood data include information on the racial composition, the proportion of persons living in poverty, the proportion of young adults who are high school drop outs, and the proportion of families that are female-headed for the neighborhood in which the family of each child in our sample lived for each of the years from 1968 to 1985.

Second, to estimate our structural model of the determinants of schooling choices (p. 350), we imputed expected income values with and without a high school degree to each observation. These income values are obtained from information on a cohort of 1,373 youths included in the PSID, who are aged 30 to 34 in 1989 (or aged 8 to 12 in 1968, the first year of the survey).[6] We use personal incomes for each year from age 19 to age 29 of this cohort to generate expected income streams if a high school graduate and if not graduating, discounted to age 16 (p. 351).

A structural model of the high school graduation choice

The estimates in most previous literature relate educational outcomes to a set of parental choice/opportunity and community characteristics by means of reduced form equations. The aim is to include an extensive set of exogenous family-based characteristics so as to minimize potential unobserved variables' problems. That approach, however, neglects the fact that, in making education choices, children's decisions are likely to reflect the expected income returns to incremental schooling. As a result, the reduced form estimates of schooling choices may attribute to background, family choice, and neighborhood variables effects properly attributed to economic returns associated with incremental schooling. In our work, we use predicted values of incomes both with and without a high school degree in a structural model of the decision of whether or not to complete high school.

The nature of the structural model

In this model, we hypothesize that the decision of individuals regarding whether or not to graduate high school depends in part on the expected difference in lifetime income if one does or does not graduate. Our model is based on the standard assumption of utility maximization where individuals face the choice of whether or not to graduate high school. The income flows associated with each option determine the well-being (utility) expected in each option. While our focus is on the dichotomous decision of graduation or not, we present a more general model which would apply to decisions over multiple schooling options.

Let U_{in}^* be the utility of individual n conditional upon the selection of option i (graduation or not) within this binary set of education choices; Y_{in}^* is a random vector of realized outcomes (income) for individual n, conditional on the selection of alternative i; S_n is a vector of exogenous characteristics and past choices of child n; F_n is a vector of family characteristics and parental choices made prior to the schooling choice of individual n; and C_n is a vector of society's choices and opportunities afforded individual n prior to the individual's schooling choice.

In the presence of uncertainty regarding the outcome of alternative education choices, Y_{in}^*, the objective of the child is to choose whether to graduate or not in order to maximize expected utility:

$$EU_{in}^* = EU^*(Y_{in}^*, S_n, F_n, C_n) \qquad (15.1)$$

subject to lifetime wealth constraints.

The individual chooses i if and only if the expected utility of option i is greater than that of option j for all $i \neq j$

$$EU^*(Y_{in}^*, S_n, F_n, C_n) > EU^*(Y_{jn}^*, S_n, F_n, C_n) \qquad (15.2)$$

for all $i \in V$, $i \neq j$.[1]

To simplify, write vector $Z_n = (S_n, F_n, C_n)$. Then, assume that the expected indirect utility of alternative i, U_i, can be characterized as:

$$U_i = Z_i\beta_1 + E(Y^*|Q, i)\beta_2 + e_i \qquad (15.3)$$

The child knows that Y^* depends on the schooling choice that is made. The child also believes that Y^* depends on the realization of an unobserved random vector Q, where Q depends on prior choices of society (C), the child's parents (F), and the child's own prior choices (S).

If we let $E(Y^*|Q,i)$ denote the child's expected value of Y^*, conditional on Q and the hypothesized choice of i, and e_i denote the unobserved random component of the utility associated with alternative i, then the child chooses the alternative that maximizes expected utility $= Z_i\beta_1 + E(Y^*|Q,i)\beta_2 + e_i$. In other words the child chooses alternative iff:

$$Z\beta_1 + \{E(Y^*|Q,i) - E(Y^*|Q,j)\}\beta_2 > e \qquad (15.4)$$

where $Z = Z_i - Z_j$, $e = e_j - e_i$ for all $i \in V$, $i \neq j$.

In fact, the choices made by older children in this model are not random – they would be repeated if an individual faced the same choice set and the same information. Therefore, the probability of the individual choosing alternative i is:

$$\Pr_i = \Pr[e < Z\beta_1 + \{E(Y^*|Q,i) - E(Y^*|Q,j)\}\beta_2] \text{ for all } i \in V, i \neq j \qquad (15.5)$$

Estimating expected incomes, with and without a high school degree

In modeling the decision of whether or not to complete high school in the context of (15.5), the central economic variable is the difference in the child's perception of Y_i^* with and without a high school degree $[\{E(Y^*|Q,i) - E(Y^*|Q,j)\}]$. Other variables included in the model control for exogenous individual characteristics of the child (age, sex, race), elements of F such as family structure, parental education, whether the mother worked as the child grew up, the income of the family and its source, the geographic mobility of the family, and elements of C including the proportion of youths who are high school drop outs and the proportion of workers in successful occupations in the neighborhood in which the child grew up.

A variety of factors influence the child's perception of education-conditioned values of Y_i^*, including the unemployment rate in the area, early career incomes of high school drop outs and high school graduates in the community, and the availability of financial assistance for post-graduation schooling. We predict the value of the expected income associated with option i, $\hat{Y}_i^*$ from individual-specific characteristics and an equation estimated over persons with education i:

$$Y_i^* = Q_i\alpha + v_i \qquad (15.6)$$

where α is estimated coefficients from a tobit model fit over observations with schooling level i, Q_i is a vector of exogenous predictor variables, and v_i is an error term.

Our procedure implicitly assumes that at age 16, youths form their expectations of future education-conditioned incomes by observing the realized incomes of persons like themselves who are in their late teens and twenties – hence, our use of conditional income terms constructed over individuals aged 19 to 29. If youths fail to place weight on outcomes observed for individuals in middle age or older, our expected income terms would be superior to estimates of full lifetime education-conditioned incomes. Because the sample over which (15.6) is estimated is aged 19 to 29, we use as predictor variables only those based on circumstances or events during the individual's ages 12 to 15. Note that by including incomes during the late teens and early twenties, we capture the opportunity cost of choosing additional schooling beyond high school.

We divide this older cohort sample into those who have and those who have not graduated from high school. As a first step, we fit a reduced form probit equation to "explain" the selected high school graduation/ not high school completion outcome for this sample. From this equation, we calculate an inverse Mills ratio (lambda) variable for each person in the older sample, to correct for selectivity in our second-stage income estimation. The results of this estimation are available from the authors, on request.[8]

In a second step, for both the group of high school graduates and the group that did not complete high school, we ran 11 tobit equations (one for each year from age 19 to 29) with personal income as the dependent variable – a total of 22 equations.[9] We included in these equations variables that are likely to be related to income – race (African-American = 1), gender (female = 1), a race–gender interaction variable, family position (if first born and average number of siblings while 12 to 15), parental education (high school graduation, some college and college graduation, for each parent), and a variety of background variables including number of years lived with one parent, number of years mother worked, whether mother had teen birth, number of years lived in an urban area, number of years head of household was disabled, the average family income relative to needs, number of years received Aid for Families with Dependent Children (AFDC), and number of years lived in each region (each measured over ages 12 to 15). The last set are included to capture the variation in regional prices and earnings, which give identification to the model provided there are not systematic regional variations in high school graduation. The lambda variable for each individual estimated in the first step was also included, in order to control for self-selection into one or the other schooling outcomes. As with the first-stage estimates, these are also available from the authors, on request.

The results of the second-stage estimates hold few surprises. Having a parent who completed college has a negative and significant effect on income for younger ages, but the coefficient becomes positive and significant in estimates for older ages. This pattern reflects the higher probability of attending college during ages 19 to 24 (and, hence, not working) for children of college graduates relative to those without a college degree. For the sample that did not graduate, having a father who graduated from high school has a negative coefficient on income for all ages. The African-American and Female variables have negative and significant coefficients, while African-American*Female has a positive and significant coefficient. The coefficient on the income–needs ratio is generally insignificant, while years spent in a Standard Metropolitan Statistical Area (SMSA) has a positive sign, and sometimes a significant coefficient. Relative to the omitted dummy variable for region (North Central), region is generally not significant for the sample that did not graduate, but living in the West is positive and Northeast is negative and significant for high school graduates. The lambda term is negative and significant in about three-quarters of the income regressions for the high school group, and one-quarter of the income regressions for the group of non-graduates.

We use the coefficients from these estimated equations (other than that on the selectivity variable) along with the individual characteristics of individuals in our primary sample to predict the level of personal income of each person for each age from 19 to 29, conditional on the individual choosing to be a high school graduate or choosing not to graduate from high school.[10] The predicted mean income and standard deviation for each of the 11 years for each of the two schooling groups are presented in table 15.1.

The patterns are as expected: predicted income for those who failed to complete high school is similar to that of high school graduates in the first few years, but the incomes for the non-graduates show slower growth after the early twenties. Predicted income for the high school graduates is generally increasing over the 11 years, and has a steeper slope. At all ages, predicted income if a graduate exceeds predicted income if not a graduate. (Note that the predicted incomes with and without a high school degree are for the same individuals.) Beginning at age 21, the relative predicted income trajectories suggest substantial gains to high school graduation.

Table 15.1   *Predicted personal incomes,[a] if high school graduate and if non-graduate*

	If graduate		If non-graduate	
	Mean	St.dev.	Mean	St.dev.
Entire sample (n = 1,705)				
Age 19	2,174.0	869.3	2,042.7	1,167.8
Age 20	3,030.2	1,211.5	2,620.4	1,400.4
Age 21	3,745.8	1,354.8	3,062.6	1,531.5
Age 22	4,324.6	1,377.0	2,404.8	1,805.9
Age 23	5,186.0	1,534.1	3,289.6	2,107.3
Age 24	5,686.4	1,792.1	3,152.6	1,931.5
Age 25	6,151,5	1,877.6	3,325.6	2,280.9
Age 26	6,895.4	2,244.7	4,273.4	2,507.1
Age 27	7,431.2	2,448.9	3,673.5	1,965.5
Age 28	7,839.9	2,521.1	4,036.3	2,350.4
Age 29	8,268.9	2,789.6	3,202.6	2,248.0
Net present value at age 16	*50,124*	*14,937*	*29,143*	*15,454*
Actual high school graduate (n = 1,437)				
Age 19	2,162.9	852.5	2,037.2	1,174.0
Age 20	2,988.4	1,203.1	2,580.1	1,407.0
Age 21	3,693.0	1,349.8	3,036.9	1,540.6
Age 22	4,264.5	1,372.2	2,250.3	1,768.9
Age 23	5,173.8	1,542.5	3,214.3	2,109.7
Age 24	5,718.3	1,794.1	3,080.0	1,931.8
Age 25	6,192.1	1,896.1	3,232.9	2,275.7
Age 26	6,920.6	2,275.6	4,346.9	2,556.3
Age 27	7,495.1	2,479.5	3,626.7	1,968.9
Age 28	7,888.6	2,559.5	4,023.8	2,364.6
Age 29	8,338.5	2,840.4	3,059.9	2,209.4
Net present value at age 16	*50,198*	*15,023*	*28,650*	*15,459*
Actual high school non-graduate (n = 268)				
Age 19	2,233.5	954.0	2,072.3	1,136.1
Age 20	3,254.6	1,234.2	2,836.1	1,346.8
Age 21	4,028.6	1,349.4	3,200.4	1,477.0
Age 22	4,647.3	1,360.6	3,233.5	1,779.3
Age 23	5,251.3	1,489.0	3,693.6	2,051.6
Age 24	5,515.6	1,774.9	3,542.1	1,885.9
Age 25	5,934.0	1,762.8	3,822.5	2,248.7
Age 26	6,760.4	2,070.5	3,879.4	2,187.6
Age 27	7,088.5	2,251.6	3,924.4	1,931.2
Age 28	7,578.9	2,291.5	4,103.7	2,275.6
Age 29	7,895.8	2,471.3	3,967.3	2,302.3
Net present value at age 16	*49,725*	*14,487*	*31,784*	*15,187*

Note: [a] US$.

In the bottom panels of table 15.1, expected incomes for the non-graduates (with their characteristics) can be compared to those of the graduates. Interestingly, the predicted incomes of the non-graduates for either schooling choice exceed those of the graduates for ages 19 to 23; after age 25, assuming high school graduation, the predicted incomes of the actual graduates diverge rapidly from those of the non-graduates. Perhaps most interestingly, non-graduates have a substantially higher expected income if they do *not* graduate than do graduates, if they do not graduate.[11]

In a final step, we calculate the present value of these predicted incomes as of age 16 (a likely age for deciding whether or not to finish high school), using a discount rate of 3 percent. The expected present value of income for the average person in the sample, if they were to graduate high school, is $50,124 (or $123,591 in 1992 $); the average expected present value if they did not graduate is $29,143 ($71,857), for a difference of $20,981 ($51,734). Interestingly, the gain from graduating high school is greater for those who, in fact, do graduate ($53,132 in 1992 $) than for those who fail to graduate ($44,238).

Structural model estimates of the high school graduation choice

The difference in the individual expected present value income estimates – the one for "if graduate" *minus* the other for "if non-graduate" – serves as the central economic determinant of the decision of whether or not to graduate high school.[12] Estimates of these economic responses are provided in table 15.2. We present a series of models that progress from including only the difference in expected incomes (the expected gain from graduating high school), to increasingly comprehensive specifications. A second set, which includes an interaction variable – the product of the expected income term and a dummy variable for non-African-American male – are shown in columns (5)–(8).[13]

The strongest influence of the expected gain is in the first equation which includes only the expected present value income gain terms. In all equations but one, the expected gain term is statistically significant. The coefficient on the income gain variable decreases as the set of non-income variables is expanded, but always suggests that the larger the expected gain from graduating high school, the higher the probability of graduating.[14]

The other variables all have the expected sign, and are consistent with the reduced form results found in other studies. The race and gender variables suggest that African-American females are more likely than others to graduate once a variety of other factors is taken into account.

Table 15.2 *Structural model of determinants of high school graduation, full sample, probit estimation (N = 1,705)*

Variant	Base (1)	Spec A (2)	Spec B (3)	Spec C (4)	Base (5)	Spec A (6)	Spec B (7)	Spec C (8)
Constant	0.46	0.26	0.70	1.14	0.47	0.51	0.85	1.30
	[4.93**]	[1.99**]	[4.11**]	[3.72**]	[5.00**]	[3.10**]	[4.31**]	[4.08**]
Expected income[a]								
$Y_{HS} - Y_{NO}$	0.27	0.19	0.13	0.09	0.25	0.33	0.22	0.22
	[6.15**]	[3.13**]	[2.12**]	[1.28]	[5.46**]	[3.99**]	[2.58**]	[2.20**]
$(Y_{HS} - Y_{NO}) \times$ non-African-American male					0.05	−0.28	−0.18	−0.23
					[1.40]	[2.54**]	[1.54]	[1.87**]
Background								
African-American		−0.10	0.16	0.16		−0.63	−0.18	−0.28
		[0.90]	[1.28]	[1.09]		[2.65**]	[0.70]	[1.02]
Female		−0.13	−0.11	−0.09		−0.77	−0.51	−0.61
		[1.12]	[0.91]	0.72]		[2.76**]	[1.78*]	[1.99**]
African-American × female		0.56	0.53	0.52		1.27	0.98	1.10
		[3.21**]	[3.00**]	[2.76**]		[3.83**]	[2.87**]	[3.01**]
Parental choice/circumstances								
Religion			0.11				0.11	
			[0.74]				[0.78]	
First born			0.25				0.23	
			[2.07**]				[1.88*]	
Number of siblings[b]			−0.04				−0.04	
			[1.30]				[1.23]	
Number of years lived with one parent[b]			−0.29	−0.20			−0.27	−0.17
			[2.51**]	[1.42]			[2.27**]	[1.21]
Highest parental education = high school graduate		0.54	0.41	0.40		0.53	0.41	0.39
		[5.87**]	[4.27**]	[4.00**]		[5.82**]	[4.26**]	[3.95**]
Highest parental education=some college		0.89	0.74	0.69		0.94	0.77	0.72
		[5.49**]	[4.39**]	[3.90**]		[5.67**]	[4.51**]	[4.03**]
Highest parental education = college graduate		1.20	0.92	0.81		1.23	0.94	0.84
		[6.06**]	[4.48**]	[3.73**]		[6.23**]	[4.59**]	[3.88**]
Years in poverty[b]			−0.38	−0.11			−0.38	−0.10
			[2.41**]	[0.52]			[2.45**]	[0.50]
Years in poverty × AFDC[b]				−0.01				−0.01
				[0.40]				[0.38]

Variant	Base (1)	Spec A (2)	Spec B (3)	Spec C (4)	Base (5)	Spec A (6)	Spec B (7)	Spec C (8)
Years mother worked[b]			0.31 [2.73**]	0.25 [2.01**]			0.29 [2.55**]	0.24 [1.93*]
Years in SMSA[b]				−0.10 [0.91]				−0.10 [0.85]
Number of location moves[b]				−1.26 [5.61**]				−1.28 [5.67**]
Years in family with disabled head[b]				−0.65 [4.24**]				−0.67 [4.35**]
Neighborhood attributes								
% of families headed by a female				−0.00 [0.48]				−0.00 [0.66]
% of youths who are drop outs			−0.02 [4.77**]	−0.02 [3.76**]			−0.02 [4.71**]	−0.02 [3.78**]
% of households headed by a person with a high status occupation				−0.00 [0.36]				−0.00 [0.39]
Adult unemployment				0.01 [0.36]				0.01 [0.71]
Log likelihood	−721.82	−674.89	−646.01	−614.54	−720.83	−671.66	−644.82	−612.78

Notes:
[a] Coefficient estimates for expected income are multiplied by 10,000.
[b] Averaged over ages 6 to 15 (except number of siblings which is averaged over ages 12 to 15).
** Significant at the 5 percent level.
* Significant at the 10 percent level.
t-values are given in parentheses.

Young adults who have parents with more education are themselves more likely to receive more education (to graduate), while those who spend more years during ages 6 to 15 living with a single parent – or who experience more geographic moves, or whose mothers worked fewer years – are less likely to graduate. Growing up in a poor family seems to play a role – those who spent more years growing up in a family with income below the poverty line are somewhat less likely to graduate – although a larger impact appears to be related to growing up in a family

Table 15.3 *Simulation of impact of increasing present value of expected income on probability of dropping out of high school[a]*

	Without non-black male interaction				With non-black male interaction			
	Base (1)	Spec A (2)	Spec B (3)	Spec C (4)	Base (5)	Spec A (6)	Spec B (7)	Spec C (8)
Base probability	0.157	0.157	0.157	0.157	0.157	0.157	0.157	0.157
10% increase	0.128	0.138	0.144	0.148	0.128	0.134	0.141	0.144
25% increase	0.092	0.112	0.126	0.135	0.094	0.105	0.120	0.126
Absolute change								
10% increase	−0.029	−0.019	−0.013	−0.009	−0.029	−0.023	−0.016	−0.013
25% increase	−0.065	−0.045	−0.031	−0.022	−0.064	−0.064	−0.037	−0.031
% change								
10% increase	−18.5	−12.1	−8.3	−5.7	−18.4	−14.6	−10.2	−8.3
25% increase	−41.4	−28.7	−19.7	−14.0	−40.8	−33.8	−23.6	−19.7

Note: [a] Specifications are from table 15.2.

with a parent who is disabled. The neighborhood where one grew up also seems to play some role: those living in areas with a greater proportion of high school drop outs are themselves less likely to graduate. Other neighborhood indicators do not suggest a significant association with the probability of graduating high school.

Depending on the specifications we accurately predict the outcome for 84–85 percent of the observations. The proportion is very high for those who graduated; we correctly predict the non-graduation outcome in 15 percent of the cases.

In table 15.3, we present the simulated effect of increasing the expected income from high school graduation by both 10 percent and 25 percent while holding constant the values of the other variables. The increase in the expected income if graduating (translated into a difference in the present value of future income streams) seems to be an important factor in determining the choice of whether or not to graduate. We simulate that a 10 percent increase in future expected income conditional on being a high school graduate reduces the probability of dropping out and not graduating by 1–3 percentage points (depending on the specification), or by about 6–18 percent; a 25 percent increase is simulated to decrease this proportion by 2–6 percentage points, or by about 14–41 percent.

Conclusions

Rather than testing a single hypothesis regarding the determinants of educational attainment, as most studies have done, we have introduced a rather full range of background, economic, family, and neighborhood variables into the analysis, including variables consistent with several of the hypotheses that have been the subject of other studies.

When a very rich set of determinants is included, both gender and race influence the education choice; *ceteris paribus*, being African-American and female is associated with a higher likelihood of graduating from high school. The amount of parental time available while growing up – including the presence of two parents in the home – is positively related to educational attainment. Where a child fits in the birth order of the family also affects educational opportunities and attainments; being first born appears to increase the amount of education attained. Both the educational level of the parents – especially having a parent with a college degree – and the economic resources available to the family (proxied by the number of years that the family was in poverty) are related to educational success. Significantly, the stresses encountered by a child while growing up – especially the number of geographic moves that are experienced and the presence of a disabled family head – seem to inhibit the likelihood a child will graduate from high school. In terms of neighborhood factors, we found that the proportion of youths aged 16 to 19 in the vicinity who are high school drop outs appears to negatively and significantly affect the probability that individuals will themselves complete high school.

In addition to the effects of parental and governmental decisions, we find that the child's expected income returns to graduating from high school are influential in the education decision. Consistent with economic models, as expected returns increase, the child is more likely to graduate from high school. These results suggest that policy makers would do well to increase the income returns to high school graduates. This should reduce the rate of non-graduation – by increasing the income returns to additional schooling, or decreasing the costs. Doing so may increase the number of youths who choose to graduate, leaving a smaller group of non-graduates who experience no gain in well-being. In order to deal with this group of low earners an alternative policy would be to supplement the incomes of high school drop outs through non-work-related income transfers, minimum wage increases, or low wage employment subsidies. While this would improve the incomes and economic well-being of these lower wage workers, it would have the adverse side-effect of increasing the number of youths who choose not to graduate.

Appendix: summary statistics for variables in prediction equation for older youth sample

Table 15A.1   *Means and standard deviation (N=1,373)*

	High school graduate		Not graduate	
	Mean	Std.dev.	Mean	Std.dev.
Number of siblings	2.8858	1.9548	3.5980	2.2213
First born	0.1764	0.3813	0.0819	0.2750
Average number of years[a] lived with one parent	0.2571	0.4128	0.3099	0.4327
Average years mother worked	0.5435	0.4290	0.4678	0.4037
Average years on AFDC	0.1165	0.2739	0.2091	0.3194
Mother high school graduate or higher			0.1462	0.3543
Mother high school graduate	0.3860	0.4870		
Mother some college	0.0607	0.2389		
Mother college graduate	0.0524	0.2230		
Father high school graduate or higher			0.1170	0.3223
Father high school graduate	0.1947	0.3961		
Father some college	0.0724	0.2592		
Father college graduate	0.1048	0.3065		
African-American	0.4567	0.4983	0.5673	0.4969
Female	0.5341	0.4990	0.4561	0.4995
African-American × female	0.2621	0.4399	0.2866	0.4535
Average years lived in SMSA	0.7386	0.4194	0.7091	0.4311
Average years in family with disabled head	0.1862	0.3453	0.3260	0.4167
Mother gave birth as a teen	0.1814	0.3855	0.2982	0.4588
Average income–needs ratio	2.3559	1.8575	1.3212	0.9069
Average years in West	0.1387	0.3433	0.0994	0.3001
Average years in Northeast	0.1697	0.3736	0.0702	0.2562
Average years in South	0.4172	0.4908	0.5629	0.4964
Inverse Mills ratio (lambda)	0.1897	0.1791	−1.3338	0.4312

Notes

1   See Haveman and Wolfe (1984).
2   See for example, Alwin and Thornton (1984), Krein (1986), Graham, Beller and Hernandez (1994), Manski (1987), Manski *et al.* (1992), Hill and Duncan (1987), Datcher (1982), Corcoran *et al.* (1992), Haveman, Wolfe and Spaulding (1991), and Haveman and Wolfe (1994).
3   Haveman and Wolfe (1994) and Haveman and Wolfe (1995). In addition,

there is a rather extensive literature on school-based determinants of children's educational attainments. See, for example, Hanushek (1986), who reviews the school production function literature.

4   A more complete description of the data is found in Haveman and Wolfe (1994).

5   The matching was done by combining geographic codes added by the Michigan Survey Research Center to 1970 and 1980 Census data. Using 1970 and 1980 Census data, we assign neighborhood values to the neighborhood in which each family in the PSID lived to Census data. In most cases, this link is based on a match of the location of our observations to the relevant Census tract or block numbering area (67.8 percent for 1970 and 71.5 percent for 1980). For years prior to 1970 we use 1970 data; for years after 1980 we use 1980 data while for years 1971–9 we used a weighted combination of 1970 and 1980 data (weights are 0.9 (1970) and 0.1 (1980) for 1971; 0.8 (1970) and 0.2 (1980) for 1972, and so on).

6   Again we arrange the data so that they are age- rather than year-specific, and convert all income values into 1976 $.

7   $E(.)$ denotes the child's subjective expected value of utility conditional on information available prior to making the choice.

8   In our sample of 1,373 older youths, 1,202 graduated while 171 did not. The variables included in this equation include parental education (dummy variables indicating high school graduation, some college or college completion for each parent); race, gender, and a race–gender interaction term; family position (first born, average number of siblings), if the individual's mother first gave birth as a teen, and background variables measured over ages 12 to 15 (years in each of three regions, years lived in an urban area, years head of household was disabled, years lived with one parent, years mother worked, years family received AFDC, and the average ratio of family post-tax income relative to needs). Also included (and used as identifiers) are the person's own health (two dummy variables indicating if fair or poor; if excellent), the years the family lived in poverty, and average total income.

9   We ran a separate tobit equation for each year rather than the more traditional age–income profile with dummy variables for each year in order to allow the effects of background characteristics to vary by age. For example, having a parent who is a college graduate is expected to have a negative effect on personal income at young ages because the individual is more likely to be out of the labor market and obtaining education; however, at older ages, having a parent who graduates from college is expected to have a positive effect on personal income.

10 In using the coefficients to predict income at each age if a graduate and if not a graduate for our primary sample, we do not use the lambda term – that is, we make an unconditional prediction. In order to avoid reducing or increasing the expected income by omitting this term, for each age for both schooling options we add the mean expected value of the lambda times its coefficient to the constant term for each prediction.

362   Robert Haveman, Kathryn Wilson and Barbara Wolfe

11   These predictions can be interpreted as the impact of providing a high school
     degree to all persons in our sample. If non-graduates are simulated as
     graduating, they would increase their income substantially. Their incomes in
     early years would be greater than those of actual graduates, but they would
     face a lower rate of growth. This interpretation, however, requires the heroic
     assumption that the income-generating process would not be affected by a
     sudden increase in the proportion of persons graduating high school.
12   Using maximum likelihood estimates of a switching model of education and
     choice when treating selection as endogenous, Manski (1987) was unable to
     obtain convergence. He then estimated a model similar to ours, and finds the
     results "amazingly sensible" (p. 306), given the difficulty of obtaining
     convergence.
13   We also attempted to create a present value term for a longer period of time
     by extending the ages over which we had expected incomes. Unfortunately,
     that required us to use the values over ages 19 to 29 that we obtained. When
     we do so using either the individual's growth trend or age 29 income, our
     results are generally consistent with those reported.
14   This is so except for non-African-American males for whom differences in
     the expected income gain seems to play no significant role, once background,
     family, and neighborhood variables are included.

References

Alwin, D. and A. Thornton, 1984. "Family origins and the schooling process:
     early versus late influence of parental characteristics," *American Sociological
     Review*, 49, 784–802

Corcoran, M., R. Gordon, D. Laren and G. Solon, 1992. "The association
     between men's economic status and their family and community origins,"
     Journal of Human Resources, 27, 575–601

Datcher, L., 1982. "Effects of community and family background on achieve-
     ment," *Review of Economics and Statistics*, 64, 32–41

Graham, J., A. Beller and P. Hernandez, 1994. "The effects of child support on
     educational attainment," in I. Garfinkel, S. McLanahan and P. Robins
     (eds.), *Child Support and Child Well Being*, Washington, DC: Urban Institute
     Press, 319–56

Hanushek, E., 1986. "The economics of schooling: production and efficiency in
     public schools," *Journal of Economic Literature*, 24, 1141–77

Haveman, R. and B. Wolfe, 1984. "Schooling and economic well-being: the role
     of non-market effects," *Journal of Human Resources*, 19, 377–407

     1994. *Succeeding Generations: On the Effects of Investments in Children*, New
     York: Russell Sage Foundation

     1995. "The determinants of children's attainments: a review of methods and
     findings," *Journal of Economic Literature*, 33, 1829–78

Haveman, R., B. Wolfe and J. Spaulding, 1991. "Childhood events and circum-
     stances influencing high school completion," *Demography*, 28, 133–57

Hill, M. and G. Duncan, 1987. "Parental family income and the socioeconomic attainment of children," *Social Science Research*, 16, 39–73

Krein, S.F., 1986. "Growing up in a single-parent family: the effect on education and earnings of young men," *Family Relations*, 35, 161–8

Manski, C., 1987. "Academic ability, earnings and the decision to become a teacher: evidence from the National Longitudinal Study of the high school class of 1972," in D. Wise (ed.), *Public Sector Payrolls*, Chicago: University of Chicago Press, 291–312

Manski, C., G. Sandefur, S. McLanahan and D. Powers, 1992. "Alternative estimates of the effect of family structure during adolescence on high school graduation," *Journal of the American Statistical Association*, 87, 25–37

16 Equivalence scales and household welfare: what can be learned from household budget data?

Richard Blundell

Introduction

The use of equivalence scales is commonplace in public policy. They are essential whenever comparisons of economic well-being are to be made across households of differing demographic composition – in particular whether, and at what level, re-distribution may be required between households of different types to ensure horizontal equity. They are also an important component in assessing whether the relative (or equivalized) gains of a particular tax or benefit reform reflects the differing needs of households with different composition. It has often been argued that observed expenditures from household budget surveys can and should be used to measure equivalence scales. But what can really be learned from household budget surveys?

The focus in this chapter will be directly concerned with equivalence scales that are designed to measure the costs of children. These costs can be seen as the additional expenditure needed by a household with children to restore its standard of living to what it would have been without them. To implement this, one might think of comparing the expenditures of two households, one with and one without children, yet sharing a common level of welfare. The difficulty in this is in finding a criterion which might allow one to identify when two households of different composition are at a common living standard. While economic analysis of demand behavior can provide important information on the way household expenditure patterns change in response to demographic change, it cannot identify preferences over composition itself and cannot identify costs of children without making assumptions about these preferences. In other words, the analysis of demands for goods by demographically different households identifies preferences *conditional* on household composition. In contrast, a complete welfare comparison between households should depend on preferences over goods *and* household composition (unconditional preference orderings).

It is important to note that this issue of equivalence scale measurement does not depend on whether demographic or composition variables are *exogeneous* in the demand equations for goods. The identification of equivalence scales from demand data is difficult because demands reveal only *conditional* preference orderings, regardless of whether households choose demands and demographic attributes simultaneously, sequentially, or independently. The determination of household composition is irrelevant to these identification findings. Indeed, the identification results apply to the measurement of constant utility cost differences associated with any household-specific characteristic, including, for example, the valuation of health disabilities or of public goods like environmental amenities.

Given this identification problem it is reasonable to look for sources of prior or alternative information. This can come in terms of *sensible* – but untestable – restrictions on behavior. Or it can come from the use of additional data, in particular the adoption of psychometric data on comparisons of well-being which was at the heart of much of Aldi Hagenaars' own research.

The remainder of this chapter is structured as follows. The next section briefly reviews the equivalence scale literature. The identification problem is then addressed directly and equivalence scales are related to general cost-of-living measures. The value of household budget data is then assessed and the value of additional information is considered. This includes a discussion of the value of psychometric data and also the use of consumption growth and savings data in a life cycle model which tracks households as they change their demographic composition as a method of measuring scales. The final section draws some conclusions.

Equivalence scales

Equivalence scales attempt to measure the proportionate increase (or decrease) in income necessary to maintain a certain level of household welfare given some change in demographic circumstances. It might seem straightforward that changes in expenditures should be useful in this comparison. However, as has been understood for some time (see Pollak and Wales, 1979, or Fisher, 1987, for example), without prior restrictions, consumer expenditure patterns cannot identify all the parameters required for making welfare comparisons across households. A family with children will certainly have different costs in terms of expenditures (and labor supply) but they will also have different benefits. Without prior restrictions on the form of these benefits, it is impossible to make constant utility comparisons using expenditure data alone. Presumably we can assume that, for the most part, parents with children choose to have them. Even if they did not, or if with hindsight they would have made different decisions, parents generally obtain some positive benefit from the presence of children. This benefit has to be set against the costs in any "utility" constant comparison. However, this does not imply that equivalence scales should be set to unity if children are optimally chosen, since the utility of the children themselves is required to be accounted for in any interpersonal welfare comparison across households of different sizes. The consumption allocations going to children still matter for making interpersonal comparisons.

Expenditure differences across families with different numbers of children will not fully capture the benefits but they might be expected to reflect the costs. If the consumption costs of children could be fully recovered then to a large extent the equivalence scale problem would largely be solved. However, even this is difficult, since costs will in general depend on a reference level of utility. Any sensible measures of costs will therefore be comparable only at some particular level of "utility." The simple and most popular forms of equivalence scales attempt to address this point by making assumptions about the way in which costs of children impact on overall parental utility so that simple comparisons across families can be made.

Fixed costs, Rothbarth and Engel scales

One strategy is to assume that all costs of children are fixed. In this case, the same costs are paid by all families of a particular demographic structure and equivalence scales can be estimated without worrying about the constant utility comparison. This is often referred to as "demographic translating" (see Pollak and Wales, 1981). However, it is not convincing, since it would seem reasonable to assume that families on higher income generally spend more on children than those on lower incomes. Empirical studies of household budget allocations typically bear this out (e.g. Blundell, Pashardes and Weber, 1993).

Another alternative is to assume that some goods – so called "adult goods" – are not affected by children. Tobacco and alcohol, or perhaps adult clothing, are typical examples. If the presence or otherwise of children has no impact on these expenditures then they can be used to construct "comparison" groups across adult families with different demographic membership. This is the Rothbarth method (see Deaton, Ruiz-Castillo and Thomas, 1989). But this kind of "separability" between children's and adult goods seems unduly strong. It is not enough that children do not consume adult goods, for the comparison group idea to work children must have *no impact* at the margin on the parents' consumption of these goods (see Blackorby and Donaldson, 1995; Browning, 1992). Yet the presence of young children clearly can increase the relative "cost" for their parents of drinking in bars, of smoking in the home, and even of new adult clothes!

Engel scales sound more convincing at face value. These are scales where the comparison group is a family with the same budget share for some basic necessities – maybe food or food, clothing and domestic energy (housing is usually treated separately). Equivalence scales then measure the additional income needed for families with children to bring their overall budget share of these basic goods in line with a similar family with no children. However, finding goods which satisfy the conditions necessary for Engel scales can also be difficult. Essentially budget shares for such goods, when written in terms of prices and utility (compensated budget shares), must be independent of the number of children (see Browning, 1992). It is only then that, for a given price regime, expenditure shares on such goods reflect family utility or welfare.

Nonetheless, Engel scales continue to have a powerful attraction in policy making circles and it may be that for poor households, where equivalence scales are used to define some comparable poverty line, expenditure shares on basic necessities do provide a rough but measurable guide to comparative welfare levels. In general, it seems easier to argue for the use of household budget data for comparisons across "poor" families.

Barten scales and scales that are independent of base utility

Further alternative methods of measuring equivalence scales are available, and an attractive one is the Barten scale in which the prices of goods each have their own demographic scaling factor (see Barten, 1964). As Gorman so neatly put it "the price of a penny bun to a family of three is three pennies." Prices of goods that children consume are scaled up, this guarantees that children are "costly," and for many goods it probably matches the expenditure effect rather well. Age effects for each household member can then be estimated non-parametrically, as in the cubic spline approach of Blundell (1980). Nonetheless, the Barten scales only allow children to affect expenditure patterns in the same way that prices affect such patterns.[1] It is probably the case that the impact of children on expenditure patterns is more general and, in any case, their impact on utility is hardly as simple as the impact on prices, otherwise very few children would be chosen.

As a final possible alternative, suppose that equivalence scales are independent of the base or reference utility level (see Lewbel, 1989; Blackorby and Donaldson, 1988). The costs of children are then proportional to overall costs. Again, in this case complete identification of equivalence scales is possible. While this assumption is commonly made in empirical demand work (see, for example, Jorgenson and Slesnick, 1983, 1987; Ray, 1983), it does appear to be a strong restriction. It might be thought that poorer households allocate a larger share of any budget to children. In some sense, this is the converse of the fixed cost case in which the consumption costs of children are the same whatever the level of overall costs.

A generally more attractive strategy would seem to let the household budget data itself determine how children affect demands and then see what sensible methods can be used to define comparison groups. The more general approaches of Lewbel (1985) and Ray (1986) fall into this category and provide an attractive basis for thinking about whether the restriction in the above models on the way children affect household budget behavior is plausible.

Testable restrictions, prior assumptions, and the use of additional data

In each of these cases there appear to be three separate issues: (1) Is the form of the equivalence scale restricting observable patterns of demand in some testable way? (2) Is the scale able to capture the consumption costs of children? (3) Is the scale convincingly capturing the benefits as well as the costs of children?

Many of the popular forms of equivalence scales do impose restrictions that are more than sufficient to identify true welfare comparisons. Indeed, they generally impose testable restrictions. The statistical analysis of family budgets, as originally put forward by Prais and Houthakker (1955), can therefore be used to distinguish between many equivalence scales and evaluate which, of the many popular forms available, is most in line with observed behavior. However, since the restrictions required to fully identify equivalence scales are only partially testable, welfare comparisons will always require prior assumptions or additional information not usually available in budget surveys. The testable implications of many standard equivalence scales and the role of prior information is the main contribution of the Blundell and Lewbel (1991) study.

To generate equivalence scales from expenditure patterns using behavioral models that are coherent with the data still requires a leap of faith. Neither of the issues (2) or (3) can be addressed by the statistical analysis of budget data alone. Both require some prior restrictions or assumptions on how to define an appropriate comparison group, whether it be for the measurement of consumption costs alone or for the *net* benefits (or costs) of children. How acceptable are these restrictions?

A new line of research supplementing the use of subjective valuations together with budget survey information provides a promising development. This work draws on the important earlier research by Hagenaars (1986), Kapteyn and van Praag (1976), and van Praag and van der Sar (1988), and has been taken forward by Kapteyn (1994) and also very recently in the careful non-parametric estimation by Melenberg and van Soest (1995).

Finally, it is worth noting that attempts to estimate the "costs of children" from household budgets have concentrated attention largely upon observing differences in the composition of spending in a single period. It would seem interesting to ask to what extent the presence of children coincides with a reallocation of life cycle expenditure, and not simply a reallocation of "within-period" expenditure shares. Households clearly save in anticipation of times when children are present and, given this behavior, expenditure in all periods of the life cycle will depend upon the complete demographic profile of the household in all time periods.

Equivalence scales and cost-of-living indices

The identification problem

For any given price vector p, demographic characteristics z, reference characteristics z^0 and utility level u, we can define an equivalence scale by

$$I(p, z, z^0; u) = \frac{c(p, z; u)}{c(p, z^0; u)} \qquad (16.1)$$

This ratio is simply the minimum cost for a household having characteristics z necessary to attain a given utility level u divided by the corresponding cost of attaining utility level u for a reference household with characteristics z^0.[2]

The calculation of equivalence scales requires recovery of the cost function $c(p, z; u)$ from demand data (see Deaton and Muellbauer, 1980a for a detailed description of the interplay between estimated demands and the recovery of the cost function). However, for equivalence scale measurement there is a serious identification problem in doing so (see

Pollak and Wales, 1979). The cost function defines the utility level only up to some increasing monotonic transformation which can depend in a fairly arbitrary way on the demographic composition z. Pollak and Wales (1979) argue that equivalence scales that are calculated from demand data cannot be used for welfare comparisons. This seems to be an overly negative assessment. Consumer demand data can be used to recover the *conditional* cost of attaining each indifference curve in consumption space, i.e. conditional preferences, and hence contains some information on relative costs.

The usual approach to equivalence scale estimation is to assume a particular (conditional) cost function c, and to calculate equivalence scales I. As the above discussion shows, the resulting equivalence scale estimates depend on a subjective value judgment. Some empirical applications make this judgment more or less explicit (e.g. Jorgenson and Slesnick, 1983, 1987 in their construction of inequality measures), but the results are no less subjective for that.

The question that needs to be addressed is: what information about equivalence scales can be identified from demand data on household budgets? This is the central focus of the Blundell and Lewbel (1991) paper in which it is shown that demand for goods provides no information about equivalence scales in a single price regime. That is, for any observed demand system, a cost function can be found that rationalizes the demand system and yields any possible values for equivalence scales in any one given price regime p. Given the true values of equivalence scales in one price regime, budget data can be used to uniquely recover the true values of all equivalence scales in all other price regimes. It is therefore useful to turn our attention to the relationship between equivalence scales and cost of living indices.

Cost-of-living indices

For any price regime p, any reference price regime p, and any demographic characteristics z, define a cost of living index $L(p, p^0, z; u)$ by

$$L(p, p^0, z; u) = \frac{c(p, z; u)}{c(p^0, z^0; u)} \qquad (16.2)$$

see Afriat (1977). Each $L(p, p^0, z; u)$ equals the cost for a household having characteristics z and facing prices p to attain a given base utility level u, divided by the cost of the same household to attain the same utility level u when facing prices p. Unlike equivalence scales, the schedule of cost-of-living indices $L(p, p^0, z)$ are identical for all choices of the cost function c that yield the same observed demand equations, and so are uniquely determined by the demand data alone.

Consider a specific equivalence scale given by:

$$\frac{c(p, z; u)}{c(p, z^0; u)} = \frac{L(p, p^0, z; u)}{L(p, p^0, z^0; u)} \frac{c(p^0, z; u)}{c(p^0, z^0; u)} \tag{16.3}$$

It follows from (16.3) that the equivalence scale in price regime p equals the product of a ratio of household specific cost-of-living indices (elements of $L(p, p^0, z; u)$ and $L(p, p^0, z^0; u)$), which are identified from demand data alone times the corresponding equivalence scale in the base price regime p^0. This simple decomposition shows that any equivalence scale that researchers report based on demand estimation is the product of relative cost-of-living indices uncovered by the data, multiplied by an arbitrary constant that the researcher has implicitly selected by his choice of equivalence scale.

Options for estimating equivalence scales

Given the results of the previous section, there appear to be only three options for estimating equivalence scales in a static Marshallian consumer demand framework. These are (1) report only what can be unambiguously calculated from demand data, or (2) make some reasonable, though untestable, assumptions to arrive at a unique scale, or (3) augment demand equations with additional data about preferences over z or psychometric data about attained utility levels. Each of these options is discussed in turn before we move to an intertemporal or life cycle setting for our equivalence scale analysis.

Testable result only

If we wish to have results that depend on the observable demand equations, then the only component of equivalence scales that can be estimated is "relative" equivalence scales, which are ratios of cost-of-living indices for different demographic groups (the first term on the right hand side of (16.3)). From our discussion above we see that nothing can be inferred about the rest of (16.3) using demand data alone.

A simple technique for constructing relative equivalence scales is to select a base price regime, then construct the unique cost function c that rationalizes the observed demands. This representation of the cost function makes all base period equivalence scales equal one so, for this representation only, equivalence scales calculated in the usual way for any z, p, and u will equal the ratio of cost-of-living indices for the different households, which by definition are relative equivalence scales. This is admittedly a much weaker result than knowing the full structure of equivalence scales, but relative equivalence scales are all that can be identified from the demand equations.

Analysis incorporating reasonable utility assumptions

If actual equivalence scale estimates are required using only demand data then an untestable assumption must be made. This is not necessarily more offensive than the standard assumptions required for welfare analysis, such as interpersonal comparability, as long as one is explicit about the dependence of the resulting estimates on this assumption.

In some cases, more specific structure in the demand equations may suggest a unique "natural" choice. An example of demand structures that lead to a single "natural" choice is the *IB* property, defined as the situation in which equivalence scales are independent of the base level of utility u at which the cost comparison is being made. Formally, *IB* means that I in (16.1) does not depend on u. *IB* can be viewed as a functional form property of the cost function, since equivalence scales are *IB* if and only if the cost function c equals $m(p, z)G(p, u)$ for some functions $m(\ )$ and $G(\ )$, yielding equivalence scales of the form $m(p, z)/m(p, z)$. The *IB* property places testable restrictions on the (conditional) demand equations. In general, *IB* also implies a unique choice of equivalence scales (see Blundell and Lewbel, 1991).

Blackorby and Donaldson (1988) and Lewbel (1989) independently analyzed the restrictions on demands and cost functions implied by the *IB* property (Blackorby and Donaldson call the *IB* property "equivalence scale exactness"). Many empirical studies in equivalence scale estimation posit cost functions that possess the *IB* property (examples are Engel scales, homothetic demands, and the models of Jorgenson and Slesnick 1983, and of Ray, (1983). However, the demographically translated Linear and Quadratic Expenditure Systems of Pollak and Wales (1981) do not necessarily satisfy the *IB* restriction. Similarly, the extensions of Deaton and Muellbauer's Almost Ideal model estimated in Blundell, Pashardes and Weber (1993) do not in general support the *IB* restriction.

In all these cases, the assumption made is "natural" only in the sense of having the least complicated expression of the dependence of utility on z. When nothing else is known about the dependence of the true measure of welfare on z, this simplest form is attractive from a purely descriptive point of view. Moreover, if one has prior beliefs about (or alternative estimates of) equivalence scales, the estimates that result from any assumption can be checked for reasonableness against these priors.

Using a time series of repeated cross-sections Blundell and Lewbel (1991) have estimated an empirical demand model which contained a reasonably general specification of demographic effects. The specification was a demographic generalization of the Almost Ideal consumer demand model of Deaton and Muellbauer (1980b), in which both the intercept and slope parameters of the share equations are allowed to be demographically dependent. They considered the restrictions that would be consistent with equivalence scales that are independent of base (or reference) utility. This restriction was rejected. They then proceeded to estimate the various components of equivalence scales that are identified from family budget data alone and assessed the sensitivity of the estimated scales to various popular restrictions.

Use of additional data

Psychometric data

It may be possible that additional data in the form of revealed preference for characteristics z (e.g. treating geographic location or household size as a choice variable) can be used to identify equivalence scales in a single price regime, or one may have opinions about equivalence scales arrived at by introspection. The extensive work by van Praag and his colleagues (see van Praag, 1995; van Praag and Kapteyn, 1973; van Praag and van der Sar, 1988, for example) provides an important attempt to use psychometric data in the form of an Income Evaluation Question to overcome the identification problem. By asking households of different composition and income levels how they value an extra unit of income, one can attempt to identify the broad features of the monotonic transformation that cannot be recovered from Marshallian demand analysis. In either case, the discussion above suggests how such information could be combined with estimates of relative equivalence scales to yield estimates of true equivalence scales. Of course, revealed preference over characteristics cannot be used for attributes that are not subject to choice, such as race or age. This work is further reviewed in Kapteyn (1994) and developed further in the careful semi-parametric work reported in Melenberg and van Soest (1995).

Consumption growth and savings data

An additional source of data is to look at the pattern of consumption expenditures over time as households change their demographic profile.

This cannot fully identify equivalence scales but it can add significantly to the information content of household budget data. Modern models of intertemporal consumer behavior seek to explain changes in consumption from one period to the next in terms of expected changes in prices, interest rates and other attributes, and unexpected events that influence the path of consumption (see Hall, 1978). By working with individual household data over time, focus can be placed on the influence demographic variables, and their evolution, have on intertemporal consumption patters, allowing an extension to the standard equivalence scale literature. This extension to the equivalence scale literature contributes additional terms to the estimated equivalence scale and thereby reduces the identification issues discussed above.

It is important therefore to assess whether it is changing needs or intertemporal substitution that dominates the response of life cycle expenditure profiles to demographic change. If children make consumption more expensive, then they would tend to lead to substitution away from child rearing periods. However, increases in needs in periods when children are present will tend to counteract this effect. Banks, Blundell and Preston (1994) estimate consistent life cycle expenditure and single-period expenditure share models that allow simulation of life cycle expenditure profiles for households with differing demographic futures.

Assume that consumers choose their most preferred allocation of expenditures over time subject to the constraint that the discounted value of life time expenditures equals the present value of life time wealth. Additive separability of utility over time allows us to separate the optimization problem into two stages. Total consumption is first allocated between time periods, and then, subject to this upper stage allocation, each period's consumption is distributed between commodity groups (Gorman, 1959).

Under such assumptions, within-period preferences may then be represented by an indirect utility function $v(x,p,z)$ where x is the (discounted) total expenditure allocation to the period and p is the vector of discounted commodity prices. Intertemporal utility is given by the discounted sum of monotonic transformations of these indirect utilities in which the monotonic transformation $F(v(x,p,z)z)$, may depend on demographic composition z. As Blundell, Browning and Meghir (1994) show, within-period behavior can identify only the indirect utilities $v(.)$ while intertemporal expenditure allocation may allow us to recover the monotonic transformation. That is, optimization leads to a chosen consumption path along which the marginal utility of within-period (discounted) expenditure remains constant (see, for instance, Browning, Deaton and Irish, 1985). The implied equation describing the dynamics of consumption provides a means of estimating the information necessary to identify $F(.).$[3]

To estimate the costs of children in the sense mentioned in the Introduction, i.e. the additional expenditure needed by a household with children to restore its welfare to what it would have been without them, requires knowledge not only of preferences over goods but of joint preferences over goods and demographic characteristics. Standard demand data models can at best help us to identify only the parameters of $v(.)$. Intertemporal models, however, can recover the way in which z effects the derivatives of F with respect to z and therefore capture the impact children have on reallocations of expenditure across the life cycle as well as within the period. That is, changes in consumption patterns resulting from changing demographic profiles provide important additional information. This idea is implemented in the Banks, Blundell and Preston (1994) paper in which changing needs over the life cycle are shown to have a significant impact on expenditure decisions. This in turn implies an important adjustment to the standard within-period equivalence scale measures.

A critical requirement underlying this intertemporal analysis is to be able to follow households over time. Panel data is therefore all but essential for estimation and may reflect why such analysis is so uncommon in equivalence scale measurement. For example, MaCurdy (1983) follows such a procedure using the Michigan Panel Study of Income Dynamics (PSID) which now covers in excess of twenty years. However, an alternative is possible where repeated cross-section data is available. Browning, Deaton and Irish (1985) utilize such data to form pseudo-panels of age cohorts from the repeated cross-sections available through the Family Expenditure Surveys (FESs) in the United Kingdom. This procedure is also adopted in the Blundell, Browning and Meghir (1994) and Banks, Blundell and Preston (1994) studies.

Summary and conclusions

In any policy-based study of family welfare it is inevitable that some comparison across households of different demographic composition will be required. Equivalence scales attempt to formalize this comparison and base it on the objective statistical analysis of consumer behavior. Table 16.1 sets out some previous estimates of equivalence scales by author and country of origin. The estimates show a wide variation. However, this chapter has stressed throughout the importance of correctly specifying the way in which demographics enter demand systems and the potential sensitivity of estimated scales to untested restrictions such as those

Table 16.1 *Some equivalence scale estimates*

Source	Country	Scale (%)
Muellbauer (1977)	United Kingdom	44
Muellbauer (1980)	United Kingdom	52
Lazear and Michael (1980)	United States	42
Van der Gaag and Smolensky (1982)	United States	22
Ray (1986)	United Kingdom	12
Browning (1992) Engel scale	Canada	52
Browning (1992) Rothbarth scale	Canada	18
Jorgenson and Slesnick (1987)	United States	72

Source: Browning (1992).

implicit in the Rothbarth or Engel scales. Moreover, our discussion relating equivalence scales to cost-of-living indices has shown the dependence of estimated scales on relative prices and therefore the sensitivity to the time at which the survey was conducted.

This chapter derived the precise aspects of equivalence scales that can be completely identified from empirical consumer demand analysis alone. We have shown that, without some prior information, household budget data alone provide no information about the equivalence scales in any one price regime, but that if equivalence scales in any price regime are known, then empirical demand analysis can be used to estimate the true equivalence scales in all other price regimes. An alternative way to express this result is that demand equations can be used to construct distinct cost-of-living indices for households of any given composition, but demand analysis alone provides no information about the relative cost-of-living of changing household composition in any selected reference price regime.

There are several possible responses to this issue. One is to combine demand data with other types of data (e.g. psychometric data) to estimate equivalence scales. This is an area in which Hagenaars' earlier work on the use of such data in constructing poverty lines is now bearing fruit in the derivation of comparison groups for equivalence scale measurement. A further source of additional data discussed above is the use of consumption growth over time for households going through periods of changing demographic composition. This has been shown to effectively improve the measurement of scales over budget data alone.

An alternative to these is to report only the component of equivalence scales that is identified from demand data, which is cost-of-living indices for each household type. The final possibility is to make plausible identifying assumptions concerning the properties of equivalence scales, such as independence of base utility, or the assumption that unconditional preference orderings depend on demographics only through Barten scales, for example. These identifying assumptions also have testable implications for demand data. Rejection of these testable implications means rejection of the proposed equivalence scale assumption, but failure to reject can never guarantee that the proposed assumptions hold. If more information is desired, the researcher should then explicitly state what identifying assumption about utility structure is being made to construct equivalence scales, remembering that such assumptions can never be completely tested with demand data.

Notes

This research is part of the ESRC Centre for the Microeconomic Analysis of Fiscal Policy at the Institute for Fiscal Studies. Special thanks are due to James Banks, Arthur Lewbel, and Ian Preston who helped develop many of the ideas referred to here. Material from the FES made available by the CSO through the ESRC data archive has been used by permission of the Controller of HMSO. Neither the NSO nor the ESRC Data Archive bears any responsibility for the analysis or interpretation of the data reported here. The usual disclaimer applies.

1 Barten scales can be generalized a little by allowing children to reduce the price of certain goods – i.e. having children might make staying at home more enjoyable for parents and effectively reduce the price of consumption in the home and of leisure time.
2 As can be seen from this equation, equivalence scales are independent of reference utility if and only if the cost function can be written $m(p,z)G(p,u)$. This assumption that "costs of children" are proportionate is clearly a restriction on preferences (see Blackorby and Donaldson, 1989).
3 With certainty about future real incomes, for instance, marginal utility of consumption – the derivative of $F(.)$ with respect to x – evolves according to the familiar stochastic Euler equation (see Hall, 1978 or MaCurdy, 1983, for example).

References

Afriat, S.N., 1977. *The Price Index*, Cambridge: Cambridge University Press
Banks, J., R.W. Blundell and I. Preston, 1994. "Life-cycle expenditure allocations and the consumption costs of children," *European Economic Review*, 38, 1391–1410
Barten, A.P., 1964. "Family composition, prices, and expenditure patterns," in P. Hart, L. Mills and J.K. Whitaker (eds.), *Econometric Analysis for National Economic Planning*, 16th Symposium of the Colston Society, London: Butterworth, 277–91

Blackorby, C. and D. Donaldson, 1988. "Adult-equivalence scales and the economic implementation of interpersonal comparisons of well-being," University of British Columbia, *Discussion Paper*, 88–27

1989. "Adult-equivalence scales, interpersonal comparisons of well-being, and applied welfare economics," University of British Columbia, *Discussion Paper*, 89–24

1995. "Measuring the cost of children: a theoretical framework," in R.W. Blundell, I. Preston and I. Walker (eds.), *The Measurement of Household Welfare*, Cambridge: Cambridge University Press, 51–69

Blundell, R.W., 1980. "Estimating continuous consumer equivalence scales in an expenditure model with labour supply," *European Economic Review*, 14, 145–57

Blundell, R.W. and A. Lewbel, 1991. "The information content of equivalence scales," *Journal of Econometrics*, 150, 49–68

Blundell, R. W., M. Browning and C. Meghir, 1994. "Consumer demand and the life-cycle allocation of household expenditures," *Review of Economic Studies*, 161, 57–80

Blundell, R.W., P. Pashardes and G. Weber, 1993. "What do we learn about consumer demand patterns from micro data?," *American Economic Review*, 83, 570–97

Blundell, R.W., I. Preston and I. Walker, 1995. "An introduction to applied welfare analysis," in R.W. Blundell, I. Preston and I. Walker (eds.), *The Measurement of Household Welfare*, Cambridge: Cambridge University Press

Browning, M., 1992. "Children and household economic behaviour," *Journal of Economic Literature*, 30, 1434–75

Browning, M., A. Deaton and M. Irish, 1985. "A profitable approach to labour supply and commodity demands over the life-cycle," *Econometrica*, 53, 503–44

Deaton, A.S. and J. Muellbauer, 1980a. *Economics and Consumer Behaviour*, Cambridge: Cambridge University Press

1980b. "An almost ideal demand system," *American Economic Review*, 70, 312–26

1986. "On measuring child costs: with applications to poor countries," *Journal of Political Economy*, 94, 720–44

Deaton, A.S., J. Ruiz-Castillo and D. Thomas, 1989. "The influence of household composition on household expenditure patterns: theory and Spanish evidence," *Journal of Political Economy*, 97, 179–200

Fisher, F.M., 1987. "Household equivalence scales and interpersonal comparisons," *Review of Economic Studies*, 54, 519–24

Gorman, W.M., 1959. "Separable utility and aggregation," *Econometrica*, 27, 469–81

Hagenaars, A.J.M., 1986. *The Perception of Poverty*, Amsterdam: North-Holland

Hall, R., 1978. "The stochastic implications of the life-cycle permanent income hypothesis," *Journal of Political Economy*, 86, 971–87

Jorgenson, D.W. and D.T.S. Slesnick, 1983. "Individual and social cost-of-living indices," in W.E. Diewert and C. Montmarquette (eds.), *Price Level Measurement*, Ottawa: Statistics Canada, 241–53

1987. "Aggregate consumer behaviour and household equivalence scales," *Journal of Business and Economic Statistics*, 5, 219–32

Kapteyn, A., 1994. "The measurement of household cost functions: revealed preference versus subjective measures," *Journal of Population Economics*, 7, 333–50

Kapteyn, A. and B.M.S. van Praag, 1976. "A new approach to the construction of family equivalence scales," *European Economic Review*, 7, 313–35

Lazear, E. and R. Michael, 1989. "Household equivalence scales and welfare comparisons," *Journal of Public Economics*, 39, 377–91

1990. "Family size and the distribution of *per capita* income," *American Economic Review*, 70, 91–107

Lewbel, A., 1985. "A unified approach to incorporating demographic or other effects into demand systems," *Review of Economic Studies*, 52, 1–18

1989. "Household equivalence scales and welfare comparisons," *Journal of Public Economics*, 39, 377–91

MaCurdy, T.E., 1983. "A simple scheme for estimating an intertemporal model of labor supply and consumption in the presence of taxes and uncertainty," *International Economic Review*, 24, 265–89

Melenberg, B. and A. van Soest, 1995. "Measuring the costs of children: parametric and semiparametric estimators," *Working Paper*, Tilburg University

Muellbauer, J., 1977. "Testing the Barten model of household consumption effects and the cost of children," *Economic Journal*, 87, 460–87

1980. "The estimation of the Prais–Houthakker model of equivalence scales," *Econometrica*, 48, 153–76

Pollak, R.A., 1983. "The theory of the cost of living index," in W.E. Diewert and C. Montmarquette (eds.), *Price Level Measurement*, Ottawa: Statistics Canada, 87–162

Pollak, R.A. and T.J. Wales, 1979. "Welfare comparisons and equivalence scales," *American Economic Review*, 69, 216–21

1981. "Demographic variables in demand analysis," *Econometrica*, 49, 1533–52

Prais, S.J. and H.S. Houthakker, 1955. *The Analysis of Family Budgets*, Cambridge: Cambridge University Press

Ray, R., 1983. "Measuring the costs of children: an alternative approach," *Journal of Public Economics*, 22, 89–102

1986. "Demographic variables and equivalence scales in a flexible demand system: the case of AIDS," *Applied Economics*, 18, 265–78

Van der Gaag, J. and E. Smolensky, 1982. "True household equivalence scales and characteristics of the poor in the United States," *Review of Income and Wealth*, 28, 17–28

Van Praag, B.M.S., 1995. "Ordinal and cardinal utility: an integration of the two dimensions of the welfare concept," in R.W. Bundell, I. Preston and I. Walker (eds.), *The Measurement of Household Welfare*, Cambridge: Cambridge University Press

Van Praag, B.M.S. and A. Kapteyn, 1973. "Further evidence on the individual welfare function of income: an empirical investigation in The Netherlands," *European Economic Review*, 4, 33–62

Van Praag, B.M.S. and N.L. van der Sar, 1988. "Household cost functions and equivalence scales," *Journal of Human Resources*, 23, 193–210

17 Equivalence scales and the distribution of well-being across and within households

David Johnson

Introduction

Measures of economic well-being should account for the differences in household size and composition. Equivalence scales are often used to adjust measures of well-being, such as poverty and inequality measures, by differences in household size and composition. Recent research shows how different equivalence scale adjustments can yield different measures of poverty and inequality (see Phipps, 1993; Atkinson *et al.*, 1995; Buhmann *et al.*, 1988; and Coulter, Cowell and Jenkins, 1992).

Using equivalence scales to adjust for differences in well-being across households usually assumes that there is no difference in well-being among the members within the household. Recently, researchers have shown that inequities that exist within the household can increase inequality. Haddad and Kanbur (1990) show that inequality in food consumption within the household dramatically increases inequality. Woolley and Marshall (1994), Davies and Joshi (1994), and Borooah and McKee (1994) examine the inequality between men and women, and Lazear and Michael (1988) examine the inequality between adults and children.

To obtain measures of the inequality among individuals, household well-being must be converted into individual well-being. This requires two measurement adjustments: an adjustment for economies of scale across households of different sizes and an adjustment for the distribution of resources that occurs within the household. The purpose of this chapter is to examine both of these adjustments and their impact on inequality measures.

First, we show that different equivalence scales change inequality. We also show that there is a U-shaped relationship between equivalence scale elasticity and inequality measures, confirming the results of Buhmann *et al.* (1988) and Coulter, Cowell and Jenkins, (1992). Our results are unique in that we estimate the scales that we use to adjust the inequality measures rather than using previous estimates. Second, we show that intra-household inequality increases the inequality among individuals, confirming the results of Haddad and Kanbur (1990) and Lazear and Michael (1988). We examine the distribution between adults and children to illustrate the importance of the intra-household distribution in assessing inequality. (In contrast, other research has focused on the intra-household distribution between husbands and wives.) We show that inequality measures can depend more on the assumptions concerning the intra-household distribution than on the choice of equivalence scale.

To examine well-being across households, we estimate different equivalence scales using expenditure and characteristics data from the US Consumer Expenditure Survey (CES). To compare our results with those of Buhmann *et al.* (1988) and Coulter, Cowell and Jenkins, (1992), we estimate scales with a constant elasticity, i.e. the percentage change in the equivalence scale due to a percentage change in household size is constant across household sizes. The scale elasticities that we obtain range from 0.35 to 0.91, similar to previous estimates. We then show that these different equivalence scales cause inequality measures to vary by 10–20 percent. These results are similar to those in Coulter, Cowell and Jenkins (1992).

Using only equivalence scales to adjust for differences across households implicitly assumes that everyone in the household receives the same level of equivalent resources. If household members do not share equally, then the inequality measure will be biased downward. To incorporate the intra-household adjustment, we assume that the distribution within the household follows a simple sharing rule in which each household member receives a certain percentage of the household resources. We use the distribution between adults and children to illustrate the importance of the intra-household adjustment. Our sharing rules depend upon the number of adults and children in the household, rather than the income earnings distribution between husbands and wives, as in other research.

By assuming that children receive a certain share of adults' consumption, we show that the level of the share significantly changes the inequality measures. Using shares from Lazear and Michael (1988), we show that the inequality measures increase by 25–50 percent. Using the ratio of expenditures on children's clothing to expenditures on adult clothing as a measure of the intra-household distribution, we show that inequality increases by 10–15 percent.

This chapter is organized as follows. The next section provides an overview of equivalence scale methods which are used to compare well-being across households. We then present the methods of determining the intra-household distribution sharing rules used to adjust the well-being of individuals within the household. We then present the data, and the results. The final section draws some conclusions and suggests extensions to the analysis presented in the chapter.

Equivalence scales and the well-being of households

Equivalence scales are used to adjust the economic resources of households with different characteristics in order to compare their respective levels of well-being. In general, equivalence scales can depend on a variety of characteristics, e.g. number, gender, and age of adults and children. To simplify the comparison, we focus on the household size characteristic.

By viewing the characteristics as household size, n, and the reference household as a one-person household, these scales can represent the economies of scale within a household. If there were no economies of scale in the household, then a two-person household would require twice the income of the reference household. Following Buhmann *et al.* (1988), an equivalence scale with constant elasticity, e, is given by n^e. While the constant-elasticity formulation of the equivalence scale essentially ignores the intra-household distribution, we use it to compare our results to other research that examines the effects that equivalence scales have on inequality measures.

The equivalence scale for an n-person household is defined by the ratio of the income, or cost, levels of the n-person household to the one-person reference household such that the households obtain the same level of utility. Using the notation of Blundell (1995), we define the scale, I, in terms of the costs functions, i.e.

$$I(p,u,n) = \frac{C(p,u,n)}{C(p,u,1)}$$

This equation implies that the scales can depend on the level of utility, u, and hence on the particular functional form of the utility function, $u(.,.)$. This means that the assumptions made about the measure of household well-being may affect the values of the equivalence scales. Whereas Browning (1989) tests for whether certain assumptions hold, we estimate various scales to examine the effects on inequality measures.

We use eight methods to estimate equivalence scales: three partial Engel scales, one Barten–Gorman scale and four scales that satisfy equivalence scale exactness.[1] To obtain constant-elasticity scales, we assume that the household characteristics enter the estimations as the logarithm of household size.[2]

The most common equivalence scale is the Engel scale, which uses the share of income spent on food as a proxy for well-being, i.e. two households are equally well off if they spend the same share of their income on food. A generalization of the Engel scale, the partial Engel scale (or Iso-prop scale) is defined for any basket of goods, such as food, shelter, and clothing. The share of income spent on this basket of goods is used as a proxy for well-being. We use food to calculate an Engel scale and two baskets of goods to calculate two Iso-prop scales.[3] Iso-Prop I consists of food, shelter, utilities, and apparel and Iso-Prop II includes all of Iso-Prop I expenditures *plus* health care expenditures.

Whereas the partial Engel scales use a basket of goods to measure well-being, Barten–Gorman scales (introduced by Barten, 1964 and extended by Gorman, 1976) use a utility function that depends on a variety of goods to measure well-being. We follow Smeeding *et al.* (1994) in estimating an extended linear expenditure system to derive the cost function (see also van der Gaag and Smolensky, 1982). Using a seven-commodity expenditure system, we obtain the Barten–Gorman scales by estimating linear Engel equations for each expenditure category.

Recent estimates of equivalence scales use a flexible functional form for the cost function. Pollak and Wales (1992), Blundell and Lewbel (1991), and Blundell (1995) have shown that transformations of the utility level, $F(u,n)$, can change the equivalence scale while leaving the consumption behavior of the household unchanged. As a result, estimates of consumption-based equivalence scales will depend on the assumptions made about $F(u,n)$. To eliminate the multiplicity problem caused by these transformations, these studies rely on the results in Blackorby and Donaldson (1991) and Lewbel (1989) to restrict the class of equivalence scales to those that satisfy equivalence scale exactness, i.e. those that are independent of the reference level of utility.

As Blundell (1995) points out, demand data cannot fully identify the scales; further assumptions about the structure of the utility function are necessary. In this chapter, we use four methods to estimate equivalence scale exactness scales with flexible cost functions; three use an Almost Ideal Demand system and one uses a Translog functional form.

In the Almost Ideal models, we assume that the scales have the following functional form:

$$I(p,n) = (n^{d_0}).\Pi p_i^{d_i(n)}$$

where d_0 represents the scale elasticity. To identify the scales, we use three different assumptions about the form of $d_i(n)$. First, we estimate price-dependent scales by assuming that $d_i(n) = d_i n$ (as in Johnson and Garner, 1995). Second, we estimate Full Engel scales by assuming that $d_i = 0$ for each i. Third, we assume that $d_i(n) = d_i \ln(n)$ and follow Pashardes (1991) to identify d_0 by using an averaging procedure that is similar to that used by Buhmann et al. (1988) to determine the elasticity of a scale; we refer to this equivalence scale as the Averaged scale.

The final method of estimating equivalence scale exactness entails estimating a translog demand system with Barten–Gorman scales. This is consistent with Jorgenson and Slesnick (1987), in which the aggregation assumptions imply equivalence scale exactness. The scales are identified by assuming that the scales are also of a translog form.

The intra-household distribution and the well-being of individuals

Using equivalence scales and focusing on the well-being across households usually assumes that each household member attains the same level of well-being. The level of individual well-being may not, however, be the same for all household members because it depends on the intra-household distribution of resources. Recent research challenges the traditional assumption that the household is the basic economic unit (see Antonides and Hagenaars, 1990; Hartog, 1995). In this chapter, we assume that the household maximizes a household welfare function, $W(u_1, \ldots, u_n, n)$, where u_i is the utility level of the ith member of the household. If each member's utility depends upon the total consumption, x, of the household then the household's well-being can be written as $u(x,n)$, the same utility function used to define the equivalence scales. In this case, the well-being of the household members will depend on the structure of $W(.)$ and each $u_i(.)$.[4]

We assume that the household's welfare function assigns weights to the utility of adults and children in the household such that adults receive the same utility as each other and children receive the same utility as each other. Without information about each member's utility function, we assume that each member's well-being depends upon his or her own consumption. We assume that the intra-household distribution between adults and children follows a simple sharing rule, that is, that children receive a certain share of adults' consumption.

Since the purpose of this research is to examine the effects of intra-household distribution, we simply assume the presence of these sharing rules (as do Borooah and McKee, 1994). Further research would involve deriving these sharing rules based on the individual income and bargaining power of the household members (as in Jenkins, 1991; Browning et al., 1994). Our sharing rules depend only upon the number of adults and children in the household. We examine two methods of using the distribution of consumption within the household to determine the sharing rules and compare these methods to a minimal sharing method and a marginal cost method.

All of these methods can be expressed in terms of a sharing parameter, θ, which represents the fraction of an adult's consumption that a child receives. For a household with total consumption, x, and household size, n (A adults and K children), the equivalent consumption for each household member assuming equal sharing is $x/I(n)$, where $I(n)$ is the equivalence scale for household size n. Assuming that children receive only a share, θ, that an adult receives, the equivalent consumption of a child is $\theta x/I(n)$.

In our first method we use the shares presented in Lazear and Michael (1988). They use the 1972/73 CES data to estimate the effect that the presence of children in the household has on adult expenditures. Their estimates provide the share of total expenditures that children receive holding other household characteristics, e.g. income and education,[5] constant.

In our second method we derive the shares by assuming that the relative expenditures on clothing for adults and children within the household reflect the share of total expenditures, i.e. the per-child expenditures on children's clothing divided by the per-adult expenditures on adult clothing provides the share of adult expenditures received by a child.

A minimal sharing method (see Jenkins, 1991; Jenkins and O'Leary, 1995) implies that each person in the household receives consumption in proportion to their individual income. While adults receive their equivalent income (their own income divided by the equivalence scale), children receive the difference between total household resources and adult equivalent resources. In our analysis, we assume equal sharing between adults. The children receive the difference between total household resources and the sum of the equivalent consumption of the adults. In this case, each child receives

$$\frac{1}{K}\left(x - A\frac{x}{I(n)}\right)$$

which can be given by $\theta x/I(n)$, where $\theta = I(n) - A/K$. Notice that unless the value of the equivalence scale is greater than the number of adults, the share is negative.

Borooah and McKee (1994) suggest a marginal cost method in which the children's share is simply the difference between the equivalence scales for a household with children and one without children. They

suggest that the equivalence scale can be decomposed into need parameters, e_i, for each household member, such that $I(n) = \sum e_i$. They
assume that the need parameters for the adults are given by the
equivalence scales for adult-only households, i.e. $e_A = I(A)/A$. Hence,
the equivalent consumption received by an adult is

$$\frac{I(A)}{A} \frac{x}{I(n)}$$

and the equivalent consumption received by a child is

$$\frac{(I(n) - I(A))}{K}$$

To obtain a comparable share for the children, we divide the consumption of the children by that of the adults, implying that

$$\theta = \frac{A(I(n) - I(A))}{I(A)K}$$

For scales with a constant elasticity, this method yields the counter-
intuitive result that the sharing parameter increases with the elasticity of
the scale. In other words, equivalence scales representing fewer economies of scale in the household imply that the children's consumption is
greater. As a result, a scale elasticity of one implies that the sharing
parameter is also one.

In the first two methods, the sharing parameter does not depend upon
the equivalence scale, while in the minimal sharing and marginal cost
methods the sharing parameter does depend on the scale. When the
sharing parameter is independent of the scale elasticity, we can compare
the effects of the scale elasticity and the sharing parameter by using a
child's equivalent consumption. Using a scale with constant elasticity
implies that the child's equivalent consumption is $\theta x/n^e$. In a household
with two adults and two children, changing the elasticity from 0.25 to 1.0
causes the child's equivalent consumption to fall such that the child's
consumption for an elasticity of 1.0 is 35 percent of the consumption
when the elasticity is 0.25. The child's consumption would also fall by a
similar amount if the sharing parameter were changed from 1 to 0.35
(using an elasticity of 0.25). This suggests that changing either the scale
elasticity or the sharing parameter has similar effects on the child's
consumption.

Another way to compare the relative effects of these two adjustments
is to examine their effect on inequality. Using an analysis similar to that
presented in Jenkins and Cowell (1994), we can examine the effect that

changing each parameter (e and θ) has on inequality for fixed values of the other parameter. For example, changing the value of θ from 1.0 to 0.25 increases inequality by an average of 50 percent, whereas changing the elasticity from 0.25 to 1.0 increases inequality by only 25 percent.

The data

The quarterly expenditure and household characteristics data are from the US CES Interview portion beginning with the second quarter of 1987 through the first quarter of 1991; over 81,000 consumer units were interviewed during this period. Each "consumer unit" represents an economic household such that a consumer unit must be either a group of related individuals or a group that shares in the purchase of some expenditures. We use a random sample of these households which are designated by the Bureau of Labor Statistics (BLS) as complete income reporters and have positive values for total expenditures and income, and non-negative health expenditures.[6] The resulting data set is mainly multi-person households in which singles comprise 28 percent of the sample and households with children comprise 38 percent of the sample.

We use expenditures for consumption only; expenditures for gifts and capital improvements, and allocations to savings are excluded. Expenditures are grouped into seven commodity groups: food, shelter, apparel and upkeep, transportation, fuels and utilities, health care, and other expenditures. For the flexible functional form scales we use price data from the Consumer Price Index (CPI) – the seasonally unadjusted consumer price indices in thirty areas for the first six commodity groups, and a weighted average price for other expenditures.

The results

In this chapter, we estimate eight equivalence scales: Engel, Iso-prop I (food, shelter and utilities, apparel), Iso-prop II (food, shelter and utilities, apparel, and health), Barten–Gorman, Full Engel, Price-dependent, Averaged and Translog. The demand systems are estimated using SUR, while the Engel curves are estimated using standard OLS. Table 17.1 provides the equivalence scale estimates and their respective constant elasticities (listed in order of increasing elasticity). The scales implicit in the US poverty thresholds are also provided for comparison.[7]

As in previous estimates, the Iso-prop scales and the Barten–Gorman scales yield low elasticities, while the Translog scale and Engel scale yield high elasticities. The high value of elasticity of the Translog scale is similar to the estimates obtained by Jorgenson and Slesnick (1987). In

Table 17.1 *Equivalence scale methods and estimates*

Household size	Poverty	Iso-prop II	Barten–Gorman	Iso-prop I	Averaged	Full Engel	Price-dependent	Engel	Translog
1	1.00	1.00	1.00	1.00	1.00	1.00	1.00	1.00	1.00
2	1.28	1.27	1.36	1.33	1.36	1.51	1.56	1.78	1.88
3	1.57	1.46	1.57	1.58	1.62	1.93	2.03	2.49	2.72
4	2.01	1.62	1.72	1.78	1.84	2.29	2.44	3.15	3.54
5	2.37	1.75	1.83	1.95	2.03	2.62	2.81	3.80	4.34
6	2.68	1.86	1.93	2.10	2.20	2.92	3.16	4.41	5.13
Scale elasticity	*0.56*	*0.35*	*0.38*	*0.42*	*0.44*	*0.60*	*0.64*	*0.83*	*0.91*

addition, the elasticity of the Iso-prop I scales is consistent with the estimates obtained by Phipps and Garner (1994) and the elasticity of the Barten–Gorman scale is similar to those obtained by van der Gaag and Smolensky (1982) and Smeeding *et al.* (1994). Given the structure of the constant-elasticity scales, a specified percentage increase in the scale elasticity does not yield the same percentage increase in the values of the scales.[8]

Inequality across households

To examine the effect that each of these scales has on inequality, we deflate total expenditures for the household by each of the scales in table A.1. Assuming equal sharing within the household, this yields an equivalent expenditure for each household member, $x/I(n)$. We calculate the Gini index and three generalized entropy inequality measures – Theil entropy coefficient, mean logarithmic deviation, and $CV^2/2$ (see Coulter, Cowell and Jenkins, 1992). These measures are person-weighted, i.e. they are calculated by multiplying the population weights provided by BLS by the household size.

Table 17.2 shows the different inequality measures for each equivalence scale method and, for comparison, the measures using the scales implicit in the US poverty thresholds. These measures can be used to illustrate the results in Coulter, Cowell and Jenkins, (1992); the scales change each inequality measure in a U-shaped manner.

The Gini coefficient varies by about 10 percent, ranging from 0.353 to 0.390 and the Theil entropy varies by 20 percent. These results are similar to those in Coulter, Cowell and Jenkins, (1992). Since all of the inequality measures are minimized at an elasticity of about 0.38, inequality increases with the elasticity for all but one of the scales. This further suggests that using estimated scale elasticities significantly changes inequality.

Inequality within households

While the above analysis assumes equal sharing in the household, in this section we use different sharing methods to adjust the equivalent consumption of the children, $\theta x/I(n)$. These shares are shown in table 17.3. The Lazear and Michael shares are the values of Φ presented in table 5.12 in Lazear and Michael (1988). These shares represent the average values over households with the same number of adults and children.

The clothing shares are calculated from the data set by using the average ratio of per-child to per-adult clothing expenditures for each

Table 17.2 *Equivalence scale methods and inequality estimates*

Inequality measure	Poverty	Iso-prop II	Barten–Gorman	Iso-prop I	Averaged	Full Engel	Price-dependent	Engel	Translog
Gini	0.364	0.356	0.353	0.357	0.357	0.364	0.367	0.382	0.390
Theil entropy	0.242	0.233	0.230	0.234	0.235	0.242	0.246	0.265	0.276
Mean log deviation	0.226	0.215	0.212	0.216	0.217	0.225	0.229	0.250	0.262
CV	0.362	0.354	0.349	0.354	0.355	0.363	0.368	0.396	0.413

Table 17.3   *Intra-household distribution methods and sharing parameters*

Household composition	Lazear/ Michael share[a]	Average clothing	Minimal share	Borooah/ McKee share
One adult, one child	0.57	0.67	0.40	0.52
One adult, two children	0.53	0.48	0.35	0.47
One adult, three or more children	0.52	0.73	0.33	0.43
Two adults, one child	0.40	0.89	0.20	0.55
Two adults, two children	0.38	0.85	0.25	0.52
Three or more adults, one child	0.21	0.68	0.00	0.57
Three or more adults, two children	0.18	0.67	0.15	0.54
Three or more adults, three or more children	0.17	0.76	0.20	0.52

Note: [a] See Lazear and Michael (1988, table 5.12).

combination of adults and children. While these shares represent group averages, future research will entail estimating household-specific shares.

For comparison, table 17.3 includes the shares using the minimal sharing method (with the equivalence scales given by Fuchs, 1986, as used in Jenkins, 1991) and the Borooah and McKee shares. Since the Borooah and McKee shares depend upon the equivalence scale, the shares given in table 17.3 are those implied by an equivalence scale with an elasticity of 0.6.

The Lazear and Michael method yields smaller shares (averaging about 0.37) than the clothing shares (averaging 0.75). The minimal sharing shares are smaller than either of the two methods used here and the Borooah and McKee shares are in between the two methods.

The effects that these different sharing methods have on inequality are shown in table 17.4. Since the share that a child receives is less than one in all methods, the inequality measures increase for all scales. With the children receiving less than 40 percent of adults under the Lazear and Michael method, inequality measures increase much more than under the clothing share method. The Lazear and Michael method causes the Gini to increase by 25 percent on average and the Theil entropy to increase by 50 percent, while the clothing share method causes the Gini and Theil indices to increase by 7 percent and 14 percent, respectively. In comparison, the Borooah and McKee method depends on the elasticity, and the changes range from 25 percent to 1 percent for the Gini and 50 percent to 2 percent for the Theil entropy.

Comparing the results of table 17.4 to those implied by the minimal

Table 17.4 Inequality measures, by equivalence scale and intra-household distribution methods

Method/inequality measure	Poverty	Iso-prop II	Barten–Gorman	Iso-prop I	Averaged	Full Engel	Price-dependent	Engel	Translog
Lazear/Michael									
Gini	0.459	0.443	0.445	0.447	0.448	0.461	0.464	0.484	0.494
Theil entropy	0.374	0.350	0.352	0.356	0.358	0.376	0.382	0.416	0.434
Mean log deviation	0.395	0.360	0.363	0.368	0.371	0.396	0.403	0.445	0.466
CV	0.555	0.528	0.530	0.534	0.536	0.561	0.570	0.624	0.655
Clothing share									
Gini	0.389	0.374	0.375	0.377	0.378	0.390	0.393	0.413	0.423
Theil entropy	0.274	0.256	0.257	0.260	0.261	0.275	0.279	0.308	0.323
Mean log deviation	0.263	0.241	0.243	0.246	0.247	0.263	0.269	0.300	0.316
CV	0.409	0.388	0.390	0.392	0.395	0.413	0.420	0.462	0.486
Borooah/McKee									
Gini	0.405	0.443	0.444	0.430	0.427	0.405	0.402	0.394	0.394
Theil entropy	0.295	0.349	0.351	0.329	0.325	0.295	0.291	0.281	0.282
Mean log deviation	0.295	0.379	0.382	0.346	0.338	0.292	0.285	0.268	0.267
CV	0.440	0.509	0.510	0.483	0.477	0.438	0.432	0.421	0.423

sharing rule may provide a means of determining a reasonable range for the sharing parameter since the minimal sharing shares are the lowest. The minimal sharing rule increases the Gini by 30 percent (from 0.355 to 0.460) and the Theil entropy by 63 percent (from 0.229 to 0.374). Since these results are similar to those using the Lazear and Michael shares, the Lazear and Michael shares may provide a reasonable lower bound for the sharing parameters.

We can compare the relative effects of the scale elasticity and sharing parameter by again examining their respective effects on a child's equivalent consumption. Increasing the elasticity from 0.38 to 0.91 is similar to using an average sharing parameter of 0.50 (and an elasticity of 0.38). This further suggests that the Lazear and Michael shares are at the lower end of a reasonable range.

Woolley and Marshall (1994) and Borooah and McKee (1994) both decompose the Theil index to illustrate the importance of intra-household inequality. Borooah and McKee use a sharing rule to distribute the resources between husbands and wives. By assuming that the wives receive about 40 percent that the husbands receive, they find that intra-household inequality accounts for almost 40 percent of the inequality.

We can decompose the Theil index to obtain estimates of the inequality between adults and children, which represents intra-household inequality. This decomposition shows that intra-household inequality accounts for 40 percent of the overall inequality for both the minimal sharing rule and the Lazear and Michael shares. In comparison, the clothing shares suggests that between-group inequality represents only 10 percent of the overall inequality.

Conclusions

This chapter has attempted to examine different methods of adjusting differences in well-being across and within households and to compare the effects that the choice of equivalence scale and intra-household distribution rule have on inequality measures.

We provide estimates of eight different equivalence scales which produce a variety of elasticity estimates. We show that these elasticities significantly change various inequality measures and that they have the predicted U-shape relationship with inequality.

We also examine four different methods of intra-household distribution between adults and children. These methods show that inequities within the household also have a large effect on inequality. In our analysis, inequality depends more on the assumptions concerning the intra-household distribution than on the choice of equivalence scale.

While we assume that the economies of scale within the household are separate from the intra-household distribution methods, a more integrated model is needed to fully examine the effects of intra- and inter-household inequality. One alternative would be to estimate two-parameter scales as discussed in Jenkins and Cowell (1994), which may account for some of differences in intra-household distribution between adults and children.

Finally, following the research suggested by Aldi Hagenaars (as described in Hartog, 1995), the analysis in this chapter can be used to examine the inequality between men and women. This would include developing a more complete model of the intra-household distribution of resources as presented in Browning et al. (1994), as well as expanding the definition of resources to account for time spent in home production.

Notes

The author wishes to thank the editor, Stephen Jenkins, and two anonymous referees for helpful comments and valuable suggestions. The views expressed in this chapter are those of the author and do not reflect the policies of the Bureau of Labor Statistics (BLS) or views of other BLS staff members.

1   See Johnson (1995) for a more complete description of these estimation methods.
2   The elasticity for the Barten–Gorman scale is estimated following the procedure described in Buhmann et al. (1988).
3   The Engel and Iso-prop scales use the share of total expenditures (instead of income) as their base so that they are more comparable with the other demand system methods.
4   Johnson (1992) discusses the importance of the structure of the utility functions for intra-household decision making.
5   Gronau (1991) uses a similar methodology and obtains estimates of the adult's share of consumption. While his share falls with more children, the child's share is relatively constant for one, two, or three children.
6   See Johnson and Garner (1995) for a detailed description of the data set and USDL (1991) for the definition of consumer units and complete income reporters.
7   See US Bureau of the Census (1991). The elasticity for the poverty scales is derived by using the procedure described in Buhmann et al. (1988).
8   For example, the Translog elasticity is 140 percent larger than the Iso-prop II elasticity which implies a 140 percent increase in the value of the scale for household size five, yet only a 50 percent increase for household size two.

References

Antonides, G. and A. Hagenaars, 1990. "The distribution of welfare in the household," Erasmus University, Rotterdam, mimeo
Atkinson, A.B., K. Gardiner, V. Lechêne and H. Sutherland, 1995. "Comparing

poverty rates across countries: a case study of France and the United Kingdom," chapter 4 in this volume

Barten, A.P., 1964. "Family composition, prices and expenditure patterns," in P. Hart *et al.* (eds.), *Econometric Analysis for National Economic Planning*, 16th Symposium of the Colston Society, London, 277–9

Blackorby, C. and D. Donaldson, 1991. "Adult-equivalence scales and the economic implementation of interpersonal comparisons of well-being," in J. Elster and J. Roemer (eds.), *Interpersonal Comparisons of Well-being*, Cambridge: Cambridge University Press, 164–99

Blundell, R., 1995. "Equivalence scales and household welfare: what can be learned from household budget data?," chapter 16 in this volume

Blundell, R. and A. Lewbel, 1991. "The information content of equivalence scales," *Journal of Econometrics*, 150, 49–68

Borooah, V.K. and P.M. McKee, 1994. "Intra-household income transfers and implications for poverty and inequality in the UK," in J. Creedy (ed.), *Taxation, Poverty and Income Distribution*, Aldershot: Edward Elgar, 69–86

Browning, M., 1989. "The effects of children on demand behavior and household welfare," McMaster University, mimeo

Browning, M., F. Bourguignon, P.A. Chiappori and V. Lechêne, 1994. "Income and outcomes: a structural model of intrahousehold allocation," *Journal of Political Economy*, 102, 1067–96

Buhmann, B., L. Rainwater, G. Schmauss and T. Smeeding, 1988. "Equivalence scales, well-being, inequality, and poverty: sensitivity estimates across ten countries using the Luxembourg Income Study (LIS) database," *Review of Income and Wealth*, 34, 115–42

Coulter, F., F. Cowell and S. Jenkins, 1992. "Equivalence scale relativities and the extent of inequality and poverty," *Economic Journal*, 102, 1067–82

Davies, H. and H. Joshi, 1994. "Sex, sharing and the distribution of income," *Journal of Social Policy*, 23, 301–40

Fuchs, V., 1986. "Sex differences in economic well-being," *Science*, 232, 459–64

Gorman, T., 1976. "Tricks with utility functions," in M. Artis and R. Nobay (eds.), *Essays in Economic Analysis*, Cambridge: Cambridge University Press, 211–43

Gronau, R., 1991. "The intrafamily allocation of goods – how to separate the adult from the child," *Journal of Labor Economics*, 9, 207–35

Haddad, L. and R. Kanbur, 1990. "How serious is the neglect of intra-household inequality?," *Economic Journal*, 100, 866–81

Hartog, J., 1995. "Escape from *Cittadella neoclassica*: reflections on the work of Aldi Hagenaars," chapter 2 in this volume

Jenkins, S., 1991. "Poverty measurement and the within-household distribution: Agenda for Action," *Journal of Social Policy*, 20, 357–83

Jenkins, S. and F. Cowell, 1994. "Parametric equivalence scales and scale relativities," *Economic Journal*, 104, 891–900

Jenkins, S. and N. O'Leary, 1995. "The incomes of UK women: limited progress towards equality with men?," chapter 18 in this volume

Johnson, D., 1992. "Team behavior in the family: an analysis of the rotten kid theorem," Bureau of Labor Statistics, *Working Paper*, 217

1995. "Equivalence scales and the distribution of well-being across and within households," Bureau of Labor Statistics, *Working Paper*

Johnson, D. and T. Garner, 1995. "Unique equivalence scales: estimation and the implications for distributional analysis," *Journal of Income Distribution*, 4, 215–34

Jorgenson, D. and D. Slesnick, 1987. "Aggregate consumer behavior and household equivalence scales," *Journal of Business and Economic Statistics*, 5, 219–32

Lazear, E. and R. Michael, 1988. *Allocation of Income within the Household*, Chicago and London: University of Chicago Press

Lewbel, A., 1989. "Household equivalence scales and welfare comparisons," *Journal of Public Economics*, 39, 377–91

Pashardes, P., 1991. "Contemporaneous and intertemporal child costs," *Journal of Public Economics*, 45, 191–213

Phipps, S., 1993. "Measuring poverty among Canadian households," *Journal of Human Resources*, 28, 162–84

Phipps, S. and T. Garner, 1994. "Are equivalence scales the same for the United States and Canada?," *Review of Income and Wealth*, 40, 1–17

Pollak, R. and T. Wales, 1992. *Demand System Specification and Estimation*, Oxford: Oxford University Press

Smeeding, T., J. Merz, T. Garner, J. Faik and D. Johnson, 1994. "Two scales, one methodology – expenditure based equivalence scales for the United States and Germany," Cross-National Studies in Aging Program, *Project Paper*, 8

US Bureau of the Census, 1991. *Poverty in the United States 1990*, Series P–60, no. 175, Washington, DC: US Government Printing Office

US Department of Labor (USDL), Bureau of Labor Statistics, 1991. *Consumer Expenditure Survey, 1998–89, Bulletin* 2383, Washington, DC: US Government Printing Office

Van der Gaag, J. and E. Smolensky, 1982. "True household equivalence scales and characteristics of the poor in the United States," *Review of Income and Wealth*, 28, 17–28

Woolley, F.R. and J. Marshall, 1994. "Measuring inequality within the household," *Review of Income and Wealth*, 40, 415–31

18 The incomes of UK women: limited progress towards equality with men?

Stephen P. Jenkins and Nigel O'Leary

Introduction

This chapter describes the trends in the relative incomes of adult men and women in the United Kingdom and investigates how changes in these differentials relate to labor market trends.

Our analysis of income trends begins with an analysis of poverty, as the "feminization of poverty" has been a focus of the debate about gender income differentials. We show that over the last twenty years in the United Kingdom the degree of female over-representation amongst the poor has fallen. In other words, if we look at the bottom of the income distribution, the position of women relative to men has improved. However, when we compare the entire distribution for women with the entire distribution for men, we find that evidence of progress towards parity is more mixed. Women's income gains relative to men appear to have been concentrated at the bottom end of the distribution and average income for women has fallen slightly relative to the average for men.

To investigate the causes of such trends, it is natural to focus on the labor market since labor earnings on average form a large proportion of personal income. Indeed, most economic research on gender differentials to date has focused on work hours and wages. We show that the links between changes in labor market relativities and changes in income relativities are not straightforward.

The first complicating feature we emphasize is the pattern of income sharing within households: a person's income depends not only on her earnings, but also on the composition of her household and on the pattern of within-household income sharing. It has been conventional to assume that incomes are pooled and shared equally, and we do so too when deriving estimates. However we also show that if one assumes minimal within-household income sharing, then there is more concrete evidence of continuing progress towards income parity.

398

The second feature of the labor market–income linkage we emphasize concerns the labor market trends themselves. We show that it is not sufficient to point to reduced gender differentials in average earnings and in participation rates as evidence of increased income parity between the sexes. Trends in full-time and part-time work rates and in their relative rewards are important for explaining the limited progress towards income parity.[1]

Our highlighting of the intimate but complex links between the distribution of income, the labor market, and within-household interactions, is a reiteration of a theme which underlay much of Aldi Hagenaars' research (see especially Hagenaars and Wunderink-van Veen, 1990).

The definition of income

Our principal measure of a person's income is the equivalent net income of the household to which he or she belongs. This measure is widely acknowledged in the United Kingdom to provide a good feel for differences in personal access to economic resources, and is used in both official and academic analyses. Household net income is the sum across all household members of income from employment and self-employment, investments and savings, occupational and private pensions, cash social assistance, and social insurance benefits (including state retirement pensions) *less* direct taxes (income tax and National Insurance contributions), in units of £ per week. To take account of differences in household size and composition, household incomes are deflated by the relevant official ("McClements") equivalence scale rate;[2] to take account of inflation, all incomes are expressed in April 1993 prices. We calculated incomes for all persons – adults and children – but, given our subject, the analysis focuses on income distributions for adult women and men only.

These income distribution definitions assume in effect that, within each household, the incomes received by all household members are fully pooled and then shared out equally. Hence within a married couple household, a wife is assumed to enjoy the same income as her husband, regardless of the amount of money each of them brings in or actually receives (which is unobserved). Hence, to the extent that traditional role models persist, our estimates are likely to under-estimate the true male–female income differential. A further consequence of the equal sharing assumption is that estimates of trends in income distribution relativities between the sexes will be driven by differential movements in the distributions for single men and women and for singles compared to multiple adult households (and the relative sizes of these groups).

An alternative income imputation strategy is to assume "minimum sharing" within households (Jenkins, 1991). In this case, people are assumed to retain the income that comes into the household in their own name, i.e. their "independent income" from sources such as earnings, income from savings, and pensions. By construction, increases in female earnings show up directly in female incomes in this case, but the true gender income differential will be over-estimated because the imputation method ignores within-household sharing, and sharing undoubtedly occurs to some extent.

The extent to which the polar assumptions about sharing lead to different pictures of the trend in women's relative incomes depends on the pattern of income changes which actually occurred. For example if women's income growth is concentrated amongst single people then the equal sharing and minimal sharing distributions would point to the same trend (since sharing is not relevant in this case). If women's income growth is concentrated amongst couples rather than singles, the impact on trends also depends on what happens to husbands' incomes. If these remain much the same on average, then both sharing assumptions would point to the same trend. But if higher incomes for wives coincide with lower incomes for husbands on average, then the equal sharing assumptions will under-estimate the increase in women's independent incomes. It turns out that this pattern has been important in the United Kingdom, and especially during the 1980s (see p. 408).

We have an open mind about which within-household sharing assumptions provide the better measure of women's economic well-being. Which is better depends on what actual sharing practices are, and also on the extent to which "independent income" generation *per se* is believed to contribute to economic well-being (the concept of interest in this chapter.[3] The equal sharing assumption is ubiquitous, used to derive the main United Kingdom official income statistics and the basis of most other empirical work in the United Kingdom and elsewhere. However, gender breakdowns are rarely produced on this basis (at least in the United Kingdom), and we believe it is useful to have some to put alongside the usual breakdowns. In any case, there are some recent United Kingdom studies of independent income trends which we can use to make comparisons with our equal sharing estimates.

The data

We use two collections of income microdata, both derived from the Family Expenditure Survey (FES), a national continuous household survey which is the primary UK source for information about incomes. The CCJ data sets (Coulter, 1991; Coulter, Cowell and Jenkins, 1994), provide distributions for 1971, 1976, 1981, and 1986. Information about 1979, 1981, 1988/89, and 1990/91 comes from the UK Department of Social Security's (DSS) HBAI data sets (DSS, 1992, 1993). Although the net income distributions are defined slightly differently in the CCJ and HBAI data sets, earlier work by one of us has shown that they are sufficiently similar to justify splicing together results about trends to get a picture of what happened between the beginning of the 1970s and the beginning of the 1990s.[4]

Are women still over-represented amongst the poor?

To answer this question requires some definitions: what we mean by "poor" – which means specifying a poverty line and a poverty index – and what we mean by "over-representation" of women relative to men.

We use two different types of poverty lines, each of varying degrees of generosity, in order to check the robustness of our results. The first type is a "relative" poverty line, defined as a fixed fraction of the contemporary average income $(z_t = \theta.\mu_t)$ so that in real terms the poverty lines vary over time. The second type is an "absolute" poverty line, defined as a fixed fraction of average income in 1979 $(z_t = \theta.\mu_{1979})$; the poverty line is fixed in real terms throughout in this case. For each type of line we use three different fractions of the average : $\theta = 0.4, 0.5, 0.6$.[5] Three poverty indices from the Foster, Greer and Thorbecke (FGT) (1984) class are employed: P_0 is the proportion of people with incomes below the poverty line (the headcount ratio, summarizing poverty incidence); P_1 is the average normalized poverty gap (incorporating poverty intensity aspects); and P_2 is the average squared normalized poverty gap (also encapsulating inequality amongst the poor).

"Over-representation" of women relative to men is straightforward to define for poverty indices which are decomposable by population subgroup. For these indices, aggregate poverty amongst adults can be written as the weighted sum of the poverty amongst men and the poverty amongst women. Using the FGT index class P_α for illustration, we have

$$P_\alpha = \nu_f \cdot P_{\alpha f} + (1 - \nu_f) \cdot P_{\alpha m} \qquad (18.1)$$

where ν_f is the proportion of adults who are female, $P_{\alpha f}$ is poverty amongst women, and $P_{\alpha m}$ is poverty amongst men. The female share of total poverty is therefore simply $\nu_f \cdot P_{\alpha f}/P_\alpha$, and the male share $(1 - \nu_f) \cdot P_{\alpha m}/P_\alpha$. For investigating over- or under-representation amongst the poor, a natural benchmark is the composition of the poor were poverty to be independent of gender, in which case a fraction ν_f would be female, and a fraction $(1 - \nu_f)$ male. We therefore define an index of women's over- or under-representation by comparing their poverty share to their population share:

$$R_{\alpha f} = 100 \cdot [(P_{\alpha f}/P_\alpha) - 1]$$
$$= 100 \cdot \left[\frac{(P_{\alpha f}/P_{\alpha m})}{\nu_f \cdot (P_{\alpha f}/P_{\alpha m}) + (1 - \nu_f)} - 1 \right] \qquad (18.2)$$

If $R_{\alpha f}$ is greater than 0, women are over-represented amongst the poor relative to men: e.g. $R_{\alpha f} = 5$ indicates that the contribution of women's poverty to overall poverty is 5 percent greater than their population share. A fall in $R_{\alpha f}$ over time towards 0 indicates a trend towards income parity between the sexes along the poverty dimension. Since the proportion of women in the adult population has changed hardly at all over the two decades 1971–91 ($\nu_f \approx 52\%$), trends in the extent of over-representation are largely determined by the ratio of female poverty to male poverty $(P_{\alpha f}/P_{\alpha m})$.[6]

Our results are shown in table 18.1. Relative poverty lines are used in the top panel; absolute poverty lines in the bottom panel. The estimates assume equal income sharing within households; we return to the sharing issue later.

The main impression given by the numbers is that women's over-representation amongst the poor fell between the beginning of the 1970s and the beginning of the 1980s, but that there was little or no further progress in the subsequent decade. However this conclusion depends somewhat on which set of estimates one looks at, a point to which we shall return.

Consider first the results for the headcount ratio and a poverty line of half the contemporary average, as these are perhaps the most commonly used poverty line and index in Britain. The CCJ data show that in 1971 the headcount ratio for women was 11.3 percent, and for men 8.6 percent, which implies an over-representation score for women of some 13 percent above parity. By 1976, the degree of over-representation index had fallen somewhat more, to 11 percent. By 1981, the women's and men's headcount ratios were 8.4 percent and 8.0 percent, giving $R_{0f} = 3$, a fall of 10 percentage points towards parity since 1971. However between 1981 and 1986, the over-representation index increased again slightly, from 3 to 5 (men's poverty rates increased from 8.0 percent to 9.9 percent and women's from 8.4 percent to 11 percent). This suggestion from the CCJ data that 1970s trends ground to a halt during the 1980s is

Table 18.1 *Trend in women's over-/under-representation amongst the poor ($R_{\alpha f}$), 1971–1990/91*

	R_{0f}			R_{1f}			R_{2f}		
$\theta =$	0.4	0.5	0.6	0.4	0.5	0.6	0.4	0.5	0.6
Poverty line $= \theta \times$ contemporary average income									
CCJ data									
1971	7	13	14	2	8	12	0	4	9
1976	6	11	13	8	9	11	9	9	10
1981	−2	3	8	−3	−1	3	−3	−2	0
1988	−1	5	8	−1	1	4	−2	−1	1
HBAI data									
1979	5	13	16	0	6	11	−2	1	6
1981	−1	3	9	−2	0	4	0	0	1
1987	1	7	10	−1	3	6	−1	1	3
1988/89	6	9	11	−5	4	8	−13	−5	2
1990/91	6	11	12	−3	4	8	−9	−3	2
Poverty line $= \theta \times$ £188.19 p.w.									
CCJ data									
1971	9	14	13	4	10	2	1	6	10
1976	7	11	13	8	9	11	9	9	10
1981	−5	1	5	−4	−2	1	−2	−3	−1
1986	1	−1	4	−2	−1	0	−3	−2	−1
HBAI data									
1979	5	13	16	0	6	11	−2	1	6
1981	−1	3	9	−2	1	4	0	0	1
1987	−2	4	7	0	0	3	0	0	1
1988/89	−3	6	9	−14	−6	2	−18	−14	−7
1990/91	−8	3	8	−11	−6	0	−12	−10	−6

Note: Values of $R_{\alpha f} > (<) 0$ indicate over-representation (under-representation) of women amongst the poor (see text, p. 402). Estimates derived assuming equal income sharing within households.

supported by the HBAI estimates. Poverty rates for both sexes grew substantially: e.g. between 1979 and 1990/91 the headcount ratio increased from 9.0 percent to 21.2 percent for women and from 6.7 percent to 16.8 percent for men. Although the over-representation index fell substantially between 1979 and 1981, from 13 to 3, it then increased over the subsequent ten years. By 1990/91, the index was 11, only two percentage points lower than in 1971.

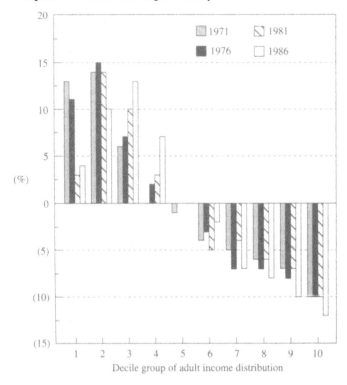

Figure 18.1a Over-/under-representation of women, by decile group, CCJ data, 1971–86
Source: Authors' calculations from CCJ data; see text for details

If we look at what happens when we vary the generosity of the poverty line or the poverty index, we get some interesting new information. First, with the least generous poverty lines ($\theta = 0.4$), or poverty indices other than the headcount ratio, there is clearer evidence of progress towards parity continuing during the 1980s. (There were even years when women were slightly under-represented amongst the poor relative to men.) This effect is more obvious for the estimates based on the absolute poverty lines – which are lower in real terms during the 1980s than the corresponding relative poverty lines.[7] This evidence suggests that the improvement in women's incomes relative to men is more pronounced the more we focus on the bottom of the income distribution rather than further up. To investigate this hypothesis further, we need to move from looking at poverty to looking directly at men's and women's income distributions as a whole.

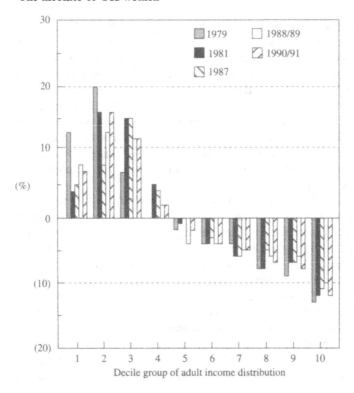

Figure 18.1b Over-/under-representation of women, by decile group, HBAI data, 1979–1990/91
Source: Authors' calculations from HBAI data; see text for details

Comparisons of men's and women's income distributions as a whole

We look first at the extent to which women are over- or under-represented relative to men in each successive tenth of the adult income distribution (still assuming equal sharing for the moment). The measure of over-representation is constructed using the same principles used when we looked at poverty. We compare the actual proportion of women in a given decile group with the proportion expected if income were independent of gender (women's population share), expressed as a percentage difference. The index is positive when women are over-represented in a decile group, and negative when they are under-represented. Our estimates are graphed in figure 18.1a (CCJ data) and figure 18.1b (HBAI data).

Figures 18.1a and 18.1b show that women continue to be over-represented amongst poorer income groups of the adult distribution and under-represented amongst the richer income groups. As for trends over time, the picture is not so clear. Perhaps the most distinct trend is the shift of women from the poorest fifth of the distribution to the next poorest fifth. During the 1970s and early 1980s there appears to be a decline in women's over-representation in the two poorest tenths matched by an increase in over-representation in the third and fourth poorest tenths. Towards the end of the 1980s this pattern appears to go into reverse a little. No clear trend is apparent amongst the richest income groups.[8]

For a second perspective, form two of Pen's (1971) parades, one for men and one for women. Imagine that everyone in the population is stretched vertically so that her/his height is proportional to her/his income: differentials in income translate into differentials in height. Everyone is then lined up within each parade in order of income shortest (poorest) at the front, and both parades march past us within one hour. If the income distributions for women and men were the same, then the heights of the two parades would be the same at each corresponding point in the processions. They are not of course: women are shorter than men at virtually all points in the parade. But what about the trends during the 1970s and 1980s? Did the height differentials between the parades get smaller and, if so, in which parts of the parades?

Table 18.2 provides information about this.[9] The middle person in the women's parade for 1971 had an income of £160 p.w.; the middle man in 1971 an income of £172. In 1986 both were taller and the corresponding incomes (medians) were £200 and £220. The ratio of the two incomes changed little however, falling from 0.93 to 0.91. There was minimal change in median differentials during the 1980s too.

This picture of "no change" persists when we look towards the tallest end of the parades. For example, the ratio of the income of the woman a tenth of the way from the end (the 90th percentile) to that of the corresponding man changes little through to the end of the 1980s. The upper quartile and mean income differentials remained much the same, too. It is only when we compare people at the very front of the parades that there appears to be some improvement in relative income (albeit a small one). The ratio of the tenth percentile for women to that for men increased from 0.93 in 1971 to 0.99 in 1986 – though it remained largely unchanged thereafter. Similarly, the lower quartile ratio increased from 0.90 to 0.94 between 1971 and 1986, but fell again between 1987 and 1990/91.

Table 18.2 *Income distributions for adult women and men compared, 1971–1990/91*

	Mean	Tenth percentile (y_{10})	Lower quartile (y_{25})	Median (y_{50})	Upper quartile (y_{75})	Ninetieth percentile (y_{90})
	Ratio = women's value ÷ men's value					
CCJ data						
1971	0.94	0.93	0.90	0.93	0.95	0.95
1976	0.94	0.95	0.92	0.93	0.94	0.95
1981	0.94	0.99	0.93	0.92	0.94	0.95
1986	0.93	0.99	0.94	0.91	0.93	0.95
HBAI data						
1979	0.92	0.94	0.89	0.91	0.93	0.94
1981	0.93	0.99	0.92	0.91	0.94	0.94
1987	0.93	0.97	0.91	0.91	0.93	0.93
1988/89	0.93	0.96	0.89	0.91	0.93	0.94
1990/91	0.91	0.96	0.88	0.89	0.93	0.92

Note: Estimates derived assuming equal income sharing within households.

In sum, the data suggest that improvements in income parity between the sexes were largely at the bottom of the distribution (which is why they were picked up by the poverty analysis). Moreover the biggest improvements occurred before the mid-1980s.

"Independent income" estimates of women's progress towards income parity

Arguably a women's independent income provides a better measure of the income she actually enjoys than the equally shared incomes we have used so far (see the Introduction). Our ability to analyze independent income trends using the CCJ and HBAI data sets is limited because they were constructed for other purposes, and so we also draw on recent work by others for the United Kingdom. We focus on Webb's (1993) results because his work is the closest in approach to ours.[10]

Webb (1993) estimates the extent of over- or under-representation of women in successive deciles of the adult income distributions for 1971, 1981, and 1991. He finds that the over-representation of women in each of the poorest five decile groups, and under-representation in each of the richest five decile groups, decreased in each successive ten-year period. In 1971, the proportion of women in the poorest tenth of the adult distribution was about 70 percent higher than the proportion expected on the basis of their representation in the adult population as a whole. In 1981, the proportion was about 60 percent higher; in 1991, just below 50 percent higher.[11]

Positive and negative evidence of progress towards income parity between the sexes is provided by Webb's (and others') independent income results. The positive feature is the continuing trend towards parity. The negative feature is the amount of progress actually made. Independent income differentials between men and women were, and remain, large. Arguably a fall in over-representation in the poorest tenth from 70 percent to 50 percent in two decades represents a relatively slow decline. If parity of independent incomes is the goal, there is much progress still to be made.

There is a straightforward explanation for the reductions in these gender income differentials: the growth in women's employment earnings combined with the decline in men's earnings because of higher unemployment. Webb shows this by breaking down total household income into its component sources, and calculating the share of the total and each source which is received by women (1993, table 14).[12] Women's share of total household income increased from 27 percent in 1971 to 32 percent in 1981 and 36 percent in 1991. Virtually all this trend is attributable to the rise in women's share of household income from employment which "rose from a little over a fifth to around one third in twenty years" (Webb, 1993, p. 32).

We provide a more in-depth look at these changes using family type breakdowns based on the single-family households in the CCJ data. Table 18.3 shows the share of total household gross income contributed by earnings from employment and self-employment of the household head, of the head's spouse (if present) – these are the most important independent income sources – and by other types of income.[13] The "all families" figures underline Webb's point about the importance of the growth of women's share of household income from earnings relative to that for men. The breakdowns by family type demonstrate this even more clearly: for married couples with children, husband's earnings comprised about four-fifths of total household gross income in 1971, but two-thirds in 1986. Over the same period wife's earnings share rose from 8 percent to 12 percent. There is a similar trend for childless married couple families.

These changes for married couples provide a clue about why independent income estimates provide more clear cut evidence of women's progress towards income parity continuing during the 1980s than the equal sharing estimates do.[14] Our conjecture is that during the 1970s the

Table 18.3 *Composition of household gross income amongst one-family households, by family type, 1971–86*

		Earnings of head		Earnings of spouse		Other income	
		Share[a]	(%>0)[b]	Share	(%>0)	Share	(%>0)
All families	1971	73	(90)	10	(44)	17	(90)
	1976	69	(88)	12	(48)	19	(90)
	1981	62	(82)	12	(48)	25	(96)
	1986	56	(76)	12	(41)	32	(96)
Single male	1971	80	(86)			20	(75)
	1976	80	(87)			20	(70)
	1981	73	(77)			27	(82)
	1986	64	(69)			36	(86)
Single female	1971	49	(63)			51	(90)
	1976	43	(57)			57	(91)
	1981	46	(59)			53	(96)
	1986	42	(50)			58	(94)
Single female	1971	26	(51)			74	(97)
and children	1976	23	(48)			77	(100)
	1981	28	(53)			72	(100)
	1986	20	(42)			80	(100)
Married couple,[c]	1971	69	(91)	19	(62)	11	(82)
no children	1976	64	(90)	23	(65)	13	(85)
	1981	58	(84)	23	(66)	18	(93)
	1986	53	(80)	25	(65)	23	(94)
Married couple[c]	1971	81	(96)	8	(48)	10	(96)
and children	1976	79	(95)	11	(55)	10	(95)
	1981	70	(89)	11	(59)	19	(100)
	1986	66	(88)	12	(53)	22	(100)

Notes:
[a] Share is income source as % of total gross household income.
[b] %>0 is % of families with positive income.
[c] Household heads in married couple families are assumed to be males.

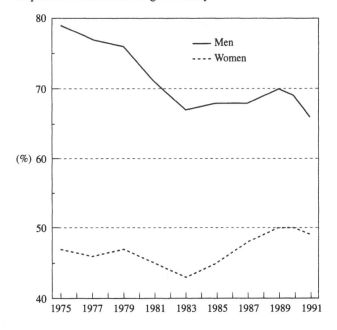

Figure 18.2 Proportion of men and women working, 1975–91
Source: General Household Survey, 1991, table 5.3, men and women aged 16 and over.

relative income gains for wives were greater than the relative income declines for husbands, whereas during the 1980s wives' income gains were more than offset by declines for husbands on average (due to the increasing rates of male unemployment). This story explains why, during the 1970s, the independent income and equal sharing estimates both showed progress by women and also why, during the 1980s, the independent income estimates again showed progress, but the equal sharing estimates much less so – because total household income, and hence the wife's share of it, was greatly affected by higher male unemployment.

Labor market trends and women's progress towards income parity

How are labor market trends related to the limited progress women have made towards income parity with men? Two of the most oft-cited stylized facts about recent labor market trends are that more women go out to work now (and fewer men), and that women's pay has risen relative to men's: see figures 18.2 and 18.3. Since 1975, the proportion of women working has increased from 47 percent to 50 percent whereas the

Figure 18.3 Female: male median earnings ratio, full-time workers with pay unaffected by absence, 1968–92, percent
Notes: 1983–90: workers on adult rates; 1968–83: men aged 21+ women aged 18+.
Source: New Earnings Survey (Atkinson and Micklewright, 1992, table BE3).

proportion of men working has fallen dramatically, from about four-fifths to two-thirds. Median full-time female weekly earnings were 54 percent of the median full-time male weekly earnings in 1970, but 69 percent twenty years later. By contrast with the results so far, these stylized facts suggest significant progress towards income parity by women. A key to solving this apparent puzzle is provided by examination of other labor market trends: in participation in full-time and part-time work, and in the relative rewards for the two types of work.

Although figure 18.2 shows secular increases in paid work for women and declines for men, the picture of narrowing differences in participation is exaggerated because like is not compared with like. The decline in men's work has been in full-time work, whereas the growth in women's paid work has primarily been in part-time work, and amongst married

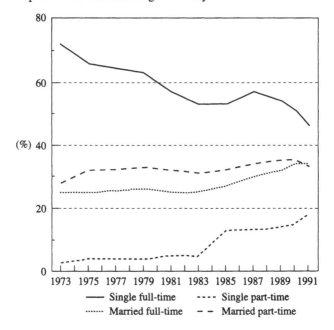

Figure 18.4 Full-time and part-time work rates, women aged 16–59, 1973–91
Note: "Single" excludes widowed, separated, and divorced.
Source: General Household Survey, 1991, table 5.10.

women (see figure 18.4).[15] Indeed the full-time participation rate for single women fell from 73 percent in 1973 to 46 percent in 1991, a very large fall even when one takes account of the early-1990s' recession.[16] Demographic trends have reinforced these trends slightly, too, since the number of married women declined relative to the number of single women over this period (UK OPCS, 1992, table 2.16).

The full-time/part-time changes also explain why figure 18.3 provides an exaggerated picture of increasing incomes for working women: the rise in the relative earnings which it illustrates is for full-time workers, but it is the relative earnings of part-timers which are increasingly relevant.[17] Figure 18.5 shows that median female part-time earnings declined relative to median full-time earnings for men or for women between the mid-1970s and the beginning of the 1990s.[18]

The reasons why women's gains appear skewed towards the bottom of the distribution rather than the top are likely to be closely associated with job trends. Income growth for the poorest men – increasingly likely not to be working – was less than for the poorest women. The richest women were increasingly likely to be married women, especially childless

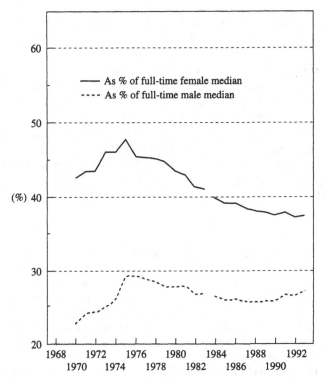

Figure 18.5 Median part-time earnings for females relative to median full-time earnings for females and males, workers with pay unaffected by absence, 1968–92
Notes: 1984–92: men and women on adult rates; 1970–83: men aged 21+, women aged 18+.
Source: New Earnings Survey.

ones (see, for example, Webb, 1993, table 13) but their independent income was more likely to comprise part-time earnings than full-time earnings, the income source with a disproportionate contribution to the richest men's household income packages. For women working full-time, even though their chances of working in the higher occupational classes (disproportionately occupied by men) have improved over time, "there is some doubt about how high up the job hierarchy women actually penetrated" (Hutton, 1994, p. 26).

In sum, there is good news and bad news about women's progress toward income parity with men in the United Kingdom. The good news is that progress over the last two decades has been in the right direction (assuming that income increases translate into personal economic well-being increases). The bad news is that the amount of progress has been relatively limited, especially during the 1980s. The result is a "divergence between the reality and perceptions of change" (Hutton, 1994, p. 24). The same divergence exists in the United States as well, according to Fuchs (1986, 1988), and for much the same reasons. In both countries there continues to be conflict between career and child raising, conflict which affects women disproportionately. These tensions will probably persist, and women's progress towards income parity remain slow, as long as part-time work remains relatively less well rewarded than full-time work, and as long as barriers to women building full-time work careers persist. Improving child care availability and affordability and part-time work terms and conditions are more sensible ways to engineer further reductions in the gender income gap than still higher male unemployment rates.

Notes

Revised version of a paper presented at the International Conference on "The Distribution of Welfare and Household Production (*in memoriam* Aldi Hagenaars)," Leiden (August 28–29, 1994). The chapter draws on research on "The distribution of full income in the UK," funded by the Economic and Social Research Council, and carried out in conjunction with J. Gershuny, B. Halpin, and S. Ringen. Jenkins' research was also supported by a Norman Chester Senior Research Fellowship at Nuffield College, Oxford. Thanks are due to our discussant Joop Hartog and to an anonymous referee for their helpful comments.

1 A third aspect relevant to the explanation for women's limited progress to economic parity, not addressed in this chapter, is the trends in relativities in non-labor income (e.g. pensions and benefits).

2 The McClements scale is the semi-official United Kingdom one. The scale rate for a married couple is 1, for a single person living alone it is 0.61. Rates for children are smaller, and vary with age.

3 If a woman starts going out to work, arguably there are positive enhancements to her independence *per se* and social contacts, and to labor market experience affecting future earnings. Nonetheless overall personal economic well-being might be reduced on balance if the reason for going out to work is financial exigency and the forgone leisure time is sufficiently highly valued.

4 Extensive adjustments to the public use FES microdata are required to derive income distributions which are consistently defined over time. See Jenkins (1994) for further details of the differences between the data sets and comparability checks.

5 We calculate the average income across all persons in the population (adults and children), but do the poverty breakdowns only for adults. For United Kingdom poverty breakdowns for children as well as male and female adults, see Jenkins (1994).

6 See Jenkins and O'Leary (1994), appendix tables A1 and A2 for the trends in ν_f, $P_{\alpha f}$, and $P_{\alpha m}$.

7 An earlier study of poverty breakdowns by gender for the United Kingdom in 1968, 1977, and 1986 by Wright (1992, 1993), found women's over-representation declining between 1968 and 1977, but no clear trend for 1977–86. These results are broadly consistent with our own, although based on some different definitions. Wright interprets his non-clear-trend result as providing no support for the feminization of poverty hypothesis. However, contrary to Wright's suggestions, most previous United Kingdom authors make no claims about trends in over-representation *per se*, only that women are over-represented relative to men *per se* – the trends they refer to are changes in knowledge about this (women's over-representation has become less "invisible"). See Glendinning and Millar (1987).

8 The CCJ and HBAI data appear to provide conflicting views about what happened for these groups during the 1980s, but as all the changes are quite small, these differences can probably be discounted.

9 The quantiles of the distributions for men and women used to calculate the ratios reported in table 18.2 are given by Jenkins and O'Leary (1994). That paper also provides a third perspective on gender differentials, comparing pictures of income frequency density functions.

10 See Davies and Joshi (1994), and also Hutton (1994). Davies and Joshi break down poverty and inequality in 1968 and 1986 by sex, comparing results derived using the equal sharing and minimal sharing assumptions. Hutton uses pseudo-panel data to analyse life cycle and birth cohort dimensions of the income differentials between the sexes. Her results clearly demonstrate that the trends described here persist even after controlling for cohort differences. (These gender income differentials are lower for younger cohorts, but are still relatively large.)

11 The 1991 figure is about twice as large as the one implied were equal sharing assumptions used instead (Webb, 1993, figure 3). Webb's estimate in this case of about 25 percent over-representation for the poorest decile is much larger than the 7 percent over-representation we show in figure 18.1b. Webb's figure 3 is not directly comparable with ours for (at least) two reasons. First, we look at 1990/91 (pooled data for 1990 and 1991) rather than 1991. Second, our net income definition is different: we include (pooled) housing benefit incomes and he does not.

12 These factors are also documented by Davies and Joshi (1994), and Hutton (1994).

13 Gross household income = net household income prior to the deduction of taxes and National Insurance contributions. The distributions summarized in the table are not equivalized, and are for households not persons. We drop multi-family households from the analysis so that we can classify households unambiguously by family type. Similar breakdowns for single-family households with a head aged 20 to 59 years showed the same patterns, and so are not reported. Breakdowns by income source are not possible with the HBAI data.

14 The fact that we calculate a decrease in the over-representation index

416   Stephen P. Jenkins and Nigel O'Leary

between 1979 and 1981 (and 1976 and 1981 with the CCJ data) suggests that the beginning of the 1980s was indeed the turning point.

15 For more information about long-term trends in women's employment rates, see Hakim (1993). She argues (p. 114) that "the much trumpeted rise in women's employment in Britain is found to have consisted entirely of the substitution of part-time for full-time jobs in the post-World War Two period up to 1988," and she draws attention to the historically remarkable nature of the sustained increase in female employment starting at the end of the 1980s.

16 We offer two explanations for the trend. First, youth unemployment rates rose significantly, and young people are more likely to be single than married. Second, there were growing numbers of never-married women with children, and their labor force participation rates fell dramatically: between 1977–9 and 1989–91, the full-time rate more than halved, from 25 percent to 11 percent (UK OPCS, 1992, table 5.15). Notice that widowed, divorced, or separated women are not counted as single women in figure 18.4. Between 1973 and 1991, the decline in full-time participation for previously married single women, from 41 percent to 36 percent, was not large as for other single women (UK OPCS, 1992, table 5.10).

17 Figure 18.3 does, however, suggest an additional factor contributing to the slowdown in progress towards income parity: observe that the rate of decline in the female–male median earnings differential was lower in the 1980s than the 1970s.

18 One potential caveat arises because the New Earnings Survey (NES) excludes significant numbers of part-time employees with low weekly earnings. Employee National Insurance numbers are used to select the sample for the NES, and part-time employees with low weekly earnings are more likely to fall below the National Insurance contribution threshold, and so be less likely to be sampled. However, because the threshold has fallen in real terms, the growing part-time–full-time differential might partly reflect a sample selection effect (higher proportions of part-timers with relatively low earnings being included in the sample).

References

Atkinson, A.B. and J. Micklewright, 1992. *Economic Transformation in Eastern Europe and the Distribution of Income*, Cambridge: Cambridge University Press

Coulter, F.A.E., 1991. "The Family Expenditure Survey and the distribution of income," *Economics Discussion Paper*, 04/91, University of Bath

Coulter, F.A.E., F.A. Cowell and S.P. Jenkins, 1994. "Family fortunes in the 1970s and 1980s," in R. Blundell, I. Preston and I. Walker (eds.), *The Measurement of Household Welfare*, Cambridge: Cambridge University Press, 215–49

Davies, H. and H. Joshi, 1994. "Sex, sharing, and the distribution of income," *Journal of Social Policy*, 23, 301–40

Department of Employment (various years). *New Earnings Survey*, London: HMSO

Department of Social Security (DSS) 1992. *Households below Average Income: A Statistical Analysis 1979–1988/89*, London: HMSO

  1993. *Households below Average Income: A Statistical Analysis 1979–1990/91*, London: HMSO

Foster, J.E., J. Greer and E. Thorbecke, 1984. "A class of decomposable poverty indices," *Econometrica*, 52, 761–76

Fuchs, V.R., 1986. "His and hers: gender differences in work and income, 1959–1979," *Journal of Labor Economics*, 4, S245–S271

  1988. *Women's Quest for Economic Equality*, Cambridge, MA: Harvard University Press

Glendinning, C. and J. Millar (eds.), 1987. *Women and Poverty in Britain*, Brighton: Harvester Wheatsheaf

Hagenaars, A.J.M. and S.R. Wunderink-van Veen, 1990. *Soo Gewonne, soo Verteert. Economie van de Huishoudelijke Sector* (Easy Won, Easy Gone. Economics of the Household Sector), Leiden and Antwerp: Stenfert Kroese Uitgevers

Hakim, C., 1993. "The myth of rising female employment," *Work, Employment and Society*, 7, 97–120

Hutton, S., 1994. "Men's and women's incomes: evidence from survey data," *Journal of Social Policy*, 23, 21–40

Jenkins, S.P., 1991. "Poverty measurement and the within-household distribution: Agenda for Action," *Journal of Social Policy*, 20, 457–83

  1994. "Winners and losers: a portrait of the UK income distribution during the 1980s," *Economics Discussion Paper*, 94–07, University of Wales, Swansea

Jenkins, S.P. and N. O'Leary, 1994. "The incomes of UK women: limited progress towards equality with men?," *Economics Discussion Paper*, 94–10, University of Wales, Swansea

Pen, J., 1971. *Income Distribution*, Harmondsworth: Penguin

UK Office of Population Censuses and Surveys (OPCS), 1992. *The General Household Survey 1991*, London: HMSO

Webb, S., 1993. "Women's incomes: past, present, and prospects," *Fiscal Studies*, 14, 14–36

Wright, R.E., 1992. "A feminisation of poverty in Great Britain?," *Review of Income and Wealth*, 38, 17–25

  1993. "A feminisation of poverty in Great Britain? A clarification," *Review of Income and Wealth*, 39, 111–12

Index